ABUSE AND MALTREATMENT OF THE ELDERLY
Causes and Interventions

Edited by
Jordan I. Kosberg

John Wright • PSG Inc
Boston   Bristol   London
1983

Library of Congress Cataloging in Publication Data
Main entry under title:

Abuse and maltreatment of the elderly.

Bibliography: p.
Includes index.
1. Aged—Abuse of—Addresses, essays, lecturers.
I. Kosberg, Jordan I., 1939–   . [DNLM: 1. Aged.
2. Crime. 3. Crisis intervention. 4. Violence.
WT 30 A167]
HV1451.A28 1982   362.8′8′0880565   82-11093
ISBN 0-7236-7025-0

Published simultaneously by:
John Wright • PSG Inc, 545 Great Road, Littleton,
Massachusetts 01460, U.S.A.
John Wright & Sons Ltd, 823–825 Bath Road,
Bristol BS4 5NU, England

Printed in Great Britain.
Bound in the United States of America.

International Standard Book Number: 0-7236-7025-0

Library of Congress Catalog Card Number: 82-11093

This book is dedicated to the
memory of Don R. Baker,
friend and colleague.

CONTRIBUTORS

Marilyn R. Block, PhD
Director, National Policy Center
  on Women and Aging
University of Maryland
College Park, Maryland

Noel A. Cazenave, PhD
Assistant Professor of Sociology
Temple University
Philadelphia, Pennsylvania

Lawrence J. Center, Deputy Director
Criminal Justice and the Elderly
  Program
The National Council of Senior
  Citizens
Washington, DC

Lynn A. Curtis, PhD
President, The Eisenhower
  Foundation for the Prevention of
  Violence
Washington, DC

Richard L. Douglass, MPH, PhD
Associate Research Scientist
Institute of Gerontology
The University of Michigan
Ann Arbor, Michigan

Gordon E. Finley, PhD
Professor of Psychology
Florida International University
Miami, Florida

Val J. Halamandaris, JD
Director of Oversight and Senior
  Counsel
Select Committee on Aging
U.S. House of Representatives
Washington, DC

Tom Hickey, DrPH
Professor of Health Gerontology
School of Public Health
The University of Michigan
Ann Arbor, Michigan

Nancy R. Hooyman, PhD
Director, Projects on Aging
Associate Professor of Social Work
University of Washington
Seattle, Washington

Victoria Holt Jaycox, Director
Criminal Justice and the
  Elderly Program
The National Council of
  Senior Citizens
Washington, DC

Victor Kassel, MD
Salt Lake City, Utah

Imre R. Kohn, PhD
Consultant, The Eisenhower
  Foundation for the Prevention of
  Violence
Washington, DC

Jordan I. Kosberg, PhD
Professor of Gerontology
Department of Gerontology
University of South Florida
Tampa, Florida

Elizabeth E. Lau, MSSA, ACSW
Medical Geropsychiatric Program
Lutheran Medical Center
Cleveland, Ohio

Jersey Liang, PhD
Research Associate
Institute of Gerontology
Wayne State University
Detroit, Michigan

Jean Luppens, MA
Director, Chronic Illness Center
Cleveland, Ohio

Susan O. Mercer, DSW
Associate Professor of Social
  Work
University of Arkansas at
  Little Rock
Little Rock, Arkansas

Carol Ann Miller, RN, MSN
Medical Geropsychiatric
  Program
Lutheran Medical Center
Cleveland, Ohio

Paul Nathanson, JD
School of Law
University of New Mexico
Albuquerque, New Mexico

Mary Rose Oakar,
  Congresswoman
U.S. House of Representatives
Washington, DC

Claude D. Pepper, Congressman
U.S. House of Representatives
Washington, DC

Eloise Rathbone-McCuan, PhD
Director Social Work Program
University of Vermont
Burlington, Vermont

John J. Regan, JSD
Professor of Law
Hofstra University
Homestead, New York

Elizabeth Reynolds, RN
Coordinator of Inservice
  Education
Plantation Hospital
Plantation, Florida

Mary C. Sengstock, PhD
Professor of Sociology
Wayne State University
Detroit, Michigan

Kenneth Solomon, MD
Associate Director for Education
  and Planning
Levindale Hebrew Geriatric
  Center and Hospital
Baltimore, Maryland

Sheila Stanton, RN, BS
Nova University
Plantation, Florida

Peter A. Stathopoulos, PhD
Professor of Social Welfare
School of Health and Social
  Welfare
Katee, Patras
GREECE

Suzanne K. Steinmetz, PhD
Professor of Individual
  and Family Studies
University of Delaware
Newark, Delaware

Joanne L. Steuer, PhD
Assistant Research Psychologist
Department of Psychiatry and
  Biobehavioral Science
University of California,
  Los Angeles
Psychogeriatrics Unit
Brentwood VA Medical Center
Los Angeles, California

Ann Travis, MSW
George Warren Brown School of
  Social Work
Washington University
St. Louis, Missouri

Emilio C. Viano, PhD
Director, National Institute of
  Victimology
Washington, DC

Barbara Voyles, MSW
George Warren Brown School
  of Social Work
Washington University
St. Louis, Missouri

Jacqueline C. Walker, RN, MSW
State Ombudsman
Department on Aging
State of Connecticut
Hartford, Connecticut

CONTENTS

Foreword   xi

Introduction   xiii

1   **Victimology: An Overview**   1
     Emilio C. Viano

Section I   **The Problems**   19

2   **Fear of Crime in the Elderly**   21
     Gordon E. Finley

3   **Personal Crimes Against the Elderly**   40
     Jersey Liang
     Mary C. Sengstock

4   **Frauds Against the Elderly**   68
     Claude D. Pepper

5   **Consequences of Institutionalization of the Aged**   84
     Susan O. Mercer

6   **Fraud and Abuse in Nursing Homes**   104
     Val J. Halamandaris

7   **Domestic Neglect and Abuse of the Elderly: Research Findings and a Systems Perspective for Service Delivery Planning**   115
     Richard L. Douglass
     Tom Hickey

8   **Dependency, Stress, and Violence Between Middle-Aged Caregivers and Their Elderly Parents**   134
     Suzanne K. Steinmetz

9   **Victimization by Health Professionals and The Psychologic Response of the Elderly**   150
     Kenneth Solomon

10   **A Geriatrician's View of the Health Care of the Elderly 172**
            Victor Kassel

Section II   **Special Groups of Vulnerable Elderly 185**

11   **Elder Abuse and Black Americans: Incidence, Correlates, Treatment and Prevention 187**
            Noel A. Cazenave

12   **The Mentally and Physically Impaired Elderly Relative: Consequences for Family Care 204**
            Jean Luppens
            Elizabeth E. Lau

13   **Special Problems and Vulnerability of Elderly Women 220**
            Marilyn R. Block

14   **Abuse of the Physically Disabled Elderly 234**
            Joanne L. Steuer

15   **Policy Responses to Problems Faced by Elderly in Public Housing 251**
            Lynn A. Curtis
            Imre R. Kohn

16   **The Special Vulnerability of Elderly Parents 263**
            Jordan I. Kosberg

Section III   **Interventions 277**

17   **Protective Services for the Elderly: Benefit or Threat 279**
            John J. Regan

18   **Protective Services for the Elderly: Connecticut's Experience 292**
            Jacqueline C. Walker

19   **An Overview of Legal Issues, Services, and Resources 303**
            Paul Nathanson

20   **A Comprehensive Response to Violent Crimes Against Older Persons 316**
Victoria Holt Jaycox
Lawrence J. Center

21   **Consumer Advocacy and Abuse of Elders in Nursing Homes 335**
Peter A. Stathopoulos

22   **Family Intervention: Applying the Task-Centered Approach 355**
Eloise Rathbone-McCuan
Ann Travis
Barbara Voyles

23   **Elderly Abuse and Neglect: Community Interventions 376**
Nancy R. Hooyman

24   **Elderly Abuse in a Hospital: A Nursing Perspective 391**
Elizabeth Reynolds
Sheila Stanton

25   **Intervention for the Victimized Elderly and Sensitization of Health Professionals: Therapeutic and Educational Efforts 404**
Kenneth Solomon

26   **Federal Legislation to Protect the Elderly 422**
Mary Rose Oakar
Carol Ann Miller

Index 437

Impaired hearing or vision, slowed motor and mental response, decreased coordination, and a host of other physical and mental impairments — and the anxiety they cause — make elderly individuals vulnerable to the crimes of troubled, desperate people or swindlers. This vulnerability becomes apparent in reports of beatings and other crimes of violence against old people as well as in news of fraudulent or exploitative schemes.

Over the past 15 years, there has been a growing movement aimed at preventing such crimes and, in those unfortunate instances when they occur, helping the victims to recover from the physical losses and psychological traumas which may result. Interest in this comes from young and old, relatives, neighbors and friends of victims, health care professionals, representatives of legal and social service organizations, and researchers.

The first evidence that elderly persons are being physically abused by their caregivers appeared in the social science research literature of the late 1960s, only after public attention had been turned to the tragic prevalence of child abuse and domestic violence. Since that time, studies have shown that elder abuse is universal. Although the most vulnerable elders seem to be poor frail women, unmarried or widowed, who are unable or unwilling to move from urban environments, the victims of abuse are rich and poor, male and female, and of all races and ethnic backgrounds. Abuse occurs in the home, in the community, as well as in such professional settings as physicians' offices, hospitals, and long-term care institutions. Abuse can be perpetrated or, even worse, ignored, because of negative attitudes directed toward the elderly in our society. When crimes do occur, negative self-image may keep the elderly from reporting them to the authorities. Abuse may also result from another common misconception — the idea that the family is always the most appropriate source of loving care for a sickly older person. In fact, family members may face conflicting demands in meeting the needs of children and parents as well as their own career and retirement needs. Families in our society are often asked to care for aged parents without any preparation for how to do so or any social support to ease the inevitable emotional and financial burdens.

A great deal of attention has been directed toward robberies, assaults, and other violent crimes, although there has been some question in recent years about the actual extent of such crime involving elderly victims. Still, these crimes receive a great deal of coverage from the media, are frequently the subject of discussions among elderly persons and cause unnecessary anxiety among people who fear losing what little they have. My own impression is that older people attempt to protect themselves by locking themselves into their apartments, particularly at night. Their fear often spurs them into action which may, on the one hand, lead to the impression that they are no more vulnerable than any age group or, on the other hand, further isolate them and make them more vulnerable.

The experts who contributed to *Abuse and Maltreatment of the Elderly: Causes and Interventions* outline the full extent of this victimization, from the obvious crimes perpetrated by thieves and con men to the often unreported, equally destructive, instances in which a frustrated adult child strikes out against a dependent parent, and to the subtle, often hidden, psychological abuse and neglect which can take place at the hands of a relative, a neighbor, or even a professional who has been trained to help. More importantly, this volume deals with what can be done by legislation and other interventions on behalf of older people, and on the foundation which has already been established by successful model programs across the United States.

Robert N. Butler, MD
Former Director, National Institute on Aging and
presently Brookdale Professor of Geriatrics
Mount Sinai Medical Center
New York, New York

INTRODUCTION

There is a growing awareness about the victimization of the elderly. Such adversity includes crime on the street and in the home by strangers, maltreatment within institutional settings, fraud and deception, and abuse by informal care providers (family, friends, and neighbors). While only a relatively small percent of the elderly have been victimized, fear, anxiety, and suspicion are fairly common reactions by an elderly person. Unfortunately, victimization of the elderly is often invisible to the general public. Victimization can occur within homes, within institutions, on crowded and busy streets, and through the mail. Individuals are the victims—not large groups—and only periodically does publicity reach the general public. There is no organized group of elderly victims of fraud, abuse, maltreatment, and criminal behavior who band together, and demand justice and public action.

It is the intent of this book to provide an overview of the causes and consequences of victimization, and possible interventions by those who are committed to working with and for the elderly and who have professional responsibilities for maintaining the rights, safety, and health of elderly individuals. The book should also be useful to the general public. The problems discussed in this book exist; undoubtedly, they are under-reported. The first step to resolving any problem is to recognize that it exists and to be sensitive to it. The second step is to acquire an understanding of the dynamics associated with its causes; to be aware of conceptual, theoretical, and interrelational issues. Finally, with knowledge about problems and causes the last step is intervention—doing something to prevent the problem from occurring or to treat the elderly victim after it has occurred.

After an initial chapter on an overview of victimology, the book is divided into three sections. Section I presents chapters which discuss the various problems faced by the elderly: crime and the fear of crime, maltreatment within institutional settings, elder abuse and violence occurring within the family, fraud and exploitation, and the consequences of ageism by health care professionals. Section II focuses on groups of elderly who are especially vulnerable to victimization and includes chapters on aged black Americans, the mentally and physically impaired or disabled, elderly women, the aged who reside in public housing or urban areas, and elderly parents. Section III includes chapters which discuss a variety of interventive possibilities, such as individual and family treatment, community organization and advocacy efforts, legal and health professional activities, state and local programs, and national legislation.

It should be noted that there is some overlap in material between sections and between chapters. This is inevitable and underscores certain commonalities between different types of problems and the interrelationships among causes, consequences, and interventions. Additionally, authors who wrote on the problems facing the elderly felt compelled also to address — conceptually or programmatically — possible solutions to the problems — while authors discussing actual or possible interventions felt it necessary to pay attention to the background of problems. It is hoped that this degree of interrelationship between chapters strengthens the ability of the book to provide a comprehensive and coherent picture of adversities which can affect the elderly.

Inasmuch as the causes of and solutions to victimization of the aged are not within the purview of any one discipline, the authors were selected to represent a range of backgrounds, experiences, and present positions. Whether from Capitol Hill in Washington, DC, state and local programs and organizations, or from academe, the authors of chapters in this book are dedicated to the identification and understanding of and the solutions to a most significant problem in contemporary society.

The editor of this book would like to acknowledge the role of William T. Strauss, MD, Medical Director of John Wright • PSG, who encouraged the creation of a comprehensive and authoritative book about victimization of the elderly. Also to be thanked for her assistance in the preparation of the chapters is Nancy Wright Buckhannan, a graduate student in the Department of Sociology at the University of South Florida.

Finally, this book is not written to sensationalize the various types of adversity toward the elderly. It is hoped that only a very small percentage of elderly are victimized, abused, maltreated, and exploited. Possibly the problems are decreasing in frequency. But as long as the problems exist, layman and professional alike need to remain cognizant of the existence of this victimization. With awareness and understanding of the problems, interventions — from individual treatment to local programs to state and federal legislation — should result. The purpose of this book, then, is to sensitize, educate, and encourage action.

1 Victimology: An Overview

Emilio C. Viano

In today's society, crime is a definite reality which every day affects the lives of thousands. Even those who do not experience it first-hand are affected by its pervasive and sinister presence. The mass media and our insatiable thirst for news and excitement greatly contribute to our awareness of its different manifestations. Films depicting violence and mayhem are often big box-office successes, just as headlines emphasizing criminal exploits sell.

Crime rates, particularly those reflecting personal victimization, are on the increase in an apparently never-ending spiral; youths become involved in delinquent behavior earlier and earlier in their lives. It is true, of course, that rising crime rates reflect, in part, our sophisticated research and data collection techniques, which generate a volume of information at times difficult to comprehend and digest.

What has emerged in recent years, however, is a realization of the victim as an integral part of the crime situation. This has not been an easy process, and many still remain unconvinced. In any society obsessed with success and one-upmanship, there is little time and sympathy for those who succumb, even if innocently and unjustifiably, to criminal victimization. The very fear of crime that is an integral part in the life of many makes rejection of the victim even more urgent and imperative, as if to exorcise the possibility of becoming one. Ostracism of the victim—like that of persons affected by a dreadful disease—is a well-established defense mechanism that deprives victims of much needed support and comfort, and deprives society of the chance to develop and exercise helping skills and humanitarian concerns.

It has taken courage and determination for those few who in recent years have attempted to reverse the tide and bring the victim's needs and reality to the attention of an oblivious, indifferent, and hurried public. The movement has grown, focusing first on sexual assault and child abuse, then on domestic violence, and more recently on the victimization of the elderly, of parents at the hands of their children, and of the survivors of victims of homicide.

The crucial role the victim and the witness play in the criminal justice system has also received increased attention. The stereotyped television and movie version of how crimes are solved notwithstanding, in real life it is what the victim/witness knows and shares with the police that makes solving the crime possible. Similarly, it is the victim/witness's willingness and ability to testify effectively that will make the prosecutor's efforts worthwhile and successful. The ever-increasing number of victim/witness programs based in police departments and prosecutors' offices reflects the system's awareness and recognition of the victim/witness's importance. Some believe that the system's inability to cope with crime and its prosecution without the citizens' cooperation will make the role played by the victim/witness increasingly important and sought after.

Of course, there are also the skeptics and cynics. They point out that police and prosecution interest in the victim/witness is motivated more by the benefits to be reaped by the system than by genuine humanitarian interest. They also stress that victim/witness services are the latest addition to a panoply of social services and thus the most vulnerable to budget reductions and reallocation of monies. There is some truth to this, but the unmistakable fact remains that our society has finally been awakened to the victim's needs, just as previously it was awakened to the poverty and lack of civil rights of many. Whatever may happen in the future to the current status of the victim/witness movement, it will have left an indelible imprint on our consciousness.

The Victim: Concept and Terminology

The concept of victim appears among the most ancient ones of humanity. Inextricably connected with the idea and the practice of sacrifice, the notion of victim belongs to all cultures. Most religions, for example, are fundamentally sacrificial. Early ritual literature from all regions of the world offers abundant clues to the study of sacrifice and of its victims — human, divine, animal, or inanimate. The epics and mythology provide sufficient evidence pointing to the existence of different types of sacrifices and victims, and they contain a wealth of symbolic elements connected to those rituals and practices.

Even before the development of scholarly studies on the subject, several writers focused their attention on the victim. The novels of Daniel Defoe (*Moll Flanders, Colonel Jack*), the satirical work on murder by Thomas de Quincey (*On Murder Considered as One of the Fine Arts*), a novel by Franz Werfel (*Nicht der Mörder, der Ermordete ist Schuldig*), some passages in *The Prophet* by Kahlil Gibran — all express important observations on the victim and his relationship with the offender.

During the 19th century and the first four decades of the 20th century, few scholars discussed the victim's role in a criminal situation. Although the founders of the science of criminology were themselves aware of the crucial importance of the criminal-victim relationship, it was not until the 1940s that high interest in the victim developed. Von Hentig's paper entitled "Remarks on the Interaction of Perpetrator and Victim" (1941) and his book, *The Criminal and His Victim* (1948); Mendelsohn's paper, "New Bio-Psycho-Social Horizons: Victimology" (1957); and Ellenberger's study on the psychological relationship between the criminal and his victim (1954) all underlined the importance of studying the criminal–victim relationship to obtain a better understanding of crime and its origins and implications. Since then, numerous scholars have focused their efforts on this aspect of crime. As a result, a considerable body of literature about victims has developed.

Meanwhile, a movement for the recognition of the victim as deserving more effective remedy than the traditional action in tort was begun by the English penal reformer Margery Fry (1951, 1957). Her call for reform was first heard in New Zealand in 1963. In that year, the New Zealand Parliament established the first crime compensation tribunal, with discretionary power to award public compensation to the victim or his dependents where he had been injured or killed through the commission of certain specified offenses. In the following year, the Tory government in England announced a similar but nonstatutory program. In America, the first jurisdiction to adopt the compensation principle was California. Its program was enacted in 1965 and put in operation two years later. Since that time, similar or related programs have been established in some 30 states in the United States and in all Canadian provinces. Australia and Sweden are two other countries that have adopted a special program of victim compensation.

Experts have suggested a different approach for the compensation of crime victims: insurance. Insurance protection is now offered in several countries to corporate clients against kidnapping and arson demands.

Meanwhile, other important facets of the victim's situation have come under scrutiny and have spurred action. Students and professionals in the criminal justice system have become increasingly aware that a victim of a criminal becomes — more often than not — also the victim of the criminal justice system. Once the victim reports his victimization to the police, the gateway to the criminal justice system, he or she is routinely faced by postponements, delays, reschedulings, and other abuses. All this means loss of earnings, waste of time, frustration, and the painful realization that the system does not live up to its ideals and does not serve its constituency, but instead serves itself. As a consequence, many innovative proposals have been advanced, such as the creation of central citizens complaint and service bureaus; witness coordinators at police stations, courthouses, district attorneys' offices, and defenders' offices; participation of the victim in plea bargaining by prosecutors; reports, at some point, by police to victims on whether they are making progress in investigating and solving their cases; the provision of the services of an ombudsman who would assist victims of crime by intervening in the crisis, acting as a community facilitator, and referring the victims to the community's resources; the establishment of Rape Crisis Centers, Spouse Abuse Shelters, and other victim assistance organizations.

Survival, Collective and Individual Responsibility, and the Victim: Historical Developments

Through the centuries, the role, importance, and visibility of the victim have varied considerably. This reflects the historical evolution of legal concepts; the diverse approach to the examination of ideas like responsibility, participation, and precipitation; and the need and desire intensely felt and expressed through the American and French revolutions, to erect solid and unbreakable barriers between the unbridled power of the state and the citizen suspected of a crime. The last development tipped the scales of the justice system in favor of the defendant and relegated the victim for centuries to a minor and secondary role in the decision-making process of the criminal justice system. Not until the 1970s would a concerted, international effort be made to reverse the trend and regain a foothold for the victim in the proceedings of justice.

Thus, the history of the justice system is being slowly rewritten from the perspective of the victim, revolutionizing tenets and perspectives taken for granted for centuries. It was not always this way. There was a time when the interests of the victim were of paramount importance in the administration of justice, and reflected the absolute need of the individual to retaliate ruthlessly against an aggressor to ensure his own survival. During these earliest days of humankind, law and order were in the hands of the individual who had to take the law into his own hands. He made the law, decided on the punishment, and then carried it out, being victim, police, prosecutor, judge, and executioner all in one. Revenge was the main justification behind this individualist form of justice; deterrence was its main goal. The need for security and survival and for preventing future attacks led early humans to retaliate ruthlessly in kind and even to conduct what today we call preemptive raids. The criminal-victim relationship at this time was not based on the concepts of responsibility and punishment, but rather on a raw struggle for power and survival.

With the development of more complex social structures like the family, the extended family, the clan, and the tribe, the guilt for the offense and the responsibility for carrying out the revenge were transferred from the individual to the collectivity. The concept of "collective responsibility" dominated human justice transactions for centuries, until the concepts of person, individual responsibility, and guilt were developed by Greek and Roman philosophers in the centuries before and after the birth of Christ and then adopted and diffused by Christianity. Collective responsibility made it possible to rationalize and justify revenge and retribution against any member of the offending group, not necessarily only against the individual transgressor, carried out by any member of the group to which the victim belonged.

This approach, richly reflected in countless documents of antiquity, including the Bible, stemmed not only from the realization that there is strength in numbers but also from the awareness of the group as the necessary unit for survival, with members sharing a commonality of purpose, destiny, responsibility, and mutual defense. While each and every individual and his contributions were vital to the success of the group, it was also true that no individual could survive alone. It was the group as a whole that possessed the spiritual power, the collective strength, and the flow of life that were imperiled and diminished by victimization and that had to be restored through revenge against the offending group. Among certain cultures, particularly in the Pacific, this conception of collective responsibility became enshrined into ritual warfare lasting for centuries. It reflected the desperate need of each group constantly to redress their collective balance of power. This, however, would inevitably lead to retaliation and revenge on the part of opponents that would tilt the balance again in their favor and start the cycle all over again. In many cases, this deadlock was not broken until the intervention of colonial powers who found it uncivilized, disruptive, or incomprehensible. Actually, the concepts of revenge, vendetta, blood-feud, and collective responsibility have clearly survived throughout the centuries even in "civilized" countries, particularly in those where law enforcement and the administration of justice have been weak and corrupt and the people have had to take the law into their own hands along family and tribal lines. In many regions of the world, including many countries in the Mediterranean, in the Pacific, and in some areas of the United States (e.g., Appalachia), blood-feud is still practiced today, at times leading to the extinction of entire family lines. The concept of collective responsibility and retribution is still applied from time to time today when racism, discrimination, persecution and warfare make it useful to justify and rationalize what otherwise could not be condoned. The genocide of the Armenians, the Jews, and the Gypsies during this century in Europe and the military atrocities of many worldwide wars testify to that.

The blood-feud, however, was slowly discredited and supplanted by several forces and ideas; they included the increased stress on individual responsibility popularized by Christianity and particularly by Protestantism; the increased complexity of society characterized by the rise of cities, commerce, banking, and legal institutions; and the slow but steady ascendancy of the state as *the* arbiter of disputes, the maker and enforcer of the law, and the guarantor of the peace.

Americans should readily grasp this historical development by relating it to the history of their own country, particularly to the settlement of the West. It was there that, at least initially, settlers had to take the law in their own hands; fight others along family or clan lines; and struggle for survival against encroachment, displacement, and wholesale destruction. The feuds between ranchers and farmers are but one example of this bloody and violent saga. The process of bringing law and order to the American West was slow and difficult. Some may think it is still under way. The same variables that affected the drive against blood-feuds in antiquity applied here as well: urbanization, commerce, the rise of the bourgeoisie, and the consequent redefinition of what is important, tolerable, or allowable.

In medieval Europe merchants, bankers, scholars, and priests saw revenge inspired by a subjective, albeit collective, perception of wrongdoing as a threat to their interests and ideals. From their respective viewpoints, they saw it as disruptive of the public peace and stability needed for commerce to prosper, or as a challenge to their philosophical or theological vision of humanity and of the world characterized by the central and supreme place bestowed upon the earth in the cosmic system and upon man standing alone — as an individual — before God above all other realms of nature. The transition to a more peaceful accommodation of the blood-feud was not only demanded but made possible by several concepts developed throughout the centuries when, for instance, commerce changed from bartering to payment in money for goods. This required a mental and cultural leap from a real to a symbolic exchange which opened the way for similar transactions related to offenses. Instead of "an eye for an eye" (a tenet which already represented an advance over more ruthless retaliation), society was now ready to accept symbolic compensation and restitution by means of money or other goods. Thus, cultural, social, and economic evolution made it possible to translate physical or mental hurt into economic goods and to equate them satisfactorily. Payment was made directly to the victim or his family. It varied according to the nature of the crime and the age, rank, sex, and prestige of the offended party. Thus, it reflected social order and class distinctions that had become progressively more complex, underlining what was now the differential ranking of the importance of each individual vis-à-vis the survival of the groups.

A crucial development that also took place at this time, culminating centuries later in the creation of the modern state, was the progressively more prominent role that an increasingly bureaucratic government took in the conduct of the affairs of the community and in the administration of justice. Slowly but steadily, the power of the state over compensation gradually increased until it became practically complete as we know it today. The compensation that used to restore the loss of the victim and also to symbolize his revenge and satisfaction, became a "fine" benefiting the state and meant to punish the offender. The interests of the victim became secondary to those claimed by the government as the representative of the larger concerns of the community which superseded those of the victim, should there be a clash.

The evolutionary circle was now complete. At the beginning, the victim's judgment and needs were the controlling factor in meting out justice; now, the community in its most impersonal form was playing that role. The victim was nothing more than another witness whose participation in the justice process was meant to serve not his interests but those of the state, at the state's complete discretion. True, the victim continued to be the cause or the reason for the justice system to become mobilized and to proceed against the accused, but the victim had lost control over the fate of the criminal and over the procedure leading to the disposition of the case and was now entirely excluded from the settlement of the case.

While the dates and times when these events took place vary from culture to culture and from region to region, there is no doubt that this is the role and the place universally occupied by the victim in today's "civilized" systems of justice.

That is why the current resurgence of interest in the victim represents a true break with tradition, challenges the existing system and status quo, and holds great promise for genuine innovation at the theoretical, legislative, and programming levels.

New Perspectives Opened by Victimological Research

Three kinds of interest are recognizable in the work of the growing number of students of victimology:

1. Scientific, that is, a principal interest in the causal association of victim and offender acts and characteristics.

2. Social engineering, reflected by those concerned directly with measures to reduce the hazards of victimization, including efforts to increase the chances of offender detection and prosecution.

3. Legal and moral, displayed by those concerned with more accurate and just assignments of responsibility, blame, fault, guilt, culpability, or mitigation. Some of these measures entail fundamental alterations of systems of law, social welfare, and administration of justice.

Research focusing on the victim has brought new perspectives into the social sciences:

1. Students of crime who focus on the individual and his characteristics have a new set of research targets. In the past, the offender has been almost exclusively at the center of interest. Much effort has been spent in attempting to find out what peculiarities, anomalies, mental disorders, or personality defects could explain criminal behavior. Now questions are raised about the victim — from a victim's perspective. Many talk about victim proneness, victim recidivists, victim in need, or latent victim. This obviously implies that there may be something in those who are victimized, particularly in those who are repeatedly victimized, that may shed light on their victimization.

2. Victim-focused research and interest has somewhat redressed the balance in crime-related research. In the past, society has been preoccupied in assigning the offender a certain societal role and keeping him in it. This labeling of the offender has been accomplished by describing him as a different kind of person; evil, sick, mentally deranged, an outsider, or an outcast. The victim has also been seen and described as an innocent party whose unlucky fate it was to fall victim to a violent crime. Victimology, by introducing a new perspective, has contributed to the softening of these stereotypes. One could almost say the balance has already swung too far in the other direction, and for a good reason: a new scapegoat has been found to explain criminal behavior, the victim. Some criminologists, or would-be ones, have quickly seized the opportunity to claim that victims of assault have no one else but themselves to

blame if they were attacked when walking, let us say, in a dark alley; or that victims of sexual assault provoked the attack by wearing attractive clothes, or by accompanying their acquaintance to a secluded place, or by hitchhiking. Others, more radical in creed, do not hesitate to point out that, for example, stores and not customers are responsible for shoplifting, because they display their wares in an enticing way.

In general, one can say that the distinction between the criminal and his victim — which in former days was deemed to be clear-cut — has become vague and blurred at least in some cases. In particular, the relationship between the perpetrator and the victim has been determined to be much more intricate than the rough distinctions of "innocent versus guilty" acknowledged by criminal law.

This approach to the explanation of crime and victimization is particularly attractive if one, accepting the officially reported rates of crimes, believes that most crime is localized in certain areas of the cities and affects a certain segment of the population. Then, one can easily consider both criminals and victims as being of the same stock, predisposed to unlawfulness, provocative, and easily provoked. The same individuals may alternatively or even simultaneously be offenders and victims, while the majority of the population is safely outside, looking on with dismay, amusement, or indifference.

3. This refocusing of the dynamics of the crime situation has influenced policymaking. In the past, the major emphasis in the war against crime was on punishment and deterrence. The goal was to affect the motivation of the offender by making it costly to engage in deviant behavior. Victim-centered research has modified this by pointing out the role the victim can play before, during, and after the commission of crimes. Many think it is reasonable to focus on the victim's behavior and to change it to prevent crimes effectively. Thus, pressure and incentives have been offered to potential victims to improve the safety and security of their dwellings, to adopt certain precautionary measures when leaving their homes, to use more sophisticated locks, to install television cameras in shops and banks, to hire private guards, to buy insurance, or to engrave their most costly belongings with identification numbers.

Society has acknowledged that the victim plays a role in his own victimization and that, by taking certain steps, he can avoid being victimized. It thus follows that if he is actually victimized, it may be at least partially his fault. In other words, society has transferred part of the social cost and part of the blame from the criminal to the victim. In some countries, like Scandinavia, some have demanded a total transfer of such costs to the victim, when it was proposed, for example, that owners of supermarkets and department stores should not have the right to prosecute shoplifters and that banks should accept responsibility and absorb the loss for forged or bad checks. Thus, what is generally deemed to be crime would be redefined as an occupational risk of which the banker or department store owner should be aware, and whose consequences must be accepted without retaliation.

There is perhaps no other area of concern and debate where the complexity of life and the tensions inherent in today's changing of roles and increase in individual freedoms clash more strongly with the stark realities of crime and violence which severely limit individual rights and activities. That women should limit their pursuit of careers, leisure, and recreation because there are rapists and murderers waiting for the right occasion to strike is ideally unacceptable. That women should, however, pursue work and pleasure with the awareness that danger exists and therefore institute reasonable steps that prudence demands is a reality of life, however disappointing it may be.

From this step to the conclusion that any woman or man sexually or otherwise assaulted, robbed, or even killed was "asking for it" and could have prevented it would constitute a rash judgment often unsupported by the facts. Being vulnerable is not the same as "asking for it;" asserting, within reason, one's right to the free pursuit of life is also not the same as "asking for it".

The problem at times lies in a clash of perceptions, values, and life-styles. On the one hand, it is unfair to ask the potential victim to limit his or her behavior because of what others may think or do; on the other, it is unrealistic to ignore or disregard what those clashes may generate, if they exist, and not take reasonable precautions.

Thus, the person who shows a large amount of cash in public or as a tourist in a foreign land that has a low per capita income and who subsequently is robbed, theoretically should have had the right to display his wealth, regardless of the circumstances. Realistically, however, he acted imprudently by attracting attention. Were the robbers innocent because of his behavior? Of course not. Was the victim blameless? Of course not, but he was at least imprudent. Did he "ask for it?" Not necessarily. Being dumb or flashy or arrogant does not mean asking to be robbed, although it may lead to robbery.

There are, of course, many variables that can modify this situation and change the equation of guilt and innocence, provocation and vulnerability, stupidity and prudence. For example, being robbed and even hurt at a wealthy and exclusive club by a fellow millionaire is so unexpected and out of place that almost everyone would hold the victim blameless, even though he openly displayed his wealth. On the contrary, being robbed in a country where many have difficulty earning in a year the large bill a tourist casually displays when paying for something may change our verdict. Some radical thinkers may even assert that the robbery actually represented a long overdue and symbolic redistribution of world wealth and was therefore entirely legitimate.

In conclusion, the complexity of every situation dictates that we be careful in assessing blame and responsibility, particularly on the victim. To blame the victim because he is an easier scapegoat or because it fits into our prejudices and preconceptions does not represent an advance in our understanding of crime and of reality. But that very complexity also demands that in real life prudence and reason temper the exercise of our rights and the testing of new frontiers.

4. An important new perspective opened by victimological interest affects the operations of the criminal justice system. After what Schafer (1977) describes as "the golden age of the victim," the victim's input in the criminal justice system has been next to nil. Many feel that the victim is the most disregarded component in criminal justice proceedings. After the victim has reported his victimization and has provided information to the police, he may not hear from the police or the prosecutor for long periods, or even not at all. Cases have been disposed of without any consultation or contact of the victim. If and when the victim is called for the trial, he falls into the category of witness—in this case, witness for the state—and is entitled to all the delays, postponements, and other frustrating experiences awaiting such a person at the courthouse. The newly focused attention on the victim has vividly brought to light the victim's plight at the hands of the criminal justice system. Attention on the victim also calls for a reexamination of the whole issue of what is justice, what is crime, what is the appropriate remedy to victimization. Most if not all laws reflect middle-class values. Thus, justice, crime, punishment, and remedies rest on such middle-class foundations. But most of the known victims belong to the lower class. Consequently, there is an inherent inequity in the criminal justice system, since the opinions of one socioeconomic class dominate and dictate the perception, assessment, and disposition of matters deeply affecting another. Victimological research, therefore, is showing how the input of the victim should be sought when developing systems for the compensation of victims of crime, and how the concept of "relative loss" should be introduced in debate and deliberations for compensation.

Limitations and Risks of Research
Focusing on the Victim

Research focusing on the victim will develop further, achieve further refinements, and engineer new breakthroughs. There are, however, some dangers that may develop as a consequence of victimological research.

1. Some researchers may simply shift their focus from the individual criminal to the individual victim. This type of research would generate findings of little use for decision-makers, because it would not consider problems stemming from societal conditions and the cultural influences.

2. The growth of research focusing on the victim may involve distortion in what is actually selected as the object of inquiry. There may be an excessive concentration of interest and research efforts on crimes of violence, sexual offenses, and swindle. Some large groups of crimes have been neglected, one suspects, mostly because there is no clearly identifiable victim. One could mention, for example, consumer-related issues; victims of omission and neglect rather than of commission; victims that are not identifiable individuals but organizations or classes of people. Thus, victimologists have generally accepted the most common, least controversial, more easily applicable definition of who the victims are and who may be a victim. The current debate about consumer problems, the environment, poverty, and malnutrition, the inequitable distribution of wealth, the struggle of minorities and women to gain recognition and economic power, the failures of the justice system, the scandals surrounding the treatment of old people, the mentally retarded, and the mentally ill require that an enlarged list of victims receive the attention of scholars, researchers, and decision-makers.

3. It is important to begin examining and studying victimization at the hands of the state and of the power structure. Most current victimological research falls along traditional lines of inquiry, focusing on individual-to-individual relationships rather than looking at the more diffuse and subtle, but by no means less important, relationships of power and oppression. More attention must be devoted to the recurrent instances of genocide, displacement, and persecution of select groups at the hand of other, more powerful ones; the various forms of colonialism; the misuse of psychiatric labels and facilities to suppress dissent and stifle opposition or unorthodox, innovative behavior; the acceptance and support of belief systems to justify oppression, discrimination, and their various manifestations like ageism, sexism, and racism. In other words, it is important for victimologists not to repeat the same errors of atomized thinking, researching, and theorizing that have characterized a portion of criminological research. Victimology has a bright future, if its development is steered in the right direction.

Victimology and the Elderly

In the next 50 years the number of elderly people in America will rapidly increase as the result of many recent medical advances. In the eyes of many, this also means a tremendous increase in the numbers of people who are, almost by definition, vulnerable, dependent, and in need of protection. The current controversy over the future of the Social Security system has catapulted old age and its concomitant financial and health problems into the national consciousness in a stark and unavoidable way. The potential for intergenerational warfare is there, with the old clinging to what they perceive are their earned rights and benefits and looking with distrust and fear at the younger generation, whom they perceive as lacking the traditional and solid values of bygone days; meanwhile the young seethe with anger and resentment at the burden they must increasingly carry to support those they consider no longer useful and productive.

The victimization of the elderly must, indeed, be placed within the context in which aging itself has been made into a process of progressive victimization. There is no doubt that in American society, for example, becoming old means becoming less of something on the way to losing everything. The celebration of youth as the optimum and enviable season of being alive and human means also that the progressive loss of youth entails the progressive loss of humanity and of life's strengths. If, in the eyes of many, becoming old means becoming less human, it is easy to see how a wide spectrum of victimization of the elderly can take place and be justified. Stripping people of their humanity to victimize them with impunity, legitimacy, and even righteousness is a process long used by humankind. Some fear that a reincarnation of the same process may lead some day a society restive under the burden of a massive Social Security system to unburden itself of at least its most helpless aged. The complexity of moral and legal judgments and the quicksand nature of our collective judgment are vividly demonstrated by the disparate perceptions of liberalized abortion, euthanasia, and "death with dignity" as expressions either of freedom of choice or of legalized genocide and organized oppression.

The connection between the diffused victimization we have built into aging as a process and the actual victimization of the aged by criminals is not difficult to see. That the elderly may be a more popular target of victimization than others is readily explained by the fact that they are seen as *legitimate* or *deserving* victims, whose diminished humanity, usefulness, and productivity make their victimization not only desirable, but even necessary and justified. The use of the elderly victim as an agent of self-legitimization (Fattah, 1976) through the steps of

- denial and reification of the victim reduced to the status of "non-being,"
- devaluation of the victim's personal worth based on some of his attributes or qualities,

- blaming the victim, and
- defining the victimization as an act of justice

is particularly evident in the senseless crimes of brutalization, deprivation, intimidation, and suicide targeted on the elderly. What is new is not
the dynamics, justifications, and actions but only the increasing number
of "legitimate" and vulnerable targets due to current population shifts:
the aged.

Possible intergenerational warfare appears in the controversy about
whether or not the elderly are truly more victimized than the young
(Goldsmith, 1974; Gubrium, 1974; Cook and Cook, 1976; Malinchak,
1978). Do the elderly truly constitute a unique class of crime victims? Are
crimes against them dealt with most effectively when they are considered
a distinct category of criminal activity? Is it justified in today's climate
of fiscal crisis and restraint to develop and maintain programs and projects especially targeted to assist elderly victims or to prevent crimes
against the aged instead of directing these efforts to benefit the general
population?

These are some of the questions that need an equitable and realistic
answer. Victimization of the elderly is the most crucial and urgent one
facing victimology today. While study, debate, reform, and innovation
are still under way in areas like sexual assault, domestic violence, child
abuse and neglect, the sheer number of Americans moving towards old
age dictates that we openly confront the topic of victimization of the aged.
On the one hand, compassion, humanitarian concern, and vested interests may lead some to emphasize the elderly's vulnerability and to demand massive intervention, thus unwittingly confirming the deep,
negative cultural values about the old that also justify victimizers' actions. On the other, reliance on data showing the young to be the most
victimized group and the desire to avoid fragmentation of efforts along
age lines may lead to downplaying the needs and expectations of the
aged, thus neglecting them, abandoning them to criminals, or greedy
relatives, and also alienating a powerful political force. The challenge
facing victimology is to devise a balanced, equitable, and humane solution to this pressing problem. Victimologists will have a rare chance to
test the worth of their work.

Victimology Today: Redressing the Balance

The current movement is laying the foundation for redressing the
situation and for instituting a system that recognizes the vital role and the
importance that the victim/witness plays in the successful accomplish-

ment of justice. This implies a partnership with the victim/witness in investigation and solution of crimes, in prosecution, in sentencing, probation, and parole stages. The degrees of input and power in decision making granted the victim may vary or be open for debate and even struggle, but the current lack of success of the justice system to control the epidemic of violent crime makes it imperative to consider a bold and drastic departure from past patterns.

Let us make sure that working for recognition of "victims' rights" does not mean turning the clock back on the many positive strides and reforms recently introduced to benefit the suspect, the accused, the defendant, the convict, and the exconvict. Contrary to taking a "zero-sum" approach to the issue, many maintain that gains for the victim can and should mean gains for the offender's rehabilitation and treatment as well. Ideas and programs benefiting the victim such as speedy trial, restitution, and compensation can constitute the foundation for alternatives that benefit the offender as well. Ultimately, it is society (all of us) that gains from better justice.

In this perspective, victimological concerns and programmatic interventions are extremely important, first, to redress the balance in the justice system to take into account more fairly the concerns, interests, and needs of the victim; and, second, to strengthen the foundations and fabric of society by demonstrating to everyone affected by crime and its aftermath that mutual care, concern, and compassion are the forces that inspire our behavior.

While fear of crime could make the country helpless and unable to deal with this problem, or cripple our ability to lead a full life, we also have the challenge of channeling fear, rage, and grief into avenues for change, including stronger community ties. At a time of fiscal conservatism and escalating costs, it is vital that the importance, innovativeness, and usefulness of victimology and of victim/witness services be clearly understood and strongly supported.

The victim/witness movement holds great promise, as a force for genuine change in society's attitudes and patterns of caring for its members and as an opportunity to stand up to crime in a positive, caring, and also preventive way. It is to be hoped that it will be able to gain momentum, avoid theoretical and programmatic pitfalls, and attain full potential as a crucial movement in contemporary social history.

BIBLIOGRAPHY

Birren JE: *The Psychology of Aging.* Englewood Cliffs, NJ, Prentice-Hall, 1965.
Bradley WM: Class corridor safety for seniors project, *The Police Chief* 1976; February.

16

Brooks J: Compensating victims of crime: The recommendations of program administrators, *Law and Society Review* 1973;7, Spring.

Butler RN, Lewis MI: *Aging and Mental Health: Positive Psychosocial Approaches.* St. Louis, MO, C.V. Mosby, 1973.

Butler RN: *Why Survive? Being Old in America.* New York, Harper & Row, 1975.

Clemente F, Kleiman MB: Fear of crime among the aged. *Gerontologist* 1976;16: 207–210.

Condit TW, Greenbaum S, Nicholson G: *Forgotten Victims — An Advocate's Anthology.* Sacramento, CA Office of Criminal Justice Planning, Alameda Regional Criminal Justice Planning Board, 1977.

Cook FL, Cook TD: Evaluating the rhetoric of crisis: A case study of criminal victimization of the elderly. *Social Service Rev* 1976;50:641–642.

Crime Against Aging Americans — The Kansas City Study. Kansas City, MO, Midwest Research Institute, 1975.

Crime Against the Elderly: L.E.A.A.'s Elderly Crime Victimization Programs, No. 1977-241-090/64, National Institute of Law Enforcement and Criminal Justice, U.S. Department of Justice, L.E.A.A., Washington, DC: Government Printing Office, 1977.

Crime Prevention Handbook for Senior Citizens. Kansas City, MO, Midwest Research Institute, 1977.

Crime Prevention Handbook for Senior Citizens. Washington, DC: Law Enforcement Assistance Administration, June 1977.

Dadich GJ: Crime, the elderly and community relations, *The Police Chief* 1977; February.

Ducovny AM: *The Billion Dollar Swindle: Frauds Against the Elderly.* New York, Fleet Press, 1969.

Elderly Crime Victimization (Federal Law Enforcement Agencies — L.E.A.A. and F.B.I.), Hearings before the U.S. Congress, House Select Committee on Aging, Subcommittee on Housing and Consumer Interests 94th Congress, 2nd Session, held April 12–13, 1976. Washington, DC: Government Printing Office, 1976.

Ellenberger H: Relations psychologiques entre le ciminel et al victime. *Rev Intern de Criminol et Police Tech* 1954;8:103–121.

Ernst ML, Jodry F, Friedsam HJ: *Reporting and Non-Reporting of Crime by Older Americans.* Denton, Texas: Center for Studies in Aging, North Texas State University, 1976.

Fattah EA: The use of the victim as an agent of self-legitimization: Toward a dynamic explanation of criminal behavior, in Viano E (ed): *Victims and Society.* Washington, DC, Visage Press, 1976.

Federal Bureau of Investigation, White Collar Crime Section, Criminal Investigative Division, Anatomy of an advanced-fee swindle. *Police Chief* 1977; September.

Forston R, Kitchens J: *Criminal Victimization of the Aged: The Houston Model Neighborhood Area,* Community Service Report No. 1, Center for Community Services, School of Community Service. Denton, TX, North Texas State University, 1974.

Fry M: *Arms of the Law.* London, Gollanez, 1951.

Fry M: Justice for victims. *The Observer* July, 1957;7:8.

Gertz MG, Talarico S: Problems of reliability and validity in criminal justice research. *Journal of Criminal Justice* 1977;5:217–224.

Glaser D: *Adult Crime and Social Policy.* Englewood Cliffs, NJ, Prentice-Hall, 1972.

Goldsmith J: Community crime prevention and the elderly: A segmental approach. *Crime Prevention Review,* State of California: Attorney General's Office, July, 1975.

Goldsmith J: Police and the older victim: Keys to a changing perspective. *The Police Chief* 1976; February.

Goldsmith J, Goldsmith SS: *Crime and the Elderly—Challenge and Response.* Lexington, MA, Lexington Books, 1976.

Goldsmith J, Tomas NE: Crimes against the elderly: A continuing national crisis, *Aging* 1974; June/July.

Goldsmith SS, Goldsmith J: Crime, the aging and public policy. *Perspective on Aging* 1975;4:(3) May/June.

Griffith L: *Mugging: You Can Protect Yourself.* Englewood Cliffs, NJ: Prentice-Hall, 1978.

Gross PJ: Law enforcement and the senior citizen. *The Police Chief* 1976; February.

Gross S, Lipstein DJ: Crime prevention education for the elderly in Baltimore city. *The Police Chief* 1977; October.

Gubrium JF: *The Myths of the Golden Years: A Socio-Environmental Theory of Aging.* Springfield, IL, Charles C Thomas, 1973.

Gubrium JF: *Time, Roles and Self in Old Age.* New York, Human Sciences Press, 1976.

Gubrium JF: Victimization in old age: Available evidence and three hypotheses. *Crime and Delinquency* 1974; July.

Hahn PH: *Crimes Against the Elderly—A Study in Victimology.* Santa Cruz, CA, Davis Publications, 1976.

Hentig H von: *The Criminal and His Victim.* New Haven, CT, Yale University Press, 1948.

Hentig H von: Remarks on the interaction of perpetrator and victim. *J Am Inst Crim Law Criminol* May–June 1940; March–April 1941;303–309.

Hypes D: New approaches to crime prevention. *The Police Chief* 1975; May.

Jones R: *The Other Generation: The New Power in Older People.* Englewood Cliffs, NJ: Prentice-Hall, 1977.

Kahana E: *Perspectives of Aged on Victimization, Ageism, and Their Problems in Urban Society.* Detroit, MI, Wayne State University, 1974.

Langer E: Growing old in America: Frauds, quackery, swindle the aged and compound their troubles. *Science* 1963;140:470–472.

Malinchak AA, Wright D: Older Americans and crime: The scope of elderly victimization. *Aging* 1978; 281–282, March/April, pp 10–17.

Mendelsohn B: Une nouvelle branche de la science bio-psycho-sociale: La victimologie. *Rev Intern de Criminol et Police Tech* 1957;11(2):95–109.

Mendelson MA: *Tender Loving Greed—How the Incredibly Lucrative Nursing Home "Industry" is Exploiting America's Old People and Defrauding Us All.* New York, Alfred A. Knopf, 1974.

Myth and Reality of Aging in America, a study prepared by Louis Harris and Associates, Inc for The National Council on the Aging, Inc, Washington, DC, 1975.

Pope CE, Feyerherm W: A review of recent trends: The effects of crime on the elderly. *The Police Chief* 1976; February.

Quinney R: *The Social Reality of Crime.* Boston, MA, Little Brown, 1970.

Riley M: *Aging and Society,* 3 vols. New York, Russell Sage Foundation, 1972.

Ritchey LW: Crime: Can the older adult do anything about it? *The Police Chief* 1977; February, 40–41.

Schafer S: *Victimology: The Victim and His Criminal.* Reston, VA: Reston Publishing, 1977.

Shimizu M: A study on the crimes of the aged in Japan. *Acta Criminol Med Legal Jap* 1973;39:No. 5/6, December.

Shook HC: Who pleads for the victim? *The Police Chief* 1978; January.

Slicker M: A public policy perspective: The elderly and the criminal justice system. *The Police Chief* 1977; February, 23–25.

Springer JL: *Consumer Swindlers and How to Avoid Them.* New York, Henry R. Regnery, 1970.

Sundeen RA, Mathieu JT: The fear of crime and its consequences among elderly in three urban communities. *Gerontologist* 1976;16:211–219.

Sunderland G: Crime prevention for the elderly. *Ekistics* 1975;39:91–92.

Sunderland G: The older American: Police problem or police asset?, *F.B.I. Law Enforcement Bulletin* 1976;45:No. 8, August.

Taylor I, Walton P, Young J: *The New Criminology.* New York, Harper and Row, 1973.

Tighe JH: A survey of crime against the elderly. *The Police Chief* 1977; February.

Viano E: *Victims and Society.* Washington, DC, Visage Press, 1976.

Willis RL, Miller M: Senior citizen crime prevention programs, *The Police Chief* 1976; February.

Youmans EG: Some views on human aging, in Boyd RR, Oakes CG (eds): *Foundations of Practical Gerontology,* Columbia, SC: University of South Carolina Press, 1973.

SECTION I
The Problems

The first section of this book discusses the problems of abuse and maltreatment of the elderly and is preceded by a chapter in which Emilio C. Viano discusses the theoretical and historical development of victimology. The author also identifies research issues related to the victim and to the criminal justice system. Victimization of the elderly is discussed within the context of cultural and societal values and practices. Gordon E. Finley discusses the interface between victimization risk and fear of crime, the causes and consequences of fear of crime by the elderly, and factors associated with fear. Also discussed are efforts to reduce both fear of crime and the commission of crime against the elderly.

Two chapters focus on different types of crime against the elderly. The first, by Jersey Liang and Mary C. Sengstock, looks at personal crimes against the elderly, using national data on the extent, characteristics, and consequences of personal victimization of the elderly. The reactions of victims is discussed, with implications for research, policy development, and the criminal justice system. The second chapter, on fraud, is written by Congressman Claude D. Pepper who describes 13 types of fraud against the elderly. The congressman illustrates his discussion with case examples from past hearings of the House Select Committee on Aging and identifies those who are responsible for reducing crimes of fraud.

Institutions for the aged have been the subject of many books and articles. Two chapters in this book are about institutional care. The first, by Susan O. Mercer, traces the development of institutional care and describes the characteristics of institutionalized elderly populations. The chapter also looks at the subtle implications of institutionalization which include symbolic and actual loss of autonomy, privacy, control, and choice, and can result in learned helplessness and self-destructive behavior. Val J. Halamandaris discusses different types of criminal fraud and abuse perpetrated by some nursing home owners and administrators over the past few years (as obtained from state and federal records). The offenses include, among others, theft, misrepresentation, fraud, kickbacks, and the involvement of organized crime.

The abuse of the elderly by family members has recently been "discovered," although it probably only characterizes the care by a very small proportion of family members. Susan K. Steinmetz has written a chapter on violence between the elderly and their middle-aged children and has related the problem to issues of stress and dependency. Conclusions were based on findings from a study of families who care for elderly relatives,

on the stress that occurred, and on methods for resolving the problems. Richard L. Douglass and Tom Hickey survey the literature on domestic neglect and abuse of the elderly and discuss conceptual problems and common causes. The authors also develop a system of human services for prevention and intervention at different levels.

Two physicians have each written a chapter on health professionals as a cause of and solution to the problem of maltreatment of the elderly. Kenneth Solomon, MD, discusses negative attitudes toward geriatric clients and consequences for care and treatment. The psychological effects of victimization, such as feelings of helplessness and coping abilities, are discussed. A geriatrician in private practice, Victor Kassel, MD, critically assesses medical care for the elderly in the United States: the role of the physician, needed policy changes, and attitudes of geriatric patients toward physicians. Also discussed are limitations in federal programs, geriatric patients in hospitals, and the dying process and death of an elderly person.

Collectively, these chapters provide a comprehensive overview of the various types of adversity facing the elderly: fear, crime and fraud, maltreatment within institutional settings, abuse by family members, and second-class professional and institutional care by health care providers and institutions.

2 Fear of Crime in the Elderly

Gordon E. Finley

Fear of crime in the elderly is best understood within the broader context of crime and the elderly. This, in turn, is best understood in a short-term historical perspective. National interest in crime and the elderly began to develop in the late 1960s and reached a height of public outrage during the mid-1970s. Four issues were raised during these years.

First, interest centered on the idea that the elderly were selected for victimization more frequently than other age groups. This notion was quickly corrected by a series of national surveys that indicated that, with the possible exceptions of the inner-city elderly and crimes of personal larceny, the elderly were undervictimized compared to other age groups. Second, it was believed that the physical and financial consequences of victimization were greater for the aged than for any other group. It is now believed that it is difficult to distinguish the aged from other victims in this regard.

Third, interest focused on the psychological consequences of victimization being greater for the elderly than for other age groups. This, too, has come to be questioned. Fourth, interest centered on the idea that the *fear* of crime was greater in the elderly than in any other age group, and this idea turned out to be true.

One in four is not a good score. Why then should the consensus of professionals and the media be so poorly supported by empirical data? There are a number of possible explanations: (1) the issues were embedded in a larger political-moral context that distorted perceptions; (2) the sensational and heartrending examples of the consequences for particular elderly, which peppered initial publications on the topic, personalized the issue and created an emotional outrage that distorted perceptions; (3) there was a rush to the bandwagon by politicians and social scientists alike; (4) there was an initial focus on case studies of the elderly that neglected comparisons with younger age groups; (5) journalism replaced empiricism as our source of knowledge; (6) because the elderly frequently are viewed as a homogeneous category, it was assumed that these extreme and sensational cases were representative examples; (7) individual and neighborhood differences as concepts for analyzing data were overlooked; and (8) simple and firm conclusions were sought when the underlying reality was complex. Often public concerns do not square with scientific evidence (Cook, 1978). A detailed account of the emergence of crime and the elderly as a policy issue may be found in Cook (1981).

It should be kept in mind that fear of crime among the elderly is not all bad. This fear has an important role in reducing actual victimization, as it does for all age groups. However, beyond a certain point it may have consequences which are deleterious.

Let us now consider the four issues introduced earlier. The chapter then will review what we know today about the correlates of fear of crime in the elderly, and conclude with suggestions for reducing the fear of crime and for future research.

Victimization Risk and Fear of Crime: The Paradox

The most obvious explanation for fear of crime is that it is a rational response to a real danger. In some cases it is. Jaycox (1978) and Smith (1979) persuasively argue that at the neighborhood level, elderly persons—like all age groups—clearly perceive the difference between safe and dangerous neighborhoods, and their fear corresponds accurately to these realistic differences. Smith (1979) further emphasizes that it is the propinquity of the inner-city elderly to the perpetrators of crime against them (unemployed, black youth, living in the inner city) that causes high levels of fear.

The paradox and the irrationality of the high levels of fear of crime in the elderly come from comparisons not across neighborhoods but across ages. The clearest presentation of the paradox may be found in the Congressional testimony of Hindelang and Richardson (1978). Listed below are six of their eight conclusions derived from analyses of the 1974 and 1975 National Crime Surveys.

1. Elderly Americans (for our purposes here those 65 years of age or older) have a substantially greater fear of criminal victimization than do younger Americans.
2. Elderly Americans in urban areas and in the United States as a whole have a higher rate of personal larceny (e.g., purse snatching) than do Americans in some younger age groups.
3. However, elderly Americans have far lower rates of homicide, robbery, rape, assault, burglary, larceny from the household, and motor vehicle theft victimization than do younger Americans.
4. Elderly Americans are less likely to be injured and less likely to be confronted with weapons in criminal victimizations than are younger Americans.
5. Elderly Americans are no more likely than younger Americans to be victimized by juveniles.
6. Elderly Americans have not experienced a recent upsurge in criminal victimization.

The one area of crime in which the elderly may be overvictimized, in addition to personal larceny, is fraud. Little data are available, in large part because of underreporting due to embarrassment. Possible frauds include: consumer fraud, medical fraud, confidence games, bunco, prepaid funeral schemes, health insurance fraud, income security schemes, medical quackery, get-well-quick plans, work-at-home-get-rich-quick-schemes, retirement real estate deals, nursing home fraud, and home and automobile repair deals (Braungart, Hoyer and Braungart, 1979). Although not commonly considered as such, medical fraud might well be viewed as a death-hastening crime. Regrettably, the elderly are not more fearful of fraud, which might lower their victimization rates.

Physical and Financial Consequences for the Elderly

The early consensus was clear: high levels of fear of crime resulted from the belief that the elderly suffered greater physical and financial consequences than did other age groups (e.g., Conklin, 1976; Cunningham, 1977; and Goldsmith and Tomas, 1974). However, in an article based on analyses of the 1973 and 1974 national surveys, Cook et al

(1978) challenged this consensus and concluded that:

> The data reported here offer scant systematic support to persons who believe that, when elderly Americans are victimized by criminals, they suffer more severe financial or physical hardship than younger persons. . . . Such findings suggest the inappropriateness and incompleteness of the current consensus that older Americans suffer more than others from crime. The consensus is inappropriate because it is not correct for most crimes, and it is incomplete because it fails to differentiate between age trends for different types of consequences (p 346).

A recent study of the economic, social, and psychological impacts of criminal victimization on the elderly also found surprisingly little immediate or delayed impact (Quay et al, 1980).

Psychological and Behavioral Consequences for the Elderly

The early consensus again was clear. Sensational vignettes peppered the media and professional papers showing horrible psychological consequences. Two headlines provide a sense of the media coverage: "The Elderly: Prisoners of Fear" (*Time,* November 29, 1976); and "Way of Life of Old People Curbed by Fear of Crime" (*New York Times,* April 12, 1976). Finley (1978) noted similar consequences for those attending classes at a Miami Beach Senior Activities Center. Most elderly felt very uncomfortable taking courses late in the afternoon and refused to come at night. Fear of crime served to keep these seniors off the streets at night, isolated in their rooms spending their evenings in intellectually unstimulating and socially impoverished environments. The impact of this on intellectual, social, and emotional functioning is not likely to be positive.

What, then, do the scant but existing data suggest? Perhaps the strongest evidence for the effects of an individual's level of fear of crime on his or her behavior comes from Garofalo (1980), whose analyses are derived from the 1975 National Crime Survey and a supplemental attitude questionnaire administered to a subsample of about 70,000 persons 16 or more years of age. The fear of crime index was, "How safe do you feel or would you feel being out alone in your neighborhood at night?" The behavioral impact question was, "In general, have you limited or changed your activities in the past few years because of crime?" For each of the four levels of fear of crime, the following percentage of respondents indicated that they did limit or change their activities because of crime: very safe, 20%; reasonably safe, 34%; somewhat unsafe, 58%; and very unsafe, 73%.

Further evidence comes from a study of black elderly living in inner-city Washington, DC (McAdoo, 1979). Ninety-five percent of the respondents felt that they had been forced to change their activities because of crime; 66% indicated that they were reluctant to go out during the day; 88% indicated that they were afraid to go out alone at night.

Sundeen and Mathieu (1976) report on the fear of crime and its consequences for the elderly in three urban communities: core (downtown areas of transition), "slurb" (middle-class urban city), and retirement (walled condominiums). Over 40% of the respondents in each of the settings reported doing the following: (1) core: obtain a whistle, install special locks, lock door during day, change behavior and activities, and stay home at night; (2) slurb: install special locks, lock door during day, change behavior and activities, and stay home at night; (3) retirement: obtain property theft insurance and stay home at night. The behavioral variable which stands out for all samples is staying home at night. The percentage for core was 65%, for slurb 47%, and retirement 55%. However, Lawton (in press) noted:

> Repeatedly in looking at the research in this area one is struck by the contrast between the extreme anxiety over crime as expressed by older people, and on the other hand, the smaller-than-expected effects of crime on their behavior or psychological wellbeing, at least as demonstrated thus far. . . . In a series of path analyses viewing fear of crime as an outcome of other background, environmental, and crime-related variables, and as a penultimate independent variable for the final dependent variable (wellbeing of a variety of types), fear of crime showed large and significant direct effects on morale, housing satisfaction, and neighborhood satisfaction. No effects on behavioral aspects of wellbeing (activity participation, contacts with friends, or contact with relatives) were observed.

Perhaps the greatest impact of fear of crime is on other feelings, rather than on behavior. As Skogan (1977) noted: "The relationship between expressed fear and actual behavior is problematic. It is not always possible to predict behavior on the basis of attitudes. Our behavior is shaped by a variety of opportunities and constraints that may cause us, perhaps even unwillingly, to act in ways that are discrepant with our expressed fears, beliefs, or preferences." Perhaps one avenue of future research is to explore the affective correlates and consequences of fear of crime, as well as the behavioral.

Fear of Crime Among the Elderly: Correlates and Causes

The need to understand why the elderly have such a high fear of crime has been put cogently by Cook et al (1978):

We do not yet have sophisticated and well-tested models of the causes of fear among different groups of Americans over 65. A real need exists to generate and test such models because, of the major crime problems confronting elderly Americans, fear seems to be the factor that distinguishes the crime-related experiences of elderly Americans from others (p 347).

A number of conceptual models recently have appeared in the literature which attempt to organize the existing data in a meaningful way (Balkin, 1979; Garofalo, 1979; Skogan, 1978; Yin, 1980). However, no model to date appears to have improved on the conceptual organization of: what, when, where, who, and why?

What   Intuitively, the *what* ought to be easy. However, due to the absence of conceptual clarity and methodological consistency, it is not. There are four major problems. First, Skogan (1978) has questioned whether or not fear of crime is a psychological construct of any particular significance. Second, Yin (1980) has emphasized the need to distinguish the determinants of fear of crime from the consequences. Third, Furstenberg (1971) argued that we must distinguish between the fear of crime (a fear of one's own chances of victimization) and the concern for crime (the seriousness of the crime situation in the country). Fourth, it has been pointed out by many authors that existing empirical studies use radically different types of questions to tap fear of crime in different studies.

Our approach will be to pull out the central trends and conclusions of the current literature. Future researchers, however, must resolve these issues if our knowledge is to advance.

When   There is no controversy with *when*. Fear of crime is strikingly greater at night than during the day.

Where   Organizing the data according to *where* fear of crime occurs provides the opportunity to locate the cause rationally in the environment.

1. *Culture.*   Comprehensive cross-cultural studies of crime, or fear of crime, and the elderly appear to be nonexistent. In a recent monograph, Smith (1979) sought to prepare such a cross-cultural review but gave up because of the paucity of data. Two recent cross-cultural reviews (Finley, 1981; Finley, 1982) also uncovered little in the way of cross-cultural survey data. However, there was some suggestion in the anthropological literature of considerable fear among the elderly in *some* traditional societies. The fears centered on the theft of their possessions or their murder to obtain their possessions or positions. Such a comparison of the most traditional and the most industrialized societies would be of great interest. For investigators interested in conducting cross-cultural studies, discussions of methodological and collaborative issues can be found in Finley (1979), Fry and Keith (1980), and Shanas and Madge (1968).

While attention to this topic appears to be limited mostly to the United States, one survey was located in South Africa. Schurink (1978) undertook a survey of blacks in Soweto and of coloreds in the Cape Peninsula. Interestingly, and in sharp contrast to the United States, fear of robbery and assault were highest among 40 to 49 year-old persons rather than among the elderly. Consistent with United States data, the lowest rate of fear was among the 18 to 29-year-olds. While fear of crime was not related to sex in the Cape Peninsula, it was in Soweto. Clearly, more cross-cultural studies are needed to determine the universality of findings obtained in the United States.

2. *Size of city.* Fear of crime generally is greatest in large urban areas and in the inner city. Fear of crime generally declines with decreasing city size and suburban status and is least in rural areas (Baumer, 1978; Clemente and Kleiman, 1977; and Lebowitz, 1975).

3. *Neighborhood.* Neighborhood is seen by many as the most powerful determinant of fear of crime (Baumer, 1978; Bishop and Klecka, 1978; Furstenberg, 1971; Jaycox, 1978; Lawton, in press; McPherson, 1978; Smith, 1979; Sundeen and Mathieu 1976). The elderly, along with people of all ages, can tell the difference between safe and dangerous neighborhoods and their fear of crime varies vertically.

4. *Level of community integration.* Gubrium (1974) suggested that high levels of social integration would be related to low levels of fear of crime, and the subsequent literature generally confirms his notion (Conklin, 1976; Lawton, in press). Dramatic support comes from Sundeen (1977) who reported that: "High levels of fear of burglary are related to a low sense of participation in one's community, to a low estimate of the likelihood that one's neighbors would call the police if they saw the respondent being victimized, to prior victimization, and to neighborhood environment." Garofalo and Laub (1978) argue that fear of crime must be examined in the broader frame of a concern for community, for the quality of life, and for community change.

5. *Age integrated-segregated public housing.* Although there is some controversy, Lawton and Yaffe (1980) appear to have the soundest conclusion. In a national study of 100 public housing projects, they found no correlation between age integration and actual crime rates. However, there was a correlation between age-integrated public housing and *fear* of crime among elderly tenants. This fear presumably arises from the intermingling of the elderly and the likely perpetrators of crimes against the elderly.

6. *Locale of crimes.* Compared to other age groups, more crimes occur to the elderly in or near their homes, perhaps causing them to feel that their castle is no longer safe (Antunes et al, 1977; Conklin, 1976).

Who

1. *Age.* With a few exceptions, (Ragan, 1977) fear of crime sharply increases with increasing age (Baumer, 1978; Braungart, Braungart and Hoyer, 1980; Clemente and Kleiman, 1977; Garofalo, 1980). Perhaps the clearest view of age trends may be seen in Figure 2-1, which shows the percentage of persons of both sexes at several age levels, who reported that they felt "somewhat or very unsafe being out alone at night in their own neighborhood" (Hindelang and Richardson, 1978). Generally, these age changes have been attributed either to an increase in perceived vulnerability (Lawton, in press) on the part of the elderly or a perceived immense difficulty in recovering from the physical, medical, or financial consequences of victimization on the part of the elderly (Skogan, 1978). As Garofalo notes, "The shift away from the extended family structure, public and private retirement policies, as well as purely physical changes such as declining health, all operate to place the elderly in positions that maximize feelings of vulnerability" (Garofalo, 1980).

It is of even greater interest that from 1967 to 1974, the differential between the levels of fear of crime between the youngest and oldest samples increased dramatically. In 1965 the difference was 3% while in 1974 it was 14% (Cook and Cook, 1976). Similar findings for the years 1965 and 1976 have been reported by Cutler (1980).

2. *Sex.* Women at all ages are strikingly more fearful than men, Figure 2-1, and this powerful effect has been noted by many authors (Baumer, 1978; Braungart, Braungart and Hoyer, 1980; Clemente and Kleiman, 1977; Garofalo, 1980; Lebowitz, 1975). Many authors attribute this sex difference to role socialization and perhaps to a greater willingness of women, as compared to men and especially young men, to admit feelings of fear.

Another interesting perspective can be seen in Figure 2-1 by examining the differences in fear levels between the youngest and oldest age groups for each sex. The age differential for women is 22% whereas for men it is a striking 42%. If these cross-sectional data can be taken to approximate longitudinal data, there are marked changes in perceived vulnerability for males throughout the life cycle but comparatively little change for females. Finally, it should be emphasized that women, from one point of view, are more vulnerable than men. From birth, men are physically heavier and more muscular than women. This, as well as the socialization variables noted above, could cause feelings of greater vulnerability in women.

3. *Income, Education, and Race.* Although demographically distinct, the covariance of these variables regarding fear of crime is most likely mediated by socioeconomically determined housing in high crime neighborhoods. Most surveys find that fear of crime increases as income

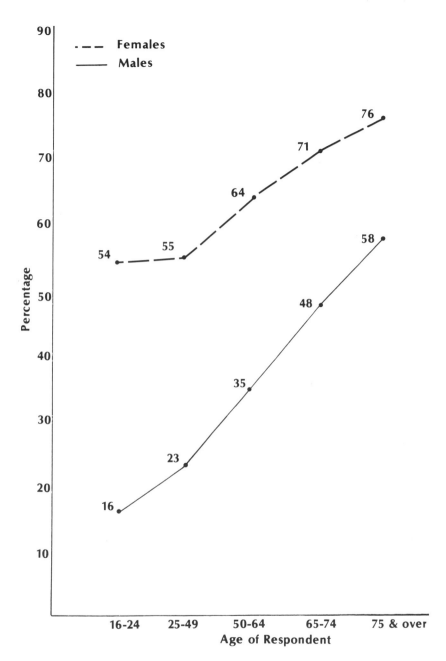

Figure 2-1 Percentage of male and female respondents reporting feeling somewhat or very unsafe being out alone at night in their own neighborhoods (26 American cities, 1973–74).

decreases for the elderly as well as for other age groups (Baumer, 1978; Clemente and Kleiman, 1977; Garofalo, 1980; Lawton, in press; Lebowitz, 1975). Fear of crime also increases as level of education decreases (Baumer, 1978; Clemente and Kleiman, 1977). Blacks, generally, are more fearful of crime than whites (Baumer, 1978; Braungart, Braungart and Hoyer, 1980; Clemente and Kleiman, 1977; McAdoo, 1979; Ragan, 1977).

4. *Health Status.* Poor health is related to high fear of crime (Braungart, Hoyer and Braungart, 1979). Sundeen (1977) reports that poor health is related to fear of being robbed in the streets, but not to burglary or fraud, a reasonable expectation, except for the possibility of medical fraud.

5. *Marital Status.* The most fearful elderly are those who have never married, followed by divorced, separated, or widowed elderly women (Braungart, Braungart and Hoyer, 1980). This variable, however, may co-vary also with living arrangements wherein older persons living alone are more fearful than those who live with others (Braungart, Braungart and Hoyer, 1980; Lebowitz, 1975).

6. *Previous Victimization.* It was formerly believed that overvictimization of the elderly caused high levels of fear. However, more recent literature suggests that previous victimization experiences can explain only a small part of the high levels of fear of crime in the elderly (Baumer, 1978; Garofalo, 1980; Lawton, in press).

Present research, however, is not adequate to address the issue. "After" fear of crime must be related to each and every kind of "before" crime, as well as the individual's fear of crime before the victimization experience. It is most unlikely that vandalism will have the same impact as the murder of one's spouse. The directions for future research are clear.

7. *Indirect Victimization.* Some authors (Baumer, 1978; Finley, 1978; Yin, 1980) have suggested that because the elderly spend a great deal of time talking with each other about crime, sharing both their own victimization experiences as well as those of family and friends, a form of indirect victimization is created that heightens fear of crime. However, the elderly would be unlikely to be devoting so much attention to the topic unless it already was a salient issue for them in the first place.

8. *Avoiders.* As noted by Lawton (in press), Furstenberg found that people who engaged in avoidance, but not mobilization behavior, had higher levels of fear of crime. Cohn, Kidder, and Harvey (1978) found that people who engaged in crime prevention (presumably mobilization behaviors) had lower levels of fear of crime than those who engaged in avoidance behaviors. The respondents also reported that they would feel less fear and more in control if they were preventing crimes (mobiliza-

tion) rather than preventing victimizations (avoidance). Such studies have clear implications for the reduction of fear of crime but require experimental testing first.

Why   There is no simple reason *why* elderly persons are more fearful than other age groups. If one examines all the known correlates of fear of crime in the WHO and WHERE sections of this chapter, it is apparent that there are plausible reasons for believing that each variable might be a causative factor in the fear of crime in the aged. In reality, each and every one of them very likely *is* a factor increasing the fear of crime in one or more elderly persons. In short, the search for a single solution is likely doomed to failure.

One helpful analytic approach is to separate the factors into rational and irrational categories. It should be clear from the foregoing that the variables grouped into the WHEN and WHERE categories are rational and tied to reality. Thus, in all likelihood, reducing the fear of crime as it is related to these factors probably is going to require doing something about the reality of crime. This means either (1) actually reducing the crime related to those circumstances or (2) hardening the target so that individuals in the WHEN and WHERE circumstances feel more secure.

By elimination, most of the irrationality of fear of crime in the elderly is left in the WHO category. However, many of the WHO variables also are tied to reality since they collectively are tied to a major WHERE variable, neighborhood. These neighborhood variables are income, education, and race. Additional WHO variables also tied to reality likely would be health status and marital status. Avoiders are a special category to be considered under the reduction of the fear of crime.

In short, we are left with the major irrational variables being age and sex. Both of them are irrational in that they bear no relationship to the reality of potential victimization. The most common explanations for the irrationality of fear by the members of these categories are socialization for women and vulnerability or fear of the consequences for the elderly.

Lawton (in press) argues for perceived vulnerability as the key factor which, in turn, is caused by the inherent changes of normal aging. He also attributes the unrealistically high levels of fear to the unpredictability of criminal action. The solution to the problem is captured in concepts such as perceived control, perceived competence, territoriality, and mobilization behavior.

Skogan (1978) argues that the fear of crime is caused by a fear of being unable to recover from the consequences. "While the issue is complex, I think a simple summary answer can be found: The aged fear crime because they have fewer resources for coping with victimization and its consequences." He further notes that the elderly are distinctly worried about personal attack and assaults on their persons rather than property offenses.

Perceived vulnerability and fear of the inability to recover from the consequences appear plausible. Fear of crime levels well beyond any reasonable risk of victimization certainly appear irrational to younger adults. To understand such irrational levels of fear, young or middle-aged readers perhaps can benefit by recalling some incident in their own lives when they were confined to bed for a protracted period of time, when they were on crutches or had an arm or other part of the body incapacitated, or when they felt extraordinarily weak, yet were obliged to carry on in an urban environment. Under such circumstances, it becomes possible to empathize with the elderly and to feel that they are indeed in a weakened position to fend off threats and dangers and to feel that victimization, on top of all one's other problems, would be too much to bear. From such a perspective, the irrationality of the feared consequences for the elderly perhaps are not so irrational. If one fears permanent physical damage or loss of life from victimization, *any* risk, no matter how small, is too great a risk.

Reducing Crime Against the Elderly

Our focus is on the fear of crime. However, much emphasis has been devoted to the reduction of victimization of the elderly. Although the relationship between such target-hardening measures and fear of crime remains uncertain, reducing the incidence of victimization inherently is a worthy goal. For this reason, references will be given to materials which are directed to senior citizens and to professionals.

The following materials are directed toward senior citizens: AARP/NRTA, (1973); Dade County Public Safety Department, (undated); and National Institute of Law Enforcement and Criminal Justice, LEAA, United States Department of Justice, (1977). The following materials are directed toward professionals: Bishop, Klecka, Oldendick, and Tuchfarber (1979); Center (1979); D'Angelo (1977); Florida Department of Administration (1978); Gross (1979); Jaycox (1980); Nitzberg (1979a); Nitzberg (1979b); and Smith (1979). Smith (1979) provides an extremely thorough and comprehensive review for professionals.

Reducing Fear of Crime Among the Elderly

Perhaps the first question is: Why bother? Skogan provides a cogent answer for the elderly, for all ages, and for cities themselves:

The fear of crime greatly affects the quality of urban life. It affects it directly through its impact upon our use of the streets and parks, the bustle of social activity, shopping, and recreation, and the diversity and anonymity that have long characterized city dwelling. It affects it indirectly through the debilitating impact of crime upon social intercourse, community morale, and even the economic base of the city. When shops and restaurants close, when downtown streets become lonely canyons in the evening, and when families rearing children flee the central city, we all suffer the consequences. The fear of crime has a social, political, and economic reality of its own. (Skogan, 1977).

As we approach fear reduction, it would be wise to recall the words of Furstenberg (1971): "It is difficult to devise strategies for decreasing the amount of fear, it is harder still to think of ways of reducing the public concern about crime." Equally important is the reality that many of the suggestions to follow are unlikely to be feasible for many political, social, and economic reasons. Finally, most of the programs fall within the realm of untested ideas. Few, if any, fear-of-crime-programs have been empirically evaluated. Nowhere is effective and efficient program evaluation more needed.

Although not directed specifically toward the elderly, the most comprehensive review of strategies for reducing fear of crime has been prepared by Henig and Maxfield (1978). They emphasize that there are no cost-free policies, and group the existing possibilities into four approaches.

1. *Probability of Victimization.* This approach assumes that there is a direct relationship between fear and probability of victimization. Thus, to reduce fear, one reduces the incidence of crime. However, "we know little more about reducing actual crime than we know about reducing fear." (Henig and Maxfield, 1978).

2. *Psychological Correlates of Fear.* Psychological approaches stress the importance of symbolic reassurances to those who are afraid. They suggest either increasing symbols of security or reducing symbols of threats to security, such as exposure to strangers. Possible confidence building strategies include: tell-the-truth campaigns, moderating the media, show of force, role models, and crime compensation.

3. *Social Disintegration.* The sense of community is involved here. The cure is to increase interaction among user groups and the police, and to develop the feeling that others will come to one's assistance if necessary.

4. *Physical Environment.* Restructuring the urban environment to reduce both crime and fear of crime includes correcting poor lighting, blind spots, and columns; improving circulation of people; building neighborhood cohesion; and increasing surveillance.

There are risks to all interventions, not the least of which is that such programs will attract robbers and criminals as well as the desired office workers and shoppers. The power of such programs to induce careless-ness through the dropping of one's guard also is important, as is the possibility of backlash effects which increase fear.

Other suggestions include: (1) broad and comprehensive social reform such as better housing, increased Social Security benefits, greater income, and more limited measures to provide safe niches for the elderly in dangerous areas (Sundeen and Mathieu, 1976); (2) requiring landlords to install protective devices in apartment units, establishment of "safe zones" in high crime areas where there would be security, supervised recreation, and transportation, and providing victim insurance (Furstenberg, 1971); (3) developing interpersonal and social networks that can be depended on for assistance, providing secure public transpor-tation, and the social-psychological supports of organized neighborhoods (Sundeen, 1977); (4) achieving a feeling of security through increasing ac-tual or perceived competence, teaching control of the environment through differentiating safe from dangerous situations, and engaging in mobilization rather than avoidance behaviors. Specific programs might include: educational efforts; services to minimize vulnerability; victim-assistance services; and community organization efforts (Lawton, in press); (5) since "only crimes against persons appeared to have any direct impact upon the fear of crime" (Skogan, 1977), reducing crimes against the person would be an appropriate goal. Burglary also is psychologically important because it forcefully shows that the moat to one's castle can be bridged; and (6) increasing territorial attitudes and behaviors (eg, build fences, post no trespassing signs, maintain surveillance of property) and shifting psychological orientations from passive to active mastery (Pat-terson, 1978; 1979).

However, none of these really addresses the two irrational variables of sex and age. It would appear that not much can be done with the sex variable. If it is the case that high levels of fear of crime exist in women of all ages, there is little room to lower this fear in elderly women who have had these feelings for their entire lives. This assumes that we are not dealing with a time-of-measurement effect. If it does reflect time-of-measurement, then historical changes must occur to change the level.

For the age variable (this affects elderly women as well as men) an educational program to inform elderly persons of their realistically low levels of victimization might lessen perceived vulnerability (assuming that they do not fall into one of the realistic WHERE categories). Fur-ther, a program geared to attenuating the physical and financial losses of elderly victimization might well also reduce feelings of vulnerability. The gist of these messages would be that: You have little realistic chance of becoming a victim. However, should victimization befall you, we will be there to help physically, medically, and financially.

Future Research

It is important to conclude with two suggestions which have the possibility of significantly enhancing our knowledge of fear of crime in the elderly.

1. Researchers in fear of crime have forgotten Kurt Lewin's famous formula B = f (P,E). Behavior (fear of crime) is a function both of the Person and the Environment. We probably now know just about all that we ever will know about the environmental determinants of fear of crime in the elderly. What is needed is information on the personality correlates of persons who are highly fearful and those who are less fearful, holding constant different environmental contexts and demographic characteristics. We specifically need more data on the feeling and affective correlates of fear of crime. Fear of death would be an important variable to examine as would neuroticism and anxiety.

2. With the exception noted above, we also probably now know about all we ever will know about the correlates of fear of crime in the elderly. Now is the time to test experimentally the existing correlations to determine which of them will receive experimental support.

A recent study by Shotland et al (1979), although not of the elderly, is a prototype for the kind of research which is required. These researchers asked respondents to read fictitious crime stories that the news media supposedly had not reported and then to complete one scale measuring an emotional response to the fictitious crime and one scale measuring a potential behavioral response to the fictitious crime. Most of the variables reviewed in this chapter could be programmed factorially into fictitious crime stories and the responses of both elderly and younger subjects could be obtained. The importance of this study lies in its promise of a fruitful experimental technique. If all the factors discussed in the present literature were tested factorially, we would know far more about fear of crime in the elderly than we do today. The present literature contains a bountiful supply of hypotheses for experimental testing.

CONCLUSION

Six conclusions can be drawn from the present review:

First, many of the early conclusions were flawed and thus unsupported by subsequent empirical research. Among the flawed ideas were: the elderly had higher rates of criminal victimization than other age groups, the physical and financial consequences of victimization were greater for the elderly than for other age groups, and the psychological consequences were greater for the elderly than for other age groups.

Second, there now are a number of empirically determined predictors of high levels of fear of crime in the elderly including: nighttime, large urban areas, bad neighborhoods, communities with low integration, age-integrated public housing, low income, low education, poor health, being female, being black, being unmarried, living alone, and engaging in avoidance behaviors. Many of these predictors are, of course, also predictors of the risk of victimization.

Third, the paradox of low victimization yet high fear remains. The best explanations to date attribute these high levels of fear to feelings of personal vulnerability or to the feeling that the consequences of victimization would be too great. It is as if the elderly were asking themselves: What is the potential cost to me?

Fourth, three directions for future research are suggested: more information is required on the personality and affective correlates of very fearful and less fearful persons in similar environmental and demographic circumstances; experimental testing of the current explanations of fear is required; and improvements in conceptual and methodological quality would advance the field.

Fifth, the literature contains many ideas regarding the reduction of the fear of crime in the elderly. However, most of these ideas remain to be evaluated.

Finally, it may be helpful to return to the aphorism of W.I. Thomas (1928): "If men define situations as real, they are real in their consequences." The elderly appear to define their personal vulnerability, their risk of victimization, and the perceived consequences of victimization as real. High fear of crime is the natural consequence of that definition of reality.

I would like to thank Esther Galicia for her assistance in gathering the materials for this chapter and Rose Serchuk for her comments on an earlier draft.

BIBLIOGRAPHY

AARP/NRTA: *Your Retirement Anti-Crime Guide.* Long Beach, American Association of Retired Persons/National Retired Teachers Association, 1973.

Antunes GE, Cook FL, Cook TD, Skogan WG: Patterns of personal crime against the elderly: Findings from a national survey. *Gerontologist* 1977; 17:321–327.

Balkin S: Victimization rates, safety and fear of crime. *Social Problems* 1979; 26:343–358.

Baumer TL: Research on fear of crime in the United States. *Victimology* 1978; 3:254–264.

Bishop GF, Klecka WR: Victimization and fear of crime among the elderly living in high-crime urban neighborhoods. Presented at the annual meeting of the Academy of Criminal Justice Sciences, 1978.

Bishop GF, Klecka WR, Oldendick RW, Tuchfarber AJ: *An Impact Evaluation of the National Elderly Victimization Prevention and Assistance Program.* Washington, DC: National Council of Senior Citizens, 1979.

Braungart MM, Braungart RG, Hoyer WJ: Age, sex, and social factors in fear of crime. *Sociological Focus* 1980;13:55–66.

Braungart MM, Hoyer WJ, Braungart RG: Fear of crime and the elderly, in Goldstein AP, Hoyer WJ, Monti PS (eds): *Police and the Elderly.* New York, Pergamon, 1979.

Center LJ: *Evaluation of the National Elderly Victimization Prevention and Assistance Program.* Washington, DC, National Council of Senior Citizens, 1979.

Clemente F, Kleiman MB: Fear of crime in the United States: A multivariate analysis. *Social Forces* 1977;56:519–531.

Cohn ES, Kidder LH, Harvey J: Crime prevention vs victimization prevention: The psychology of two different reactions. *Victimology* 1978;3:285–296.

Conklin JE: Robbery, the elderly, and fear: An urban problem in search of solution, in Goldsmith J, Goldsmith SS (eds): *Crime and the Elderly.* Lexington, MA, D.C. Heath, 1976.

Cook FL: Crime and the elderly: The emergence of a policy issue, in Lewis D (ed): *Reactions to Crime.* Beverly Hills, CA, Sage, 1981.

Cook TD: Research revisited: Crime against the old. *APA MONITOR* 1978; 9:1–11.

Cook FL, Cook TD: Evaluating the rhetoric of crisis: A case study of criminal victimization of the elderly. *Social Service Review* 1976;50:632–646.

Cook FL, Skogan WG, Cook TD, Antunes GE: Criminal victimization of the elderly: The physical and economic consequences. *Gerontologist* 1978; 18:338–349.

Cunningham C: *Crimes Against the Aging: Patterns and Prevention.* Kansas City, Midwest Research Institute, 1977.

Cutler SJ: Safety on the streets: Cohort changes in fear. *Int J Aging Human Development* 1980;10:373–384.

D'Angelo S: Senior home security program. *The Police Chief* 1977;44–45.

Dade County Public Safety Department: *Your Personal Guide for Burglary Prevention.* Miami, Dade County Public Safety Department, undated.

Finley GE: Fear of crime and some consequences for the elderly, in *Research into Crimes Against the Elderly.* Select Committee on Aging, House of Representatives, Part II. Washington, DC, Government Printing Office, pp 84–87, 1978.

Finley GE: Collaborative issues in cross-national research. *International Journal of Intercultural Relations* 1979;3:5–13.

Finley GE: Aging in Latin America. *Spanish-Language Psychology* 1981;1: 223–248.

Finley GE: Modernization and aging, in Field T, Huston-Stein A, Quay H, et al (eds): *Review of Human Development.* New York, Wiley-Interscience, 1982, pp 511–523.

Florida Department of Administration, *Florida's Plan to Reduce Crime Against the Elderly,* vols 1 and 2. Tallahassee, 1978.

Fry CL, Keith J (eds): *New Methods for Old Age Research.* Chicago. Center for Urban Policy, Loyola University, 1980.

Furstenberg FF Jr: Public reaction to crime in the streets. *American Scholar* 1971;39:601–610.

Garofalo J: Victimization and the fear of crime, in Bittner E, Messinger SL

38

(eds): *Criminology Review Yearbook,* vol 2. Beverly Hills, Sage, 1980.

Garofalo J, Laub J: The fear of crime: Broadening our perspective. *Victimology* 1978;3:242–253.

Goldsmith J, Tomas NE: Crimes against the elderly: A continuing national crisis. *Aging* 1974;10–13.

Gross PJ: Crime prevention and the elderly, in Goldstein AP, Hoyer WJ, Monti PJ (eds): *Police and the Elderly.* New York, Pergamon, 1979.

Gubrium JF: Victimization in old age: Available evidence and three hypotheses. *Crime and Delinquency* 1974;245–250.

Henig J, Maxfield MG: Reducing fear of crime: Strategies for intervention. *Victimology* 1978;3:297–313.

Hindelang MJ, Richardson EH: Criminal victimization of the elderly. In *Research into Crimes Against the Elderly.* Select Committee on Aging, House of Representatives, Part I. Washington, DC, Government Printing Office, pp 62–74, 1978.

Jaycox VH: The elderly's fear of crime: Rational or irrational? *Victimology* 1978; 3:329–334.

Jaycox VH: *Using Anti-Crime services to Reach Elderly Women in Need.* Washington, DC, National Council of Senior Citizens, 1980.

Lawton MP: Crime, victimization, and the fortitude of the aged. *Aged Care and Services,* in press.

Lawton MP, Yaffe S: Victimization and fear of crime in elderly public housing tenants. *J Gerontol* 1980;35:768–779.

Lebowitz BD: Age and fearfulness: Personal and situational factors. *J Gerontol* 1975;30:696–700.

McAdoo JL: Well-being and fear of crime among the Black elderly, in Gelfand DE, Kutzik AJ (eds): *Ethnicity and Aging: Theory, Research, and Policy.* New York, Springer, 1979.

McPherson M: Realities and perceptions of crime at the neighborhood level. *Victimology* 1978;3:319–328.

National Institute of Law Enforcement and Criminal Justice, LEAA, *Crime Prevention Handbook for Senior Citizens.* Washington, DC, Government Printing Office, 1977.

Nitzberg R: *Trainer's Manual: Crime Prevention for Senior Citizens.* Washington, DC, National Council of Senior Citizens, 1979a.

Nitzberg R: *Guide to Training Materials in Crime Prevention and Victim Assistance for the Elderly.* Washington, DC, National Council of Senior Citizens, 1979b.

Patterson AH: Territorial behavior and fear of crime in the elderly. *Environmental Psychology and Nonverbal Behavior* 1978;2:131–144.

Patterson AH: Training the elderly in mastery of the environment, in Goldstein AP, Hoyer WJ, Monti PJ (eds): *Police and the Elderly.* New York, Pergamon, 1979.

Quay HC, Johnson VS, McClelland K, et al: The economic, social, and psychological impacts on the elderly resulting from criminal victimization. Presented at the Annual Meeting of the American Society of Criminology, San Francisco, November 5–8, 1980.

Ragan PK: Crimes against the elderly: Findings from interviews with Blacks, Mexican Americans, and Whites, in Rifai MAY (ed): *Justice and Older Americans.* Lexington, MA, D.C. Heath, 1977.

Schurink WJ: The fear of crime among the Blacks of Soweto and the Coloureds of the Cape Peninsula. *Humanitas* 1978;4:291–296.

Shanas E, Madge J: (eds) *Methodological Problems in Cross-National Studies in Aging*. New York, S. Karger, 1968.

Shotland RL, Hayward SC, Young C, et al: Fear of crime in residential communities. *Criminology* 1979;17:34–45.

Skogan WG: Public policy and the fear of crime in large American cities, in Gardiner JA (ed): *Public Law and Public Policy*. New York, Praeger, 1977.

Skogan WG: The fear of crime among the elderly, in *Research into Crimes Against the Elderly,* Part II. Select Committee on Aging, House of Representatives. Washington, DC: Government Printing Office, 1978.

Smith RJ: *Crime Against the Elderly: Implications for Policy-Makers and Practitioners*. Washington, DC: International Federation on Aging, 1979.

Sundeen RA: The fear of crime and urban elderly, in Rifai MAY (ed): *Justice and Older Americans*. Lexington, MA, D.C. Heath, 1977.

Sundeen RA, Mathieu JT: The urban elderly: Environments of fear, in Goldsmith J, Goldsmith SS (eds): *Crime and the Elderly*. Lexington, MA, D.C. Heath, 1976.

Thomas WI: *The Child in America: Behavior Problems and Programs*. (with D.S. Thomas). New York. Knopf, 1928.

Yin PP: Fear of crime among the elderly: Some issues and suggestions. *Social Problems* 1980;27:492–504.

3 Personal Crimes Against the Elderly

Jersey Liang
Mary C. Sengstock

Objectives

This chapter concerns criminal victimization of the elderly. It presents a systematic body of national statistics about various aspects of personal crimes against the aged. They include the risk of personal victimization, the profile of the incident, the consequences of the victimization, and the victim's reactions to the crime. Efforts will also be made to view criminal victimization in a multivariate context; consequently, the relationship between victimization and factors such as individual and structural characteristics will be examined. Finally, policy implications will be discussed.

This research was supported by a grant from the AARP-NRTA Andrus Foundation. Data used in this study were made available by the Inter-University Consortium for Political and Social Research. The data were originally collected by Census Bureau for the Law Enforcement Assistance Administration. Neither the original collector of the data nor the Consortium bears any responsibility for the analyses or interpretation presented here. The assistance provided by Becky Warfel and Sara Barrett is gratefully acknowledged.

Crime against the elderly is a national problem of great concern. As early as 1971, the White House Conference on the Aging deemed that protection of the elderly should be a top priority and that physical and environmental security standards must be developed as basic elements of all housing projects serving the aged.

Although crime rates against older Americans are generally lower than those against other age groups (Antunes et al, 1977; Hindelang, 1976), criminal victimization of the elderly deserves special attention because of the potentially serious consequences of crime and the increased vulnerability of the aged (Goldsmith and Goldsmith, 1976; Cunningham, 1973; Hahn, 1976). Older people are often trapped in situations which make them particularly vulnerable to crime. Living on limited, fixed incomes, a great number of the elderly reside in or near high crime areas. Their greater reliance on public transportation or on walking also increases exposure to criminal attack. For an older person, even relatively minor injuries can cause serious and perhaps permanent damage. And the loss of a few dollars has a dramatic impact on someone with limited financial resources.

Another aspect of criminal victimization is the perceived threat or fear of crime. Due to their heightened vulnerability and the serious consequences of crime, the elderly are more fearful of crime than are younger persons (Clemente and Kleiman, 1976). This fear often leads to withdrawal from the community and a reduction in social activity (Hahn, 1976; Midwest Research Institute, 1977). Thus, the quality of life of the elderly may be seriously affected.

Although considerable knowledge has been gained during recent years, conventional studies of criminal victimization of the elderly are limited in several aspects. The reporting of national crime rates against the elderly has usually been done by treating all those 65 and over as one group, thus masking important differences among subgroups (United States Congress, 1977). On the other hand, Skogan (1975, 1976) pointed out that there are many, relatively small-scale, localized victim surveys that cannot be generalized about. There is still a lack of detailed national statistics regarding criminal victimization of the elderly. One major purpose of this study is to present systematic national statistics concerning the pattern of crimes against the elderly, the consequences of these crimes, and aged persons' responses to crime. Thus, findings of regional or local victimization surveys can be validated.

Although the impact of a number of variables (eg, sex, age, race, income, environment) on victimization has been examined, it is generally restricted to descriptive and bivariate analyses (Midwest Research Institute, 1977; Antunes et al, 1977). Little effort has been made to examine relevant factors simultaneously or to integrate them. In this chapter, results from several multivariate analyses of victimization are

42

presented. These results are especially useful for the planning of comprehensive crime prevention programs and provide valuable information for resource allocation and identification of target populations.

Data

The data for this research came from the National Crime Survey (NCS) conducted by Census Bureau for the Law Enforcement Assistance Administration. NCS was designed to achieve three primary objectives: (1) to develop detailed information about the victims and consequences of crime; (2) to estimate the numbers and types of crimes not reported to police; and (3) to provide uniform measures of selected types of crimes permitting reliable comparisons over time and between areas. The surveys provide measures for the following types of crimes, including attempts: rape, robbery, assault, burglary, larceny, and auto or other motor vehicle theft. Crimes such as murder and kidnapping do not lend themselves to this type of survey and therefore are not covered.

The National Crime Survey has two distinct samples: the National Sample and the Cities Sample. Although both samples use virtually the same questionnaire forms, there are notable methodological differences between the two. The National Sample, consisting of about 72,000 sample units, is enumerated on a continuing basis. Periodic independent surveys of households in 26 major central cities have also been conducted. The National Sample yields approximately 60,000 household interviews in the 50 states and the District of Columbia for a six-month period. About 12,000 sample units in each survey city were designated for the Cities Sample. From this sample, the number of units where interviews were taken averaged roughly 10,000 per city.

All persons aged 12 and older in selected households and group quarters were interviewed. Each respondent was asked a series of screening questions to determine if he or she were victimized during the six-month reference period. Questions designed to obtain data on the characteristics and circumstances of the incident were asked for each report of an incident. These included items such as time and place of occurrence; injuries suffered; medical expenses incurred; number, age, race, and sex of offender(s); relationship of offenders to victim (stranger, causal acquaintance, relative); and other detailed data relevant to a complete description of the incident. Legal and technical terms, such as assault and larceny, were avoided during the interview. The incident was classified at a later time into more technical definitions based on the presence or absence of certain elements. In addition, data were collected to obtain information on such subjects as education, migration, labor force status, occupation, and income. A detailed description of the design of NCS is contained in Hindelang (1976).

The present research is primarily based on data from the National Sample collected between 1973 and 1976. Only respondents 65 years of age or older are included in this analysis. This resulted in four national samples of older people, each including between 21,000 and 22,500 respondents. Furthermore, only personal victimization (ie, rape, robbery, assault, and personal larceny with contact) is examined. Personal victimization is quite different from property victimization such as household larceny, burglary, and auto theft. For instance, property victimization by definition does not involve any direct confrontation between the victim and the offender. Victims of property crimes are neither physically attacked nor injured. Financial loss and property damage are usually the only consequences. Furthermore, in the case of a property victimization, the victim is the whole household rather than the individual. Consequently, it seems appropriate to examine personal and property victimizations separately.

Given the stratified, multistage cluster sampling design used in NCS, data are also weighted to adjust for the probability of selection and within-stratum nonresponse. The weights used in the present study are for victimizations rather than incidents. One victimization is counted for each person victimized during an event while one incident is counted for each event regardless of the number of victims involved. For example, if a robbery involved five victims, five victimizations would be counted but only one incident would be recorded. The victimization or person weights generally range between 1000 and 2000. In the actual analysis, the person weight is further divided by a factor of 1000.

It should be noted that in any personal crime incident more than one criminal act can take place. For instance a rape may be associated with a robbery. In classifying these crimes, each incident was only counted once, by the most serious act that took place during the incident. The ranking of seriousness was made in accordance with the system developed by the FBI. In this system, the order of seriousness is rape, robbery, assault, and personal larceny.

Organization of the Chapter

This chapter covers five dimensions of personal crimes against the aged. They include (1) the risk of personal victimization, (2) the profile of the incident, (3) the consequences of victimization, (4) the aged victims' reactions to victimization, and (5) policy implications of these findings.

THE RISK OF PERSONAL VICTIMIZATION

This section considers the types of personal crimes against the aged and the victimization rates of various sociodemographic subgroups. In addition, the risk of personal victimization is also examined in a multivariate context.

Based on the NCS conducted between 1973 and 1976, the total number of personal victimizations suffered by the elderly is approximately 265,000 each year. Table 3-1 presents a detailed breakdown of these victimizations. As indicated, assaults account for half of the victimizations, personal larceny with contact for 28%, and robbery for 21%. Rape and attempted rape are rare.

According to Table 3-2, yearly personal victimization rates for the aged range from 11 to 14 per 1000. However, there is considerable variation among different subgroups of the aged. For instance, the risk for urban dwellers can be up to five times as high as that for rural residents. On the other hand, older people who are married, white, and female tend to have lower rates of victimization. The relationships between probability of victimization and variables such as age, education, and family income are not quite as clear. With the possible exception that age may be negatively correlated with the personal victimization rate, no systematic pattern can be observed about the impact of income and education.

Although the bivariate analyses presented in Table 3-2 are useful, a multivariate analysis of risk of personal victimization provides additional information. It enables the analyst to examine the marginal increase of an independent variable while holding other variables constant. Table 3-3 presents the adjusted probabilities of personal victimization for selected values of each independent variable while holding all other variables constant at their mean value.[1]

As suggested by Table 3-3, the size of the community is one of the most important determinants of the risk of personal victimization. For example, the ratio between the victimization rate (approximately 14 to 21 per 1000) in a city of 250,000 and that in a small town of 17,000 (approximately 5 per 1000) ranges from 2.33 to 4.25. Thus, other things being equal, the odds for a city dweller to be victimized can be four times greater than that of his rural counterpart. Consistent with the previous discussion that income and education do not have a direct impact on the probability of being victimized, the adjusted probabilities are virtually unchanged at different levels of income and education.

The negative relationship between age and being a victim of per-

---

[1] These probabilities were generated by using logistic function analysis. For more details, see Liang and Sengstock: The risk of personal victimization among the aged, *J Gerontol* 1982;36:463–471.

Table 3-1
Distribution of Personal Crimes Against the Aged (NCS 1973–1976)

Type of Crime	Estimated Annual Frequency	Sample[a] Frequency	Percent
Assaultive violence	134,020	536.08	50.5
Rape	2803	11.21	1.0
Rape with theft	398	1.59	.1
Attempted rape with theft	—	0.00	0.0
Rape without theft	260	1.04	.1
Attempted rape without theft	2145	8.58	.8
Assault	131,218	524.87	49.5
Serious assault	29,698	118.79	11.2
With weapon, with theft	14,608	58.43	5.5
No weapon, with theft	4273	17.09	1.6
With weapon, no theft	7818	31.27	3.0
No weapon, no theft	3000	12.00	1.1
Minor assault	29,693	118.77	11.2
With theft	17,270	69.08	6.5
Without theft	12,423	49.69	4.7
Attempted assault	71,828	287.31	27.1
With weapon, no theft	23,023	92.09	8.7
No weapon, no theft	48,805	195.22	18.4
Personal theft without assault	130,843	523.37	49.4
Robbery	56,138	224.55	21.2
Robbery with weapon	17,700	70.80	6.7
Robbery with no weapon	20,742	82.97	7.8
Attempted robbery with weapon	7213	28.85	2.7
Attempted robbery with no weapon	10,483	41.93	4.0
Personal larceny with contact	74,705	298.82	28.2
Purse snatch	22,485	89.94	8.5
Attempted purse snatch	10,810	43.24	4.1
Pickpocketting	41,410	165.64	15.6
TOTAL	264,862	1,059.45	100.0

[a]The fractional sample frequency counts are due to the sample weights used.

sonal crimes is vividly illustrated by the adjusted probabilities. As age increases from 66 to 80, the probability of victimization decreases from 12 per 1000 to 9 per 1000 (see Table 3-3, 1973 data). This is a one-third reduction in the risk of victimization.

Marital status has a substantial impact on the risk (Table 3-3). The risk for married people is 6 to 9 per 1000; for those widowed, the risk is 10 to 12 per 1000; and for the divorced, separated, or never married, the risk is 13 to 22 per 1000. In other words, the risk of those widowed is

Table 3-2
Personal Victimization Rates per 1000 by Selected Variables

Variables	1973 (N = 21,206)	1974 (N = 21,887)	1975 (N = 22,085)	1976 (N = 22,508)
Total sample	14	11	12	11
Land use				
urban	17	13	15	13
rural-farm	3	8	1	1
rural-nonfarm	8	7	3	10
Place size				
under 2500	6	6	4	9
2500–9999	6	4	5	5
10,000–24,999	18	10	8	7
25,000–99,999	11	11	10	9
100,000–499,999	18	16	20	13
500,000–999,999	43	23	28	19
1,000,000 or more	35	24	34	30
Age				
65–69	17	12	11	14
70–74	13	12	13	10
75–79	12	11	11	9
80–84	14	8	10	14
85 +	8	8	11	5

47

Variables	1973 (N = 21,206)	1974 (N = 21,887)	1975 (N = 22,085)	1976 (N = 22,508)
Marital status				
Married	12	9	8	9
Widowed	14	12	14	12
Divorced	36	25	31	22
Separated	63	20	32	40
Never married	21	17	16	23
Race				
White	13	10	11	10
Black	23	20	16	24
Other	50	21	28	22
Sex				
Male	17	13	11	14
Female	13	10	12	9
Education				
0–6	16	12	15	15
7–12	14	10	10	10
13–16	16	15	14	19
16 +	10	21	10	12
Family income ($)				
Under 3000	15	16	15	17
3000–4999	15	11	12	11
5000–7494	9	7	7	9
7500–11,999	12	10	11	7
12,000–19,999	14	8	12	14
20,000–24,999	7	3	0	15
25,000 and over	17	7	23	10

Table 3-3
Adjusted Probabilities of the Risk for Personal Victimization

Independent Variables	1973		1974		1975		1976	
	X[a]	P[b]	X	P	X	P	X	P
Place Size by 1000	1.75	.005	1.57	.005	1.49	.004	1.71	.006
	244.06	.021	251.25	.015	211.59	.017	250.61	.014
Income by $1000	14.02	.011	13.80	.009	16.03	.008	16.52	.009
	40.25	.012	39.21	.008	44.27	.007	44.99	.009
Education by year	3.75	.012	2.76	.009	4.88	.008	4.99	.009
	15.50	.009	16.22	.009	13.87	.007	13.96	.009
Age	66.36	.012	66.30	.011	66.08	.009	66.05	.011
	80.04	.009	80.04	.007	80.09	.007	80.24	.008
Marital Status								
Married	—	.009	—	.007	—	.006	—	.007
Widowed	—	.012	—	.012	—	.010	—	.012
Divorced/Separated/Never married	—	.022	—	.015	—	.013	—	.020
Race								
White	—	.010	—	.009	—	.008	—	.009
Nonwhite	—	.015	—	.012	—	.007	—	.015
Sex								
Male	—	.015	—	.012	—	.009	—	.013
Female	—	.009	—	.007	—	.007	—	.007

[a] Values of independent variables.
[b] Adjusted probabilities.

about 60% greater than that for married people while the rate for divorced, separated, or never married persons is approximately two and one-half times that of their married counterparts.

Race and sex are also related to risk. While the adjusted probability of victimization for a white aged person is about 9 or 10 per 1000, the rate for a nonwhite person is 12 to 15 per 1000. Thus, the risk of victimization for a nonwhite aged person can be up to 66% higher than for a white elderly person. Elderly men are more likely to be victims of personal crimes than are elderly women. Specifically, an older man has a probability 70% greater than an older woman of becoming a victim of a personal crime.

Given the estimated probabilities, one can make various projections of victimization risk. Based on the 1973 data, several extrapolations are presented:

1. For a 67-year-old black man who is divorced and living in a community of one million population, the annual rate of personal victimization is 120 per 1000.

2. The victimization rate for a 67-year-old black widow who lives in a community of one million people is 40 per 1000.

3. For a 67-year-old white man who is married and lives in a large city of one million people, the risk of being victimized is 37 per 1000.

4. For a 67-year-old white woman who is currently married and lives in a suburban community of 25,000 people, the risk of personal victimization is 7 per 1000.

Although the above cases are only hypothetical, it should be noted that the differences in terms of the risk for personal victimization can vary widely. The victimization risk for an older black man may be up to 14 times as much as that of an elderly white woman, or three times as much as that of an older black woman. Thus, the present study lends support to the claim that when demographic characteristics are taken into consideration, the victimization rate can be much higher. This conclusion is also consistent with the analysis reported by Balkin (1979), that is, when the level of exposure is controlled, the risk of victimization can be much higher.

PROFILE OF THE INCIDENT

This section describes two essential aspects of the victimization, (1) the time and place of occurrence and (2) the characteristics of the offender. Due to the relatively modest number of aged personal crime victims involved, statistics concerning the profile and the consequences of the incidents were generated by pooling victims surveyed between 1973 and 1976.

Time and Place of Occurrence

Personal victimizations of the elderly are most likely to occur during the day, between 6 AM and 6 PM (67%) (Table 3-4). However, victimizations may also take place in the evening, between 6 PM and 12 midnight (29%), although the aged are rarely victimized after midnight (5%). Such a pattern perhaps reflects the life-style or activities patterns of the aged.

Regarding the place of occurrence, over one-third of personal victimizations happened either in the aged victim's own home (19%) or nearby, such as in the yard, driveway, or apartment hallway (16%). However, the majority of personal crimes against the aged happened away from the victim's home. Among those, 41% occurred on the street, in a park, field, school, or parking lot. Victimizations inside commercial buildings such as stores and banks or public conveyances accounted for 16% (Table 3-4).

Table 3-4
Time and Place of Occurrence (NCS 1973–1976)

Variables	Frequency	Percent (N = 1059)
Time of Occurrence		
Day (6 AM–6 PM)	702	67
Evening (6 PM–Midnight)	301	29
Night (Midnight–6 AM)	50	5
Place of Occurrence		
At or in own home	199	19
Near own home	179	16
Inside commercial buildings	169	16
Inside office, factory, or warehouse	8	1
On the street	432	41
Other	69	7

Profile of the Offender and Victim-Offender Relationship

Three aspects of the offender and of the offender-victim relationship will be considered, including the (1) number and types of other victims present, (2) number and characteristics of the offender(s), and (3) relationship between the offender and the victim. Characteristics of the offender and of other persons present are given in Table 3-5.

The risk of victimization may be related to the social setting in which the victim finds himself. A would-be offender is more likely to take advantage of a lone individual. As Table 3-5 shows, the aged victim was the

Table 3-5
Characteristics of Offenders (NCS 1973–1976)

	Frequency	Percent
Persons present during crime (N = 1059)		
Victim and offender only	626	59
Others present	433	41
Number of offenders involved (N = 1059)		
One	527	50
Two	230	22
Three	84	8
Four or more	65	6
Don't know	146	14
Single Offenders (N = 527)		
Age of single offender		
Under 12	3	1
12–14	25	5
15–17	57	11
Total juvenile	85	17
18–20	65	12
21 or over	343	65
Total adult	408	77
Age unknown	35	7
Sex of single offenders		
Male	454	86
Female	64	12
Don't know	9	2
Race of single offenders		
White	253	48
Black	238	45
Other	6	1
Don't know	30	6
Multiple offenders		
Age of youngest offender (N = 384)		
Under 12	21	5
12–14	58	15
15–17	80	21
Total juvenile	159	41
18–20	97	25
21 or over	97	25
Total adult	194	50
Age unknown	33	9
Age of oldest offender (N = 286)		
Under 12	6	2
12–14	31	11
15–17	73	26
Total juvenile	110	39

Table 3-5 (continued)

	Frequency	Percent
18–20	105	37
21 or over	32	11
Total adult	137	48
Age unknown	39	14
Sex of multiple offenders		
All male	309	81
All female	23	6
Mixed	39	10
Don't know	9	2
Race of multiple offenders		
All white	116	30
All black	229	60
All other	12	3
Mixed	17	4
Don't know	10	3
Relationships between offenders and victims (N = 1058)		
Victim doesn't know the offender	809	76
Victim knows the offender	249	24
The offender is:		
Family member	29	3
Well-known but not related	118	11
Acquaintance	49	5
Known by sight	53	5

only person present, other than the offender, in more than half of the cases (59%).

The offenders described by the aged victims were evenly divided between single offenders and multiple offenders (Table 3-5). Half of the victims reported only one offender, and 22% were victimized by two offenders. Only 6% reported more than 4 offenders although some reported as many as 20. Fourteen percent did not know how many offenders were involved. It has been suggested that elderly persons tend to be victimized by juveniles (Cunningham, 1976). While the NCS data do not allow fine distinctions in the ages of offenders, they do permit a distinction between juveniles and adults. As indicated in Table 3-5, 65% of the elderly victims of single offenders estimated that the offender was 21 years or over, and another 12% estimated that the offender was 18 to 20, giving a total of 77% of the offenders who would be legally defined as adults. Only 16% stated that the offender was under 17 years of age.

Multiple offenders were estimated to be considerably younger, however. Victims of such offenses estimated that the oldest offender was a juvenile in 38% of the cases and that the youngest offender was a juvenile in 41% of the cases. This is more than twice the number of single victims. These data question the common assumption that elderly persons are victimized largely by juveniles. However, they suggest that the stereotype of juvenile victimization of the elderly is more accurate with regard to multiple offenders than for single offender crimes. It also fits a common pattern of juvenile offenses, which are often likely to occur in groups or gangs (Haskell and Yablonsky, 1974). Victimization of the elderly is an activity which is almost exclusively male, since the victims identified 86% of the single offenders and 81% of the multiple offenders as males. Female offenders and mixed sex multiple offense groups were unlikely. The racial picture of offenders is more balanced. The race of single offenders was almost evenly divided between whites (48%) and blacks (45%). However, multiple offenders were more likely to be black (60%) than white (30%).

To summarize the characteristics of the offenders who victimize the elderly, it is useful to describe some typical cases. One type would be the offense which occurs "one-to-one," with only the victim and a single offender present. In such a case, the offender would be over 18 (probably over 21) and almost certainly a man. The chances are almost even as to whether he will be black or white. In the second type of pattern, a single victim is confronted not by one offender, but by a group of offenders. In this case, the offenders are also likely to be exclusively male, but they are more likely to be black than white. The likelihood of the offenders being juveniles also increases considerably in the multiple offenses.

Studies suggest that offenders and victims are very likely to be acquainted with each other or even be related (Wolfgang, 1958). The NCS data must be interpreted very carefully in this respect, since victims would probably be more likely to report offenses by strangers than by persons known to them. Only 24% of the aged victims reported that they knew the offender. Further, the degree of relationship in these instances was not close. Only 3% said the offender was a family member. Another 11% said he was well known, but was not a relative. The remaining 10% said he either was an acquaintance or was known by sight. One cannot conclude from these data that the elderly are the victims of persons they know well.

As suggested in an earlier study (Sengstock and Liang, 1979b), some elderly victims may be characterized as persons with a limited degree of contact with the offenders who victimize them. That study used data from the NORC survey of victims (Ennis, 1967). It was found that more than half of the victims who knew the offender did not know whether or not he had a criminal record and should be dealt with cautiously. Over 80% of these aged victims said they had perceived the offender as being either friendly or neutral. Few had known he was unfriendly or represented a threat. Thus, they were available targets for victimization.

This view that the elderly are victimized by persons with a slight degree of contact has been reached by other studies. Thus, Winslow (1973) suggests that the greatest danger of victimization tends to be in one's own neighborhood where one is "likely to be known at least by sight." And Cunningham (1976) found that elderly persons were usually victimized by persons who lived in the same neighborhood as the victim. Geis (1976) even notes that some juveniles can predict exactly when a specific elderly person will return home and then wait for the opportunity to accost him. Hence, the offender may have clear knowledge of the life style and activities of his elderly victim. But as the Midwest Research Institute study (1977) showed, the aged person often had not noticed the offender before the incident.

CONSEQUENCES OF VICTIMIZATION

The consequences of victimization mainly involve physical injuries and/or financial loss, an examination of which is presented. In addition, the extent to which the medical expenses and property loss were covered by insurance or recovered by the police is described. It should be noted that the statistics in the following analysis were generated by combining aged personal crime victims surveyed by NCS between 1973 and 1976.

Injuries

One-third (34%) of the 1069 aged victims were attacked in the course of the crime incident. Among the 355 victims who were attacked, only 31% (N = 111) reported having no physical injuries. Most (53%) suffered only one type of injury, although as many as four types of injuries happened to some (Table 3-6). The most predominant injuries were bruises, black eyes, and cuts (59%). However, there was a fair chance for the victims to suffer internal injuries or to be knocked unconscious.

Medical Attention

Nearly half (43%; N = 104) of the 244 victims who were injured required medical attention after the attack. Of these, one-third (32%; N = 34) received no treatment at a hospital; the majority, (47%;

Table 3-6
Injuries Received During Crime (NCS 1973–1976)

Injury	Frequency	Percent[a]
No injury	111	31.0
Rape	2	0.4
Attempted rape	1	0.3
Knife or gunshot wound	9	2.5
Broken bones, teeth knocked out	15	4.2
Internal injuries, knocked unconscious	38	10.7
Bruise, black eyes, cuts	208	58.5
Other injuries	38	10.6

[a]Since a victim may receive more than one type of injury, percentages add up to more than 100.

N = 48) received emergency room treatment only; and another 21% (N = 22) had to stay overnight or longer. Once a victim was hospitalized, however, the number of days in the hospital ranged from 4 to 180, with an average stay of 28 days, much longer than for younger victims.

Of those who were injured and required medical attention, most (74%) were covered by some type of medical insurance at the time. Medical expenses ranged up to $10,000, with an average of $637. Eighteen percent, however, listed no medical expenses. Therefore, many of those who were covered by insurance did file a claim for their medical expenses (53%). Of those who had filed claims thirty-two percent had not yet had the matter settled. Nearly two-thirds (64%), however, received all or part of the medical expenses which had resulted from this victimization. The average payment reported by the insurance or health benefits program was $305, although payments up to $1229 occurred.

Loss of Work Because of Crime

About one-fifth of the sample (21%) had a job at the time of the incident. Among those with a job, most worked for a private business (74%), while some were self-employed (19%) or employed by the government (4%). Most victims (97%) did not lose time from work. Of those who did, one-third (34%) lost from one to five days. Another 13% lost less than one day. Over half (54%) lost more than five days of work.

Theft

Theft was involved in 49% (N = 524) of the personal criminal victimizations reported, while attempted theft was reported in 27%

(N = 146) of the incidents. There were no thefts in 51% (N = 536) of the incidents. Among those crimes which involved attempted theft (N = 146), criminals were most likely to attempt to steal purses (45%) or wallets and money (43%). Criminals attempted to steal cars, parts of cars, or other motor vehicles from only three of the respondents. Other unspecified things were the targets of attempted theft 7% of the time. Nine percent of the sample reported being unsure if an attempt to steal something had been made.

The elderly victims were asked what else had happened to them in the course of the theft or attempted theft. While about half (51%) had only one thing happen, some had as many as four types of problems accompany the attempted theft. Nearly two-thirds (60%; N = 233) reported being threatened with harm, while 31% were actually attacked. Property destruction or damage or a threat or attempt to destroy property was reported by 16%. The use of abusive language or other verbal harassment was reported by 32%. Only 2% reported that there was an attempt to break into their cars.

Those who actually had something stolen (N = 524) were robbed most often of a purse (40%) or a wallet (55%). Cars, other motor vehicles, or parts of cars were rarely taken. Other stolen property was listed by 45% of the victims although the property was not specified. When cash was taken, the amounts ranged up to $9600 with an average of $135 being stolen. In only 24 out of 1059 incidents (2%) was the cash recovered. The amount ranged up to $670 with an average of $132. Nevertheless, the amount most likely to be recovered was under $20.

When property was taken, the actual value of the property ranged up to $10,000, with an average of $182. However, in half of the incidents, the property loss was less than $10 with 90% of the property losses being under $100. This value was determined mainly from the original cost (by 47%), through personal estimates of the current value (32%), or by what the replacement cost would be (19%). Very few victims decided the value of what was stolen through the police or insurance report estimates.

In most cases (75%), none of the stolen property was recovered. Ten percent recovered all of their loss and another 15% recovered some of it. Most likely to be recovered were purses (47%) and wallets (51%). Undefined "other" goods were recovered 39% of the time. The value of the property recovered, excluding cash, ranged up to $485, an average of $25, and is substantially less in value than what was taken. Among the incidents with theft involved, only 10% (N = 50) of the sample had insurance against theft. About half of those who were insured (53%) reported the loss to their insurance company. Of those, about two-thirds (64%) recovered some of their loss through their insurance coverage.

This ranged in dollar value up to $500, with an average of $117.

Damage to property that was not taken (eg, broken locks, clothing damage, car damage) occurred in 15% of the incidents. In half of the incidents (49%), the victim did not replace or repair these things but estimated the cost of replacement would average $55, ranging up to $500. Actual repair or replacement was made by 51% of the sample, who paid an average of $64, ranging up to $325. Payment in most cases was provided by someone in the immediate household (85%), while insurance accounted for 11%. Landlords paid for repairs or replacement in 17% of the cases, and unspecified other sources accounted for 4% of the replacement costs.

A Multivariate Analysis of the Seriousness of Crime

The discussion of the consequences of victimization would be incomplete without considering all of them simultaneously. For example, a victim might have been robbed, assaulted, and injured. To examine only one type of consequence at a time may yield misleading conclusions. What is needed is a measure of the seriousness of victimization suffered by each victim. Once such a measure is obtained, it is meaningful to ask the question: What type of victim suffers more serious victimization?

In this study, the level of seriousness of the victimization was measured by using the Sellin-Wolfgang (1964) seriousness scale. This scale was developed by using a magnitude estimation procedure taking into account the extent and nature of victimization. For personal crimes, five components are included, (1) injury, (2) sex offense, (3) weapon, (4) intimidation, and (5) financial loss. According to a study done by Rossi and associates (1974), respondents largely agree on the relative ordering of seriousness of various crimes. Furthermore, Blumstein (1974) demonstrated that the Sellin-Wolfgang ratings are linearly related to the FBI Crime Index.

To ascertain the correlates of the seriousness of victimization, a multiple regression analysis was conducted. The exogenous variables included age, race, sex, marital status, income, education, size of community, multiple offenders, multiple victims, and whether the offender(s) was known to the victim.

Table 3-7 presents the analysis of the relationships between seriousness of crime and various individual and structural characteristics. None of the exogenous variables exhibits a systematic effect on the seriousness of victimization. Although a few variables — income, education, size of place, and marital status — show a statistically significant effect, none of these was systematically replicated.

58

Table 3-7
Regression Analysis of the Seriousness of Victimization*

Independent Variables	1973	1974	1975	1976
Family income by $1000	.024 (.086)	.026 (.083)	$-.243^b$ (.083)	.007 (.084)
Education in year	$-.009$ (.084)	$-.038$ (.087)	$.264^b$ (.082)	$-.154$ (.085)
Age	$-.010$ (.080)	.076 (.079)	$-.053$ (.079)	.032 (.082)
Log place size	$-.076$ (.088)	$-.172^a$ (.080)	$-.067$ (.078)	$-.081$ (.093)
Marital status (1 = nonmarried)	$-.198^a$ (.086)	.031 (.083)	$-.017$ (.082)	$-.076$ (.089)
Race (1 = white)	.027 (.082)	$-.144$ (.086)	$-.075$ (.079)	$-.082$ (.085)
Sex (1 = male)	$-.098$ (.083)	.010 (.085)	.092 (.078)	.097 (.081)
Multiple offenders	.136 (.081)	.065 (.079)	.060 (.077)	.110 (.081)
Offenders known	.031 (.085)	$-.063$ (.083)	.099 (.076)	.073 (.090)
Multiple victims	$-.019$ (.082)	$-.014$ (.079)	$-.113$ (.073)	.079 (.079)
Adjusted multiple correlation	.106	.074	$.275^b$	.174

*All coefficients are standardized regression coefficients. Standard errors are enclosed within the parentheses.
$^a p$ less than .05
$^b p$ less than .01

The regression analysis seems to suggest that among the victims, the seriousness of victimization is not related to any individual or structural characteristics. However, since various subgroups have different risk of personal victimization, one may argue that certain groups of individuals suffer more just because of their higher probability of being victimized.

REACTIONS TO VICTIMIZATION

Response of the victims to their victimization has been only minimally researched. Both short-range and long-range reactions will be discussed here. Short-range reactions include the reactions of the individual victims to the immediate situation: how they respond to the offender at the time of the incident, and subsequently, whether or not they decide to call the police. Longer-range reactions include possible changes in the life-style of the victims as a result of the victimization.

Reactions to the Incidents

It is useful to summarize the existing research and to supplement it with an analysis of the data from the NCS. The Midwest Research Institute (1977) found that few elderly victims gave a direct response to the offender. Some cried out from surprise or for help, but few attempted to flee from the scene. The same lack of response was found among the NCS aged victims, three-fifths of whom made no attempt to protect themselves. This leaves a sizable minority (40%) who did make some response, however.

Most of the responses involved actions which did not directly confront the offender (Table 3-8). This type of measure accounted for 61% of the responses and was equally divided between those who screamed or yelled for help (31%) and those who ran away (30%). More direct measures accounted for 41% of the responses. These include trying to reason with the offender (21%), using or attempting to use physical force (16%), and using or brandishing a weapon (4%).

An earlier paper (Sengstock and Liang, 1979b) analyzed this topic and found that certain types of elderly were more likely than others to take some type of protective measure. Education, race, sex, and income were not significantly related to use of protective measures. Neither was age a significant factor. Thus the young old were not, as one might expect, more active in dealing with the offense than the old old. Not surprisingly, there was a clear relationship between type of crime and use of

Table 3-8
Protection Method Used

Variables	Frequency	Percent
Use of protection methods (N = 1059)		
Used some method	421	40
Used no method	638	60
Methods used (N = 421)[a]		
Used or brandished weapon	17	4
Used or tried physical force	68	16
Reasoned with offender	90	21
Screamed or yelled for help	129	32
Left scene, ran away	128	30
Other	99	24

[a]Since multiple responses were possible, percentages may add up to more than 100.

protective measures; elderly persons were more likely to take protective measures when victimized in more serious ways. Less serious personal offenses (eg, larceny without assault) were less likely to evoke attempts at self-protection.

Demographically, persons more likely to use some protective measures were married and living in smaller communities. Single persons (including widowed, divorced, and never married) and those living in large cities were less likely to take protective steps. One might suggest that residents of smaller communities would be more accustomed to expecting assistance from others and would be willing to seek it, while urban dwellers might not seek help as often because the supposedly anonymous urban mass discourages people from helping and seeking help.

The consequence of using protective measures is also important for a victim to consider in deciding whether or not to react to an offender. Some studies suggest that defensive efforts can cause the offender to injure the victim more seriously, making victims hesitant to resist (Amir, 1967; Butler, 1975). Our analysis showed that persons who attempted to reason with the offender were less likely to be injured; conversely, aged victims who used or tried to use force or a weapon were more likely to be injured. Screaming, running away, or other responses did not appear to have any significant effect upon the likelihood of injury. The old-old were more likely to be injured than the young-old, probably due to their greater frailty.

Crime Reporting

Criminal victims seem to report crime to the police in a highly selective manner. According to the NCS, the rates of nonreporting range from 13% to 85% depending on the type of crime (Hindelang and Gottfredson, 1976). It has been suggested that the total amount of crime is two to three times as high as the amount known to the police (Schneider et al, 1976). Among the aged personal crime victims, the rate of crime reporting is about 55%.

According to the literature, crime reporting is closely related to the seriousness of the crime. In addition, it may also be influenced by the characteristics of social structure and the individual (Gottfredson and Hindelang, 1979; Black, 1976; Schneider et al, 1976). There are several predictions that evolve from this finding. First, the more serious the crime, the more likely it is to be reported. Second, there is a positive link between crime reporting and variables such as income, education, and population size. Third, victims who are socially integrated (eg, married) are more likely to call the police. Fourth, crime reporting is more likely in cases involving multiple offenders or victims, while it is less likely when the offender(s) is known to the victim.

However, our multivariate analysis of the NCS data indicated that among the elderly victims the seriousness of crime is the only variable which shows a positive effect on the likelihood of crime reporting (Liang and Sengstock, 1979). None of the other variables shows a systematic effect. Table 3-9 presents the probability of reporting given various elements of victimization.[2] Other things being equal, a loss of $20 will increase the probability of reporting from about 21% to 38%. If a weapon is present in a victimization, the likelihood of crime reporting increases about 15%. If the victim is verbally or physically intimidated, the probability of calling the police will increase to between 12% and 21%. Nevertheless, statistical evidence is still inconclusive regarding the effect of verbal or physical intimidation. A minor physical injury with no medical treatment increases the chances of reporting by 5% to 38%,

Table 3-9
Adjusted Probabilities of Crime Reporting

Independent Variables	1973	1974	1975	1976
Financial loss				
None	.528	.441	.429	.485
$20	.854	.725	.805	.698
Weapon intimidation				
No	.603	.494	.566	.500
Yes	.754	.659	.567	.691
Verbal/physical intimidation				
No	.528	.522	.484	.505
Yes	.796	.666	.689	.623
Injury				
None	.494	.470	.492	.470
Injury—no treatment	.844	.517	.875	.637
Injury—emergency room	.971	.949	.771	.944
Injury—hospital stay	.917	.830	1.000[a]	1.000[a]
Rape				
No	.649	.539	.566	.549
Yes	.646	1.000[a]	1.000[a]	1.000[a]

[a]Since this is perfectly correlated with crime reporting, a probability of 1 is inserted.

[2] For greater detail concerning the estimation of these probabilities, see Liang and Sengstock: The aged personal crime victim's decision to call the police. Paper presented at the 32nd Annual Scientific Meeting of the Gerontological Society, Washington, DC, November 1979.

62

whereas having an injury requiring treatment at a physician's office or an emergency room will increase the likelihood of reporting from 28% to 48%. A serious injury that requires hospitalization increases the probability of reporting by 36% to 53%. This means that almost all victimizations involving serious injuries were reported (Table 3-9). In the event of rape, the probability of crime reporting grows by about 45%. As in the case of serious injury, this means that all rapes were reported.

One may gain additional insight concerning the process of crime reporting by examining the reasons for not informing the police as reported by the victims themselves (Table 3-10). Among the reasons mentioned, considerations of cost and reward are clearly indicated. They include: "didn't think it is important enough," "didn't want to take time," "didn't want to get involved," and "afraid of reprisal." However, it is in-

Table 3-10
Percentage Distribution of Reasons for not Reporting Personal Victimization*

Reasons	1973 (N = 129)[a]	1974 (N = 119)	1975 (N = 117)	1975 (N = 123)
Nothing could be done—lack of proof	45	52	57	35
Did not think it is important enough	21	23	19	26
Police wouldn't want to be bothered	15	10	12	23
Didn't want to take time—too inconvenient	9	7	6	0
Private or personal matter; did not want to report it	8	10	6	13
Did not want to get involved	7	6	5	2
Afraid of reprisal	8	6	7	3
Reported to someone else	12	13	13	11
Other[b]	21	13	19	26

*Since each respondent can give more than one reason, the percentages do not add up to 100%.
[a]Number of respondents who did not report crime to the police.
[b]Since the authors do not have access to the interview schedule of NCS, the meaning of this category is rather ambiguous.

teresting to note that the perception that nothing can be done and the conception that the police would not want to be bothered were reasons frequently reported. This seems to suggest that the victim's sense of control over the matter and his/her perception of the response on the part of the police also play important roles in deciding whether or not to report the crime. In the present analysis, due to the lack of appropriate measures, the effects of these variables were not examined. These effects should be considered in future research, however.

The reason, "reported to someone else," was also frequently cited as to why the police were not informed. This indicates that the police are not the only source of assistance. Unfortunately, data on the sources to whom the victims did report the crime are not available from NCS, sources that would be interesting to examine.

Long-Range Reactions: Changes in Life Style

Although NCS does not contain data on long-range reactions of the victims, it is useful to summarize findings from other studies. In addition to the immediate response to the offense, studies have shown that the reactions to a crime have a continued impact on a victim and extend into many facets of his life. The long-range impact of crime on the lives of elderly persons can be devastating. Most studies have suggested that the elderly, in general, are more fearful of victimization than younger persons (Conklin, 1976: Hindelang et al, 1978: 177–178). Fear of crime also tends to increase among the elderly who have actually been victimized (Sundeen, 1977).

This fear often leads to a decrease in social contacts (Lawton, et al, 1976; Sundeen, 1977; Schack and Frank, 1978; Butler, 1975; Conklin, 1976). Victims have also been found to decrease activities outside the home especially in the evening (Rifai, 1977; Midwest Research Institute, 1977). Such social isolation may increase the likelihood of victimization since the elderly tend to be victimized in or near their homes; conversely, neighborhoods with a high degree of social isolation often have higher crime rates (Butler, 1975; Lawton et al, 1976; Sundeen, 1977). The elderly often take security measures such as adding locks to doors and windows, leaving lights on at night, and marking personal property with crime prevention identification (Rifai, 1977; Midwest Research Institute, 1977).

DISCUSSION AND IMPLICATIONS

In the present study, a multivariate model was used to examine the risk of personal victimization among the elderly. This approach enables the researchers to assess simultaneously the relative importance of various factors in relation to victimization. One important contribution of such an approach is the integration of individual characteristics as well as environmental context in understanding criminal victimization of the aged. This information is also useful in helping policy-makers as well as service providers design comprehensive programs which serve aged victims. In particular, a multivariate model enables professionals to assess the risk of personal victimization by taking into account a multitude of variables concurrently rather than one variable at a time. This knowledge is critical for resource allocation and the identification of target populations vulnerable to criminal victimization.

The wide variation in the risk of personal victimization is impressive. Accordingly, caution must be applied when interpreting age-specific victimization rates. It has been pointed out by Balkin (1979) that the low observed rate of victimization for the elderly may be a result of the high level of fear of the older people that causes them to curtail activities substantially. To measure the "real" risk, one should adjust for the level of exposure, that is, the real risk should be defined as the probability of victimization per 1000 contacts rather than per 1000 population. Balkin demonstrated both theoretically and empirically that personal victimization rates for the aged are much higher when exposure is controlled. The fear of crime is also, in a sense, one form of victimization although not as tangible. This is because fear of crime usually creates an adverse effect on the quality of life. Also, the relationship between fear of crime and the probability of victimization may be a reciprocal one.

Gerontologists should, therefore, always be conscious of the wide variations in victimization rates among different subgroups. It seems premature to dismiss criminal victimization as a social problem for the elderly simply because they have the lowest overall average victimization rate. At the same time, it is also apparent that age should not be the sole indicator for vulnerability, size of community, marital status, sex, and race being equally important.

Three major policy implications can be drawn from the above. First, crime prevention or control programs should be targeted for high-risk groups of the elderly. Second, use of age-specific rates of victimization as the sole basis for policy making is inadequate, and rates probably should be considered. Third, attention should not be focused only on observed rates of victimization; reduction of fear of crime should be a goal.

Criminal victimization tends to be an individual-to-individual activity. Victims were often alone at the time of the offense; adult offenders, who constituted the majority of the offender group, also tended to operate alone. Thus, the elderly might best protect themselves if they developed more extensive social contacts and engaged in more group activities. Victimization and the fear of victimization tend to increase social isolation, thus making the elderly more likely targets for a would-be assailant, whereas the presence of other people may tend to discourage offenders.

The elderly must be careful with whom they associate. A number of victims indicated that they knew the offender slightly, but not well enough to know whether that person was a threat. Safety for senior citizens will best be served by programs designed to bring people together under circumstances in which they may get to know each other. It has often been noted that neighbors who are concerned about each other and watch each other's property are a good protection against crime in the neighborhood.

In the event that victimization occurs, social contacts will also assist the victim in recovering from the experience. Persons with a higher degree of isolation (such as the unmarried) were less likely to respond effectively to the offender, while persons with strong social support mechanisms were more likely to have sources to call on for help. Such responses could also assist them in recovering after a victimization experience. Crime control programs might also assist aged victims by suggesting the most effective means of responding to an offender. Our data suggest that nonviolent methods, such as reasoning with an offender, were more likely to be effective in preventing injury; direct confrontation of the offender is not recommended, particularly for an elderly person faced with an offender who is physically stronger.

Although increasing attention has been paid to the consequences of victimization, most studies are limited in two respects. First, the focus has been placed chiefly on physical injuries and financial loss whereas the psychological impact and long-term behavioral changes are not well understood. Second, in most instances, the consequences of victimization are examined one by one, but the victim is likely to experience multiple consequences. Thus, it is imperative to integrate these multiple consequences, such as in the seriousness of crime index developed by Sellin and Wolfgang (1964). Systematic applications and elaborations of this type of index should be undertaken.

The examination of reporting crime to the police is significant since nonreporting may not only prevent law enforcement agencies from taking actions against the crime but also can prevent the elderly victim from obtaining necessary services. However, the criminal justice system may not need to be overly concerned about nonreporting, especially if the unreported crimes are minor and trivial (Schneider et al, 1976). The present study indicates that seriousness of crime is the primary determinant of reporting, offering support to the belief that nonreporting is mainly due to the incidents' minor nature.

66

The aged victim's interaction with the criminal justice system is a significant part of the victimization experience. Most studies of criminal victimization stop at the point where the incident occurs. The focus has been the likelihood and nature of victimization, the circumstances under which the crime took place and the immediate consequences of the crime, and the possible means of preventing it. Little information is available concerning the victim's reaction and the manner of coping. The study of crime reporting is only the first step in understanding the interaction between the victim and the criminal justice system. The victim's experience with the police, the prosecuting attorney office and the court are meaningful subjects for future research and may yield important findings for policy-making and service planning.

BIBLIOGRAPHY

Amir M: Patterns in forcible rape, in Clinard M, Quinney R (eds): *Criminal Behavior Systems: A Typology*. New York, Holt, Rinehart, 1967.

Antunes G, Cook FL, Cook TD, Skogan WG: Patterns of personal crime against the elderly: Findings from a national survey. *The Gerontologist* 1977;17:321–327.

Balkin S: Victimization rates, safety and fear of crime. *Social Problems* 1979; 26:343–358.

Black D: *The Behavior of Law*. New York, Academic Press, 1976.

Blumstein A: Seriousness weights in an index of crime. *American Sociological Review* 1974;39:854–864.

Butler RN: *Why Survive? Being Old in America*. New York, Harper & Row, 1975.

Clemente F, Kleiman MB: Fear of crime among the aged. *The Gerontologist* 1976;16:207–210.

Conklin JE: Robbery, the elderly, and fear: An urban problem in search of solution, in Goldsmith J, Goldsmith SS (eds): *Crime and the Elderly*. Lexington, MA, Lexington Books, 1976, pp 99–110.

Cunningham CL: Crime and the aging victim. *Midwest Research Institute Quarterly* 1973;Spring:4–9

Cunningham CL: Pattern and effect of crime against the aging: The Kansas City study, in Goldsmith J, Goldsmith SS (eds): *Crime and the Elderly*. Lexington, MA, Lexington Books, 1976.

Ennis, PH: *Criminal Victimization in the United States: A Report of a National Survey*. Chicago, National Opinion Research Center, University of Chicago, May, 1967.

Geis G: Defrauding the elderly, in Goldsmith J, Goldsmith SS (eds): *Crime and the Elderly*. Lexington, MA, Lexington Books, 1976.

Goldsmith J, Goldsmith SS: (eds). *Crime and the Elderly*. Lexington, MA, Lexington Books, 1976.

Gottfredson MR, Hindelang MJ: A study of the behavior of law. *American Sociological Review* 1979;44:3–18.

Hahn PH: *Crimes Against the Elderly: A Study in Victimology*. Santa Cruz, CA: David Publishing, 1976.

Haskell MR, Yablonsky L: *Juvenile Delinquency*. Chicago, Rand McNally, 1974.

Hindelang M: *Criminal Victimization in Eight American Cities: A Descriptive Analysis of Common Theft and Assault*. Cambridge, MA, Ballinger, 1976.

Hindelang M, Gottfredson MR: The victim's decision not to invoke the criminal justice process, in McDonald WF (ed): *Criminal Justice and the Victim*. Beverly Hills, CA, Sage Publications, 1976.

Hindelang M, Gottfredson MR, Garofalo J: *Victims of Personal Crime: An Empirical Foundation for a Theory of Personal Victimization*. Cambridge, MA, Ballinger, 1976.

Lawton MP, Nahemau L, Yaffe S, Feldman S: Psychological aspects of crime and the fear of crime, in Goldsmith J, Goldsmith SS (eds): *Crime and the Elderly*. Lexington, MA, Lexington Books, 1976.

Liang J, Sengstock MC: The aged personal crime victim's decision to call the police. Paper presented at the 32nd Annual Scientific Meeting of the Gerontological Society, Washington, DC, November 1979.

Liang J, Sengstock MC: The risk of personal victimization among the aged. *Journal of Gerontology* 1981;36:463–471.

Midwest Research Institute. *Crimes Against the Aging: Patterns and Prevention*. Kansas City, MO, Midwest Research Institute, 1977.

Rifai MAY: Implications for crime prevention: The response of the older adult to criminal victimization. *The Police Chief* 1977;44(2):48–50.

Rossi PH, Waite E, Bose CH, Berk RE: The seriousness of crimes; Normative structure and individual differences. *American Sociological Review* 1974;39:224–237.

Schack S, Frank R: Police service delivery to the elderly. *Ann Am Acad Polit Soc Sci* 1978;438:81–95.

Schneider AL, Burcart JM, Wilson LA: The role of attitudes in the decision to report crimes to the police, in McDonald WF (ed): in *Criminal Justice and the Victim*. Beverly Hills, CA, Sage Publications, 1976, pp 89–113.

Sengstock MC, Liang J: Elderly victims of crime: A refinement of theory in victimology. Presented before the International Symposium on Victimology, Muenster, Germany, September, 1979a.

Sengstock MC, Liang J: Responses of the elderly to criminal victimization. Presented before the American Society of Criminology, Philadelphia, 1979b.

Sellin T, Wolfgang M: *The Measurement of Delinquency*. New York, Wiley, 1964.

Skogan W: Measurement problems in official and survey crime rates. *Journal of Criminal Justice* 1975;3:17–32.

Skogan W: *Sample Surveys of the Victims of Crime*. Cambridge, MA, Ballinger, 1976.

Sundeen R: The fear of crime and urban elderly, in Rifai MAY (ed): *Justice and Older Americans*. Lexington, MA, Lexington Books, 1977.

United States Congress: *In Search of Security: A National Perspective on Elderly Crime Victimization*. Washington, DC, Government Printing Office, 1977.

Winslow RW: *Crime in a Free Society*. Encino, CA, Dickenson, 1973.

Wolfgang M: *Patterns in Criminal Homicide*. New York, Wiley, 1958.

4 Frauds Against the Elderly

Claude D. Pepper

Senior citizens constitute 11% of the population but are almost 30% of the victims of crime in the United States. While violent crime is on the increase, a much sharper increase is reported in economic and nonviolent crimes, which is to say fraud. Reinforcement for the proposition that the elderly are easy prey for con men is apparent in replies to a recent survey of United States Police Chiefs conducted by the House Select Committee on Aging.

It has also been noted in law enforcement circles that in times of high inflation, high unemployment, and general economic turbulence, the incidence of fraud increases. Senior citizens are sought out because of their particular vulnerability. Senior citizens sometimes have relatively little background in investments; they may also be more open and trusting than the general population. In this present time of high inflation and social security reductions the elderly have been more and more pushed by fear to gamble on an investment or business opportunity presented by an earnest young salesman who appears to have their in-

68

terest at heart. Equally as appealing are schemes advertised in newspapers offering seniors a way to augment their incomes while working at home. Senior citizens who have severe medical problems very often are tempted by the "siren song" of a promised cure touted in a local magazine for $9.98. As they approach retirement, many seniors are attracted by advertisements suggesting they could buy property in sunny Florida or Arizona. Unfortunately, many of these seniors fall victim to the peculiar species of con men who specialize in defrauding the aged.

What is fraud? Most people know it means being cheated, being swindled. Lawyers talk in terms of depriving another of his personal property by trick, deceit, stealth, or false representation with intent to keep the money thus obtained and convert it to one's personal use.

Why are senior citizens victimized at a rate much higher than the population in general? The best answer to this question was provided to our Committee by a convicted con man who was making over $1.5 million profit a year through a scheme to sell counterfeit coins. He appeared before the House Select Committee in September 1981, and answered this very question. He said:

> The elderly are vulnerable, they make easy marks for the con man. There are many reasons for this.
> For one thing, they grew up in a different, more trusting, less cynical era. For another thing, the elderly usually have some money somewhere; either they bought a house 30 years ago and it has appreciated tremendously or a spouse has passed away leaving the proceeds of a life insurance policy.
> The third thing is that they are not accustomed to spending a lot of money or investing throughout their lifetimes, and they make easy marks for fast-talking salesmen because of their limited business experience.
> After a person retires he obviously has much more leisure time and does not really know what to do with the time, and it's such a change after maybe working at a job for 30, 40 years and all of a sudden having all of this leisure time on their hands, they try to find something to do.
> The final factor is what I call a desire for immortality; they are often consumed with the desire to do something or leave a little something for their children or grandchildren. All these factors together with the notion of continuing to provide for themselves in independence throughout their later lives combine to make them easy targets and deserving of special protections.

The convicted con man continued with these thoughts:

> I think prevention is the ultimate cure, because in many cases after the elderly are swindled they are just too embarrassed or too heartbroken to admit that they have been swindled, so prevention is the ultimate cure.

The one thing I have learned from being in prison is there are a million schemes from phony stocks and commodities to land deals which can be targeted against the elderly, and there are thousands of con men in prisons who are being reeducated who can hardly wait to get out to try some of the new schemes that they have learned in prison.

There is so much money involved and the chances of getting caught, prosecuted, and sentenced to jail are so slim that many con men look at jail time as an acceptable professional risk.

The House Select Committee on Aging has conducted numerous hearings on the subject of fraud and abuse. Six hearings were held in 1981 alone. The Committee continues to receive literally thousands of complaints every year from older Americans who feel they have been wronged. The Committee cannot resolve all of these complaints but we do our best to do so or refer them to the appropriate agency which might be able to solve the problem or at least investigate the charge in detail.

The following case histories are taken from the files of the House Select Committee on Aging. The examples were chosen because they were typical and illustrative. It is not suggested by these examples that each and every professional or industry in the United States is dominated by rogues who seek to take advantage of the elderly. Thankfully, the con men are in the minority, but the damage they do to legitimate business and professionals is great. These examples are provided with the hope of informing the public about what can happen. As noted, the cases are illustrative not exhaustive; many similar cases can be found in the files, hearings, and reports of the Select Committee.

TYPES OF FRAUD

Work at Home Schemes

Senior citizens are enticed by advertisements in their local papers which tell them that they can earn several hundred dollars a month stuffing or addressing envelopes. They have to pay a fee of $15 to $100 to do so. Typically, they lose their money, and the firm is never heard from again. Other advertisements implore the elderly to watch television and get paid for doing so or to make wreaths and plaques at home which the company promises to buy back from the person. As always, there is an obligatory fee to participate and the company seldom if ever buys back the products. Senior citizens are also attracted to schemes which purport to put them in the nursery/plant growing business or the earthworm business. Once again many, if not all, of these schemes perpetrated through the United States mail are a fraud.

For example: Mr. S.H. of El Cajon, California was one of several people in that region defrauded by a Texas firm which encouraged investors to grow earthworms. The company said that it would buy back the adult worms at $44 a pound and falsely asserted that large profits would be possible because it had developed a special large worm which ran 350 to the pound. Mr. H. invested $11,130 because of the representations made to him. All he ever received was $231 which the company paid him for one shipment before it went out of business.

Securities

Senior citizens, like the general population, are sometimes netted in phony security schemes. A classic example involved Progressive Farmers Association (PFA). PFA was touted as a farmer's cooperative whose purpose was to build a chain of retail stores where farmers could sell directly to consumers. The company sold notes, bonds, and stocks over a five-year period, all of which were worthless because the company officers were converting the proceeds to their own use after paying salesmen their commission. Some 6000 people were fleeced for more than $12 million in the scheme which operated in Missouri and Oklahoma.

For example, Mr. R.M. of Greenfield, Missouri, a 73-year-old farmer, lost $84,000. Mr. C.D. of Iberia, Missouri, who was 58 and retired on disability because of a heart condition, lost $49,926.

Franchises

Franchise operations are big business. They constitute about 25% of all retail sales and 13% of the gross national product. Franchising developed when small businessmen with a popular product and limited capital were looking for a means of expanding. Under this arrangement, the company offers a trade-named, quality product, operating know-how, equipment, and supplies in a given territory to individuals in return for their initial investment and usually a percentage of gross revenues.

Most franchise investments are above board, but the lure of high profits has made them an ideal device for con men. The Federal Trade Commission contends that its trade rule on franchises which requires that each investor be presented with detailed information which is on file with the commission has served to limit the number of such frauds recently. Some district attorneys and consumer fraud experts say that frauds continue to increase.

Some of the most popular franchise frauds relate to sun tanning salons, ice cream parlors, and travel and vacation operations. Fast food franchises are extremely popular. At the hearing, a witness from Pennsylvania testified about how she and others each lost $25,000 in a fast food restaurant franchise that featured homemade pies.

A more exotic example involves a North Carolina man who was among more than 1000 bilked by a company that sold franchises to manufacture and sell cockroach traps. Investors paid $600 for the franchise, plus additional sums for materials. They were told that there was an established market for the product and a sales crew standing by to sell the product which was touted as being superior to everything on the market. They were told they had exclusive rights to make the product and distribute it in the territory they purchased. None of these promises turned out to be valid. The product turned out to be a small cardboard box which they had to assemble with a sticky nonpoisonous substance attached to it. The idea was that once the roaches entered the box, they would get caught in the sticky material. The investor made a number of these traps but the company refused to buy any of them. He tried to sell them himself at the company's suggested price of $13 each, only to find a similar and better product for sale in stores for less than $1. Court records place the total losses at more than $500,000.

Distributorships

Senior citizens sometimes respond to advertisements which purport to offer exclusive rights to distribute a particular product in a certain geographic area. Among the most popular are vending machine and jewelry distributorships.

For example, thousands of people were defrauded by a vending machine company based in Delaware. Mr. E.F. of Virginia Beach, Virginia lost $6950. He said he responded to an advertisement that said that he could make a guaranteed $600 a week in profits for full-time and $150 a week in profits per week for part-time work. He said that every promise the company made to him was broken: (1) inferior machines were substituted for what he paid for without his consent, (2) the machines broke down constantly and the company failed to repair them as promised, (3) his territory was not protected as promised, (4) the locations were far from acceptable, generating little traffic, (5) he received no training as promised, and (6) the company failed to meet its guarantees.

Commodities

Gold, silver, oil, coal, sugar, wheat, and foreign currencies all can be sold on the commodities market. Fortunately, most firms are reputable, but there is a growing number of outlaw firms who illegally sell off-exchange instruments to the unwary. There are two basic ways to invest. The first is to pay the entire price and take possession of the item. The second is to buy on margin which involves putting up a percentage of the total purchase price with the balance being due on a certain date in the future.

Typically, commodity schemes involve a "boiler room operation," a room with perhaps 100 telephones with salesmen making cold calls or calls to people who have responded to newspaper advertising. High pressure sales are the method of operation. Seniors often believe that they are paying the full price for a commodity only to learn that they are paying a nonrefundable fee for the privilege of buying to come up with the money needed to meet one or more margin calls made by the company when the price of a commodity drops. Still others pay money and receive nothing at all.

For example, Mr. R.C. of Monona, Wisconsin, age 63, lost $66,000 in a gold investment. He was told that he would have to come up with an additional $314,000. Mr. G.C. of Quakertown, Pennsylvania, lost $83,000 in a similar swindle; all he received was 35 gold coins worth $14,000. Mr. D.H., age 73, of Reidsville, North Carolina, lost $53,454 in silver investments.

Medical Quackery

The Committee has conducted a number of hearings relating to medical quackery and sale of unproven remedies through the United States mail. Representatives of the Arthritis Foundation testified that at least a billion dollars a year are lost in phony arthritis claims alone. The United States Postal Service described a broad range of "cures" for cancer, heart disease, and virtually any other medical problems that are sold through the mails. The Postal Service says that 60% of all medical quackery is targeted at the elderly. Here are some examples from Committee files:

- The Postal Service cracked down on a promoter who was selling so-called "guaranteed" cancer cure kits. The kits contained bottles of seaweed solution and live bacteria, selling for $700. Postal officials said injection of the solution could have resulted in illness or even death.
- Phony arthritis cures, from special foods and diets to expensive machines, are common. The Arthritis Foundation estimates that at least $1 billion a year is wasted on such

phony cures. An estimated 25 million Americans, many of them elderly, suffer from arthritis, for which there is no known cure.

- Youth restorers and wrinkle removers abound. The Postal Service says fully 60% of "fountain of youth" preparations and medical "cures" in general are marketed to the elderly.
- One scheme involves a system of eye exercises purportedly to improve nearsightedness, farsightedness, and glaucoma. The regimen includes looking directly at the sun, a potentially dangerous practice that can result in eye damage.

Land Fraud

Seniors are prime targets for land fraud. Postal Service officials testified before the Aging Committee about promoters who sold land in Florida that was under water. One of the victims was a survivor of the German concentration camp Dachau, and he lost $30,000 in reparation payments he had received as compensation for his imprisonment.

The latest version of this kind of abuse involves the selling of interval ownership or so-called time-sharing rights in various properties. Seniors and others are typically sold the right to use a condominium for one week a year. They are told they have this right forever and that the property will appreciate in value so that they will recover their investment if they care to sell. What many find is that the property does not appreciate, and they cannot sell their interest except at a great loss. Still others learn that there are undisclosed fees which must be paid for every time the "owner" uses his condominium.

Home Improvement Fraud

Home improvement rackets are one of the most popular schemes. A North Carolina promoter was convicted in 1978 of contracting to remodel kitchens. He would begin the work asking for half of the money in advance and the other half when the job was near completion. He would convince seniors he needed the second payment early to buy essential supplies. The seniors were left with kitchens which were torn apart; obviously, they lost their money. Other examples included:

- In May, 1979, Mrs. H, a 68-year-old widow, called XYZ Roofing and Skylight Service requesting repairs to her skylight. A repairman, George, came to her home, looked at her skylight, and said he would do the job. Mrs. H asked for an estimate on the total job, but George was evasive and said he would give it to her later. George worked, along with five other men, on Mrs. H's roof for three weeks. After each week George would detail additional needed repairs, and ask for payment for his workers. Mrs. H continued to ask for the final estimate, and George continued to be evasive. By the end of three weeks Mrs. H had paid $31,000.00 to George and his workers, and George presented the final bill as $35,400. A few weeks later there was a severe rainstorm and the roof leaked, causing extensive damage to all the rooms on the second floor of Mrs. H's home. Mrs. H repeatedly tried to call the XYZ Roofing and Skylight Service and each time there was no answer. Mrs. H then had a reputable mason estimate the cost of the work done by the XYZ Roofing and Skylight Service, and his estimate was "a maximum of $6000 for the entire job." George is now being sued by a number of his clients.

- In July, 1978, Ernest L. Bowers, principal in E.L. Bowers Construction Company, was convicted on 11 mail fraud counts for use of the mails in a home improvement scheme which caused an approximate $47,000 loss to victims in the Charlotte, North Carolina area. Bower arrived in Charlotte in approximately March, 1977, rented office space in a prestigious building and advertised extensively, principally in the local Sunday newspaper. His advertisements offered a special discount on the job of remodeling homes by the addition of an extra room, kitchen renovation, and installation of cabinets, counters, sinks, and the like. Homeowners answering the advertisement were signed to contract calling for one-third payment upon signing the contract, one-third upon delivery of materials to the site of the renovation, and one-third upon completion of the work. Soon after delivery of material a Bowers salesman would visit the homeowner and collect the second payment. Little or no work was done thereafter, and what was done was of such poor quality that the homeowner would have to have it ripped out and redone at a later date. Shortly after the delivery of the materials, also, the homeowner would receive notice of a lien filed against this property by the materials supplier for the amount of the money owed on the building materials which had been delivered to his home. Bowers was indicted in March 1978, and later sentenced to five years imprisonment.

Funeral Abuses

Committee files also include numerous complaints against funeral directors. Typical complaints involve everything from failure to disclose prices and misrepresenting legal requirements to failure of the funeral home to inform family that it has obtained a body from a hospital or nursing home. The Federal Trade Commission has been considering the promulgation of rules to protect the consumer in this area. Here are some examples of unhappy experiences which some families have endured:

- A woman from Washington and her mother were severely castigated for picking out a less expensive coffin for a deceased relative. The funeral director said that he "wouldn't be caught dead" in such a cheap coffin.

- In New York, a man paid $600 to have his father interred in a mahogany coffin. Unusual circumstances brought to light the fact that his father was buried in a pine box.

- An Illinois woman was told she had to disclose the amount of her insurance before she could arrange the burial of her aunt. The cost of the funeral, coincidentally, equalled the amount of the insurance.

- When sudden infant death struck the grandson of Mrs. G, she helped her daughter plan and pay for the funeral. She tells the story of what turned out to be a nightmare for the family. One day last year, the baby died at 7 AM and that morning at 9 AM the family received a phone call from a funeral director who called himself "Bishop W" who said he would like to come over and console the family. When he arrived, the director had more than consolation in mind. He offered to bury the child complete for $475. Although Mrs. G had other funeral homes in mind for the funeral, the price sounded right. The next time Mrs. G saw the "Bishop" was at the graveside when he drove up in a flashy red sedan. The family was shocked to see a small casket containing the child on the back seat of the car. Upon closer inspection, the family was horrified to see that the casket was filthy and in a state of disrepair. The casket was lifted from the back seat and taken to graveside in front of the astonished family and friends. It soon became evident that there was a problem. The obviously disturbed "Bishop" tried without success to force the casket into the cement grave liner. Again and again he failed. The "Bishop" asked the family to leave before the closing of the grave so that he could do his work in private but they refused. Again he tried to force the casket which clearly was too big for the liner. Finally, the lid of the casket popped off from all the pressure being exerted on the sides. The "Bishop" hurriedly returned the casket to the back seat of the big red Lincoln leaving the funeral party shrieking. The family's hysteria subsided in a few days when they were told that the cemetery had built a larger liner for the casket, and they set another date for the graveside service. The family was to receive another rude surprise. When they and all the mourners arrived for the service, they found that the burial had already taken place. Mrs. G believes that the family was subjected to deep humiliation by the "Bishop" at a time when they were most vulnerable and that he engaged in unfair, unprofessional, and improper tactics. She was not aware that under her state law the kind of solicitation involved in this case is illegal. The family was so disturbed by the experience that they have contacted an attorney and are filing suit.

Hearing Aids

Approximately 30% of the 25 million Americans over age 65 have some kind of hearing impairment. The figure increases to 90% among those in institutions, such as nursing homes and retirement homes. Hearing aids are a great blessing to the elderly. They restore a valuable and important dimension to human life. Hearing aids vary greatly in price and effectiveness. Most senior citizens do not fall victim to the con men who take advantage of the elderly by deceptively representing how a hearing aid works. For example, the elderly are sometimes told that the quality of sound heard through a hearing aid will be as natural as that heard through a normal ear; that hearing aids will retard or arrest the progression of hearing loss; that hearing aid models or features are "new" when they are virtually identical to models or features that have been on the market for years; that hearing aids will enable wearers to hear out of their essentially dead ears; that hearing aids can be "prescribed" with the same precision and results as eyeglasses and drugs; that hearing aids can operate without batteries; and that an unaided ear will deteriorate. All of these statements are untrue.

The most common abuses also include the sale of hearing aids that are used. This fraud is compounded by the sale of hearing aids which are defective and do not work. Here are some examples from the Committee's files:

- An elderly woman with only one aid was told by a dealer that she would need amplification in both ears because without amplification the other ear would suffer and cause brain damage. The woman was scrimping to make ends meet and could not spend hundreds of dollars on unneeded hearing aids but was nevertheless saving to purchase a second aid.

- A 79 year old woman had owned one aid for some time. When she visited a new dealership, however, she was sold a second aid for her other ear, which was clinically dead.

- An elderly woman purchased binaural hearing aids with the assurance that her hearing would gradually come back if she wore the aids regularly. She wore the aids for 3 to 4 years with no improvement in her hearing.

Pension Fraud

Fraud and abuse in pension and employee benefit plans are significant problems. Hearings by the Senate Permanent Subcommittee on Investigations, Chaired by Senator Sam Nunn, and by the House Select Committee on Aging have disclosed significant problems. Whether established by private employers or through the collective bargaining process, employers and employees agree to set aside a certain amount of wages in a trust to pay for health care, to purchase life and disability insurance and to pay retirement benefits when workers retire. These trust funds are supposed to be managed by fiduciaries, who are legally responsible to protect the funds against fraud, waste, abuse, and mismanagement. Fortunately, they are successful most of the time. However, the sheer volume of the money invites abuse. There are about 1.5 million employee benefit plans in the United States at the present time with combined assets of some $600 billion, the largest private pool of private capital in the United States today. Needless to say, this pool of money is inviting prey for the "sharks" of the financial world.

The Congress reacted in 1974 by passing the Employee Retirement Income Security Act (ERISA) which imposes on officers of these trusts a fiduciary duty to manage the funds as would a "prudent man" and makes them personally liable for any improper diversion of these funds. The Congress has imposed the duty of enforcing ERISA's fiduciary provision on the Department of Labor. Unfortunately, there is abundant evidence that the Department of Labor has abrogated its responsibility to enforce this and other provisions of ERISA. It is also clear that employee benefit trust funds are being looted on a scale that few have dared to dream possible.

November 1981, hearings by our Committee included testimony from individuals who arrived at retirement age only to find there was no money in the fund. This applied to employees with money in private (employer) as well as union pension plans. Representatives from the New York, Pennsylvania, and New Jersey Crime Commissions testified about the involvement of organized crime which they had found in some pension and welfare plans.

The Committee also heard from alleged syndicate chieftain James "Jimmy the Weasel" Fratianno who is presently in Federal custody and is enrolled in the witness protection program. The former syndicate crime leader described his direct involvement in this area:

> Let me talk a little bit about the technique involved in this racket. There are billions of dollars sitting around in trust funds set up by employers and unions. All you do is find out who controls the money. Then you go and see if you can work out a deal. You do something for them and they do something for you. It works like this:
>
> 1. You can pay a union officer or a trustee some money up front.
> 2. You can pay him a kickback when you get the contract.
> 3. You can do him a favor. You can do a favor for a friend of his.
> 4. If that doesn't work, you can find out who his superior is and put pressure on the man to come through.
> 5. If this doesn't work you might try threats of physical violence.
> 6. Finally, if all else fails you might break the guy's leg or worse.
>
> The technique is the same whether you are selling a dental plan, a medical plan, life insurance, or whether you are out to get a loan on highly favorable terms.
>
> It might surprise you how easy it is to get a loan without signing any documents if you know the right people. The sad part is that the average employee doesn't have any remote idea of how much money is being stolen. He doesn't feel it. So money is stolen from the trust fund. So what? There is more where that came from. What happens is that the union asks for higher fringe benefits and the employer has to pay and the cost is passed along to the consumer.
>
> With this process occurring over and over again involving huge amounts of money, is it any wonder that we have the kind of inflation that we have?
>
> In my opinion the possible abuse of trust funds is a serious problem. The Justice Department and the FBI are doing an excellent job but they do not have the resources that they need to do the job.

Medicare and Medicaid Fraud

The Medicare and Medicaid programs were enacted in 1965 to provide needed health care benefit to the poor, blind, disabled, and aged. They have provided a valuable service. No two programs have been better received among those they were intended to help. No one would suggest that either program be curtailed or eliminated. There are many people who suggest that the programs, particularly Medicaid, could be better managed.

Medicare is a 100% federal national health insurance program for the elderly. By contrast Medicaid is a joint federal-state grant-in-aid program available to the poor elderly, the blind, and the disabled. Both entities have the responsibility to police Medicaid, but there is evidence that neither the states nor the federal government are doing what they should.

In 1975, hearings by our Committee disclosed that 20 states had never audited a single provider or convicted a single Medicaid practitioner of fraud since the beginning of the program in 1965. In 1981, our Committee wanted to see how many of the states had obtained convictions the prior year. We learned that 18 states had no convictions. The Department of Health and Human Services is also responsible. Congress created the Office of Inspector General in that Department to consolidate government antifraud activities. The Senate Aging Committee released a report in December 1981 which showed that the Inspector General had referred only 41 cases for prosecution and that only 5 convictions had resulted in 1980.

In May 1980, the Federal Bureau of Investigation testified before our Committee that "corruption has permeated virtually every area of the Medicare/Medicaid health care industry. Based on our experience, the methods to commit fraud are virtually unlimited." The FBI said that their investigation in Los Angeles showed that "kickbacks and rebates were a way of life" and that crooks have absolutely no fear of being caught and prosecuted. Examples follow:

- A dentist was indicted on 471 counts which included submitting invoices for services never performed, soliciting signatures in invoices for work never performed, billing repeatedly for the same services including several sets of false teeth for the same patient, and billing for the work done by another dentist. He was alleged to have billed twice for making an extraction and to have drilled holes in perfectly healthy teeth. He was convicted, sentenced to 90 days in jail, and reinstated in the Medicaid program.

- A nursing home owner was convicted of diverting several million dollars from the Medicaid program in New York City. The money was used to provide the operator with an opulent life style. The Medicaid program was charged for the purchase of a number of items not related to patient care, including paintings by Renoir and Matisse.

- A podiatrist who billed for seeing over 50 patients a day was charged and convicted of submitting false billings. He charged for performing surgery on the feet of several Medicaid patients when in fact he had only clipped their toenails.

Insurance Frauds

The Aging Committee and Postal Service have documented numerous cases where seniors have been victimized by unscrupulous and unethical insurance agents. Elderly people have been defrauded in the purchase of duplicative and virtually worthless insurance policies. One senior was bilked of $40,000 in premiums and a 93-year-old-woman was sold maternity insurance for what she thought was a supplementary Medicare policy. Major scandals involving the sale of health insurance to the elderly have erupted in half of the 50 states. Here are more case histories:

- An 80-year-old Pennsylvania woman spent over $50,000 on 31 policies over a three-year period. She took out a $3000 loan from a bank to make insurance payments.

- A Pennsylvania widow, also near 80, was spending $100 of her $109 old age pension on insurance. She said she sold baked goods and dipped into her small savings to survive.

- An 87-year-old Wisconsin woman purchased 19 different policies from 6 agents representing 9 companies and costing $4000. As in these other cases, the policies were largely worthless because of duplication.

- A Florida couple, age 82 and 78, delayed repairing their refrigerator, television, or stove because they were trying to keep up with $2882 yearly premiums on 19 separate insurance policies.

- An Ohio woman bought 13 different policies over a two-year period, costing her more than $9000 or 68% of her income.

Our Committee concluded that $1 billion out of the $4 billion which was spent for Medicare supplementary health insurance was wasted in the purchase of duplicative and, therefore, worthless insurance.

Our Committee recommended, and the Congress passed, a bill which makes it a federal crime for insurance agents to indulge in overselling and/or to pose as representatives of the federal Medicare program when they are trying to sell insurance. The bill also authorizes the use of a federal seal of approval by those companies which meet or exceed Federal minimum standards. The seal is an indication to senior citizens of policies which provide a reasonable return on their investment.

WHO IS RESPONSIBLE TO POLICE THESE FRAUDS

The primary jurisdiction with respect to stopping fraud and other crimes rests with the states. In addition to criminal jurisdiction, which is exercised through the state's attorney generals and district attorneys, there is residual authority under some state civil fraud statutes. However, the act creating the Commodities Futures Trading Commission (CFTC) preempted state law and made the CFTC the exclusive agency to police commodities. This has caused some resentment among state officials.

The Securities and Exchange Commission continues to police securities fraud fairly effectively. The Federal Trade Commission has authority to issue trade regulations to protect consumers and has done so in the area of franchise. Finally, the single most effective agency in deterring fraud against the elderly is the United States Postal Service. The Postal Service has a section called the Inspection Service with trained investigators under the direction of the Chief Postal Inspector. The Postal Inspector has been instrumental in bringing a great number of these schemes to an end through the mail fraud statute.

The problem with the Postal Service, however, is that it lacks the authority it needs to move quickly. The Chief Postal Inspector was the prototype for the Inspector General's offices created in every other government agency and, yet, Congress has not given the Chief Postal Inspector the authority (ie, the power of subpoena) that it has given to all the other departmental inspector generals.

SOLUTIONS

The best answer to fraud is an informed consumer. Senior citizens must learn to be less trusting and more skeptical. If something sounds too good to be true, it probably is. Government and consumer groups must seek to educate the public but more must be done.

Law enforcement agencies at both the state and federal level must increase their efforts to find and prosecute lawbreakers, especially those who prey upon the poor, the helpless, and the elderly.

The Postal Service needs additional authority to do the job. Our Committee has sponsored a reform measure, H.R. 3973, which has been cosponsored by about 280 members of the House of Representatives, as of this writing. The bill gives the Chief Postal Inspector the subpoena authority that he needs. It would also provide for fines to be levied against those mail order hucksters who continue to sell questionable products and to defraud the public thereby, after they have been found guilty of misrepresentation and ordered to stop the conduct. Violation of a judicially imposed stop order would result in fines of $10,000 for each violation. The outlook for passage seem good since the identical bill was sponsored in the Senate by Senator David Pryor.

The combined efforts of all parties from the federal and state governments along with senior citizens and consumer organizations are needed if there is ever to be hope of reducing the incidence of fraud perpetrated against the aged.

5 Consequences of Institutionalization of the Aged

Susan O. Mercer

Understanding the consequences of institutionalization on our aged and finding ways to minimize or counteract its negative impacts have become major concerns in recent years. There are currently 23 million Americans 65 years of age or older. It is projected that by the year 2030 this number will double to 55 million. The 75-year or older age group will then be the same size as the over 65-year-olds today. Furthermore, it is reported that the rate of entry into nursing homes is 25 times higher in the 75 years and older age group, compared with the 45 to 64 age group (Kane et al, 1980).

Institutionalized persons are our focus. This chapter will review the literature on the impact of institutionalization, particularly related to the loss of control and choice, and the concomitant effects of learned helplessness with relocation to a long-term care facility. In addition, a brief historical development of long-term care facilities and the characteristics of long-term care residents are presented. Implications of the literature conclude the chapter.

The Advent of Long-Term Care Facilities

Certainly not all of the aged population are poor, alone, sick, or in need of specialized care. However, the increasing number of aging individuals is directly reflected in the growing number of institutional beds created for their care and maintenance.

Since the so-called "homes for the aged" are a relatively new development, it is of interest to note who were the providers of care for the aged from an historical perspective.

Although in ancient times the numbers of persons who survived to old age were comparatively few by modern standards, still social concern for the aged antedates biblical times and the early Christian period. Generally, those surviving few were revered and cherished not only for their age, but also for the wisdom represented and accumulated during their years. Some cultures in the modern world still practice this reverence. Historically, the care of the aged was viewed as the natural and logical responsibility of the person himself, his immediate family, or clan. This was generally rooted in a religious philosophy and, as a rule, family networks and support systems were large and accepted these responsibilities.

Society progressed into the Elizabethan days, and when the individual could not care for himself or his family, governmental responsibility developed to care for the "homeless, the sick, the poor or the paupers" (Randall, 1965). Cohen (1974) related to this viewpoint when he stated that the early records reflected public concern with: "The disabled, the handicapped, the aged, widows with children, full orphans, remnants of families surviving epidemics, Indian raids and massacres, the mentally feebleminded and deranged, victims of chronic diseases, the unemployed, and the victims of crop failure."

Early developments in the colonial period in the United States consisted of these "public homes" and "asylums" where a heterogeneous grouping of persons accepted as socially disadvantaged was housed. In addition, there were early "outdoor relief" (noninstitutional) systems of care which consisted primarily of subsidies for families for the care of a disabled or senile member. Both types of these early care facilities were characterized by a blending of charity and economic aid as well as a sense of stern morality. By 1712, the concept of the almshouse had developed, and by 1769 the Philadelphia almshouse had paid physicians in attendance. After the American Revolution, there was increasing emphasis on the use of almshouses as the most suitable and financially sensible way to meet the needs of the socially disadvantaged. It was not uncommon in these facilities for the more able persons to be contracted out for work in return for their care (Cohen, 1974; Randall, 1965).

Although there is no question that significant changes have been made since these times, the concept of the long-term institution as a method of solving problems of the disadvantaged owes its beginnings to the history of this period, even though that history is far from glorious (Cohen, 1974).

Eventually the practice of bringing together such a heterogeneous grouping of persons was regarded as unsound and undesirable. It became such a concern that homes for the aged began to develop under church and other private sponsorship and were operated by voluntary, independent management, frequently supported by charitable organizations. In some communities, such as Boston, by the end of the 19th and the early years of the 20th century there are records of movements to improve the lives of elderly persons outside of institutions as well as improve the institutions themselves by removing children, persons with infectious and communicable diseases and the insane to settings which could better handle their special needs. Some individuals recorded as being a part of this movement were Florence Nightingale ("equally motivated by discipline, soap, and prayer") and settlement leaders such as Jane Addams, John L. Elliott, and William H. Matthews. Nevertheless, the institution persisted until late in the 1920s and early 1930s as the primary solution for care of the physically and economically disadvantaged and the elderly (Randall, 1965).

The depression of the 1930s changed the complexion of public welfare in significant ways. By 1933, it is estimated that 25 million persons in 7 million households depended upon relief for their basic livelihood. The depression led to the development of such social programs as the Social Security Act, which has had a lasting impact on the philosophy and practice in social welfare services. With the severe unemployment during the depression, the immediate effect of old age assistance was to remove persons 70 years or older from the job market. By 1937 the eligibility age for assistance was reduced to age 65. The facts suggested that the establishment of the retirement age was an outgrowth of economic needs and was not a solution per se for the elderly, but for the younger workers needing to come into the job market (Cohen, 1975; Randall, 1965).

Much has been written of the weakening of the family structure and the increased need for institutional care of the aged. It appears that the demands of living and working conditions in the modern world frequently necessitate the generations having separate living arrangements. The historical facts indicate that economic security, mobility, improved health, and better education have had an impact on and altered the traditional living patterns (Randall, 1965).

The concept "long-term care facility" is generally defined as an institutional setting providing care for an extended period of time. Such care can be offered in nonprofit homes for the aged, county-supported homes, and proprietary nursing homes. While licensing definitions dictate which facilities presumably provide the highest level of care (skilled, intermediate, and minimum), this definition is incomplete as licensure policies vary from state to state. It can be assumed that nursing homes embrace a range of facilities from extended care facilities to essentially independent, self-care quarters (Cohen, 1974).

The literature is replete with criticisms citing the evils of nursing homes. Comfort (1976) stated that "if old people were unpeople, it would not matter that the institutions provided are often a disgrace, a rip-off, and generally run in a manner which would lead to prosecution if they were advertised as animal hospitals. Care of the old is rapidly becoming one of the fastest growing branches of organized crime." Former Utah Senator Moss (1977) wrote that the "average senior citizen looks at a nursing home as a human junkyard, a prison . . . a kind of purgatory, halfway between society and the cemetary . . . or as the first step of an inevitable slide into oblivion," and proceeded to cite dire consequences resulting from negligence on the part of the nursing home personnel. Nader (1971) described persons living in a nursing home as "an aggregation of poverty, sickness, loneliness, and powerlessness." Jorgensen and Kane (1976) stated that "the few homes that are humane, competent, and mindful of their resident's needs for activity and meaning in their day highlight the staggering gap between what should be attainable in an affluent society and what is too frequently the reality for nursing home residents." Vladeck (1980) refers to a nursing home as "unloving care." Although he observes that nursing home care has improved dramatically in the past decade, his passionate analysis offers little hope that these institutions can be transformed to offer quality care. Posner (1974) suggested that nursing home care is oriented toward the least competent person. If this is true, the logical conclusion is that normal, competent behavior may be perceived as atypical, unprepared for, and inappropriate.

It is evident that nursing homes are a diverse grouping of institutions which share primarily the facts that they are designed for care of the aged person and are subsequently licensed. Being diverse, they vary on a continuum of goodness and badness or adequacy and inadequacy. In discussing the variance of nursing homes, Tobin (1974) said that:

> Beneath the surface of these highly charged judgments is a hypothesized chain of causality; starting with little funds for actual care . . . leading to a paucity of skilled personnel . . . leading to practices of non-individualizing their residents . . . leading to absence of a beneficial psychosocial environment . . . and eventuating in something we call poor quality of care.

Five major causes of substandard nursing homes were reported by the Subcommittee on Long-Term Care of the United States Senate Committee on Aging (Smith, 1973). These are set forth for the reader to make his own conclusions. No doubt many others could be added to the listing. First, there is a lack of a clear national policy with regard to the infirm elderly. Second, there is a system of long-term care with inherent or built-in financial incentives in favor of poor care. Third, there is the absence of the physician from nursing homes and, in general, a de-emphasis on geriatrics in medicine. Fourth, there is a reliance on untrained or inadequate nursing staff. Finally, there is a lack of enforcement of existing standards.

Cohen (1974) cited a 1939 Census study estimating that at that time there were 1200 institutional facilities for the aged in the United States with a total bed capacity for 25,000 persons. By 1954 the facilities had increased to 25,000 with the bed capacity increasing to 450,000. It is presently estimated that the total number of institutional facilities has declined slightly but the bed capacity has more than doubled to over a million nursing home beds. The figure thus represents from 4% to 5% of persons over 65 years of age. Total numbers are not large, but the impact of these institutional situations is felt not only by the individuals, but by family members within every generation (Brody, 1974; Cohen, 1974). Nursing homes too frequently are a last way station, a repository for our nation's aged. There are many reasons why the aged reside in an institutional setting. With all of the multiplicity and range of problems as well as positive advantages, nursing homes are deeply entrenched in our care system for the aged and we should not underestimate the realistic need for the kinds of services that nursing homes provide. It is thus appropriate to examine what kinds of persons reside in these institutions and what is the known impact of the institutionalization.

Characteristics of the Nursing Home Resident

There are two primary reasons why aged persons are living in nursing homes. First, the person probably has one or more disabling and chronic conditions. Second, the person is probably dependent because of age-related decreases in family, economic, and personal resources. The demographic characteristics of the nursing home resident are sketchy and frequently contradictory. However, health, length of residence, age, sex, race, and marital status were sorted out as the most relevant among variables.

Health   Gottesman and Hutchinson (1974) and Grintzig (1970) discussed the findings from a study of 920 nursing homes which indicated that only 5% to 15% of nursing home residents are excessively disabled by deafness, blindness, or serious illness. However, despite the fact that the larger proportion are not seriously disabled, about 50% were reported to "require" help with activities of daily living.

Although the data on senility and confusion among residents appeared difficult to interpret because of varying definitions of these disorders, it is concluded from a study of 1144 residents in Michigan that approximately one-fourth to one-third of nursing home residents were likely to be confused most of the time whereas about two-thirds were fully alert or confused only on occasion. (Gottesman, 1971).

The health care received by many institutionalized aged tends to emphasize drugs, especially psychotropic drugs, but to limit personal and physician attention (Spasoff et al, 1978). Health status and needs are difficult to assess specifically, although obviously chronic illness and associated disability accelerate with age. A thorough review of the health status is discussed by Kovar (1977).

Length of residence A 1970 study provided data that indicated that 30% of nursing home residents had been institutionalized for one year or less; 23% between one and two years; the remaining 47% had been institutionalized for more than two years. The median time of residence in nursing homes was estimated to be about two years (Gottesman, 1974). About 31% of nursing home admissions come from hospitals; 13% come from other nursing homes; the remainder enter the nursing home directly from their own home (Moss, 1977).

Age Within the nursing home population, 88% of the population is 65 years of age or older, the remaining 12% being younger. Of the residents 16% are between 65 and 74 years; 39% between 75 and 84 years, the remaining are 85 years of age or older. The median age is 82 (Moss, 1977).

Sex Women are present in nursing homes in a somewhat larger proportion than in the elderly population at large. It is surmised that since women have a greater life expectancy than men, they have a greater likelihood of being ill and alone in later life. By current data, women are said to outnumber men in nursing homes three to one. Men in nursing homes are likely to be somewhat younger than women. Men also are more likely to be divorced or never married and less likely to be widowed (Moss, 1977).

Marital status Table 5-1 depicts the point that a person is more likely to be in an institution if he does not have a family that can or will provide care. Single persons are more likely to be institutionalized; divorced and separated persons also are more vulnerable (Gottesman and Hutchinson, 1974).

Race Although the statistics on racial division are incomplete, it is

90

Table 5-1
Persons Residing in Long-Term Care Facilities
by Marital Status (Percentage)

Marital Status	Under Age 65	65–74 Years	75 and Over
Male			
Married	15	20	22
Widowed	10	12	28
Divorced/Separated	17	12	9
Single	58	46	37
Female			
Married	13	34	22
Widowed	26	29	50
Divorced/Separated	13	11	6
Single	48	26	22

Adapted from: Characteristics of residents in nursing and personal care homes in United States Department of Health, Education and Welfare, National Center for Health Statistics, *Vital and Health Statistics* Series 12, No 19, June–August, 1969 (as cited in Brody, 1974, p 35).

believed that blacks comprise only 4% of the nursing home population, while national figures reported show that blacks represent 11% of the United States population of all ages. A national study reported by Brody (1974) also showed that homes of black residents generally have younger residents and a higher proportion of men.

In summary, the nursing home resident is likely to be white, female, widowed, and alone. Most enter the nursing home from their own homes, and the median residence period is approximately two years. Some 20% (Moss, 1977) will return home, but the majority will die in the nursing home or in the hospital following transfer from a nursing home. Admission to a nursing home thus appears to be a final step. There are physical and social causes for so few aged returning to their homes. A person entering a nursing home may relinquish his original housing which cannot be replaced anywhere near the original cost. Admission to a nursing home may also lead to severing of community ties and loss of access (Kane and Kane, 1980). It is also true that most nursing homes are custodial and not rehabilitative and, thus, few provide the services of encouragement to return to independent living (Austin and Kosberg, 1976).

The Impact of Institutionalization

A major condition conducive to emotional or mental health is a sense of autonomy and control. Deprivation of these feelings frequently leads to apathy and depression. Brody (1971) suggested that the demise of self-determination, the necessity to turn to others for care, and the need to surrender the directions of one's personal life are the most negative effects of life within an institution.

All persons develop certain life-styles. Major parts of this life-style include sleeping and eating patterns, exercise, and interactional and recreational patterns. Additional dimensions include intellectual outlets, occupational interests, religious beliefs or nonbeliefs, and sexual satisfaction. In the older person, this life-style has been developing over many decades and is well established. Suddenly, an institution imposes a different style of living on the person (Wolk and Reingold, 1975). A number of studies indicate increased negative effects immediately before and after admission to an institution (Costello and Tanaka, 1961; Markus et al, 1972; Bourestom and Pastalan, 1981), although others have failed to find debilitating efforts attributable to relocation (Lieberman, Tobin and Slover, 1971; Wittels and Botwinick, 1974; Borup, Gallego and Hefferman, 1980). Residents have a tendency to lose interest in and contact with the outside world and become passive (Kasl, 1972). Resident passivity is not entirely disadvantageous to the institutional staff—the institution may tend to encourage the residents into a common mold and treat them as dependent and sick and, thus promote what has been called the infantilization of the elderly (Gresham, 1976). The human costs of institutionalization are thus great.

Understanding what institutionalization means to the aged person is comprehending what a major departure it represents from what is considered normal living within a family unit or in the community. The person's range of choices is restricted even in the most basic activities. These restrictions include, for example, food, bedtime, rising time, dressing or not dressing, frequency and timing of baths, being with others or being alone, the use of alcoholic beverages, and being examined medically or not. The adjustment to these demands and externally controlled patterns of daily living make severe demands on the individual (Cohen, 1974).

A year-long study which had focused on identifying beneficial and detrimental aspects of life in an institution was reported by Halbfinger (1976) who found that the residents did not form close relationships with others in the nursing home and felt that the home provided few, if any, supports for the development of sustaining friendships or relationships. There was also little exercising of self-determination, but rather a tendency to submit to an orderly routine, a routine related to the requirement of the staff and the need for an "efficient operation." The residents stated they viewed certain institutional practices as arbitrary, and the end results were feelings of "frustration, helplessness, hopelessness, and powerlessness." The beneficial aspects were apparent in the areas in which the residents were offered activities most closely resembling their preinstitutional experience and when relationships with staff followed a mutual gratification model. The most notable satisfaction in this study was the religious program within the home.

Townsend (1962) captured the essence of institutionalization for many aged persons when he wrote:

> People live communally . . . with a minimum of privacy and yet their relationships with each other are slender. Many subsist in a kind of defensive shell of isolation. They are subtly oriented toward a system in which they submit to orderly routine, noncreative occupation, and cannot exercise much self-determination. . . . He has too little opportunity to develop the talents he possesses and they atrophy through disuse. He may become resigned and depressed and may display no interest in the future or in things not immediately personal. He sometimes becomes apathetic, talks little, and lacks initiative. His personal habits and toilet may deteriorate. Occasionally he seems to withdraw into a private world of fantasy.

The loss of privacy can infringe on the aged persons' sense of territoriality. The loss of territory has been suggested as precipitating some of the behavioral difficulties. The social withdrawal observed in the aged person following institutionalization has led to the suggestion that the artifacts of institutionalization includes self-isolation as a way to compensate for loss of physical privacy (Nelson and Pellick, 1980; Lawton, 1970).

Table 5-2 outlines the symptoms, development, and prognosis of the process of institutionalization. This process is also referred to by the authors (Yawney and Slover, 1973) as the social breakdown syndrome or the syndrome of psychosocial degradation.

It is commonly accepted that the majority of institutions have noxious effects on their residents brought about, in part, by the dehumanizing and depersonalizing characteristics of the environment. Ayllon and Azrin (1968), calling these effects "institutionalization," suggested that the result is apathy and a significant decrease in motivation that can lead to passivity and decreased activity at all levels.

Engle (1968) investigated the role of these social and psychological variables in the maintenance of health and the development of a variety of diseases. He discussed one aspect of illness of particular significance for the aged admitted to institutions; involved theories about the clinical characterization of a psychological state commonly found to precede the onset of illness. Engle called this state the "giving-up, given-up complex" and indicated that there are strong suggestions that this state of mind plays a major role in modifying the capacity of the organism to cope with illness. The pattern he described had five progressive characteristics:

Table 5-2
Stages in the Development of Institutionalization

Stages of Development	Symptoms	Prognosis
Stage of uncertainty	Loss of identity	Readily reversible
Deprived of cultural and social reinforcement	Looks for success and adaptation; is hypersuggestible	
Feels relieved of responsibility due to message: "Something is wrong with you"	Less interest in personal care; resents being treated as incompetent	Therapy is increasingly difficult
Compliant but still more competent than most residents		
Loss of contact with family and friends	Fewer letters and visits; socially awkward	
Identifies self with others in the institution	Complete psychosocial degradation	Not readily reversible

Adapted from Linder: You won't believe it. Paper presented at State of Delaware Governor's Conference on Aging, 1967 (as cited in Yawney and Slover, 1973, p 87).

1. The feelings of hopelessness, impotence, and the inability to cope with changes in the environment.
2. A depreciated self-image.
3. A loss of gratification from relationships or roles in life.
4. A disruption of the sense of continuity between past, present, and future.
5. A reactivation of memories of the early experiences related to "giving up."

Engle hypothesized that these conditions are frequently present in the aged in institutions and contribute to the emergence of disease and more rapid mental deterioration.

The intuitive and common sense viewpoint that institutionalization has a deleterious effect on the psychological well-being and physical survival and health of the aged person is supported by much empirical research. A brief summary follows.

Rowland (1977) has completed a review of the literature related to events within the environment predicting death for the aged person. She discussed three great events as being predictors of death and these were:

the loss of a significant other, relocation, and retirement. Her summary on relocation is pertinent to this discussion. She concluded that relocation appears to predict death for the aged person who is in poor health. Those aged persons whose mental functioning is impaired and who are depressed are also more vulnerable to death following relocation. Rowland cited additional studies where a significantly larger number of aged who had been depressed before relocation showed more negative reactions, such as development of serious diseases, after relocation. Whether the aged person perceived relocation as voluntary or involuntary and what the degree of change was between the old and the new environment also appeared to have a contributory effect on mortality rates.

How the relocation process is handled may also affect the mortality rates (Novick, 1967; Jasnau, 1967). This can include options such as preadmission visits and preparatory site visits to meet roommates and to get a general feel of the setting. Studies have also demonstrated that aged persons who were rated as being aggressive, demanding, active, and narcissistic were found to be most likely to survive relocation (Turner, Tobin, and Leiberman, 1972).

Schulz and Brenner (1977); Lieberman, Prock, and Tobin (1968); Lieberman, Tobin, and Slover (1971); Lieberman (1969); and Blenkner (1967) have also delineated the empirical studies related to the effects of institutionalization on the behavior and psychological well-being of the aged. Some of these studies yielded contradictory results, and there were some difficulties in design such as poor, if any, controls for equivalent health and age factors with the subjects, differing measures and classifications for psychological data, inability to use randomization of subjects in many studies, and the confounding of the many variables associated with such research. Additional problems in the home-to-institution research are that the reported higher mortality could be brought about by environmental change or also by the exposure to some aspect of the environment of the institution itself. Examples of the latter could be poor nutrition, exposure to infectious diseases, inadequate medical care and supervision, differing admission policies, and sensory deprivation (Rowland, 1977; Kasl, 1972).

As Schulz (1977) stated: "To untangle the knot of increased or decreased mortality, higher or lower life satisfaction, more or less activity, it is necessary to go beyond the descriptive explanations offered . . . and to attempt to understand the data at a broader theoretical level." He further suggested, in condensing the relocation stress literature, that we have an understanding of the important mediators of individual responses to stressful events such as institutionalization, that is, "the greater the perceived predictability or controllability of a stressor, the less aversive and harmful are its effects on the organism."

Control and Choice

The concept that most individuals seek control over their personal environment is a central ingredient in many theories (de Charms, 1968; G.A. Kelly, 1955; H.H. Kelley, 1971; Wortman, 1975). de Charms (1968) states:

> Man's primary motivational propensity is to be effective in producing changes in his environment. Man strives to be a causal agent, to be the primary focus of causation for, or the origin of, his behavior; he strives for personal causation. His nature commits him to this path, and his very life depends on it. . . . There is the desire to be master of one's fate.

He continues by saying that personal causation means a personal knowledge of being an agent of change in one's environment.

Kelly (1955), in his theory of constructive alternativism, reflected on the importance of control and predictability.

> It is customary to say that the scientist's ultimate aim is to predict and control . . . yet psychologists rarely credit the human subjects in experiments with having similar aspirations . . . . Might not the individual, each in his own personal way, assume the stature of the scientist, ever seeking to control and predict the course of events with which he is involved?

Although many persons in our society experience loss of control and the loss of the sense of personal causation, the institutionalized aged seem particularly vulnerable. For the institutionalized aged the loss is rarely temporary, but is rather a permanent life-style. The institutionalized aged have lost the important work role, plus the loss of income and all the ramifications of a diminished income. There is also the loss of an important role within the family structure. The person has frequently lost his home and the majority of his lifetime possessions. Institutionalization is generally a result of some level of physical impairment which further shrinks his realm of control and choice. Institutionalization, in and of itself, further restricts the aged individual's sense of control through the institutional regime. All of these losses are cumulative and thus more damaging.

Schulz and Aderman (1973) have indicated that the aged person's negative reactions of institutionalization are perhaps mediated by feelings of helplessness. This helplessness is "born out of the patient's perception that the institutional demands for passivity represent a real loss in his ability to control the environment . . . ." The outcomes of this real or perceived loss of control can include increased passivity, withdrawal, reactive depression, and sometimes an early and unexpected death (Schulz and Alderman, 1973; 1974).

Some research reflects that the increased helplessness and perception of loss of control begins even before the actual institutionalization occurs. Ferrari (1962 cited in Seligman, 1975; Langer, 1976) was concerned in her dissertation with freedom of control and choice factors of the aged. She interviewed persons upon admission as to how much control and choice they felt in moving to the nursing home and the extent of family pressure in the relocation process. Within the group of 17 women who stated they had no alternative, 8 died after 4 weeks in residence, and 16 of the 17 were dead within a 10-week period. According to the study, only 1 person in the group of 38 who perceived that they had an alternative had died in the initial time period. Another sample who applied for admission, but who never became residents (because of death) reflected equally startling findings. Within the group of 22 whose family made their application, 19 were dead 1 month after the application process. In a group of 18 who applied for themselves, only 4 had died within the same period. As Seligman (1975) indicated, the exact physical health status in the groups is unclear from the study, and a differentiation in health status could be a confounding factor in the findings. He stated, however, that the results may also demonstrate the deadly effect of helplessness on the aged person.

More recently, Tobin and Lieberman (1976) studied the older person waiting to enter the nursing home. They reviewed the assumed reasons that institutionalization has negative effects on the aged. These negative factors include the trauma of relocation, the feelings of separation and abandonment, and the potentially dehumanizing effects of institutional life with its subsequent lack of privacy and restrictions on movement and activity. They compared two groups of elderly persons. One group was living independently in their own homes and the second group was at home, but waiting for admission into a nursing home (application had been made and was pending). They found that the crucial time is the waiting period and that much of the deterioration takes place during this time. The noted deterioration was in mental functioning and emotional responsiveness. They postulated that the cause of this deterioration is the stress in deciding to move and thus an early onset of a sense of loss of control and hopelessness and helplessness. In a continuation of their study they stated that the impact of institutionalization itself is most acutely felt in the first few months of residence. They hypothesized that institutionalization forces aged persons into the role of patient, reinforces awareness of their inability to provide self-care, and subsequently fosters feelings of helplessness. After a year of residence, Tobin and Lieberman stated that passivity is the primary personality characteristic associated with the adverse effects of institutionalization. This passivity was found to work against the individual's capacity to adapt and resulted in greater susceptibility to stress.

Learned helplessness   In research within the institutional setting, Mercer and Kane (1979) measured the effects of choice and enhanced personal responsibility for the aged. It was anticipated that the deteriorated state of many of the institutionalized aged is, in part, the result of living in an environment which is essentially decision-free and control-free and that this deterioration is potentially and partially reversible.

A quasi-experimental design (N = 75) was used to test the hypothesis that nursing home residents who were exposed to an experimental intervention designed to increase choice and control would show less hopelessness, a higher level of activity, and a better level of psychosocial functioning than would a control group. The experimental group of residents were given a message stressing responsibility for themselves, whereas the comparison group received a message stressing the staff's responsibility for them. In addition to the message, the experimental group was permitted to make certain choices within their environment which the comparison group did not experience. Self-report measures and interdisciplinary staff raters were used. The findings demonstrated a significant decrease in hopelessness, an increase in physical activity, and improved psychosocial functioning in the experimental group. The study suggests that one useful and feasible way to blunt the impact of institutionalization is to allow the aged person to be given choices and maintain control even within the nursing home environment, and supported earlier findings reported by Langer and Rodin (1976).

The substantial correlation ($r = .62$; $p < .001$) between low levels of activity and increased hopelessness represents a provocative, but not definite association (Mercer and Kane, 1979). Although there is evidence that reduced activity can result from the loss of perceived control and the learned helplessness that ensues, there is also independent correlation that the opportunity for activity itself elevates morale and life satisfaction (MacDonald and Butler, 1973; Rodstein, 1975). Some advocates claim that regular physical exercises for nursing home residents enable them to use less medication, increase their ambulation, and enhance socialization (Nester, Anderson, and Hodes, 1981). Some authorities maintain that exercise has a beneficial effect on depression, anxiety, and tension (Fixx, 1977; Stuart, 1968).

The Mercer and Kane (1979) study was based on the theoretical concept of learned helplessness formulated by Seligman (1975). Learned helplessness is the belief that one's actions have no influence on or relationship to the outcomes of events. Learned helplessness is characterized by motivational, cognitive, and behavioral deficits that ultimately render individuals incapable of distinguishing whether or not their actions have an influence on events. Learned helplessness is manifested in ways similar to those of reactive depression, for example in sharp reduction of activity so prevalent in the institutionalized aged. More ominous, however, is the increase in mortality among nursing home residents.

Seligman (1975) strikes a poignant note as he described death from helplessness in old age:

> If a person or animal is in a marginal state, weakened by malnutrition or heart disease, a sense of control can mean the difference between living and dying. There is one aspect of the human condition that invariably entails physical weakening . . . growing old. The aged are the most susceptible to the loss of control; no group, neither blacks, Indians, nor Mexican-Americans, are in as helpless a state as our aged. The mediocre life span of Americans, relative to other prosperous nations, may be a testimony not to mediocre medical care, but to the way we treat our aged psychologically. We force them to retire . . . we place them in old age homes . . . we are a nation that deprives old persons of control over the most meaningful events in their lives. We kill them.

Schulz (1976) also hypothesized that some characteristics observed among the institutionalized aged (such as depression, helplessness, and accelerated physical decline) are, in part, attributable to a loss of control. His study assessed the effects of increased control and predictability upon the physical and psychological well-being of the institutionalized aged. Persons were randomly assigned to one or four groups. Those in three of the four groups were visited by college students, whereas the fourth group was not visited and served as the baseline comparison group. Some of the individuals could control both the frequency and the duration of visits (thereby having control and predictability); some had no control over these details but did have predictability, the third group was visited on a random schedule. The findings reflected that the controllable and predictable events (positive) had a powerful, positive impact on well-being.

The aged need the opportunity to retain as much control over their lives and environment as is realistic. Brody (1973) and Pfeiffer (1973; cited by Schulz, 1977), make the point that complete care is just as damaging as no care whatsoever. Schulz (1976), Langer and Rodin (1976), and Mercer and Kane (1979) support this view.

Langer (1975) discussed another dimension of control, the illusion of control, stating that the illusion of control can be considered "the inverse of learned helplessness . . . just as one may erroneously come to learn an independence between actions and outcomes, so too one may erroneously learn a dependence between actions and outcomes." Langer's discussion suggested that the illusion of control is not necessarily a cause of dysfunction for the person. It may even improve the well-being of the institutionalized aged. When it is not altogether possible to encourage the exercise of actual control, Langer suggested the illusion of control may be beneficial. Some may use the illusion of control to prevent others from exercising real control, but an attempt might "boomerang." The probable increase in confidence resulting from the illusion of control might sufficiently motivate an individual actually to seek out more rather than less control. Langer stated that giving so-called insignificant choices to the institutionalized aged might enable them to experience again the capacity for control and to renew a capacity to make decisions about themselves. It was further suggested that residents' subjective perceptions of the institutional environment might be critical for personal well-being.

Indirect self-destructive behavior   A relatively elusive and little researched phenomenon that can be associated with learned helplessness and loss of control in the institutionalized aged is indirect self-destructive behavior (ISDB) (Nelson and Farberow, 1980; Farberow, 1980). Terms such as partial suicide, hidden suicide, and chronic suicide are similar concepts. ISDB can be manifested in behaviors such as alcoholism, obesity, withdrawal from a social environment, and disregard for or abuse of one's health. Nelson and Farberow (1980) suggested that although some forms of ISDB are obvious in a nursing home, such as the diabetic who blatantly disregards his dietary and insulin regime, other behaviors such as smoking, accidental injuries, and refusal to get out of bed are subtle and idiosyncratic forms. The psychosocial benefits of assertive (perhaps even passive-aggressive) behavior that introduces some level of countercontrol in a controlled institutional environment might, in some instances, outweigh the self-destructive costs of such behavior.

Nelson and Farberow (1980) studied the ISDB in 99 veteran male nursing home residents. The findings suggested a relationship between the ISDB and the experience of significant loss, cognitive confusion, dissatisfaction with life, infrequent contact with family and friends, and the limited possibility of discharge from the institution; ISDB may serve a specific purpose for certain residents in a nursing home. The above combination of factors can produce a psychological state characterized by depression and hopelessness.

Nelson and Farberow (1980) further found a positive correlation between the level of observed ISDB and overt suicidal feelings as measured by the MMPI Scale. They questioned why there is not more overt suicide among the institutionalized aged population. It is reasonable to assume that suicide continues to be taboo, with social and personal injunctions exerting influence against the act. It is also possible that ISDB acts as a substitute for overt suicide, allowing the institutionalized person to achieve a partial objective of self-destruction without experiencing the social stigma, guilt, anxiety, or self-disclosure that might be present with the overt act. Thus, ISDB is a convenient mechanism for this population.

Positively, ISDB is a way, albeit dangerous, of re-establishing some sense of control over one's life. The noncompliant diabetic is at least making some decisions,.even if negative, about her own body.

The relationship between ISDB and the institutionalized aged is complex. As Nelson and Farberow (1980) suggested, additional research is needed to distinguish between ISDB which is suicidal and those non-compliant behaviors that may represent some positive coping mechanisms that simultaneously produce harmful consequences to the institutionalized aged person.

CONCLUSION

From the literature reviewed it can be concluded that the intrinsic value of control and choice in one's environment can be considered critical for the institutionalized aged. The aged inevitably experience an accumulation of losses, rarely temporary, but part of a permanent life-style compounded by institutionalization. The relocation process is traumatic and can have deleterious physical and emotional effects. With institutionalization, control, choice, and predictability are further diminished and there are many negative effects such as helplessness, depression, and hopelessness, and a loss of sense of self.

Although it is unreasonable to think that all of the negative effects of institutionalization can be eradicated, the good news is that there are some simple, inexpensive ways of counteracting some negative effects. For example, preadmission visits that permit choice and participation in the decision-making process, orientation programs for all new residents and their families, choices and controls relative to rooms, furnishings, roommates, and foods are just a few. Resident councils can provide a viable mechanism for some level of resident governance. A board of residents could be a spin-off of a council, to meet regularly with administration and key personnel. It seems important that all programs be contingent on individual assessment of each resident to insure that the control and choice being offered correspond to what he values. Professionals should have a penchant for individualization and expend energy in determining what is important to each individual.

In summary, the practical implications of the literature indicate that programs, policies, and staff education within nursing homes should be developed to maximize and enhance the levels of control, choice, and predictability available to the institutionalized aged.

In an excerpt from Gardner's play "A Thousand Clowns," the uncle stated what he wanted in life for his nephew. The message seems equally appropriate for the institutionalized aged:

> I want him to get to know exactly the special thing he is or else he won't notice when it starts to go. I want him to stay awake and know who the phonies are. I want him to know how to holler and put up an argument. I want him to show guts and see all the wild possibilities. And I want him to know the subtle, sneaky important reason he was born a human being and not a chair. (McNamara, 1974).

BIBLIOGRAPHY

Austin M, Kosberg J: Nursing home decision-makers and the social service needs of residents. *Social Work in Health Care* 1976;1:447–456.

Ayllon T, Azrin NH: *The Token Economy.* New York, Meredith, 1968.

Blenkner M: Environment change and the aging individual. *Gerontologist* 1967; 7:101–105.

Borup FJ, Gallego DT, Hefferman PG: Relocation: Its effects on health, functioning, and mortality. *Gerontologist* 1980;21:468–479.

Bourestom N, Pastalon L: The effects of relocation on the elderly: A reply to Borup JH, Gallego DT, Hefferman PG. *Gerontologist* 1981;21:4–7.

Brody EM: Long-term care for the elderly: Optimums, options, and opportunities. *J Am Geratrics Soc* 1971;19:482–492.

Brody EM: Seeking appropriate options for living arrangements, in Pfeiffer E (ed): *Alternatives to Institutional Care for Older Americans.* Durham, NC, Duke University, 1973.

Brody, EM: *Introduction to Long-Term Care Facilities: A Social Work Guide for Long-term Care Facilities.* Rockville, MD, National Institute of Mental Health, 1974.

Cohen ES: An overview of long-term care facilities, in Brody EM (ed): *A Social Work Guide for Long-Term Care Facilities.* Rockville, MD, National Institute of Mental Health, 1974.

Comfort A: Age prejudice in America. *Social Policy* 1976;7:3–9.

Costello JP, Tanaka GM: Mortality and morbidity in long-term institutional care of the aged. *J Am Geriatrics Soc* 1961;9:959–966.

de Charms R: *Personal Causation: The Internal Affective Determinants of Behavior.* New York, Academic Press, 1968.

Engle GL: A life setting conducive to illness . . . The giving-up, given-up complex. *Bul Menninger Clin* 1968;32:355–365.

Farberow NL (ed): *The Many Faces of Suicide: Indirect Self-Destructive Behavior.* New York, McGraw-Hill, 1980.

Ferrari M: *Institutionalization and Attitude Change in an Aged Population.* Unpublished PhD dissertation, Case Western Reserve University, 1962.

Fixx JF: *The Complete Book of Running.* New York, Random House, 1977.

Gottesman LE: Report to Respondents: Nursing Home Project. Philadelphia, Philadelphia Geriatric Center, 1971.

Gottesman LE, Hutchinson E: Characteristics of the institutionalized elderly, in Brody EM (ed): *A Social Work Guide for Long-Term Care Facilities.* Rockville, MD, National Institute of Mental Health, 1974.

102

Gresham ML: The infantilization of the elderly: A developing concept. *Nursing Forum* 1976;15:195–210.

Grintzig L: Selected characteristics of residents in long-term care institutions. *Long-Term Care Monograph* 1970;5.

Halbfinger JD: *The Aged in Institutions.* Unpublished PhD dissertation, Case Western Reserve University, 1976.

Jasnau KF: Individualized versus mass transfer of non-psychotic geriatric patients from mental hospitals to nursing homes. *J Am Geriatric Soc* 1967;15: 280–284.

Jorgensen LA, Kane RL: Social work in the nursing home: A need and an opportunity. *Social Work in Health Care* 1976;4:471–482.

Kane RL, Kane RA: Alternatives to institutional care of the elderly: Beyond the dichotomy (United States). *Gerontologist* 1980;20:249–259.

Kane RL, Solomon DH, Beck JC, et al: *Geriatrics in the United States: Manpower Projections and Training Considerations.* Santa Monica, CA: Rand Publication Series, 1980.

Kasl SV: Physical and mental health effects of involuntary relocation and institutionalization of the elderly. A Review. *Am J Pub Health* 1972;62: 377–384.

Kelley HH: *Attribution in Social Interaction.* New York, General Learning Press, 1971.

Kelly GA: *The Psychology of Personal Constructs.* New York, General Learning Press, 1955.

Kovar MG: Health of the elderly and use of health services. *Pub Health Rep* 1977;92:9–19.

Langer EJ: The illusion of control. *J Personality Soc Psychol* 1975;32:311–328.

Langer EJ, Rodin J: The effects of choice and enhanced personal responsibility for the aged. *J Personal Soc Psychol* 1976;34(2):191–198.

Lawton MP: Ecology and aging, in Pastalan LA, Carson, DH (eds): *Spatial Behavior of Older People.* Ann Arbor, Institute of Gerontology, University of Michigan, 1970.

Lieberman MA: Institutionalization of the aged: Effects on behavior. *J Gerontol* 1969;24:330–340.

Lieberman MA, Tobin SS, Slover D: *The Effects of Relocation on Long-Term Geriatric Patients.* Chicago, Illinois Department of Health and Committee on Human Development, 1971.

Lieberman MA, Prock VN, Tobin SS: Psychological effects of institutionalization. *J Gerontol* 1968;23:343–353.

MacDonald ML, Butler AK: Reversal of helplessness: Producing walking behavior in nursing home wheelchair residents using behavior modification procedures. *J Gerontol* 1973;29:97–101.

Markus EJ: Perceptual field dependence among aged persons. *Percept Motor Skills* 1972;33:175–178.

McNamara W: *The Human Adventure.* Garden City, NY, Doubleday, 1974.

Mercer SO, Kane RA: Helplessness and hopelessness among the institutionalized aged: An experiment. *Health Soc Work* 1979;4:91–113.

Moss F: It's Hell to be Old in the U.S. *Arkansas Gazette,* July 17, 1977.

Nader R: *Introduction to Old Age: The Last Segregation.* New York, Grossman, 1971.

Nelson FL, Farberow NL: Indirect self-destructive behavior in the elderly nursing home patient. *J Gerontol* 1980;35:949–957.

Nelson MN, Pellick RJ: Territorial markings: Self-concept and mental status of the institutionalized elderly. *Gerontologist* 1980;20:96–98.

Nester RM, Andersen DW, Hodes E: Limbering up in West Virginia. *Public Welfare* 1981;Winter:29–33.

Novick JB: Easing the stress of moving day. *Hospitals* 1967;41:64–74.

Pfeiffer E: Introduction to the conference report, in Pfeiffer E (ed): *Alternatives to Institutional Care for Older Americans: Practice and Planning.* Durham, NC, Duke University Center for Study of Aging and Human Development, 1973.

Posner J: Notes on the negative implications of being competent in a home for the aged. *Int J Aging Human Development* 1974;5:357–364.

Randall OA: Some historical developments of social welfare aspects of aging. *Gerontologist* 1965;5:40–49.

Rodstein M: Challenging residents to assume maximal responsibilities in homes for the aged. *J Am Geriatrics Soc* 1975;23:317–321.

Rowland KF: Environmental events predicting death for the elderly. *Psychol Bull* 1977;84(2):349–372.

Schulz R: Effects of control and predictability on the physical and psychological well-being of the institutional aged. *J Personality and Soc Psychol* 1976;33:563–573.

Schulz R, Aderman D: Effects of residential change on the temporal distance of death of terminal cancer patients. *Omega: J Death Dying* 1973;4:157–162.

Schulz R, Aderman D: Clinical research and the stages of dying. *Omega: J Death Dying* 1974;5:50.

Schulz R, Brenner G: Relocation of the aged: A review and theoretical analysis. *J Gerontol* 1977;32:323–333.

Seligman MEP: *Helplessness: On Depression, Development and Death.* San Francisco, Freeman Press, 1975.

Smith BK: *Aging in America.* Boston, Beacon Press, 1973.

Spasoff RR, Kraus AS, Beattle EJ, et al: A longitudinal study of elderly residents of long-stay institutions. *Gerontologist* 1978;18:281–292.

Stuart RB: *Act Thin, Stay Thin.* New York, Norton, 1968.

Tobin SS: How nursing homes vary. *Gerontologist* 1974;14:516–519.

Tobin SS, Lieberman MA: *Last Home for the Aged.* San Francisco, Jossey-Bass, 1976.

Townsend P: *The Last Refuge. A Survey of Residential Institutions and Homes for the Aged in England and Wales.* London, Routledge and Kegan Pual, 1962.

Turner BF, Tobin SS, Lieberman MA: Personality traits as predictors of institutional adaptation among the aged. *J Gerontol* 1972;27:21–68.

Vladeck BC: *Unloving Care: The Nursing Home Tragedy.* New York, Basic Books, 1980.

Wittels I, Botwinick J: Survival in relocation. *J Gerontol* 1974;29:440–443.

Wolk RL, Reingold J: The course of life for old people. *J Am Geriatrics Soc* 1975;23:376–379.

Wortman CB: Some determinants of perceived control. *J Personality Social Psychol* 1975;31:282–294.

Yawney BA, Slover DL: Relocation of the elderly. *Social Work* 1973;18:86–95.

6 Fraud and Abuse In Nursing Homes*

Val J. Halamandaris

Throughout the 1970s, the Subcommittee on Long-Term Care of the United States Senate Special Committee, chaired by Senator Frank E. Moss, documented widespread fraud and abuse among nursing homes participating in the Medicaid program. The Subcommittee concluded that much of the fraud was made possible by lax enforcement at both the federal and state level and the use of a cost-plus reimbursement formula (which Senator Moss said would "make defense contractors drool with envy"). The House Select Committee on Aging also contributed to examination of this problem documenting that 20 states had never audited a single nursing home owner or other Medicaid provider through January 1976, and that 20 states had never convicted a single nursing home owner or medical practitioner of Medicaid fraud from the beginning of the Medicaid program through this same time period. Chairman Claude Pepper of the House Aging Committee charged that the situation was "outrageous."

---

*Excerpted from *Too Old, Too Sick, Too Bad.* Authored by Mr. Halamandaris and Senator Frank Moss. Published by Aspen Systems, Rockville, MD, 1977.

The result of disclosures of widespread fraud in the Medicaid program by the House and Senate Aging Committee was legislation creating the Office of Inspector General in the Department of Health and Human Services to coordinate the Department's war on this kind of fraud and legislation authorizing 90% federal funding to the states to help them establish separate units to find and prosecute fraud.

In 1980, the Inspector General referred 42 cases for prosecution and 5 fraud convictions resulted. In this same year there were 3067 cases of potential Medicaid fraud being investigated by the states, some 228 convictions were made and 24 people actually served some time in jail. Nursing home owners/operators made up 15% of all the pending cases, 20% of the convictions, and 37% of those who actually served some time in jail. Nursing homes receive about 45% of all Medicaid funds.

Following is a brief catalogue of the kinds of criminal fraud and abuse perpetrated by nursing home owners. It is not implied that all or even the majority of nursing home owners indulge in some or all of these practices. Rather, this is a list assembled from convictions that have been obtained by the states and the federal government over the past several years.

THEFT OF PATIENTS' FUNDS

Congress has provided that every nursing home patient on Medicaid is entitled to at least $25 a month as a personal spending allowance. Nursing home owners are trustees of these funds and are obligated by federal regulations to keep the funds separate from their operating revenues. In 1975, Senator Moss asked the United States General Accounting Office (GAO) to investigate reports of wide-scale fraud involving patients' personal funds. GAO conducted an audit of 30 homes in six states. In their March 1976 report, GAO found that each of the 30 homes had failed to safeguard patients' funds in one of several ways. GAO found shortages in patients' monies, that medical supplies and services were being improperly charged to such funds, that the funds of dead or transferred patients were being retained by the facilities, or that nursing homes had invested the funds and kept the interest for themselves. In one case, an operator was using these trust funds as collateral on a personal loan.

In some cases the nursing home is not to blame. A Wisconsin nurse in January 1979 pleaded guilty to taking about $1500 from the personal accounts of patients. In the state of Washington a bookkeeper for a Spokane nursing home admitted to the theft of about $4000 in trust funds. In January 1980, the brother of a nursing home owner admitted to stealing $1192 from patients; however, in this case also admitted she stole over $18,000 from these accounts over three years. In January 1979, a Spokane nursing home administrator and former state legislator was found guilty of "borrowing" money which belonged to nursing home patients. In 1978, a Seattle-based nursing home chain was fined $15,000 for the embezzlement of trust funds. This was the second case in which a corporation was convicted of this offense in Washington. In the earlier Seattle case, the defense attorney argued unsuccessfully that his client should not be convicted because "borrowing" money from the patients funds accounts was a common industry practice.

MEDICAID ABUSES

Supplementing Medicaid

Federal regulations prohibit charging the patient or the family any amount over and above the Medicaid rate established by the states. However, the Senate Committee on Aging established that nursing homes sometimes violate this regulation. Family members might be told that if they pay extra ("under-the-table") their relative will receive better care. In New York a nursing home owner was convicted in 1975 for telling a family that, as a Medicaid recipient, their mother could expect to be placed in the dilapidated, original section of the home but, for a few dollars on the side, a bed in the new wing could be found.

A more subtle variation of the same theme requires the family to make a "gift" or "donation" as a precondition of the nursing home's accepting a Medicaid patient. In Miami, an operator required the children of a patient to sign a contract which stipulated their mother was conditionally accepted until they had paid a "gift" or "donation" to the building fund of $8500. This was in addition to the $900 a month they were to pay for their mother's care. If they decided to break their pledge to keep the mother in the facility permanently, the relatives had to pay a "pledge" of $1000. In December 1981, the Supreme Court of the State of New York released a grand jury report which found there was a pattern of soliciting charitable contributions from prospective patients and their relatives at or near the time of admission. Most of the applicants were eligible for and subsequently had their care paid for by Medicaid. The grand jury asked for the enactment of a statute, similar to the amendment which Congressman Pepper was able to add to federal law, which made such solicitations illegal. The amendment was part of Public Law 95-142.

Costs Unrelated to Patient Care

One of the most common techniques of defrauding Medicaid involves the presentation of unauthorized or improper charges for reimbursement. The Medicaid system requires nursing homes to file cost reports to show how they have used taxpayers' dollars. Such dollars must be used for the benefit of the patients and not be converted to the personal use and benefit of the nursing home owners or operators.

Charles J. Hynes, former Deputy Attorney General and Special Prosecutor for Nursing Homes in New York, provided the following list of personal expenditures which operators in his state tried to claim were related to patient care. These items were not allowed. Nursing home owners were asked to pay back money that they had used to purchase these items and in some cases were convicted of fraud. Federal statutes require that cost reports be signed by the nursing home owner under penalty of perjury. Many operators have been convicted of filing false cost reports. Several states have recently enacted legislation to require that cost reports also be signed under penalty of perjury by accountants who fill them out for the operator.

- Personal maids and servants
- Private residential landscaping
- Travel expenses
- Expensive food items
- Luggage
- Works of art (including paintings by Matisse and Renoir in one instance)
- Vast quantities of liquor
- Interior decorating
- Dental and medical care
- Pharmaceuticals
- Heating fuel for private residences
- Charitable contributions
- Political contributions
- Profits to investors
- Private automobile expenses
- Private pension plans
- Vacation expenses
- Real estate taxes
- Mink coats
- Personal investment stock
- Renovations to private homes
- Entertainment
- Legal fees
- Theatre tickets
- Tickets for sporting events
- High fidelity stereophonic equipment
- Secret personal profit

In Connecticut, eight nursing home operators and administrators have recently been arrested for defrauding Medicaid. Allegedly, in the words of columnist Jack Anderson, funds "were squandered on everything from shrimp and filet mignon to the purchase of 17 X-rated movies that were charged off to the taxpayer as 'patient entertainment'."

Placing Relatives or "Ghosts" on the Payroll

Another means of fraud used by some nursing homes is to place "ghosts" on the payroll—nonexistent persons whose salary is taken by the nursing home and for which Medicaid is charged. This procedure has more risk than placing relatives on the payroll. The question involved here is: Are they qualified and did they actually provide services to the home and its patients.

One operator charged New York Medicaid for a $21,926 salary paid to his first wife at the time the operator was living with his second wife in Florida. He also charged New York for domestic help in his Florida home, and $10,587 in fees to an engineer who was working on a new nursing home in Florida. In addition, the operator charged off $29,324 for entertainment and travel including restaurant bills from across the country and operational expenses for his yacht in Florida. A Connecticut operator last year was alleged to have kept his wife on the nursing home payroll even though she actually worked for a different family-owned company and spent much of her time in Florida.

Failure to Offset Costs with Related Income

GAO in a 1977 audit found that some nursing homes receive a great deal of income from vending machines and beauty shops which they operate. Nursing homes pass the costs of these services on to the Medicaid program for reimbursement but forget to offset the costs they are asking for by any profits they have made in the venture. The result is that a facility is reimbursed twice — "once as income and again as Medicaid reimbursement for the cost of the activity that produced the income."

Duplicate Payments from Medicare and Medicaid

In October 1980, Congress enacted a provision requiring common audits for facilities that participate in Medicare and Medicaid. Until this time, Medicare auditors would look only at the Medicare part of a nursing home's business. Medicaid would look after its part. No one was checking to see that the same expenses were not passed on to both programs. In an audit for the Senate Committee on Aging, which involved Kane Hospital, the nation's second largest nursing home located near Pittsburgh, GAO found that the facility had billed both programs to the extent of some $2 million. GAO said recently that they have since found other examples of such double billing which should be more difficult in the future.

Collecting for Patients that
Are Dead or Discharged

GAO reported in an audit of the California Medicaid program that "in 22 of the 260 (nursing home) cases examined, claims were paid after a recipient had died or had been discharged from a nursing home." At least one case of this kind of abuse brought about a guilty plea from the owner of an Ohio nursing home in May, 1981.

"Dummy" Invoices Used as Basis for Medicaid Reimbursement

Nursing homes sometimes use nonexistent or "dummy" invoices submitted by a related or friendly company to justify costs which are passed along to Medicaid. In a famous case which involved prominent political figures in Minnesota, a nursing home operator was convicted of operating this kind of scheme in 1976. In that case, court records show that phony bills were submitted by a furniture company at the request of the nursing home owner in return for the promise that he would send them a great deal of business. The phony bills, of course, were never paid but were passed along to Medicaid and generated a cash flow for the operator. Such "dummy" invoices are sometimes used to disguise illegal kickbacks.

OTHER ABUSES

Capital Items Expensed Rather Than Capitalized

GAO found in a 1977 audit that a large number of permanent improvements to nursing home structures or items, such as new kitchen equipment, were accounted for as expenses rather than capitalized for tax purposes. Expenses can be deducted entirely in one year. Capitalized items must be depreciated and, thus, deducted over several years determined by the useful life of the item. In some cases GAO found that operators had both expensed and capitalized the same costs. The result was that the facility was reimbursed twice during the useful life of the items.

Trading in Real Estate

There is a heavy traffic in the buying and selling of nursing homes. There are many reasons for this but the most important relate to tax advantages and increased Medicaid reimbursement. The Internal Revenue Service allows the operator to deduct from his taxes, in each year, an amount equal to 10% of the value of the property he purchased as depreciation. The purchase price of the nursing home becomes the basis for such depreciation. The larger the price, the more that can be taken off the operator's taxes. At the same time, if the purchase involves a minimum down payment (usually the case), most of the payments paid by the operator in the first few years will be for interest which is deductible on the operator's taxes and reimbursable from Medicaid.

The second reason for the buying and selling of nursing homes involves the reimbursement formula for Medicare and Medicaid. The formula offers the operator a return on his investment. One way to increase the return is to sell the nursing home back and forth, which has the effect of inflating its value. As the purchase price goes higher and higher, the increasing costs incurred can be passed along to Medicaid. One nursing home in New York was sold back and forth between related parties about 11 times in eight years. Operators in that state have been convicted not of trading in real estate per se but of filing false and inflated cost reports or of failure to disclose properly the owners of the nursing homes involved.

Cutting Expenses

According to sworn testimony before the Subcommittee on Long-Term Care, many nursing homes cut expenses to the point of harming patients. There are reports that some operators cut back on staff, spend as little as 50 cents a day for food, weigh meat on a stamp scale, serve "mock meatloaf" or breakfasts of coffee and one-half slice of bread, refuse to buy toothbrushes and toilet paper, or have only one thermometer for the entire home. There are other reports of cutting costs, such as keeping the heat turned low in winter and the air conditioning off in summer. The question here is when, if ever, these activities amount to fraud.

In addition, there are nursing home owners who report on their cost reports that they had 100 employees working 40 hours a week when they had only 75 employees. Or an operator might charge the program for therapy allegedly given by these employees to patients when such therapy was not given.

In 1981, law enforcement authorities in Texas issued 38 indictments involving the death of eight patients in a Texas City nursing home. The controversial charge amounts to murder by fraud or at least murder by omission. The unusual legal theory alleges that the defendants fraudulently appropriated government funds for medical care that was not delivered, which prosecutors claim was an act "clearly dangerous to human life."

It is to be emphasized that an indictment is only a formal legal charge. The defendants are innocent in the eyes of the law until proven guilty. However, the case has already served to put nursing home owners on notice that penury and cost cutting may have serious consequences if they jeopardize the health and safety of patients. For example, if a nursing home admits a patient with a diagnosis of diabetes and knows that the patient needs insulin, and yet fails to provide that insulin out of penury or negligence (or worse yet, if it charges Medicaid for insulin that is never given), the nursing home and its operators may find themselves facing criminal charges.

Hidden Charges

The Federal Trade Commission is presently considering a trade rule that would require nursing homes to disclose fully all costs to prospective customers. There are presently few federal laws which service to protect private paying patients. There are, however, a number of applicable state consumer laws. In these states nursing homes that fail to inform customers fully of costs may find themselves in violation of the law.

The kinds of violations involved would relate to the failure of a home to disclose ancillary charges. The patient's family would be told only about the monthly charge of perhaps $1500 per month but would not be told that they would be charged extra for each of the following items used: air mattresses, alcohol, baby oil, body lotion, bed sore care, bibs, catheters, chest restraints, enemas, hand feeding, incontinent care, oxygen, shampoo, plastic gloves, spray deodorant, television in the room, tissues, wheelchairs, walkers, syringes, and senile care.

Fraudulent Therapy Charges

Nursing homes either provide therapy themselves or through recreational, occupational, and physical therapists whom they hire. In recent years, there have been numerous convictions involving either the nursing home or the therapists themselves who charge for services not rendered.

In December 1978, for example, the director of a social work firm which provided psychotherapy to patients in Wisconsin nursing homes was convicted of stealing more than $17,000 from Medicaid in connection with such services. Two months before, the director of a Milwaukee agency providing psychotherapy services under the Medicaid program pleaded guilty to charges that she received $328,843 from the program for services not rendered over a two-year period.

Fraudulent Pharmaceutical Charges

In the past five years a number of pharmacists who deal with nursing homes have been convicted either of kickbacks, as listed below, or of filing false claims. For example, a Greensboro, North Carolina pharmacist in March 1980 was convicted of Medicaid fraud and ordered to return $16,000 to Medicaid. The pharmacist allegedly submitted bills for medication on behalf of nursing home patients that were never ordered or provided. Similar charges led to the conviction of a New York City pharmacist in 1981.

Kickbacks

One of the most pervasive methods of Medicaid fraud involves the payment of kickbacks. A kickback is the practice whereby a supplier is forced to pay a certain percentage of the price of nursing home supplies back to the nursing home operator ("under the table") for the privilege of providing supplies or services to the nursing home.

In May 1977 the Senate Aging Committee issued a report entitled "Kickbacks Among Medicaid Providers." The report concludes that "Kickbacks are rampant and that the 1972 law enacted by the Congress making them illegal is not being enforced." The report continues: "The evidence is overwhelming that many pharmacists are required to pay kickbacks to nursing home operators as a precondition of obtaining a nursing home's business."

The report includes example after example of these kinds of kickback arrangements. For example, an undercover operation was conducted by New York's Deputy Attorney General Hynes and involved a cooperating nursing home administrator who wore a microphone and a recording device while negotiating contracts with over 30 suppliers in New York City. As various suppliers were caught in the net, they were turned into undercover operatives cooperating with the government in exchange for consideration at the time of their sentencing. Deputy Attorney General Hynes told the Senate Aging Committee that kickbacks were found in half of the 125 nursing homes in New York City. "Our indication is that the same kind of abuses are found in all providers of service in Medicaid. Kickbacks were paid to nursing homes by linen, laundry, milk, produce vendors as well as contract cleaning firms and medical supply houses." He said the average kickback was about 25%.

The report describes illegal kickback cases in several states including California, Florida, Wisconsin, Illinois, and Utah. The most common form was cash. Kickbacks also were paid in the form of long-term credit arrangements, rental of space, furnishing supplies to the nursing home, paying for a nursing home's advertising, or paying for employees ostensibly working for the pharmacy, for prepaid vacations, gifts of cars, boats, and television sets or giving the nursing home operator shares in the pharmacy.

The report includes a letter from a former nursing home administrator who said he had partial ownership of four nursing homes although he had never invested a dime of his own money. He alleged that he declared only 30% of his annual income for tax purposes. He admitted paying physicians and hospitals $50 for each referral. He said the following were the average rates paid to nursing homes:

1. Pharmacies pay 25%.
2. Physical and occupational therapists pay 50% to 60%.
3. Food supplies were competitive except that some owners were supplied with food for their personal use.
4. Laundry did not involve rebates because the industry is controlled by organized crime.
5. Undertakers pay 20%.
6. Cemetery lot sales and tombstones may bring the operator a 20% kickback.
7. Contractors pay 10% of the gross construction price of a new nursing home.

In May 1980 agents of the Federal Bureau of Investigation testified before the House Select Committee on Aging on the results of their undercover investigation in the Los Angeles area. The agents represented themselves as interested in entering the health care field, especially the nursing home business. The FBI, in this guise, began to contact vendors to service their nursing homes. The FBI stated:

> It became immediately apparent that kickbacks and rebates were a way of life. Virtually every provider of ancillary services that we contacted made offers of rebates and kickbacks in an effort to provide the business services which would be needed to maintain a nursing home. These offers were made by clinical laboratories, therapists, X-ray services, or providers of oxygen. . . . Based on our experience, the methods to commit fraud in the Medicare/Medicaid programs are virtually unlimited. The most widely used method of paying kickbacks in this program is by cash. . . . Corruption has permeated virtually every area of the Medicare/Medicaid health care industry.

Organized Crime Involvement

In October 1978 the House Select Committee on Aging conducted a hearing on fraud and racketeering in the Medicare and Medicaid programs. The purpose of this hearing was to determine the extent to which organized crime was invading the programs. Questionnaires were sent to the attorney general, state bureau of investigation, district attorneys, and police chiefs of major cities in each of the 50 states. In addition questionnaires were sent to all 95 United States Attorneys and to the 14 organized crime strike forces.

The results were shocking. About 9 of 14 federal organized crime strike forces reported that they had evidence and pending cases of organized crime involvement in the health care field. Some 15 of the 95 United States Attorneys responded in the affirmative. Thirty-five of the states sent in at least one positive response. In some states four or five positive responses were received from law officers who had evidence of mob involvement. Asked to identify the areas where they had investigations or pending cases under way, the states mentioned nursing homes most frequently. A total of 39 positive responses related to nursing homes; pharmacies were second with 16 law enforcement officers saying they had evidence in this area; prepaid health care plans were third, with 14 affirmative responses.

SOLUTIONS

There can be only one solution to the kind of fraud described in this chapter. The Department of Justice, the FBI, the Department of Health and Human Services (especially their Inspector General) must work together to investigate cases of this nature and prosecute them to the full extent of the law. Judges must begin to give more jail sentences. The states must also begin to enforce the law, because in the words of Sir Robert Peel, "Law is not law unless it is enforced." The nation can no longer tolerate the degree of fraud that exists. Lawbreakers have no fear of being caught and prosecuted. They flout the law with impunity and mock the honest providers who follow it. This must change, and it must change soon.

7 Domestic Neglect and Abuse of the Elderly: Research Findings and a Systems Perspective for Service Delivery Planning

Richard L. Douglass
Tom Hickey

The elderly have always been a population of concern to Western society, although history documents the inconsistency of such concerns. In early 20th century England, for instance, a noted social advocate, Beatrice Webb, called upon Parliament to modify the English Poor Law and to create a Society for the Prevention of Cruelty to the Elderly. While sporadic recognition of the plight of the mistreated, dependent elderly has come into public view throughout the last 50 years, only since 1977 have considerations of neglect and abuse in the homes become a priority issue. Now, based only on minimal information, we are seeking to find solutions to the various kinds of maltreatment of the elderly found in our society. Such a "new" social problem provides an opportunity to formulate coordinated service delivery before institutionalization of specialized, uncoordinated, and potentially conflicting service delivery components. This chapter will review early evidence about the causes of neglect and abuse of the elderly, and then offer a systems analysis perspective of how different service delivery efforts can be developed to meet common objectives.

Recent Research on Neglect
and Abuse of the Elderly

Recent research on neglect and abuse of the elderly has included six sources: three case studies, two mail surveys of professionals and practitioners, and one a combination of personal interviews of practitioners and professionals and secondary data analysis (Table 7-1). These studies, conducted at the same time in relative isolation from each other, have resulted in a modest number of scientific reports, publications, conference papers and testimonial presentations before Congressional Committees.

The case studies presented by Rathbone-McCuan (1978, 1980) in Missouri and Steinmetz (1978) in Delaware were based on information gathered from social services, hospital social workers, and emergency rooms. Data collection was principally intended to raise hypotheses. The majority of cases have some information about the extent of mistreatment, characteristics of the victim and perpetrator, and the situation existing. These authors have indicated, however, that these cases probably represent the most bizarre forms of abuse and should not be widely generalized. Lau and Kosberg (1980) reviewed 404 new cases of patients over age 60 who were accepted within a 12-month period to the Cleveland Chronic Illness Center; they asked the Center staff to identify cases of abuse or neglect from the case records and provide information from their recollections of individual patients. A range of physical and psychological abuse and neglect and what the authors termed "material abuse and violation of rights" were found. Of the cases of mistreatment, 74% were judged to be physical abuse (beatings) or physical consequences of neglect and 51% included psychological abuse. Like the case studies of Rathbone-McCuan and Steinmetz, the majority of victims reported by Lau and Kosberg were also subjected to more than one form of abuse, and the majority of victims were women, widowed, dependent on others, and frail.

From these early case studies the image of mistreatment of the frail elderly in their homes began to spark the interest of other researchers. While these findings were relatively consistent, it has not been determined if the emphasis on deriving a "typical" case has actually isolated a target group, because the majority of all elderly are women who are widowed, who may be somewhat dependent on others and who have chronic health problems. Certain causal factors have been suggested including a caretaker's inability to handle the stress associated with personal care for an older person, alcohol abuse, and unresolved emotional problems between abused and abuser. Adult daughters were more likely than adult sons to be abusers, other abusers included grandchildren, siblings, or spouses. Non-relative caretakers were less likely to be identified as abusers.

Summary of Recent Studies on Neglect and Abuse of the Elderly

Principal Author(s)	Release Date	Design(s)	Method(s) of Data Retrieval	Study Site(s)
Steinmetz	1978	Case studies	–	Delaware
Rathbone-McCuan	1978	Case studies	Hospital, emergency room, police	Greater St. Louis, MO
Lau, Kosberg	1978	Case studies	Case review	The Cleveland, Ohio Chronic Illness Center
O'Malley, Segars, Perez, Mitchell, Knuepfel	1979	Mail survey to general lists and selected individuals of health, human service, police and voluntary agencies and staff	Respondent—completed questionnaire 34% response rate	Massachusetts
Block, Sinnott	1979	Soliciting cases from selected agencies	Case solicitation	Greater Washington, DC-Maryland
		Direct mail to elderly	Direct mail survey to elderly – 0.7% response rate	Members of American Psychological Association, emergency room physicians and gerontological society
		Mail survey of medical, nursing social work and aging services personnel in Greater Washington, DC	Direct mail survey of professionals, 31.4% response rate	
Douglass, Hickey, Noël	1980	Personal interviews with practitioners, providers; Police data analysis; Nursing home admission data analysis: 238 interviews + 15 anecdotal interviews	Personal interviews in field. 97% sample response rate. Secondary analyses of Detroit criminal data; Oakland County Michigan Medicare nursing home admission data	State of Michigan: City of Detroit Kent County (Grand Rapids) Lake County Marquette County (Marquette) Oakland County (Pontiac)

The utility of such research is questionable regarding questions of incidence, prevalence, or risk group identification. Such issues cannot be addressed by the case method alone. Rathbone-McCuan noted that the cases she reviewed presented no greater level of dependence, poor environment, or personal circumstances than many, if not most, situations in which the caretakers and the dependents successfully lived without neglect or abuse. Thus, while these cases have been reported as the "tip of the iceberg" of neglect and abuse of the elderly, possibly only in a minority of similar situations there is a true probability of neglect or abuse. The most important contribution of the case studies, however, has been the suggestion that more research be conducted and the generation of specific hypotheses of manifestations, cause, and magnitude of the problem.

Block and Sinnott (1979) designed a study to test three alternative case identification strategies in Metropolitan Washington, D.C. and the State of Maryland. The first method solicited case reports from health and human service agencies which produced few responses. The second method, a direct mail questionnaire to elderly living in the greater Washington, DC area inquiring about their knowledge of or experience with domestic neglect or abuse, had less than 1% of the questionnaires returned. The third approach by Block and Sinnott was to mail questionnaires to three groups: members of the American Psychological Association, emergency room physicians, and members of the Gerontological Society who lived in Maryland. Of the sample 31.4% returned questionnaires of which 13.4% were familiar with at least one case of mistreatment of an older person. The authors concluded that many of the observations of earlier case studies were supported except that the most frequent form of mistreatment was psychological and not physical. Specifically, Block and Sinnott concluded that the victims were usually frail, female, and highly dependent upon a related younger adult who was under some exceptional stress level. This information does not permit generalization.

O'Malley et al (1979) surveyed a combination of professional groups in Massachusetts about familiarity with the aged in that state. From a spectrum of professional groups 332 mail survey questionnaires were returned (Table 7-2).

The sample is primarily from medical, police, legal, or in-home services and was drawn from the private sector. A major portion is drawn from visiting nurses, in-home service workers, and police, a strong point because these individuals are likely to have experience in the homes of aged persons. There are probably too few public protective service workers or other representatives of the public services sector, however, to draw many conclusions from this stratum of the sample.

Table 7-2
Respondent Classification Distribution

Respondent Category	N	%
Visiting nurse	83	24%
Hospital social services director	56	16
Homemaker/home health aid	17	5
Home care corporation staff*	22	6
Emergency room nursing supervisor	22	6
Public welfare — protective service worker*	4	1
Private social service agency staff/social worker*	49	14
Lawyer/paralegal	24	7
Police officer	33	10
(All other categories, including multiple responses)	34	10
TOTAL	344	(99.0)

*unknown if staff or supervisory
Data from O'Malley et al, 1979.

As with the Block and Sinnott study, and to a lesser degree with that of Lau and Kosberg, a great emphasis was placed on a respondent's familiarity with at least one case of abuse or neglect of an older person. In the present case it was emphasized that 55% of the returned survey forms "indicated a citing of elder abuse within the last eighteen months." This figure verifies that these respondents had at least minimal direct experience with neglect or abuse of the elderly; it does not, however, put the respondents' experiences with the problem in perspective, relative to his work load or responsibility. The authors presented numerous descriptive findings regarding the experiences of respondents with cases of neglect or abuse, possible cause, adequacy or inadequacy of services to deal with abuse or neglect, and the respondents' suggested intervention strategies.

The principal descriptive findings from O'Malley et al verify the case and survey impressions of the studies discussed above. The victim of "Elder Abuse in Massachusetts" was reported as older than most other elderly, frail, mentally or physically disabled, female, and living with the abuser. The perpetrator (abusing person) was usually a relative who provided care for the victim. The authors also report that the abuser was "experiencing some form of stress such as alcoholism or drug addiction, a long-term medical complaint or long-term financial difficulties." The abuser, furthermore, was usually chiefly responsible for physical, emotional and financial care of the victim.

This survey has numerous strengths in the range of questions asked and the proximity of the respondents to the elderly. Its descriptive findings, while congruent in most ways with the earlier studies, are less critical in describing kinds of "abuse" than in measuring the potential and actual ways that cases are reported, referred, and treated by these respondents. The authors note, for instance, that few victims (24%) report their own plight, with equal likelihood that the respondent (24%) or a caseworker (19%) would first recognize the case as "abuse." Of the cases reviewed, 70% required a third party to bring the case to the attention of the helping professions. This is not particularly unusual in the area of child abuse; but it differs greatly from spouse abuse in which the victim is the most frequent reporting source. Thus, the vulnerability and available resourcefulness of victims of elder abuse in Massachusetts may be more analogous to child abuse than to spouse abuse.

An important finding by O'Malley et al is that the cases retrieved from their respondents were chiefly active physical trauma. This is decidedly different than the findings of Lau and Kosberg or Block and Sinnott.

Douglass, Hickey, and Noël (1980) conducted personal interviews with practitioners and professionals in five Michigan locations in 1979. The field sites included rural, urban, suburban, affluent, and depressed areas. Each study site was profiled regarding its service delivery system and a peer-nomination sample was selected for several categories of respondents in each study site. Principal respondent selection requirements were that at least one-third of the respondents' routine activities must be spent in direct service delivery, and administrative or supervisory personnel were to be excluded. This strategy was generally successful with the exception of some groups such as coroners, morticians, and clergy. The respondent distribution is shown in Table 7-3.

Table 7-3
Distribution of Respondents by Professional/Occupational Category

Respondent Category	N	%
Police officers and detectives	25	11.9%
Physicians in general and family practice	18	7.9
Nurses and aides in public and home health	27	11.8
Social workers in medical or outreach services	40	17.5
Adult protective service workers	21	9.2
Community mental health workers	16	7.0
Attorneys, legal counselors, public guardians	17	7.5
Aging services workers	17	7.5
Clergy	24	10.5
Morticians, coroners, medical examiners	23	10.0
TOTAL	228	(100.0)

Data from Douglass, Hickey, and Noël, 1980.

The respondents were about equally divided between the public and the private service sectors which differs from the study of O'Malley et al. The Michigan study also included personal interviews with a small sample of nursing home staff, secondary analysis of Detroit police data on crimes against the elderly, and nursing home admissions data. Only the field study will be reviewed here, however, since this was the major thrust of the research.

Data were collected in personal interviews which lasted from only a few minutes (for respondents with no experience with maltreatment and who considered the needs of the vulnerable adult groups to be always met) to three hours or even longer. Questionnaires were designed to guide the interview through several categories of information. The main categories were:

1. Information about the respondents and the respondents' involvement with the elderly.
2. Perceived degree to which daily needs are met by these persons upon whom the elderly depend.
3. Perceptions regarding relative frequency and dynamics of passive neglect, active neglect, verbal/emotional abuse, or physical abuse. Information on the relative likelihood of neglect or abuse resulting in serious injury or death.
4. Case-finding mechanisms.
5. Reporting and intervention activities.

Over 270 interviews were conducted, of which 228 were included in statistical analyses.

The Michigan research and subsequent analyses placed a major emphasis on three basic issues: Is there neglect or abuse of the elderly in the community? What are the characteristics of such "maltreatment," if it exists? Who sees it from the services sector, and why do they think it occurs? This study verified many of the conclusions of earlier work. While a majority of elderly dependents were viewed by respondents as generally well cared for, they felt that a minority experiences some form of neglect or abuse. By a wide margin maltreatment was viewed by the respondents as passive and neglectful, rather than active and abusive. Older women, highly dependent elderly and very sick or frail persons were regarded as most likely to be abused or neglected.

Despite methodologic differences, these studies have verified that a problem of unknown proportion does exist. A modest degree of "cross-validity" has occurred between the studies; however, differences and similarities depend on the sample designs and methods as much as on any actual dimension of neglect or abuse of the elderly.

In general, the population at risk for domestic abuse or neglect can be identified as those elderly who are most vulnerable because of advanced age, frailty, chronic disease, or physical or mental impairment, in other words those who are least capable of independent living and most dependent on others. They are generally less conscious of alternative living arrangements or means of support than others in their age cohort, and they are more likely to be aged women than men. On the average, victims will have two or more physical disabilities. However, neglect or abuse should not be ruled out if an older patient without impairment appears for treatment — it simply means that most victims will be highly vulnerable. With the aged, unlike children who survive domestic violence, vulnerability increases over time. It is relatively uncommon for incidents of neglect or abuse to be isolated, moreover, and episodes of neglectful or abusive behavior can be expected to continue and increase in a specific family as a dependent older person ages, unless some form of intervention changes the family's circumstances. Racial, socioeconomic or other social criteria have not been found to identify population segments at higher risk of being neglected or abused.

The Meaning of Maltreatment

There are different manifestations of neglect or abuse of the elderly, and various approaches to the problem of definitions of these manifestations. Table 7-4 presents the definitions as used in four principal studies which have been conducted. The meaning of the term *abuse* is generally avoided or confused with the term *neglect* since these generic terms have been used in the general domestic violence literature. If abuse implies an active, purposive set of behaviors, it is not clear why some studies have included "lack of personal care, food, supervision, or medical care" in the same category as physical assault. It is also unclear whether all respondents to mail surveys had reliable understandings of such ambiguous terms as "lack of personal care," "malnutrition," "debilitating mental anguish," or "misuse of money or property." Without follow-up questions or validity or reliability checks, it is not entirely certain that the percentages and frequencies linked to these various manifestations of maltreatment are meaningful.

The Lau and Kosberg study emphasized the predominance of physical abuse. If the Michigan conceptual definitions were used, however, most of Lau and Kosberg's physical abuse would more appropriately fit into the categories of active or passive neglect. Similarly, much of the Block and Sinnott abuse categories are actually physical consequences of neglect rather than inflicted trauma. This is the crux of the problem when

Table 7-4
Comparative Conceptual Definitions of Manifestations of Neglect and Abuse of the Elderly

Lau, Kosberg (1979)	Block, Sinnott (1979)	O'Malley, et al (1979)	Douglass, Hickey, Noël (1980)
Physical Abuse	Physical Abuse	Physical Trauma	Physical Abuse
Direct beatings (hit frequently)	Bruises, welts	Bruises, welts,	Verbal-Emotional Abuse
Lack of personal care	Sprains, dislocations	wounds, cuts, punctures, bone fractures	Active Neglect
Lack of food	Malnutrition, freezing	abrasions, lacerations,	Passive Neglect
Lack of medical care	Abrasions, lacerations, cuts, punctures	sprains, burns, scaldings	(Financial Abuse or Exploitation)[a]
Lack of supervision	Direct Beating	Debilitating Mental Anguish	
Psychological Abuse	Lack of personal care	Malnutrition	
Verbal assault	Lack of food	Sexual Abuse	
Threat	Lack of supervision	Freezing	
Fear	Tied to bed		
Isolation	Tied to chair		
Material Abuse	Psychological Abuse		
Theft of money or property	Verbal assault		
Misuse of money or property	Threat		
Violation of Rights	Fear		
Forced from home	Isolation		
Forced from nursing home	Material Abuse		
	Theft of money or property		
	Misuse of money or property		
	Poor Residential Environment		

[a]Introduced by respondents, not built into the study design.

ng to identify the common denominators of these studies. The actions nactions of the caregiver formed the basis of the definitions we chose use in Michigan. Behaviors were viewed as abusive (implying active, entional behavior) or neglectful (either active or passive). The consequences of such abuse or neglect could be equally damaging to a victim, however the *intent* or ability of the caregiver to have avoided causing harm is differentiated. Thus, we are without means of deciding the extent to which supportive assistance in the home might have prevented any of the cases of abuse or neglect in the Ohio, Massachusetts, or Maryland studies, whereas it can be expected that a majority of the passive neglect cases reported in Michigan might have been prevented with an assortment of family support services; passive neglect was the most frequently recognized form of maltreatment in the Michigan study. Definitions are vital to future research and program or policy development and must be clarified before any empirical progress can be expected. One of the conclusions of the Michigan study was that any of the active or passive, abusive or neglectful forms of maltreatment could result in serious or life threatening consequences to a frail and dependent adult. It is necessary to separate the consequences of maltreatment from the alternative actions or inactions of caretakers before future research is undertaken. Program development also must consider these factors before identifying appropriate activities within communities.

Focus on Cause

A major area of investigation in the Michigan study was that of the causes of neglect and abuse as perceived by direct service providers in the community (Hickey and Douglass, 1981a, 1981b). In this regard it is useful, we think, to keep in mind the 18th century verse about the blind men and the elephant.

All research in this area must face the possibility of being partially blinded by previous assumptions. There is, however, the need to begin such inquiry, the intention of each study to date. As the poet Saxe described, the intentions of different investigators can be identical and the capabilities comparable, yet the outcomes of research can vary according to the method of inquiry. In several important ways each existing study of domestic neglect and abuse of the elderly has been different in perspective, research strategy, and degree of parochialism. Thus, it should not be surprising that some of the findings initially seem to conflict.

In the Michigan study the first means of identifying causal factors was simply to ask each respondent what they considered the causes of neglect and abuse to be. The responses were initially coded into aggregated categories. The second question was: "In certain situations with which you are familiar, are the causes of neglect different from the causes of abuse?" The forced response portions of each answer included valid "yes," "no," "a matter of degree," and "don't know" categories. Respondents were asked to elaborate, and certain remarks were found to be frequent when these answers were coded.

The final question regarding the causes of neglect and abuse was asked of all respondents, even those who reported no experience with maltreatment of vulnerable adults. The question first required each respondent to consider these four causal hypotheses:

1. A person who relies on someone else for his care is more likely to be neglected and/or abused.
2. A child who is abused or witnesses abuse grows up to be an abusive adult.
3. Life crises in either the abused or abuser trigger abusive behavior.
4. Environmental factors (such as crowded living quarters or physical isolation) play a major part in bringing about neglectful and abusive behavior.

Then each respondent was asked to select the "most important" of the four hypotheses.

Of the different categories of respondents, only among police officers was a clear majority convinced that the causes of neglect or abuse were essentially the same. Nurses, home health aides, adult services workers, lawyers, and clergy tended to consider the causes of neglect to be different from the causes of abuse. Physicians, caseworkers, mental health workers, and morticians were about equally divided on the question.

When elaborating on their answer to the question of the causes of neglect or abuse being similar or different, the most frequently coded remark dealt with the distinction between intentional and unintentional behaviors toward an older person that resulted in neglect or abuse. Abuse was generally the result of an intentional set of behaviors. Neglect, on the other hand, was considered to be unintentional. Several respondents offered their own theories about the causes of maltreatment, frequently suggesting that unintentional neglect was the consequence of a family not having sufficient time or energy to provide adequately for a dependent adult. Other respondents who considered both neglect and abuse a result of intentional actions considered the problem to be based on the caretaker's ambivalence or resentment regarding the responsibilities of caring for a dependent person, mixed with frustration, being overwhelmed by demands of the dependent, and exhaustion or emotional stress.

The respondents identified with the causal theories in a way that at least partially reflected their training and experience. It was observed that most practitioners do not see clients or patients in a comprehensive way, but tend to address their emotional, physical, or legal problems separately. Physicians, caseworkers, and adult service workers noted that maltreatment of an aged person could be the continuation of long-standing abusiveness among family members that had little to do with the increased vulnerability of an aging person within the family. The victims themselves were considered to be at least partially responsible for their own maltreatment by more than 20% of the respondents. The victims' difficult personalities, level of dependency, or personal habits were considered as a frequent cause of neglect or abuse.

One contributing cause of maltreatment was substance abuse of the victim, perpetrator, or both. Almost without exception this referred to alcohol abuse. Of all specific categories of response to the question of causes of neglect or abuse these factors were mentioned in more than one-third of the interviews in which the respondent answered the question. Of those responses, alcohol abuse of the perpetrator was indicated twice as often as that of the victim. Half of the respondents who mentioned physical abuse also indicated that alcohol abuse was likely to have been involved, a factor mentioned by all other investigators.

From the Michigan study, the most common causes of neglect and abuse appear to include the consequences of adult caretakers becoming overtaxed by the requirements of caring for a frail dependent adult. Physical, economic, or emotional limitations can prohibit adequate recognition of the needs of an older person and prevent the caretaker from being responsive to those needs. The burden for caring, without occasional relief, can lead to despair, anger, resentment, or violence among some caretakers. A family that is already at the brink of crisis for any reason will only be more quickly thrown into a disastrous chain of events when a frail and dependent parent imposes unexpected problems and demands on the family's physical, emotional, and financial resources. Some cases of neglect or abuse are clearly malicious and intentional. Some cases involve caretakers with unresolved emotional or psychiatric problems. Also, victims have been known to provoke abuse or neglect through unacceptable, hostile, or confused behavior.

It is not now possible to determine the extent to which experience, training, professional orientation, or the context in which the respondents dealt with people most dominantly influenced their perceptions of cause. Some respondents were in the homes of abused elderly, and some only saw victims in a hospital or in an office. Some only had first-hand experience with the caretaker/abuser. The context in which people conduct their professional interaction with the elderly is associated with their assessment of neglect and abuse of the elderly. Service providers whom we expected to have the most experience with maltreatment of the elderly often did not. This finding was also highlighted in the O'Malley et al (1979) study in Massachusetts where the authors stated:

> The data . . . are interesting in their negative findings. Surveyed groups which produced the lowest citings of abuse were emergency room nursing supervisors, police and welfare protective service managers at the regional level; yet one might expect each of these professions to know of cases of elder abuse in their role as mediators of family violence. This survey can only raise the obvious question of why these key professionals cite so few instances of elder abuse.

Except for the finding regarding police, the Michigan data agree with the observations from Massachusetts. We occasionally found situations in which cases were referred to specific community resources, yet these resource personnel never recognized the referrals as abuse or neglect. If the same Michigan respondents had been better informed and sensitized to domestic maltreatment of the elderly, their interpretations of existing caseloads might be different than these initial field findings.

The importance of the respondents' niche in the community services system cannot be overemphasized as we consider the practical meaning of our research observations. Some illustrations demonstrate how respondents became aware of maltreatment of the elderly and how their views of cause differed.

A police officer with 12 years of experience in the same Detroit precinct responded that he usually became aware of cases of domestic violence or abusiveness in response to a call for help in a domestic crisis. The officer related that other members of the household were frequently known as delinquents or "troublemakers." This officer, like most of the other police department respondents, considered domestic violence to be cyclic, and child abuse, spouse abuse, and abusive treatment of the elderly were considered to be closely interrelated. Police officers in our study were familiar with family units in states of crisis with multiple problems including serious levels of mistreatment.

One mental health counselor in our sample illustrates a different dimension. While few elderly are directly involved in Community Mental Health Services in Michigan, we found that the elderly dependents of adults who are undergoing mental health treatment are frequently at the center of the problem being remedied. The mental health respondent told us that several of her adult female patients were overwhelmed by the levels of dependency of their own, elderly parents, and frequently guilt-ridden about the neglectful or abusive ways in which they cared for their parents. Thus, unlike the police officers, the mental health counselors saw the problem from the perspective of the caretaker, rather than as a family crisis.

Adult day care workers provided us with another perspective. Like the mental health workers, the day care centers provide services to only one generation of a community's family units. This time we heard from providers to the victims of neglect or abuse. The adult day care workers and senior center staff would be most likely to know of poor domestic situations as told to them by the elderly. These elderly, however, were not usually severely impaired or disabled and may have been less vulnerable than those seen in emergency rooms or other crisis-oriented situations.

Finally, the emergency room medical staff saw the most severely abused or neglected elderly victims of mistreatment. These respondents, however, seldom viewed the medical consequences of neglect or abuse within the family context and only hesitantly recognized that the victims themselves were not responsible for their injuries. The importance of recognizing that different components of a comprehensive service delivery system view the causes of neglect and abuse differently cannot be overstated (Hickey and Douglass, 1981b). Unless some degree of consistency in perspective is attained it is unlikely that uniform or complementary interventions can be developed. At worst, emerging components within the system will be in direct conflict with each others' goals and methods. Unless a more rational approach is adopted, as in the tale of the blind men and the elephant, various community health and human services systems will see the problem of neglect and abuse of the elderly at different levels of severity, within various family contexts, and usually isolated from the insights of other practitioners and professionals. How can our emerging response systems be organized so that integrated approaches are adopted?

The Development of a Response System

The whole is not necessarily greater than the sum of the parts when we consider a complex and developing system of human service delivery components. When each component views its own goals and objectives in a vacuum, independent of other components, the whole might even be less than the sum, since units which are in conflict with each others' purposes can reduce their combined effectiveness. There are scores of self-defeating systems in health and human services which demonstrate this. Thus we need to consider these new systems and use whatever knowledge we have available to ensure that the resulting systems are more effective than the simple sum of their parts. The information we have about how different types of providers and professionals view causes of domestic neglect and abuse of the elderly should put us on notice that without active coordination and cross-interpretation of theory and practice, emerging prevention or intervention system components are likely to be at cross-purposes with one another. With informed foresight, however, this situation can be avoided.

We are proposing some structure for a system of preventive and intervention services according to the basic principles of systems analysis, and relate how the ways in which providers interact with patients and clients can affect performance of components as part of a larger system. While each separate group might interact with abusive caretakers and/or victims, the absence of coordination and communication will impair the success of their combined efforts.

A system will emerge accidentally or by design, and its eventual impact will depend upon how well the system's components articulate with each other. Like all systems, the one being considered here has total system objectives; component objectives; the fixed constraints of the social environment (including economic and political factors); resources; component service units; and some form of system management or supervision.

In the present case the objectives of the system to deal with domestic neglect and abuse of the elderly cannot be fully developed, at least in a public health context. For example, the incidence and prevalence of domestic maltreatment of the elderly are unknown and can not be used as measures of system success or failure. Similarly, case-finding techniques are usually undeveloped and untested, which leads us to recognize that the initial objectives of this emerging system will have to be appropriate for initial system development, rather than for routine program performance. Thus the system's objectives will be to measure incidence and prevalence of neglect and abuse of the elderly; to initiate and test alternative means of case-finding; to develop and test alternative kinds of intervention and reporting procedures; and to identify appropriate kinds of case prevention services. These objectives will necessarily apply to different subsets of service delivery components. The implication is, however, that some form of centralized oversight is required to carry out the critical evaluation functions inherent in each of these objectives. A final developmental objective might be to define appropriate routine objectives for the system and each participating component, an objective that cannot be realized until the preliminary objectives are met and each component is communicating sufficiently with each other one.

The system's environment is crucial, and it is the area of least control by components or management. This decade is undoubtedly the worst time in the last 25 years to place a demanding social problem before the American Public. Current uncertainties regarding the national economy and widespread calls for fewer governmental services because of economic limitations need no further discussion here. Public demand for less governmental involvement in family life suggests a political obstacle to overcome before our system can become operative.

Countering these negative environmental forces are a social awakening to the needs and demands of older Americans and a recognition of the political clout of the nation's elderly. It is not possible to estimate the degree that these positive forces will counterbalance the negative ones.

At the community level it is not easy to predict the receptivity of existing social or economic forces for dealing with neglect and abuse of the elderly. There is some evidence that the problem is so distressing that community leaders will attempt to avoid public acknowledgment of it. On the other hand, in Michigan and elsewhere several grass roots programs have been started which are energetic, organized, and operating with considerable public support and political encouragement.* Possibly the most important environmental factor is public response to awareness of the plight of neglected or abused elderly. Public concern can facilitate the availability of both economic and political resources or such essential supports can be denied.

The system can take advantage of and modify or control certain factors. In the present case the resources are those individuals motivated to initiate programming; existing service delivery units which can be modified or redirected to become components in a system to deal with neglect or abuse of the elderly; and the capacity of these existing service delivery units to expand their own activities to accommodate new tasks. Another resource is its capacity to generate totally new service delivery units to fill roles that cannot be filled by existing units.

The components of the developing system will, at least initially, be the existing relevant service delivery units whose objectives and missions have been coopted to allow them to participate in new tasks and functions. Figure 7-1 is a rudimentary structure that lists many of these existing service delivery units. Once these units become organized around common goals and objectives they become components. A set of components participates in case-finding and referral to protective services in which the public unit receives duplicate referral documentation about cases being handled in the private protective services system (Figure 7-1). Victim-specific services range from restrictive to nonrestrictive and can

---

*One example of a grass roots program is in Inkster, Michigan where an RSVP program organized the city's police, mental health, aging, hospital and public health services and created the Inkster Task Force Concerned with Senior Citizen Abuse in 1979. This program is now developing case-finding and referral activities for the local population.

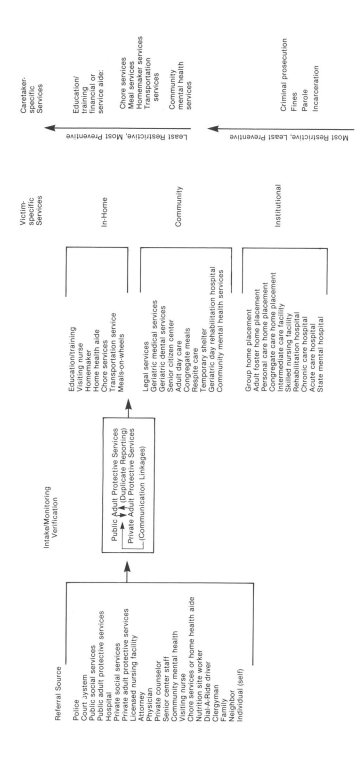

Figure 7-1 Systems of referral, intake, and service provision: neglect and abuse of the elderly.

132

be used on the probability of being preventive or curative to determine the kinds of activities included. Similarly, services for perpetrators and caretakers will range from education and training (preventive) to criminal punishment.

The system's management will be the most important single component during the developmental period. System management will facilitate activities, initiate coordination and communication, negotiate conflicts between units, and evaluate unit performance. Management will also take principal responsibility for implementing activity and component-objective modifications by ongoing evaluation. The system's developmental period will eventually culminate in a case-finding-referral-service delivery-feedback flow which will be the hallmark of a routine system. At this stage, management must determine a new set of objectives that will apply to all components of the system and participate in individual objective definitions for each separate component.

In conclusion, we can expect that service delivery planning, to deal with domestic neglect and abuse of the elderly, can lead to coordinated and effective systems rather than conflicting and ineffective separate service delivery activities. The different perspectives on domestic violence and maltreatment of the elderly, which we know exist among different kinds of practitioners and professionals, can be either an asset in a coordinated system of service delivery or a debilitating liability. It is conceivable that each service provider can learn to appreciate and be sensitive to alternative views regarding case-finding, cause, and case management, but it would be naive to assume that such enlightened cooperation and communication will happen without effort. A coordinated system, therefore, with active oversight; centralized client referral, intake, casework and disposition; component performance evaluation; and good communication linkages will lead to more satisfactory development of social responses to neglect and abuse of the elderly than accidental and haphazard program development. The lack of long-established programs in this field and the scarcity of objective information can be turned to the advantage of emerging systems because traditional ways of responding and established practice stereotypes will not need to be challenged. This perspective represents a considerable challenge for the 1980s.

BIBLIOGRAPHY

Block MR, Sinnott JD: *The Battered Elder Syndrome: An Exploratory Study.* Final Report to the United States Administration on Aging. The University of Maryland, Center on Aging, November, 1979
Douglass RL, Hickey T, Noël C: *A Study of Maltreatment of the Elderly and*

Other Vulnerable Adults. Final Report to the United States Administration on Aging and the Michigan Department of Social Services. The Institute of Gerontology, The University of Michigan, 1980.

Hickey T, Douglass RL: Neglect and abuse of older family members: Professionals' perspectives and case experience. *Gerontologist* 1981a;21:171–176, April.

Hickey T, Douglass RL: Mistreatment of the Elderly in the Domestic Setting. *Am J Pub Health* 1981b;71:500–507.

Lau EA, Kosberg JI: Abuse of the elderly by informal care providers. Paper presented at the 31st Annual Meeting of the Gerontological Society, Dallas, TX, November, 1978.

O'Malley H, Segars H, Perez R, et al: *Elder Abuse in Massachusetts.* Legal Research and Services for the Elderly. Boston, MA, 1979.

Rathbone-McCuan E: Intergenerational Family Violence and Neglect: The Aged as Victims of Reactivated and Reverse Neglect. International Conference of Gerontology, Japan, November 1978.

Rathbone-McCuan E: Elderly victims of family violence and neglect. *Social Casework* May, 1980.

Steinmetz SK: Battered Parents. *Society* 1978;15(15).

Webb B: *The Breakup of the Poor Law,* Minority Report, Commission on Relief for the Poor. London, England, 1909.

SUGGESTED READINGS

Briley M: Battered Patients. *Dynamic Years* 1979;January–February.

Churchman CW: *The Systems Approach.* New York, Delta Publishing, 1968.

Douglass RL: *The Etiology of Neglect and Abuse of Older Persons.* Proceedings, Tennessee Conference on the Abuse of Older Persons. The University of Tennessee, Knoxville, December, 1980.

Douglass RL: A Systems Perspective for Service Delivery Planning for Domestic Neglect and Abuse of the Elderly. Region X ADAMHA-Administration on Aging Joint Workshop. Portland, OR, January, 1981.

Douglass RL: Domestic Neglect and Abuse of the Elderly: Current Status of Psycho-Social Research. National Conference on Abuse of Older Persons, Harvard University, Cambridge, MA, March, 1981.

Douglass RL, Ruby-Douglass PA: Emergency medical response to domestic abuse and neglect of the elderly, in Braen GR (ed): *Management of the Physically and Emotionally Abused.* San Diego, CA, Appleton-Century-Crofts, Capistrano Press, Inc, in press.

Kosberg JI: Family maltreatment: Explanation and intervention. Paper presented at the 33rd Meeting of the Gerontological Society, San Diego, CA, November, 1980.

O'Malley H: *Elder Abuse: A Review of the Literature.* Legal Research and Services for the Elderly. Boston, MA, 1979.

Select Committee on Aging, United States House of Representatives, Ninety-Sixth Congress. *Elder Abuse: The Hidden Problem.* Committee Publication 96-220. Washington, DC, Government Printing Office, 1980.

Select Committee on Aging, United States House of Representatives, Ninety-Sixth Congress. *Domestic Abuse of the Elderly,* Committee Publication 96-259. Washington, DC, Government Printing Office, 1980.

Steinmetz SK, *The Cycle of Violence.* New York, Praeger, 1977.

8 Dependency, Stress, and Violence Between Middle-Aged Caregivers and Their Elderly Parents

Suzanne K. Steinmetz

THE GRAYING OF AMERICA

The increasing number of vulnerable elderly is one of the most distinctive characteristics of this decade. The most critical factors are the increase in the very oldest group, the increase in the dependency ratio, the loss of status, prestige, and power that often accompanies retirement, and physical and mental health deterioration experienced by many of our oldest citizens.

By the end of the century one of every five persons will be 65 years or older but the greatest change will be the dramatic increase in the number of our oldest citizens. Between 1960 and 1970 the number of individuals 75 years and older increased at a rate 3 times that of those in the 65 to 70 age group. Between 1970 and 1976 the population of 40 to 64 year olds increased just under 2%, while those 85 years and older increased by 40% (United States Bureau of Census, 1977).

This graying of America occurs because there are more older people

134

and an increase in the median age of the population to 35.5 years (Brotman, 1981). In addition to the change in the age structure, the dependency ratio (the number of young or old dependent on the middle group) has also increased. Brotman (1981) notes that for every 100 persons in the economically productive age range of 18 to 64, the number of older persons is nearly 20. While the number of dependent children is decreasing slightly, the numbers of elderly are growing, and the increase in care, time, resources, and emotional energy needed to care for an elder as opposed to caring for a child is considerable. The greater strain of caring for an elder is a result of: (1) the actual age as well as stage in the life cycle of caregivers (ie, the young are more likely to have a healthy spouse to help with care); (2) few role models and experiences available for caregivers; (3) fewer resources for caregivers; and, (4) the increasing dependency of elders as time passes.

We have, for the first time, many people living beyond their economically productive years. Economic productivity, defined in contemporary society as maintaining full-time paid employment, is the means by which people often find their identity and gain resources. Retired individuals are often forced to face living several decades on a fixed income, while suffering the loss of their identity. Thus, individuals who retire lose the status, power, and prestige that go with being an economically productive member of society.

The physical health of the type of individual who survives past 70 is likely to be different than in an earlier time. With the advent of antibiotics and other major medical advances we have many people living to old age in a deteriorating physical condition. In the past, survival of the fittest was a reality; today survival can be based on medicine or being attached to a sophisticated machine. Since life expectancy is computed by averaging the life span, or total years lived of all individuals born in a certain year, an era characterized by high rates of infant mortality would experience a lower average life expectancy. Today we have greatly decreased infant mortality and the ravages from early childhood diseases, as well as reduced loss of life through childbirth. While we have increased life expectancy, we have done little to lengthen the actual life span of individuals.

In earlier times those individuals who survived infancy and childhood to live into their sixth or seventh decade tended to be stronger and healthier. However, survival was still precarious because the diseases that were likely to affect the elderly (eg diabetes, arthritis, heart attacks, and strokes) were without effective treatment until recently. Today many survive illnesses, but are left with varying degrees of physical disability and a chronic illness.

While extending life expectancy has been a focus of biomedical research, the issue of quality of life has been minimally dealt with. The problems created by increased longevity encompass the whole family life cycle. Middle-aged children often are unable to cope with problems arising within their own nuclear families (Silverstone and Hyman, 1976; Kirschner, 1979).

As a result of these trends, we find an increasing number of three- and four-generation families in which the elder is physically, emotionally, socially, and financially dependent on younger kin for a prolonged period of time. The multigenerational family of a generation or two ago was likely to exist for a very brief period of time, while a newly married couple was building their home or when an elderly relative moved in to die. Now we have a large number of dependent elderly people relying on their kin for prolonged physical, emotional, and financial aid. Families must face this emerging family form without role models for dealing with the problems.

GENERATIONAL INVERSION

Problems Experienced by
Generationally Inversed Families

There is a lack of terminology for dealing with this new problem. The term role reversal is not sufficient because it implies a temporary reversal of roles, not a permanent change in which responsibilities, status, control, and dependency for survival as well as roles are reversed. We have found the term *generational inversion* to be most appropriate for describing these families in which the roles of being the parent and child are simply inverted (Steinmetz, 1980, 1981; Foulke, 1980). In these families it is not only role reversal but generationally linked rights, responsibilities, and expectations that are reversed.

In addition there is the inverted pyramid of elderly in which one or two brothers or sisters must bear the responsibility for four or five family members over 75 years of age who are no longer able to live independently. Generationally inversed families (those families in which the elderly parent is dependent on the children for emotional, financial, physical or mental support) are no longer unique. The existence of multiple generations with generationally inverse families is a rapidly growing phenomenon. With the rising divorce rate, which produces multiple sets of in-laws and extended kin, it is conceivable that this number will grow. Who will take care of the caretakers when the caretakers need taking care of? Whose responsibility is this?

When the children are responsible for two or more older kin, pressures and strains, varying with the degree of dependency of the elderly person, can be severe. This problem is intensified because the caretaker is frequently elderly himself. The caretaker assumes this new role while having to prepare for his own retirement, often facing increasing health problems.

Generationally inversed families must also face the emotional stress brought about when the adult child assumes the role of caregiver. The change in the role of the child from being cared for to that of caretaker may build feelings of resentment and misapprehension in both generations (Hooker, 1976; Knopf, 1975; Silverstone and Hyman, 1976). Feelings of love and respect easily can turn into guilt, hatred, and disappointment as children attempt to function in their new roles of caregiver (Cohen and Gans, 1978; Knopf, 1975).

Unresolved conflict between parents and adolescent age children often continues throughout the life cycle (Boszormenyi-Nagy and Spark, 1973; Brody, 1966), with the result that contact may remain at the level of obligatory vacation or holiday visits during the child's adulthood. In such unresolved conflicts it is unlikely that a child will shoulder the responsibility of caring for an elderly parent with open arms and a warm heart. Thus the motivation to care for the older kin may not only be out of love and concern, but also out of a sense of responsibility, duty, or guilt.

Another source of stress is the parents' inability to understand that their children are adults. A preliminary analysis of our study on elder abuse revealed that 56% of the caregivers reported that they were bothered by the elder's lack of respect for their privacy.

In some families an elderly parent is unable to relinquish power. One woman in her late 60s was unable to leave her home to be interviewed because her father, in his 90s, felt that it was his daughter's place to remain at home and answer his demands. When she would leave, he would violently attack any caretaker left with him and would turn the room into a shambles. Another respondent, also in her sixties, had to deal with an elderly mother who treated her as if she were a teenager whenever she expressed an opinion or disagreed with her. The respondent stated that her mother believed that "parents are right and always are up until the hour of death, you don't talk back. One day she told me I was talking back to her. Here I am a grandmother talking back!"

Stress and Dependency

While chronologic age is used as a major descriptive variable of adult behavior, dependency may defy chronologic categorization. Just as all toddlers do not start to walk at the same age, all 65-year-olds are not developmentally similar. One 65-year-old man may consider himself to be in his declining years, suffering from bad health, and counting the days toward retirement, while his 65-year-old neighbor may be embarking on a new career, learning to play tennis, and viewing himself as a vibrant middle-aged man. Even self-categorization is misleading. Eisendorf and Lawton (1973) found that only those over 80 years of age classified themselves as "old," and about one-half of this age group claimed they were "middle-aged."

There are a number of stresses related to dependency in generationally inversed families: economic, physical, social and emotional, and those related to mobility. As these dependency needs of the elderly increase, the stress on the caregiving family can result in abuse and neglect unless adequate resources are available (Blenkner, 1965; 1969; Steinmetz, 1980).

Another form of dependency, physical, becomes a problem (Knopf, 1975). Not only is the caregiver required to expend energy and bear the often uncompensated cost of medical needs; these services are provided with the knowledge that inadequate care could produce a life-threatening situation for an elderly parent. Physical deterioration (loss of hearing, failing vision, or decreased strength, and severe or chronic illness) place additional burdens on the caretaking family. Medical costs frequently are not compensated or at best may be undercompensated by public and private health insurance. Medical costs, therefore, compete with other expenses incurred by the caretaking family such as children's education, weddings, or providing for retirement.

In one study, families reported that psychological and emotional dependencies were the most stressful (Foulke, 1980). Foulke noted that physical dependency, even when it required increased health care responsibilities, was easier for caregivers to deal with and produced less stress than did the social and emotional dependency. Most often it was the decision-making associated with emotional dependency and increased amount of personal time required to care for a dependent elderly, which was considered stressful.

How a decision is made to have the elder move in with an adult child influences the likelihood for abuse. Burston, (1978) has suggested that a hastily made decision to have an aging parent live with an adult child may create conditions for eventual abuse. Because the decision is reached at a time when family emotions are strained, family members may feel they are forced into taking the aging parent (Douglass, Hickey, and Noël, 1980). Power conflicts (Renvoize, 1978); increased disability (Lau and Kosberg, 1979); dependencies of the older person; and the existence of a high level of family stress (Blenkner, 1965; 1969; Steinmetz, 1978; 1980) produce the potential for violence.

Abuse and Neglect of the Elderly

Although a great deal of research has been done concerning domestic violence, violence against the elderly by their adult children has been virtually ignored until recently. Research has shown that the most frequent abusers of women and children are family members; thus it is not surprising that family members predominate as abusers of the elderly. In one study 13% of service providers who responded to a mail survey reported that they knew of a case of elder abuse. However, 88% who responded were aware of the problem even if they had no cases to report (Block and Sinnott, 1979). Douglass, Hickey and Noël (1980) found that 17% of their respondents in a similar survey of professionals reported physical abuse of an elder, and 44% reported verbal or emotional abuse. In one of the first studies of elder abuse, a mail survey of over 1000 medical personnel, social service professionals, and paraprofessionals, 183 reports of elder abuse were received (O'Malley et al, 1979). Seventy percent of the reports noted that the abuse occurred twice. Furthermore, 75% of the reported victims lived with the abuser, and in over 80% of the reports, the abuser was a relative. These researchers also noted that three-fourths of the reports suggested that the abuser was experiencing some kind of stress such as alcoholism, drug addiction, medical problems, or long-term financial crisis.

During a 12-month period, the Family Service Association of Greater Lawrence (Massachusetts) received 82 referrals of elders suspected of being abused, neglected, or being in a potentially threatening situation. On investigation, one-fourth of those elders who were living with their family experienced abuse or neglect (Langdon, 1980). Baltimore police in a single year reported 149 assaults against individuals 60 years old or older. They noted that nearly two-thirds of these assaults (62.7%) were committed by a relative other than the spouse (Block and Sinnott, 1980).

In the first eight months after passage of the Connecticut Elderly Protective Service Law, 87 cases of physical abuse, 314 cases of neglect, 65 cases of exploitation, and 8 cases of abandonment were reported (Block and Sinnott, 1980). By April 1979, the total number of reported cases was 937, of which 651 concerned neglect; 166, physical abuse; 127, exploitation, 32, abandonment and 89, cases needing other kinds of assistance. Lau and Kosberg (1979) found that more than three-fourths of their cases of elderly abuse involved physical abuse and over one-half psychological. The above studies did not limit the abuse to that which occurred exclusively within the family. Furthermore, the data were reported by a third party — a social service agency, medical or legal personnel, police, or a protective service agency.

140

A STUDY OF FAMILY STRESS

The goal of this study has been to ascertain the stresses, conflicts, abuse, and maltreatment experienced in families who cared for an elderly parent. Articles describing the study and requesting volunteers were placed in state-wide newspapers, social service/professional newsletters, and monthly information packets mailed to directors of agencies providing services for the elderly. Volunteers were screened by telephone to assure that they met the criteria, and interviews were scheduled.

Although the sample was nonrepresentative, a broad range of social classes and ethnic groups was included. The nonwhite sample was increased through additional personal contact with directors of services which served predominantly elderly of minority groups. The interviews were conducted by two graduate students, a medical social worker, and an undergraduate student.

Interviews using a structured format, were conducted with 77 adult children who were presently caring for an elderly kin or had done so within the past three years. Thirteen families had provided care for two elders; a total of 103 dependent elderly were covered. In these families the elderly had to reside with and be dependent on their adult children for at least part of their basic survival needs. Therefore, cases where a mother visited for two months each winter or where mother and daughter had mutually pooled their resources to maintain a higher standard of living were not included. Interviews were taped to allow for the recording of the delivery as well as the content of the unstructured responses. Responses to the structured parts of the questionnaires were coded by the interviewers during the interview.

The caregivers were asked a series of questions designed to discover what tasks were performed by family members who cared for the elder. The reponses were categorized into six dependency categories: household management, financial, mobility, social/emotional, mental health, and personal grooming/health care. Responses were categorized into "never performed," "had performed," and "performed usually or always." In addition, respondents were asked to assess the stress they experienced as a result of the tasks under each dependency category. For example, the respondents were asked how frequently they had to provide transportation for the elder and then asked to rate, on a five-point scale, how much this bothered them. Finally, caregivers were asked to state how often they and the elder had used certain techniques to resolve problems or carry out their wishes.

Analysis of the data provided some interesting insights into the problems faced by these families.

Family Characteristics

First, the overwhelming majority of caregivers (90%) were women. Likewise, they comprised the overwhelming majority of vulnerable elderly (more than 82%), a finding consistent with other studies. Women face double jeopardy: they bear the stresses and strains of caring for an elderly woman, and they face the high probability of being in the same situation when they become older (Brody, 1979; Block and Sinnott, 1979; O'Malley et al, 1979; Steinmetz, 1980, 1981).

A second unique characteristic of this group is that the caregivers are often elderly themselves (by the standard definition of 60 or older) and yet they are caring for a still older dependent (Foulke, 1980; O'Malley et al, 1979; and Steinmetz, 1980; 1981). Although the age of caregivers ranged from 23 to 72, more than 20% were 60 years or older; about 40% were 50 years or older; and more than 60% were 55 or older.

A third, unexpected finding not considered by most other studies is the double direction of violence. While violence perpetrated on elders has been sensationalized in the media, violence by elders on their adult children has remained hidden (Steinmetz, 1980; 1981). The authoritarian father who ruled his children with an iron fist and dealt with a loss of authority or control by a beating apparently still resorted to these techniques at age 90. When the father found it to be more difficult to maintain control over children, he resorted to temper tantrums and physical outbursts. It is not difficult to understand why these elders resorted to physical violence since they had no other mechanism, such as money, prestige, mobility, or independence, with which to assert their will and gain their wishes. They had to depend on manipulations or physical control if their children were unwilling to meet their needs or their demands.

A final characteristic was that the caregivers were often caught in the middle, finding themselves caught between two or more generations. At the time that one's own family income is leveling, retirement plans were imminent, and college and wedding plans of one's children a costly expense, this middle generation often had to assume the cost of caring for elderly parents (Cohen and Gans, 1978; Silverstone and Hyman, 1976).

The value system was also strained. Where do these middle-aged caregivers put their priorities? Should priority be given to the parents who reared them or their children who may still need emotional and financial support? Caught in this dilemma the middle generations often found that there was no physical, psychological, or financial cushion for themselves. This dilemma is of major importance, because it is a dilemma that most of us will face, first as a caregiver and, later, as a dependent elder.

The effect of being caught in the middle is evident in a comment made by one of the 60-year-old respondents regarding her 84-year-old mother. She noted:

> I don't want to consider my mother a burden. I would be glad to continue to care for her if she were not unpredictable and I could. This is the selfish part—I want to do some of the things I like to do because I am not very young either.

Streib (1972) noted that studies have tended to overlook the rights and needs of adult children and blame them if they have not provided a comfortable happy arrangement for their aged parents during this crisis that may last for 10 to 15 years. In his study the average length of time for caregiving was 9.5 years. However, 30% of the families had provided care for an elder for 10 or more years; 17% provided care for 15 or more years and 10% assumed this responsibility for 20 years or more.

Provision of Care and Resulting Stress

In many of the families the elderly maintain a high degree of independence and autonomy, while in other families almost all tasks had to be performed for them. In an earlier preliminary analysis of these data, Foulke (1980) outlined four stages of dependency (Figure 8-1). The first stage is independence, a stage in which elders could live independently and perform most tasks. In reciprocal dependence, the second stage, elders do such services as baby sitting, cooking, and cleaning in exchange for heavy housekeeping, financial help, and social interaction provided by the adult child. The third stage is symmetrical dependence. Although services flow in both directions, the elder is receiving considerably more social, emotional, physical, or financial help than the adult child. The last stage, survival dependence, is arrived at when the elder is dependent on the adult for almost all his needs and services.

As Table 8-1 suggests, housekeeping tasks are the most frequently performed. When all household items were averaged, 90% of the caregivers provided this help. Only one family reported that it did not do any of the housekeeping tasks for their elderly relative. About two-thirds of the caregivers reported providing social/emotional tasks. An average of 57% of the caregivers provided help in mental health, but only six families were free from aid for any of the tasks in this category. Help with financial management and personal health care tasks were provided by caregivers in over half of the families, while 43% of the elders required help with some type of mobility. In the least frequently observed type of dependency, mobility, some type of assistance was provided by 64% of the families.

STAGE I →	STAGE II →	STAGE III →	STAGE IV →
Independence Dependence	Reciprocal Dependence	Asymmetrical Dependence	Survival Dependence
Tasks Performed by Caregiver	Tasks in Stage I plus -	Tasks in Stages I and II plus -	Tasks in Stages I, II, III plus -
grocery shopping	writing checks	understanding doctor's orders	helping make calls
transportation	paying bills	dispensing medication	protecting needs; elder cannot be left alone
running errands	managing resources	washing, setting, cutting hair	
laundry	providing social life for elder	helping with decision making	
providing emotional support to elder		assisting with walking when elder is outdoors	
		helping elder get in and out of car	
		encouraging elder to develop new interests and friends by arranging social contact	

Figure 8-1 Stages of elder's dependency with tasks required to be performed by caregiver. Adapted from Foulke, 1980.

Table 8-1
Percent of Caregivers Providing Tasks for Elderly

Categories of Dependency	Have Performed	Usually or Always Performed	Mean Frequency[a]
	%	%	$\overline{x}$
Household			
Light housekeeping	82	56	2.5
Heavy housekeeping	85	72	3.0
Laundry	88	73	3.1
Grocery shopping	95	79	3.4
Cooking	94	72	3.0
Transportation	90	76	3.2
Run errands	94	72	3.2
Emotional/Social			
Provide emotional support	94	72	3.1
Provide social life	85	65	2.8
Take relative visiting	79	49	2.4
Writing letters	45	25	1.3
Make phone calls	70	36	2.0
Reading to	32	11	0.7
Encourage/Help develop friendships	70	44	2.0
Mental Health			
Needs help with decision making	80	53	2.3
Forgetful	85	28	2.1
Gets lost	24	10	0.6
Non-rational behavior	40	12	0.9
Explosive behavior	57	10	1.1
Must be watched	54	34	1.6
Financial Dependency			
Writing checks/Pay bills	68	55	2.4
Provide financial support	29	29	1.2
Help manage resources	63	54	2.5
Pay for essentials	60	37	1.8
Pay for luxuries	53	29	1.5
Personal and Health Care			
Bathing	42	25	1.2
Dressing	51	23	1.2
Hair Care	55	37	1.8
Following doctor's orders	70	75	2.3
Giving medication	60	44	1.9
Change bedding/diaper	43	25	1.2
Mobility			
Stairs	44	28	1.3
Help in/out chair	36	12	0.8
Help in/out bed	29	17	0.8
Help with walking	64	22	1.3

[a]Answers ranged from 0 = never done to 4 = done all the time.

For those families that reported providing considerable help, the responses of "usually" or "always" followed a similar trend with household and emotional/social categories being carried out by the highest percentage of families and personal/health care and mobility categories being provided by the lowest percentage of families. However, the number of families which had to perform these tasks does not provide insight into how much stress these tasks provide (Table 8-2). For example, although all but one family reported that they provide household tasks for the elderly, only about half reported ever feeling stressed from these tasks and only about one-fifth experienced considerable stress (the combined categories of "usually" or "always"). On the other hand, mental health dependencies, performed less frequently, apparently produced the greatest stress. One category, social/emotional dependencies, not only was a frequently performed task (the second highest) but also produced an extremely high degree of stress.

It appears that instrumental tasks (ie, doing household chores, providing transportation, grooming, and special diets) although often described as very time-consuming, apparently produced little stress. However, expressive tasks such as dealing with lonely, demanding parents, or parents who were senile or had emotional or mental problems were considerably more stressful.

Methods of Resolving Conflicts

In an attempt to gain or maintain authority, various methods were used by the elderly parent and their adult children. While 85% of the adult children reported talking out problems, many noted that this talking was often done with a raised voice, or "loud tone." Screaming also was frequently used by a sizeable number of adult children and their parents (Table 8-3). The technique most frequently used by the elder to get their way was to pout or withdraw, with 61% of the elderly using this method as a means of dealing with conflict. Other psychological methods used by elderly included manipulation (43%); especially pitting one family member against another; crying (37%); using their disabilities to gain sympathy (33%); or imposing guilt (53%). Of the elderly, 71% used some form of psychological manipulation to impose guilt or sympathy.

Adult children also used a variety of methods of problem solving. Sixty-five percent sought the advice of a third party, 20% considered alternative housing, and 7% threatened to send the elder to a nursing home. Since 16% of the elders refused food or medication, it is not surprising that 3% of the children resorted to forcing food or medication. Four percent withheld food, but it tended to be done for dietary reasons, usually keeping sweets from a diabetic parent. Medication was given for health reasons rather than a control mechanism.

Table 8-2
Levels of Stress Experienced by Caregivers
In Providing Care for an Elderly Relative

Sources of Stress	Levels of Stress		
	Some	Usually or Always	Average Score
	%	%	$\overline{x}$
Household management	58	20	1.3
Provide transportation	40	8	0.7
Grooming	53	4	0.7
Physical disability	72	19	1.5
Refusal of food	54	14	0.9
Special diet	44	8	0.6
Financial dependency	56	3	0.6
Mobile but senile	82	14	1.5
Emotional/mental dependency	84	24	2.0
Lonely	72	28	1.7
Excessive demands	58	27	1.5
Lack of privacy	61	22	1.4

Table 8-3
Percent of Adult Children and Elderly Parents
Using Various Conflict-Resolution Techniques

Methods	Child to Parent	Parent to Child
Talked	85	—
Sought advice	65	—
Considered alternative housing	20	—
Threatened nursing home	7	—
Pouted/withdrew	—	61
Confined to room	1	—
Manipulated others	—	43
Imposed guilt	—	54
Used disability to gain sympathy	—	33
Forced food	3	—
Refused food	—	16
Withheld food	4	—
Forced medication	14	—
Refused medication	—	15
Screamed and yelled	40	36
Cried	—	37
Called police	—	5
Physically restrained	8	—
Threatened physical force	5	—
Slapped, hit with object, shook	1	18

As a result of conflicting demands, abusive and neglectful methods of control often become the method of last resort. Table 8-3 reveals many negative methods of control, although many times they were used for safety reasons. Physically restraining elderly parents was used by 8% of the children, threat of physical force by 5%; and hitting, slapping, and shaking by 1%. About 10% of the elderly had experienced one or more acts of violence or a threat by their adult child. The data in Table 8-3 also indicate that the violence is engaged in by both groups since 18% of the elders slapped, hit with an object, or threw something at their adult child.

CONCLUSION

An earlier article noted that our knowledge about the battered elderly parent mirrors our knowledge of the extent of child abuse in the early 1960s or the extent of our knowledge about wife abuse in the early 1970s (Steinmetz, 1978). If we were to label the 1960s as the decade of interest in child abuse and the 1970s as the decade of wife abuse studies, then one could predict that the 1980s will surely be the decade of concern about the battered parent.

There must be clarification regarding the types of families who are abusive or potentially abusive. Unlike the picture often painted by the media, it is not a selfish uncaring 35-year-old daughter who is deliberately neglecting or maltreating her 65-year-old mother. It is more likely to be a woman in her late 50s or early 60s (by census definition an elder herself) who is not only responsible for the older parent (who may be in the eighth decade), but also very likely to have some responsibility toward her own children and perhaps doing baby sitting for grandchildren and great-grandchildren so that a son or daughter is free to work.

Thus, while we are continually confronted with the message that it is a family responsibility to care for the elderly, we need to recognize that the family in some cases may consist of just one older woman, perhaps herself in need of services. Another factor is that we are a society who values independence. To be dependent on someone is an indication of failure. It is with reluctance that an older person must resign himself to being dependent on someone for whom a few decades ago he felt responsible. Unresolved parent/child conflicts of an earlier period are likely to become a serious focal point when the generations are brought closely together under the same roof. If the 20-year-old child and mother did not get along, and the 40-year-old child and mother still did not get along, why should we assume that the 60-year-old child and her 80-year-old mother would get along? If mother nagged, and was always critical and difficult to deal with at age 40, there is no reason to assume that her behavior will become totally different at age 80. Likewise, the father who ruled his children with an iron fist will not become a sweet, loving malleable man at age 90. Value systems, life-styles, child rearing and marital interaction are different among generations.

Service providers need to be aware of these differences and the effect they have on family dynamics. They need to help the elderly accept these new dependent roles and help adult children learn to "parent" their elderly parent. Service providers also need to become more sensitive to the types of services most likely to reduce stress, conflict, and abuse. Although household dependencies are the most commonly performed services, they do not seem to be the most stressful as measured by self-reported responses of stress. Services such as health and housekeeping aids, chore services, and meals on wheels provide a valuable help to the elderly and their families. However, the data suggest that the services most likely to reduce stress, and to relieve some of the burden faced by generationally inversed families, would be those designed to help with social/emotional and mental health dependency such as friendly visitors, day care, and respite care for elderly, elder "sitters," and support groups for adult children who are assuming the care for an elderly parent.

I wish to acknowledge the assistance of Deborah Amsden with the computer analysis and for her comments which were helpful in writing this paper. I also wish to thank Marge Murvine for her patience in editing and retyping countless revisions.

BIBLIOGRAPHY

Blenkner M: Social work and family relationships in later life with some thoughts on filial maturity, in Shanas E, Streib G (eds): *Social Structure and the Family*. Englewood Cliffs, NJ, Prentice-Hall, 1965.

Blenkner M: The normal dependencies of aging, in Kalish R (ed): *The Dependencies of Old People*. Ann Arbor, University of Michigan Institute of Gerontology, 1969.

Block M, Sinnott JP (eds): *The Battered Elder Syndrome: An Exploratory Study*. College Park, MD, Center on Aging, University of Maryland, 1979.

Block M, Sinnott JP: *Prepared Statement: Elder Abuse: The Hidden Problem*. Briefing by the Select Committee on Aging U.S. House of Representatives. (96) June 23, 1979. Boston, MA, pp. 10–12. Washington, DC, 1980.

Boszormenyi-Nagy I, Spark GM: *Invisible Loyalties. Reciprocity in Intergenerational Family Therapy*. Hagerstown, MD, Harper & Row, 1973.

Brody EM: The aging family. *Gerontologist* 1966;6:201–206.

Brody E: Women's changing roles, the aging family and long-term care of older people. *National Journal* 1979;11:1828–1833.

Brotman HB: The aging society: A demographic view. *Aging* 1981;315–316 (January–February):2–5.

Burston GR: Do your elderly parents live in fear of being battered? *Modern Geriatrics* Nov. 16, 1978.

Cohen SA, Gans, BM: *The Other Generation Gap: The Middle-Aged and Their Aging Parents.* Chicago, Follett Publishing Co., 1978.

Douglass RL, Hickey T, Noël C: *A Study of Maltreatment of the Elderly and Other Vulnerable Adults.* Final report to United States Administration on Aging and the Michigan Department of Social Services, Ann Arbor, November, 1980.

Foulke SR: *Caring For the Parental Generation: An Analysis of Family Resources and Support.* Unpublished masters thesis, University of Delaware, Newark, Del. May, 1980.

Hooker S: *Caring for Elderly People; Understanding and Practical Help.* London, Routledge and Kegan Paul, 1976.

Kirschner C: The aging family in crisis: A problem in living. *Social Casework* 1979;60:209–216.

Knopf O: *Successful Aging, the Facts and Fallacies of Growing Old.* New York, Viking, 1975.

Langdon B: Statement presented at the House of Representatives Select Committee on Aging (96) June 23, 1979. Boston, MA. pp 16–21. Washington, DC, 1980.

Lau E, Kosberg J: Abuse of the elderly by informal care providers. *Aging* September–October, 1979, pp 10–15.

O'Malley H, Bergman J, Segars H, et al: *Elder Abuse in Massachusetts: A Survey of Professionals and Paraprofessionals.* Legal Research and Services for the Elderly, Boston MA, 1979.

Renvoize J: *Web of Violence: A Study of Family Violence.* London, Routledge and Kegan Paul, 1978.

Silverstone B, Hyman HK: *You and your Aging Parent.* New York, Pantheon, 1976.

Steinmetz SK: The politics of aging, battered parents. *Society* (July/August): 54–55. 1978.

Steinmetz SK: *Prepared Statement: Elder Abuse: The Hidden Problem.* Briefing by the Select Committee on Aging. United States House of Representatives. (96) June 23, 1979. Boston, MA. Washington, DC, 1980, pp 7–10.

Steinmetz SK: Elder abuse. *Aging* 1981;315–316 (January/February):6–10.

United States Bureau of Census. *Current Population Reports.* 25, No. 643, Tables 2 and 5. 1977.

9

Victimization by Health Professionals and the Psychologic Response of the Elderly

Kenneth Solomon

Older people suffer more psychopathologic morbidity than any other age group. It has been estimated that 30% to 68% of the population over age 65 will have an episode of depression severe enough to inhibit functioning (Ban, 1978). The death rate from suicide is highest for white men age 75 and over, and also is extremely high for white men age 65 to 75 and for older white women (Weiss, 1974). Approximately 5% of the elderly are institutionalized (Redick, Kramer, and Taube, 1973); many of these individuals suffer from an irreversible dementia, especially Alzheimer's disease. Another large number of older people with milder forms of neurologic failure reside in the community, frequently suffering from secondary behavioral or affective disorders (Kay, 1977). This suffering then extends to anxious, stressed caretakers. In addition, the many stresses and losses that the elderly suffer lead to a wide variety of biologic, cognitive, affective, and behavioral problems, and a diminished ability to perform activities of daily living.

The community mental health center has been an integral part of psychiatric services for over 30 years. It has been the focus of major federal legislation. With deinstitutionalization, there is now impetus for the development of mental health services on a state and local level. Comprehensive services to individuals of all ages targeted as "psychiatrically underserved" have been mandated, and the elderly are defined as one of those groups. However, despite their high incidence of psychopathology, older people have not been served by the community mental health system. Less than 2% of all clients of community mental health centers are over the age of 65 (Eisdorfer, 1977). In addition, the bulk of mental health services delivered to the elderly are to those 5% who are institutionalized, not the 95% living in the community (Brown, 1975). Private psychiatric and other mental health practitioners see even fewer elderly.

The multipurpose senior citizen center is another site that generally provides a wide range of services to the elderly. The elderly attending these centers vary in levels of activities of daily living (ADL) functioning from completely independent ADL functioning to marginal ADL functioning with the aid of multiple community supports. These elderly may have both physical and psychiatric disorders that often become manifest during their participation in center activities. These symptoms may include the entire gamut of psychopathology in the elderly, from major psychiatric syndromes to anxieties associated with problems of daily living. But few senior center staff have experience with the identification and treatment of these problems (Solomon, 1980, 1981d), and virtually none have ready access to geriatric mental health services.

Physicians, especially primary care physicians and family practitioners, frequently see elderly patients in hospital, office, and clinic settings. These elderly frequently have physical complaints that mask an underlying psychiatric problem or they demonstrate a psychologic response to a physical disease. Since some family practitioners estimate that over half their practice deals with psychology to some extent, it is not surprising that many elderly with psychiatric problems are seen at the primary care level, treated by practitioners ill-trained to provide appropriate services. Analogous situations exist for other health professionals, including nurses, social workers, physical therapists, dentists, podiatrists, and attorneys.

Despite the amount of professional contact with older clients, many elderly are not receiving adequate services in general and few are receiving adequate mental health services. This is partly because these professionals rarely have had specific training or experience in identifying or assessing behavioral or emotional problems of the elderly (Levenson and Felkins, 1979); and they do not have the skills to assess the many causes of these problems. In particular, they are frequently unable to identify the results of victimization and abuse of the elderly, and they cannot identify factors in an elderly person's biopsychosocial system that increases his/her risk of victimization or abuse. Even if victimization and abuse is identified, the health worker often lacks the skills and resources for effective intervention.

In this chapter, victimization of the elderly will include an expanded definition of "abuse" offered by Block and Sinnott (1979). According to their study, "elder abuse refers to one or more of the following acts: physical abuse . . . , psychological abuse . . . , material abuse . . . , and violation of rights." Medical abuse will be added to this definition.

Elder abuse has received only minimal investigation and has only now emerged as an important issue. Research in this area has identified it as a real problem. This chapter will describe several types of victimization and abuse suffered by the elderly in America. The reinforcement of victimization by the health professional will be elucidated. The psychologic mechanism for coping with abuse will be discussed, as will the effect of coping on the elderly.

VICTIMIZATION BY HEALTH WORKERS

New psychiatric symptoms in the elderly are always triggered by current stress. The stresses experienced by the older person may be acute and episodic or chronic. The events that cause acute, episodic stress are chiefly characterized by losses in the social support system, social role, health, independence, adequate income, mobility, adequate housing, and leisure activities.

In addition to these acute, episodic stressors, there are chronic stressors to be called *victimization:* economic, attitudinal, role, and physical (Solomon, in press). The health professional is most likely to be aware of the last of these four; however, all four have an impact on the mental health of the elderly, both as nonspecific stress and as specific events that have specific effects.

Economic Victimization

Economic victimization is the form of which the health profession is least likely to be aware. It includes not only illegal "rip-offs," but also sanctioned policy such as inadequate pensions, the effects of inflation, and business schemes that bilk the elderly consumer of needed funds.

Besides being a chronic stress in the older person's life, this economic victimization has specific consequences for health care of the elderly, since Medicare may be considered a part of this economic victimization. Despite Medicare, the elderly person averages $800 to $1000 per year in out-of-pocket medical expenses. There are even greater limitations on reimbursement for psychiatric services, with "Maximum Allowable Charges" and inadequate annual limits of reimbursement. For the elderly on marginal and fixed incomes, to forego medical, and especially psychiatric, care is a necessity. For the physician, inadequate reimbursement leads to cursory, inadequate care. Other health professionals may not even be reimbursed for their services and thus simply do not provide services to the elderly.

Butler (1975) and others have documented the acute care bias of the medical system that has resulted in scant attention to chronic problems of the elderly. Historically, long-term care facilities for the aged developed outside the hospital since reimbursement mechanisms did not encourage their integration (Moroney and Kurtz, 1975). Reinforcement for isolation of the aged from the mainstream of medical thinking and medical care resulted. Government policy also has served to encourage the institutionalization of the elderly and, as yet, has not developed a significant set of options for community-based care (Butler, 1975). The nursing home industry has thrived in large measure as a result of Medicare policies and regulations which have been quite loose. Patient care then becomes considerably less important in some homes than profits (Mendelson and Hapgood, 1974).

Role Victimization

Role victimization has a more direct effect on the mental health of the elderly. Rosow (1976) suggests that all social roles have two major dimensions: the clarity of role behaviors and role expectations associated with the role and the clarity of the status of that role. Institutional roles are those in which behaviors and expectations are quite clear to all actors involved. They include most religious, occupational, family, and parental roles.

The elderly are more likely to adopt informal or tenuous roles. Tenuous roles have a clearly defined status. However, associated behaviors and expectations may be extremely unclear. The expectations of the actor in that role may be unclear or even nonexistent. Examples of tenuous roles are nominative offices; other examples are deviant roles in which status is clear (although low) and behaviors and expectations vaguely, if at all defined. Within a deviant subculture, as noted by Scheff (1970) and Zusman (1966), there is an attempt to institutionalize these deviant roles as a way to limit the psychologic effects of the dissonance between status and behavior. Stereotyping and attribution are important mechanisms in this process, when it involves the elderly (Solomon, 1978, 1979a).

Informal roles are those in which behavior and expectations are clear, but associated status is nebulous. These roles have been important for the maintenance of primary group functioning. By their nature, tenuous and informal roles are a source of stress for the elderly. Not only must the elderly grieve over the loss of institutionalized roles, but because of the discrepancy between status and expectations, tenuous and informal roles also become a continuous source of psychologic dissonance and stress for the older person. As these roles exist at the whim of the primary group or society, the tenuousness of their future is quite clear to the older person; that, too, becomes a source of stress.

Thus, role victimization is the shift from institutional to tenuous and informal roles in the elderly. Should the older person be unable to find, create, or adopt tenuous or informal roles, or should these roles become unavailable to him through illness or societal deprivation, the older person may then lapse into a state of rolelessness with subsequent alienation, anomie, apathy, and psychopathologic symptomatology (Solomon, 1981a), or may become vulnerable to other forms of abuse.

Attitudinal Victimization

Attitudinal victimization is the result of the stereotyping of the elderly in society. These beliefs (Tuckman and Lorge, 1953a) are that:

1. The elderly are politically conservative and personally old-fashioned.
2. They have limited activities and interests.
3. They are poor.
4. Physical deterioration is inevitable.
5. They disengage from family and others.
6. They have all positive or all negative personality traits.
7. They are pessimistic.
8. It is the best or worst period of their lives.
9. They are insecure.
10. Senility is inevitable.
11. They are asexual.
12. They interfere in the lives of others.
13. They are dirty.

Solomon and Vickers (1979) have defined a stereotype as "the holding in common by the members of a group of a standardized mental picture representing an oversimplified and uncritical judgment of another group." That older people are stereotyped by the general population, specifically by health care providers, has been well known for 30 years. Thus, the acceptance of stereotypes of the elderly by professionals is not different from that of the general population. The data in support of the opposite idea, that professionals are less willing to accept the stereotype of old people, are limited and nonspecific. For example, Rosencranz and McNevin (1969) found that stereotyping was less characteristic of professional and economically advantaged classes; this finding was confirmed by Ivester and King (1977). Thorson and co-workers (Thorson, Whatley, and Hancock, 1974; Thorson, 1975) showed that with more years of education, more realistic expectations were held for the aging. In all of these studies, however, professionals were not specifically evaluated.

Most published data support the concept that older people are stereotyped as frequently by professionals as by other members of the population. LeShan and LeShan (1961) noted that psychotherapists are reluctant to work with patients with a limited life span and were remote from these patients. Kastenbaum (1963) further noted that old people are less likely to receive psychotherapy than younger people, because of the low status of old people and the fact that psychotherapists rely on unexamined values and stereotypes in determining who is to receive psychotherapy. This has been reiterated by Garfinkel (1975). Dye (1979) has suggested that negative attitudes of caregivers facilitate psychologic withdrawal in the elderly.

Tuckman and Lorge (1958) found that individuals who had experiences with the aged in a lecture course accepted stereotypes of old people to the same degree as students who did not have such a course. Arnhoff and Lorge (1960) evaluated 25 fellows in gerontology, all of whom had a medical degree or doctorate, and found that this group accepted the stereotypes of old people just as other groups did. They also found that this group was more likely to advise palliative therapy rather than positive growth-oriented therapy for old people.

McGuinness and Knox (1968) found that nurses tended to rank psychogeriatric nursing as either their first or last choice of career. Interestingly enough, however, the reasons for first or last choice were similar: more bedside nursing, slow convalescence, and the dependency of the patients.

Spence, Feigenbaum, Fitzergald, and Roth (1968) evaluated the acceptance of stereotypes by freshman and senior medical students and found no difference between the two groups. They also found that in hypothetical life-threatening situations, medical students were more likely to save a young person over an old person, a woman over a man, a young woman over an old man, and a white person over a black person, but a young black person over an old white person—a response to societal stereotypes and medical training that emphasizes the chronologic age of the patient. Mills (1972) found that undergraduate occupational therapy students also held a stereotype of old people which prevented them from developing an interest in working with geriatric patients.

Cyrus-Lutz and Gaitz (1972) evaluated the attitudes of psychiatrists towards old people and found that although psychiatrists were more aware of the positive aspects of the elderly, such as their humanistic values, the importance of work to them, and their wisdom and intelligence, as well as their fear of loneliness and isolation, they tended to concentrate on negative aspects, such as memory loss and physical problems as more important to their role as a physician. Younger psychiatrists were more out-going and more comfortable with patients over the age of 65.

York, Fergus, and Calsyn (1975) found negative attitudes toward the elderly in nursing staff in nursing homes, attitudes directly correlated with the length of time the nursing personnel worked at a home; the longer the nurse worked with the elderly, the more negative the attitudes were. McConnell (1977) made a similar finding.

Hickey, Rakowski, Hultsch, and Fatula (1976) found that in-service training to a variety of caregivers to the elderly did not change their attitudes. Younger practitioners, however, tended to become less cynical, to do less stereotyping, and to have less social distance from the aged. Studies of nursing students by Kayser and Minningerode (1975), Johnson and Wilhite (1976), and Robb (1979) showed that nursing students had less positive attitudes toward the elderly than toward other groups.

Romaniuk, Hoyer, and Romaniuk (1977) found negative attitudes among the staff and clients of a psychogeriatric day treatment center. These attitudes were particularly noted in the area of patronizing comments and client self-attitudes and were modified by staff training. Job satisfaction was correlated with staff attitudes toward the elderly in a study by Montgomery and Wilkinson (1978). They studied staff at health and mental health clinics and nursing homes and generally found negative attitudes toward the elderly.

Brennan and Moravec (1978) studied the attitudes toward the elderly by the staff at a Veterans Administration Hospital and found it negative. Following a series of training sessions, attitudes and knowledge improved significantly. Similar findings in a study of medical and dental students were reported by Holtzman and Beck (1978), who also reported an association between the acquisition of knowledge of the elderly and improvement in attitudes (Holtzman and Beck, 1979).

Solomon and Vickers (1979) studied the acceptance of stereotypes of old people by medical students, house staff, and psychogeriatric team staff and found that there were significant differences between the groups; in general, medical students and house staff held to the stereotypes more strongly than geriatric staff, stereotypes that older patients had limited activities and interests, were in poor physical condition, were not important to their family, had negative personality traits, were pessimistic toward the future, were insecure, and conservative, mentally and physically deteriorated, asexual beings.

Beck et al (1979) assessed the attitudes of dental students toward old people. Negative to begin with, the attitudes became increasingly negative as the student had more experience with the elderly dental patient. The authors attributed this to the students' exposure to a majority of elderly patients with poor oral hygiene, since mildly negative attitudes toward the elderly with good oral hygiene remained unchanged. In another study, Ettinger et al (1979) reported negative attitudes of dental students toward old people.

Farrar and Miller (1979) studied the attitudes of social work students, social workers, law students, and attorneys toward older people. Their data supported the hypothesis that the elderly were not preferred clients and that these professionals had negative attitudes toward the elderly. Psychiatrists, in a study by Ford and Sbordone (1980), were found to believe many stereotypes about the elderly. Their subjects felt that older patients had a poorer prognosis and that older patients were not suitable candidates for psychotherapy.

Solomon and Vickers (1980) examined the adherence to stereotypes of older people of adult protective service workers, most of whom were social workers, the rest being public health nurses. These workers had most of the common stereotypes of the elderly and viewed older people as conservative, insecure, physically and mentally deteriorated, lonely, meddlesome, and pessimistic persons. Adherence to these stereotypes changed dramatically following intensive training sessions.

Physical Victimization

Physical victimization of the elderly includes the abuse by his children and/or spouse and the effects of crime against person and property. It also includes frequent poor treatment by health care givers, including inadequate or inappropriate diagnosis, overmedication, undermedication, inappropriate medication or surgery, and inadequate care in custodial institutions.

Failure to provide appropriate food can lead quickly to malnutrition. Failure to change soiled clothing, inadequate bathing, or lack of dental care may also increase social isolation, poor nutrition, and risk of infection. Failure to administer prescribed medications or lack of appropriate medical intervention may lead to unnecessary debility, deterioration, and institutionalization. Equally common psychologic abuse is the threat of institutionalization, abandonment, or even bodily harm.

Actual physical abuse such as beatings, imprisonments, or bondage is not as common as child or spouse battery; however, the inappropriate use of drugs for sedation or chemical restraint in the elderly is much more prominent (Covert, Rodrigues, and Solomon, 1977; Block and Sinnott, 1979). Older persons are often encouraged by their doctors or families to take too many drugs, the effects of which create confusion and loss of self-esteem.

IMPACT OF VICTIMIZATION ON THE HEALTH CARE PROVIDER

In his theory of stereotyping the elderly, the author (1978, 1979a, 1980) has identified some of the attitudinal, affective (stress-linked), and cognitive components to the process of the development of stereotypes. Included are a lack of accurate objective data about the elderly, inconsistency of behavior responses by and to the person interacting with the elderly (a cause of stress), societally defined stereotypes and labels that create specific attitudes, and the realities of the sick role and power differential between patient and healer (Parsons, 1951; Wilson, 1970; Solomon, 1979b, 1982) As Solomon and Vickers (1979) hypothesized, following Cook (1962), factual knowledge of the elderly cannot be integrated by the practitioner unless the underlying attitudes and stereotypes have been modified and learning occurs in a care context that allows positive interactions with the elderly. As the data are used by the student, the educational and care context also becomes more positive, leading to less stereotyping, positive attitudes, and further learning. Frequently confronted with problems of the elderly, service providers often feel discouraged or lose interest in working with the elderly because of their lack of understanding of their clients. Then morale at service sites suffers, and the quantity and quality of service given to the well elderly are further diminished. Moreover, the lack of understanding of the complexity of normal aging, coupled with beliefs of stereotypes of old people, often leads to misdiagnosis and inappropriate or irrelevant service delivery. As the elderly do not "respond" to these interventions, the sense of futility on the part of the staff increases, leading to a further decline in morale and quality of service delivery.

It has been pointed out by Butler (1975) and Solomon and Vickers (1979) that stereotyping frequently leads to a lack of recognition of the individuality of the older person; this leads to inappropriate or inadequate service. The older person who is stereotyped as senile or as having limited growth or therapeutic potential will not receive appropriate pharmacologic, psychotherapeutic, and sociotherapeutic interventions to enhance his functioning in the community. The behavior caused by the negative attitudes of mental health workers is likely to drive older people away from the receipt of services in community agencies into a lonely suffering or institutionalization. As noted further by Solomon (1979b, 1981a, 1982), these attitudes may be an important factor in the creation of dependency, helplessness, and depression.

Another stereotype affecting referral of elderly patients to mental health workers is that held by physicians about psychiatry and the psychiatrist. As noted by Klopott (1977) and by Solomon and Nathan (1979, in press), these negative attitudes frequently block the referral of patients of any age labeled as "psychiatric." (In one case reported by Klopott (1977), this misdiagnosis was fatal.) As the attitudes of students toward psychiatry is similar to the attitudes of their teachers (Solomon and Nathan, 1979, in press), one can surmise that there is a perpetuation of these attitudes from one professional generation to another.

These stereotypes lead to victimization of the elderly in the health care setting. The most common demeaning behavior of the health worker is patronization (Romaniuk, Hoyer, and Romaniuk, 1977). This form of social or psychologic abuse casts doubts on the elder's self-confidence and own ability. Physicians also often feel and transmit a false sense of loss of any hope for improvement or relief in a case (Duff and Hollingshead, 1968). Physician abuse of the elderly is subtle—limiting the number of Medicare recipients, refusal to make house calls, or lack of evening hours.

Abuse in the hospital begins at the door of the emergency room. The arrival of an elderly debilitated and possibly demented patient may be met with scorn. Voluntary hospitals may even refuse to admit a Medicare/Medicaid patient (Shem, 1978). All too frequently, the major problems lie with discharge of patients to nursing homes without exploring home care possibilities.

The nursing home represents another area for psychologic, financial, and physical abuse of the elderly. Increasing regulation and supervision have removed a large number of the blatantly abusive environments from these homes; however, subtle abuses remain. Poorly trained caretakers can command lesser pay but have an extremely high turnover rate. Any closeness or companionship is thwarted by an ever-changing, overworked, and inexperienced nursing staff. The frustrations of the job and the debility of the patients promote infantilization, derogation, and actual physical abuse. Mixed with the power of responsibility, it is easy to see how authoritarianism can evolve. Problem or noisy patients are sedated (Butler, 1975); restraints can be too easily overused (Covert, Rodrigues, and Solomon, 1977); failure to change incontinent patients may be used as a punishment (Schreiber, 1977). A lack of activities and isolation can lead to insufferable boredom and poor nutrition; the lack of professional services such as dentists, social workers, or therapists can result in unnecessary illness and progressive debility.

Other subtle feelings that interfere with the relationship between health care givers and elderly clients are infantilization and parentification (Solomon, in press). Since part of the stereotype of the elderly involves a belief in their supposed helplessness, health workers may treat the older patient as if he/she were a child. The author has heard many nurses call elderly residents of nursing homes "Baby" rather than by name. Or the opposite may occur, as the health worker overidealizes the older person into an omnipotent, omniscient, all-good or all-bad parent, thus blinding the worker to the richness of the older person's personality. Often, this interferes with the worker's interactions with the older person, especially concerning sexuality, vulnerability, and relationships with children. In either case, the older person becomes a substitute child or parent for the worker, and appropriate evaluative or intervention services are not delivered.

PSYCHOLOGIC EFFECTS OF VICTIMIZATION

In all chronic situations in which the individual is "one-down," the individual feels oppressed, angry, despondent, and helpless and may turn the anger onto himself or explosively outward toward other individuals or society-at-large (Brody, 1974; Ryan, 1976). Self-victimization, self-blame, and loss of self-esteem go hand in hand with a sense of powerlessness and, at times, apathy. While these phenomena have been relatively well studied in blacks and other oppressed groups, they have not been studied in detail in the elderly.

Helplessness

The major psychologic response of the abused older person is learned helplessness. More specifically, the health care delivery system creates and perpetuates learned helplessness as a coping mechanism of the victimized elderly. It does this through health workers' stereotypes of the elderly, the mechanisms of social exchange theory, and the vicissitudes of the sick role (Solomon, 1982).

In Seligman's model of learned helplessness (Seligman, 1975; Maier and Seligman, 1976), response-outcome must be independent of subject response. Thus, regardless of the apparent appropriateness of the response to the subject's needs, the response is not reinforced by the environment. Furthermore, as it becomes clear that the subject has no control over response-outcome, the subject becomes apathetic and a "giving up-given up" syndrome (Engel, 1967) develops with apathy, lack of response, and helplessness as the consequence.

The individual may also come to perceive response-outcome as not under his control, regardless of the reality of that perception. This perception colors attempts at controlling responses, and may be considered real, again contributing to learned helplessness.

Stereotypes are some of the social antecedents of learned helplessness when translated into behavior. However, this hypothesis is a difficult one to test. Simon and Wilson (1978) found that nurses who view patients as dependent and in need of care reinforced the sick, psychopathologic, and dependent behavior in their patients and negatively reinforced socially appropriate behavior. These data supplement the rich observations of Goffman (1961) and Zusman (1966) on the creation of dependency and institutionalized behavior among residents of institutions.

By stereotyping the aged person as dependent, senile, incompetent, and chronically disordered with a poor prognosis, the health worker does not respond to the older person's behavior and needs but responds to the patient's custodial or maintenance needs, as perceived by the worker. These perceptions are frequently different from the patient's own perceptions of his needs. The care provider's responses, which are not particularly rewarding to the provider, become haphazard, artificially scheduled, or perhaps even nonexistent. The older patient's individuality and individual needs become lost to the provider.

The older person may also come to perceive that all that can be done for him is in the hands of the health worker who maintains total control of response-outcome. If the old person is in an institution in which the staff is not only perceived to be in control, but in reality does control every minute of the day, then it is possible that all responses to all stimuli become independent of response-outcome. Once the older person begins to behave in a way consistent with helplessness, the contingencies of his environment, ie, the negative stereotyping of the health care provider coupled with the real effects of institutionalization, serve to reinforce helpless behavior. This further leads to a marked decrease in motivation, more dependency, and more helplessness. In an extreme, the older person may do absolutely nothing for himself.

Exchange Theory

Exchange theory hypothesizes that human interpersonal interaction is mediated by the real and perceived benefits and costs to individuals involved (Nye, 1978). Exchange theory hypothesizes certain propositions that have a consequence for the development of learned helplessness in the elderly. For example, if an interaction's long-term outcomes are perceived as equal, the individuals will choose alternatives providing better immediate outcomes. If costs are perceived as equal, the individuals will choose alternatives that will supply, or are perceived to supply, the most rewards. Finally, if costs and other rewards are equal, individuals will choose the alternatives which can be expected to supply the most social approval or least social disapproval.

In the interactions between health care providers and elderly patients, interpersonal distance increases because of contingencies inherent in the sick and healer roles and disparities of status, including education, age, roles, and to some degree, real helplessness. As Blau (1955) noted, a differential in benefits and costs, coupled with increased distance, leads to a disparity in the distribution of power in the relationship, which increases the chance of capricious behavior on the part of the provider. Response-outcome may then become independent of behavior.

In addition to an increase in interpersonal distance, health care providers perceive long-term outcome to be negative and the costs to the provider in terms of both emotional and physical energy to be high. Therefore, they are unlikely to invest much energy to minimize cost and maximize the few benefits to be gained from working with the elderly. Their behavior becomes responsive to their own needs to optimize their own "cost/benefit ratio," and may become unresponsive to the elderly patient. Thus, response-outcome becomes independent of the elderly patient's response to stimuli.

In addition, the health care provider who treats the elderly patient in a way inconsistent with stereotyping and who perceives working with the elderly as having long-term benefits at lesser costs than perceived by his colleagues, can expect to meet with disapproval of colleagues.

From the patient's point of view, the power disparity forces the patient to "play the game" by the provider's rules and to adapt to the behavior of the provider, if the patient is to benefit at all from the interaction. Playing by the provider's rules also minimizes the costs in energy to receive care, at least on a short-term basis. As old people are more likely to accept the stereotype of old people than any other population group (Tuckman and Lorge, 1953b), their expectations of themselves are further minimized and they accept the passivity and dependency necessary for care, thus further minimizing costs while maximizing short-term benefits. Unfortunately, such care is given on a long-term basis to old people and, if the "rules of the game" are not changed, costs may be diminished to zero in order to gain any benefits.

Sick Role

Introduction of the sick role into the discussion of the social antecedents of learned helplessness also means the introduction of reality. The reality is that most older persons, when they become ill, require some help. The more serious the illness, the more complex and necessary the help. Thus, any sick individual is put into a social position in which helpless and dependent behavior is expected, sanctioned, and reinforced. Indeed, as Wilson (1970) points out, the adoption of the sick role results in the development of a mutuality of roles between the ill person and the healer. The sick role, as Parsons (1951) has noted, is legitimized behavior for the ill person who then has the societal responsibility to accept whatever help is offered by someone who is defined by society as a healer.

Thus, the sick person becomes a passive, dependent, and weak individual who is at the mercy of the skills and expertise of the healer. To get well, the sick person is completely dependent upon his relationships with caregivers. In the ideal situation, the healer provides not only health, but support and permissiveness.

However, the healer also manipulates rewards for appropriate sick role behavior. Within the context of learned helplessness, manipulation of rewards can mean that the person's needs will be appropriately responded to and that the response-outcome for elderly patients will be dependent on and consistent with the response of that patient. However, because all the power is held by the healer, the healer's response and rewards may be totally independent of the patient's needs, leading to independence of response-outcome. This will set up a situation where the older person thinks he/she has no control over his health care. He/she then passively accepts whatever the healer says. This is a two-edged sword. If the healer is attuned to a model of personal growth and autonomy as well as the needs of the older patient, the responses of the healer may minimize the development of learned helplessness. Instead, the older patient will gradually become less sick and re-establish appropriate premorbid role behavior.

Stereotyping

Negative stereotyping by health care providers may lead to the elderly patient being viewed as helpless, dependent, unproductive, weak, and powerless; translating these attitudes into behavior means that the health worker will then treat the elderly person as helpless, dependent, weak, powerless, and vulnerable, a stereotype accepted by the elderly. The stereotype and behavior of the caregivers leads to minimal expectations of inner-directed behavior by the patient. The major danger of stereotyping and its resultant behavior, as has been pointed out by Solomon and Vickers (1979), is that there is a loss of awareness of the individual's needs so that services are given to the older patient regardless of their appropriateness. In other words, response-outcome becomes independent of response and this independence is perceived and expected, leading to helplessness.

The status differential between the health worker and the older patient that leads to interpersonal distance is accentuated by stereotypic behavior. The health worker who perceives minimal benefits and maximal costs when working with older patients also holds a great deal of power over the older patient because of this distance. The health provider then reduces costs by spending less time with the older patient or behaving in a way as if the older person needs things done for him/her. Or the provider may maximize benefits by reducing prognostic expectations. The resultant behavior further increases distance and the disparity of power and thereby increases the chance of independence of response-outcome. The sick role with its passivity and helplessness only serves to reinforce the stereotype of old people and gives the older person permission to relinquish responsibility of his/her self-care behavior. The acceptance of the sick role has its benefits for the older person, at least during a period of acute illness, as it leads to a reciprocity of roles with the provider, at the cost of increasing the provider's power. Again, the system is maintained.

Finally, while these interactions may all occur in the context of an outpatient medical setting, more helplessness and depression is seen in the context of total institutions for the elderly, including mental hospitals, nursing homes, and acute care hospitals. Total institutions are considered because they completely control all response contingencies of their residents' lives and therefore wield an almost omnipotent power over the lives of the elderly. In a total institution, learned helplessness in the elderly is probably more pervasive than seen anywhere else in the human social environment.

Other Psychologic Responses

The older person who experiences the stresses of victimization develops other psychologic responses. Role victimization leads to feelings of alienation and anomie, both of which have been associated with depressive symptomatology (Durkheim, 1898; Becker, 1964; Akiskal and McKinney, 1973, 1975). A loss of self-esteem accompanies the self-blame that occurs with self-victimization and the acceptance of the stereotype. Loss of self-esteem has been postulated by several authors to be another important dynamic factor in the development of depressive symptomatology (Durkheim, 1897; Becker, 1964; Bibring, 1965; Akiskal and McKinney, 1973, 1975). The anger associated with chronic victimization is turned inward, as there is no way to direct outward. This, too, is a major factor in the development of depression (Abraham, 1911; Freud, 1917; Akiskal and McKinney, 1973, 1975).

Coping Abilities

Whether or not the victimized older person will develop psychiatric symptoms depends upon his abilities to cope. The elderly have a characteristic set of psychodynamic responses to any stress, regardless of its biologic, psychologic, or social nature (Goldfarb, 1968, 1974; Solomon, 1981b, 1981c). Faced with stress, the older individual experiences a diminished sense of mastery over his internal or external environment. This diminished mastery may or may not be observable. It is the subjective experience of diminished mastery that is crucial to the development of psychopathologic symptoms.

With diminished mastery, the older person feels more helpless, with loss of control and autonomy and difficulty in making decisions. Concurrently, the older person feels ambivalently dependent on others for help in responding to the present stress.

Feelings of helplessness and dependency lead the older person to experience three possible affects. One is fear, as the older person worries about what is to become of him as he works to resolve the stress. The other affect is anger at both self and/or others, an anger over what has happened to the older person as well as an anger at powerlessness. A victimized older person feels intense rage, but it may be buried under a surface crust of resignation and uncertainty (Solomon and Zinke, 1981). A third affect, that of loss, is also frequently experienced, as most acute stresses involve the loss of a member of the older person's social support system, social role, or personal attribute.

If the older person has a history of adequate coping skills and is able to use them, he will begin to solve his problems. Any discomfort will be relatively transitory, rarely lasting more than a few days during which he may be sad, irritable, anxious, or withdrawn. As the days pass, the older person begins to handle the intensity of his affective responses to the stressor and attempts to rectify the stressful situation. These individuals are rarely seen in clinical practice because they recognize their discomfort as a normal response to stress. The discomfort rarely lasts more than several days, and they feel competent to manage these problems of daily living without professional assistance.

However, if the older individual has inadequate coping skills, psychopathologic symptoms will develop. The nature of the symptoms will depend on where the individual's affective responses fall on the fear/anger continuum. They will also be determined by the intensity of the loss (Goldfarb, 1974; Solomon, 1981c). For example, the older person who experiences fear will present symptoms of panic. There may be panic, phobia, or physical aggression toward others. There may, on the other hand, be anxiety and depression or hypochondria and illness.

There are three groups of older people with inadequate coping skills. The first group, probably the majority, has been able to cope adequately with stress throughout life. But, because of severe loss such as the death of a spouse, illness, or retirement, occurring sequentially over a brief period of time, their ego defenses and coping skills may become overwhelmed. Or their defenses may be worn down by a daily attack on them by victimization.

The second group also had adequate coping mechanisms when younger. However, because of neurologic failure, the individual is unable to use these coping skills when faced with stress. This leads to psychopathologic symptoms on top of the underlying neurologic or systemic difficulty.

The third group is the minority which demands the most time and energy from health care providers and social agencies. This group includes people who have never had adequate coping skills, people with chronic schizophrenia and mental retardation, and those with unresolved neurotic conflicts and personality disorders that may or may not have been manifested earlier (Solomon, 1981b).

Many factors assure that victimized elderly cannot successfully cope with chronic abuse. First, the abuse occurs daily, slowly whittling away at the older person's ability to cope and use his/her defense mechanisms. Since many abused elderly have various degrees of neurologic failure (Block and Sinnott, 1979), their coping skills are already compromised.

Second, victimization stimulates the affects noted above as part of the psychodynamics of coping in the elderly. Anger (turned inward), loss, fear, (learned) helplessness, enforced dependency, and diminished mastery are sequences in the development of psychopathology. True vulnerability, coupled with diminished self-esteem, self-hatred, and psychologic fatigue increase the chance of the older victimized person developing major psychopathology.

SUMMARY

This chapter has examined the abuse of the elderly in the health care system. This abuse may be perpetuated by physicians and other health workers through adherence to their stereotypes and through the provision of inadequate and inappropriate services. In addition, they perpetuate other abuses by not being sensitive to the effects of these abuses on an elderly person.

This chapter has also examined learned helplessness and other psychopathologic symptoms. Clarification of this sequence of psychologic events is necessary if the health worker is to aid elderly clients. Knowledge of the role health professionals play in development of victimization of the elderly is also necessary.

BIBLIOGRAPHY

Abraham K: Notes on the psychoanalytic investigation and treatment of manic-depressive insanity and allied conditions, in *Selected Papers on Psychoanalysis*. New York, Basic Books, 1911(1960), pp 137–156.

Akiskal HS, McKinney WT Jr: Depressive disorders: Toward a unified hypothesis. *Science*, 1973;182:20–29.

Akiskal HS, McKinney WT Jr: Overview of recent research in depression. Integration of ten conceptual models into a comprehensive clinical frame. *Arch Gen Psychiatry* 1975;32:285–305.

Arnhoff FN, Lorge I: Stereotypes about aging and the aged. *School and Society* 1960;88:70–71.

Ban TA: The treatment of depressed geriatric patients. *Am J Psychother* 1978;32:93–104.

Beck JD, Ettinger RL, Glenn RE, et al: Oral health status: Impact on dental student attitudes toward the aged. *Gerontologist* 1979;19:580–584.

Becker E: *The Revolution in Psychiatry*. London, Free Press of Glencoe, 1964.

Bibring E: The mechanism of depression, in Greenacre P (ed): *Affective Disorders*. New York, International Universities Press, 1965, pp 13–48.

Blau PM: *The Dynamics of Bureaucracy*. Chicago, University of Chicago Press, 1955; pp 6–13.

Block M, Sinnott JD: *The Battered Elder Syndrome: An Exploratory Study*. College Park, University of Maryland, 1979.

Brennan SJ, Moravec JD: Assessing multidisciplinary continuing education as it impacts on knowledge, attitudes and behavior in caring for the elderly. Presented at the 31st Annual Meeting of the Gerontological Society, Dallas, TX, Nov. 19, 1978.

Brody EB: Psychosocial aspects of prejudice, in Caplan G (ed): *American Handbook of Psychiatry*, vol 2, ed 2. New York, Basic Books, 1974, pp 492–511.

Brown BS: Goals in mental health and aging. Presented at the 28th Annual Meeting of the Gerontological Society, Louisville, KY, Oct. 28, 1975.

Butler RN: *Why Survive? Being Old in America*. New York, Harper and Row, 1975, pp 174–259.

Cook SW: The systematic analysis of socially significant events: A strategy for social research. *J Social Issues* 1962;18:66-84.

Covert AB, Rodrigues T, Solomon K: The use of mechanical and chemical restraints in nursing homes. *J Am Geriatrics Soc* 1977;25:85-89.

Cyrus-Lutz C, Gaitz CM: Psychiatrists' attitudes toward the aged and aging. *Gerontologist* 1972;12:163-167.

Duff RS, Hollingstead AB: *Sickness and Society.* New York, Harper and Row, 1968.

Durkheim E: *Suicide.* New York, Free Press, 1897(1951).

Dye CA: Attitude change among professionals: Implications for gerontological nursing. *J Gerontolog Nursing* 1979;5:31-35.

Eisdorfer C: Evaluation of the quality of psychiatric care for the aged. *Am J Psychiatry* 1977;134:315-317.

Engel GL: A psychological setting of somatic disease: The "giving up-given up" complex. *Proc Roy Soc Med* 1967;60:553-555.

Ettinger RL, Beck J, Kerber P, Scandrett F: Dental student confidence in prosthodontics and attitudes toward the elderly. Presented at the 32nd Annual Meeting of the Gerontological Society, Washington, DC, Nov. 29, 1979.

Farrar DR, Miller RH: Professional and age related attitudinal conflicts of social workers and lawyers. Presented at the 32nd Annual Meeting of the Gerontological Society, Washington, DC, Nov. 29, 1979.

Ford CV, Sbordone RJ: Attitudes of psychiatrists toward elderly patients. *Am J Psychiatry* 1980;137:571-575.

Freud S: Mourning and melancholia, in *Collected Papers,* vol 4. London, Hogarth Press, 1917(1934), pp 152-170.

Garfinkel R: The reluctant therapist 1975. *Gerontologist* 1975;15:136-137.

Goffman E: *Asylums.* New York, Doubleday, 1961.

Goldfarb AI: Clinical perspectives, in Simon A, Epstein LJ (eds): *Aging in Modern Society.* Washington, American Psychiatric Association, 1968, pp 170-178.

Goldfarb AI: Clinical perspectives, in Simon A, Epstein LJ (eds): *Aging in Modern Society.* Washington, American Psychiatric Association, 1968, pp 170-178.

Hickey T, Rakowski W, Hultsch DF, Fatula BJ: Attitudes toward aging as a function of in-service training and practitioner age. *J Gerontology* 1976;31:681-686.

Holtzman JM, Beck JD: The impact of medical and dental education on student's attitudes toward the aged. Presented at the 31st Annual Meeting of the Gerontological Society, Dallas, TX, Nov. 19, 1978.

Holtzman JM, Beck JD: Palmore's Facts on Aging Quiz: A reappraisal. *Gerontologist* 1979;19:116-120.

Ivester C, King K: Attitudes of adolescents toward the aged. *Gerontologist* 1977;17:85-89.

Johnson DM, Wilhite MJ: Changes in nursing students' stereotypic attitudes toward old people. *Nursing Research* 1976;25:430-432.

Kastenbaum R: The reluctant therapist. *Geriatrics* 1963;18:296-301.

Kay DWK: The epidemiology and identification of brain deficit in the elderly in Eisdorfer C, Friedel RO (eds): *Cognitive and Emotional Disturbance in the Elderly.* Chicago, Yearbook Medical Publishers, 1977, pp 11-26.

Kayser JS, Minningerode FA: Increasing nursing students' interest in working with aged patients. *Nursing Res* 1975;24:23-26.

Klopott Z: Attitudes of general hospital physicians toward psychiatry, psychiatrists and psychiatric patients and their effect on patient care. Presented at the Department of Psychiatry, Albany Medical College, Albany, NY, Apr. 5, 1977.

LeShan L, LeShan E: Psychiatry and the patient with a limited life span. *Psychiatry* 1961;24:318–323.

Levenson AJ, Felkins BJ: Prevention of psychiatric recidivism: A model service. *J Am Geriatrics Soc* 1979;24:536–540.

Maier SF, Seligman MEP: Learned helplessness: Theory and evidence. *J Exp Psychol: Gen* 1976;105:3–46.

McConnell SR: The effects of organizational context on service providers' attitudes toward old people. Presented at the 30th Annual Meeting of the Gerontological Society, San Francisco, CA, Nov 20, 1977.

McGuinness AF, Knox SJ: Attitudes to psychogeriatric nursing. *Nursing Times* 1968;63(supplement):127–128.

Mendelson, MA, Hapgood D: The political economy of nursing homes. *Annals Am Acad of Political Social Science* 1974;415:95–105.

Mills J: Attitudes of undergraduate students concerning geriatric patients. *Am J Occup Ther* 1972;26:200–203.

Montgomery D, Wilkinson A: Intervention in the organizational environment: Correcting the mismatch between staff attitudes and agencies' activities. Presented at the 31st Annual Meeting of the Gerontological Society, Dallas, TX, Nov 20, 1978.

Moroney RM, Kurtz NR: Evolution of long-term care institutions, in *Long Term Care.* Sherwood S (ed): New York, Spectrum Publications, 1975, pp 81–121.

Nye FI: Is choice and exchange theory the key? *J Marriage Family* 1978;40:219–233.

Parsons T: *The Social System.* New York, Free Press, 1951, pp 428–473.

Redick RW, Kramer M, Taube CA: Epidemiology of mental illness and utilization of psychiatric facilities among older persons, in Busse EW, Pfeiffer E (eds): *Mental Illness in Later Life.* Washington, American Psychiatric Association, 1973, p 229.

Robb SS: Attitudes and intentions of baccalaureate nursing students toward the elderly. *Nursing Res* 1979;28:43–50.

Romaniuk M, Hoyer FW, Romaniuk J: Helpless self-attitudes of the elderly: The effect of patronizing statements. Presented at the 30th Annual Meeting of the Gerontological Society, San Francisco, CA, Nov 20, 1977.

Rosenkranz HA, McNevin TE: A factor analysis of attitudes toward the aged. *Gerontologist* 1969;9:55–59.

Rosow I: Status and role change through the life span, in Binstock RH, Shanas E (eds): *Handbook of Aging and the Social Sciences.* New York, Van Nostrand Reinhold, 1976, pp 457–482.

Ryan W: *Blaming the Victim,* revised ed. New York, Vintage Books, 1976.

Scheff TJ: Schizophrenia as ideology. *Schizophrenia Bull* 1970;2:15–19.

Schreiber MJ: *Accidental Mental Health Care—The Inappropriate Reliance on Nursing Homes; Behavioral Drug Therapy in Nursing Homes—A Pattern of Risk.* Springfield, United States Dept. of Commerce, 1977.

Seligman MEP: *Helplessness.* San Francisco, W.H. Freeman, 1975, pp 21–74.

Shem S: *House of God.* New York, Marek, 1978.

Simon SS, Wilson BM: Nurse-patient interaction and the maintenance of mental illness. Unpublished Master's thesis, Richmond, Medical College of Virginia School of Nursing, 1978.

170

Solomon K: The development of stereotypes of the elderly: Toward a unified hypothesis. Presented at the 31st Annual Meeting of the Gerontological Society, Dallas, TX, Nov 19, 1978.

Solomon K: The development of stereotypes of the elderly: Toward a unified hypothesis, in Lewis EP, Nelson LD, Scully DH, Williams JS (eds): *Sociological Research Symposium Proceedings* (IX). Richmond, Virginia Commonwealth University, 1979a, pp 172–177.

Solomon K: Social antecedents of learned helplessness of the elderly in the health care setting, in Lewis EP, Nelson LD, Scully DH, Williams JS (eds): *Sociological Research Symposium Proceedings* (IX). Richmond, Virginia Commonwealth University, 1979b, pp 188–192.

Solomon, K: Social antecedents of depression in the elderly: The relationship between societal structure and stereotyping. Presented at the 133rd Annual Meeting of the American Psychiatric Association, San Francisco, CA May 5, 1980.

Solomon K: The depressed patient: Social antecedents of psychopathologic changes in the elderly. *J Am Geriatr Soc* 1981a;29:14–18.

Solomon, K: Personality disorders in the elderly, in Lion JR (ed): *Personality Disorders: Diagnosis and Management,* ed 2. Baltimore, Williams and Wilkins, 1981b, pp 310–338.

Solomon K: The elderly patient, in Spittell JR (ed): *Clinical Medicine,* vol 12. *Psychiatry.* Hagerstown, MD, Harper and Row, 1981c, pp 1–14.

Solomon K: Geropsychiatry training for senior center staff—Curriculum and process. *Gerontol Geriatr Ed* 1981d;2:9–13.

Solomon K: Social antecedents of learned helplessness in the health care setting. *Gerontologist* 1982;22:282–287.

Solomon K: The older man, in Solomon K, Levy NB (eds): *Men in Transition, Theory and Therapy.* New York, Plenum, in press.

Solomon K, Nathan RG: Psychiatry's image: The attitudes of physicians and medical students. Presented at the 132nd Annual Meeting of the American Psychiatric Association, Chicago, IL, May 15, 1979.

Solomon K, Nathan RG: Psychiatry's image: The attitudes of physicians and medical students. *Hillside J Clin Psychiatry* in press.

Solomon K, Vickers R: Attitudes of health workers toward old people. *J Am Geriatr Soc* 1979;27:186–191.

Solomon K, Vickers R: Stereotyping the elderly: Changing the attitudes of clinicians. Presented at the 33rd Annual Meeting of the Gerontological Society of America, San Diego, CA Nov. 25, 1980.

Solomon K, Zinke MR: Group psychotherapy with the depressed elderly. Presented at the 53rd Annual Meeting of the American Orthopsychiatric Association, New York, NY, Mar. 31, 1981.

Spence DJ, Feigenbaum EM, Fitzgerald F, Roth JR: Medical students' attitudes toward the geriatric patient. *J Am Geriatr Soc* 1968;16:976–983.

Thorson JA: Attitudes toward the aged as a function of race and social class. *Gerontologist* 1975;15:343–349.

Thorson JA, Whatley L, Hancock K: Attitudes toward the aged as a function of age and education. *Gerontologist* 1974;14:316–318.

Tuckman J, Lorge I: Attitudes toward old people. *J Soc Psychol* 1953a;37:249–260.

Tuckman J, Lorge I: "When aging begins" and stereotypes about aging. *J Gerontology* 1953b;8:489–492.

Tuckman J, Lorge I: Attitude toward aging of individuals with experiences with the aged. *J Genetic Psychol* 1958;92:199-204.

Weiss JAM: Suicide, in Arieti S, Brody EB (eds): *American Handbook of Psychiatry,* vol 3 ed 2. New York, Basic Books, 1974, pp 743-765.

Wilson RN: *The Sociology of Health: An Introduction.* New York, Random House, 1970, pp 13-32.

York J, Fergus E, Calsyn R: The implications of staff attitudes for a nursing home mental health training program. Presented at the 28th Annual Meeting of the Gerontological Society, Louisville, KY, Oct. 28, 1975.

Zusman J: Some explanations of the changing appearance of psychotic patients. Antecedents of the social breakdown syndrome concept. *Milbank Memorial Fund Quarterly* 1966;44(supplement):363-396.

10 A Geriatrician's View of Health Care of the Elderly

Victor Kassel

To be old in America today is unfortunate; to be old and sick is tragic. A growing number of social injustices weigh more heavily against the aged. Quality geriatric health care cannot be bought in America; it only can be given.

For the past 30 years, daily encounters with bias against the aged have been my experience as a full-time geriatrician in private practice. I am confronted daily with the wrongs suffered by senior citizens, not simply medical but social and psychological. The misuse of the aged also becomes part of the obstructionism to the delivery of the service to the patient by the physician, while the patient tries to live normally as a family and a community member. The geriatrician's responsibility develops into advocacy with very few allied compatriots — that is how private practice works in America. This situation is in stark contrast to that of the administrator, who delegates responsibility to the many others in bureaucracy; it is in contrast too to the usual academic, who teaches from the latest research without practical experience. These experts take moral stands for good without personal risk.

172

There are very few physicians who have chosen to limit their practice to care of the aged. Most physicians include older patients in their patient load but seem to limit the level of care given them. I take care of elderly people impaired by a variety of medical/surgical, psychiatric/psychological, and social problems. The geriatrician has an obligation to care for the patient as a person with accumulated disabilities, and to render as expertly as possible the necessary services (Kassel, 1979). Geriatrics is the counterpart for the elderly of pediatrics. Geriatric medicine has accumulated a large reservoir of information especially about the older patient. It is a speciality which is "expert in understanding senile pathology and managing the problems which result from it" (Devas, 1977). Geriatrics is a special medical study in spite of the denial by the National Institute on Aging, the American Geriatrics Society, the Gerontological Society of America, and nonpracticing physicians. These groups, in their limited understanding, are comfortable to relegate the care of the most complicated patients — the aged chronically ill — to the least trained health professionals. This is the supreme abuse directed against the aged by the nondeliverers of service, today's decision makers.

Medical Care

In the United States medical schools are just beginning to introduce classes in the care of the geriatric patient, an occurrence much later than other medical schools in the Western world. In this country there is still the stigma of ignorance that describes geriatrics as that medical practice directed to the worst patient by the worst doctors. Brickner (1978) asks applicants to his Home Health Care Program about their willingness to tolerate the scorn and amusement of fellow physicians when the accusation is made of wasting time treating the "unsalvageable people." Another of his questions deals with costs of care and concepts of rationing health resources. Why not reserve care for younger people, where there may be a profit from the investment in sickness? This is just one branch from the American tree of the antiaged bias: the denigrating of the worth of the older person.

The hearings held by Congressman Claude Pepper (Hearing before the Select Committee on Aging, House of Representatives, July 1980) echo the concern for increased health costs particularly under Medicare. Services to the aged are being cut back with growing costs for decreasing services. A solution, the Committee insists, is the Health Maintenance Organization (HMO). They are trying to legislate financial advantages for the HMO participant, when the HMO is selected for health care in preference to a solo medical practitioner. For a perceptive criticism of the concept of the HMO, see "The HMO and the Future of Medicine: Another Perspective" (*The Golden Age,* July 1980, p 1). One can hope that these committee members will recall that two of the foremost advocates of the HMO, the late Senator Hubert Humphrey and the late Dr. John Knowles, did not take advantage of the HMO opportunity during their terminal illnesses.

My own practice experience with the HMO is limited to patients who left the program to continue their care with me. Geriatric care is long term for chronic illnesses. A review of the records of geriatric patients cared for by an HMO with its ancillary, nonphysician, medical personnel, hired to render health care to the aged, leaves much to be desired. The complete physical examination rarely is done by the physician; follow-up care is supervised by a physician but not rendered by him personally; serious pathology is missed; and family support is slipshod. Much of it impresses one as malignant neglect, and our chronically ill, senior citizens are entitled to more. Geriatric quality care demands professional time; time is money, and the primary appeal of the HMO is decreased costs.

The recent mechanization of medicine with the development of superspecialists has resulted in a Cartesian dichotomy of the psyche from the soma. Rather than the physician increasing his competency in total geriatric care, he denies himself the opportunity of personal growth into a Renaissance man of medicine or into the tradition of philosopher-physician. The patient, counterproductively, with healer prestigitation, is cleaved into separate disease entities. The aged patient in this way is fragmented by ever-increasing parcelling of bits of the geriatric body into the fields of the superspecialists. No one assumes responsibility for the whole! Being of service to the sick aged person becomes of secondary importance. Rather than the healing profession's calling to service, it becomes perverted into a business with all of the accoutrements of a corporation for profit.

A recent example of the change from concerned service to timed efficiency is the infrequency of the house call. An office call or emergency room visit is more cost-effective than a house call. A former president of the American Geriatrics Society said he could see no reason why house calls were necessary. The reason for his limited understanding may be that he is not a private practice geriatrician but a superspecialist, and this may be valid for him. It is not valid for any practitioner who compassionately cares for the elderly sick and who is cognizant of their total needs and limitations.

Care of the aged ill is time consuming, and in modern medical practice, time is money. For this reason, many aged do not receive a complete physical examination. Without a comprehensive history, a thorough physical examination, and necessary laboratory work, it is impossible to develop that essential tool, the Troyka Geriatric Diagnostic Profile (Kassel, 1979). The development of this three-part information reservoir about the older person — the medical/surgical, the psychiatric/psychological, and the social problems — enables the practitioner to understand all the pathologic entities affecting the aged patient.

The ignorance of third party payers such as private insurance companies, Medicare, and Medicaid abets this neglect. For the thoroughness required for a comprehensive examination within the comfortable speed of the patient's limitations, one and one-half hours are required. One is not only trying to examine the patient, but also trying to establish a rapport. If the patient suffers from any confusion or anxiety, an intrusion upon the privacy of his body requires gentleness and repeated reassurance.

One example is the frequency of misdiagnosis of cerebral arteriosclerosis in the presence of brain failure. Following an incorrect diagnosis, the patient is given a variety of pills and capsules which are supposed to increase the blood supply to the brain. Less than 20% of these patients have cerebral arteriosclerosis, between 10% and 30% have a remedial lesion, and between 50% and 60% have Alzheimer's disease. This incorrect diagnosis leaves the family ignorant of the social implication of Alzheimer's disease, in which a patient has few medical problems until the terminal stage of the illness. Rather, the family throughout the course of the illness should be guided, reassured, and supported by the geriatrician when confronted with the problems of the patient. Continuing geriatric care is important at this time, and later too, to help the family care for the patient during the last days of severe dementia. The patient must not be abandoned during his last illness.

Progressive brain impairment leads to difficulties with swallowing, and the patient easily develops aspiration pneumonia. Should such a catastrophe happen, the family, adequately advised and cautioned previously, has had time to consider the welfare of the patient and the mechanics of treatment if the patient is admitted to a hospital intensive care unit (ICU). Some families are unsophisticated about the intrusive technology of modern intensive care units. A patient with severe dementia from a global Alzheimer's disease should not be subjected to the constellation of tubing, respirators, monitors, and proddings that are routine in these units. For the patient's sake, the family should have been counseled in the difference between prolonging life and prolonging the act of dying.

The American political process seems to wish to solve health problems by seeking immediate, inadequate remedies without cognizance of long-term destructive effects. At times, one wonders whether the aged are misled by sociopathic, self-interested profiteers. The statement by

176

Pinner et al (1959) is appropriate: "A dependent social group attempting concerted action is vulnerable to political exploitation."

The cost involved in bringing medical care to the aged is greater than that to the younger patient, because extra medical services need to be performed. The practicing geriatrician requires a larger waiting room, because usually someone must accompany the elderly to the office. Additional examining rooms are needed, because of the greater length of time required for undressing and dressing. More secretarial staff is used, because there is more paper work for an aged patient. More time is required per patient examination due to possible increased forgetfulness (a longer life means a longer medical history). More family conferences are needed to insure proper care and proper understanding in the family. The need for house calls, to provide total quality care required by an aged sick person, is an added time-factor cost. Now a precedent is being set, in full agreement with the aged patient. The aged are willing to accept a program financed less well than that of their younger counterparts. The Medicare assignment procedure as full payment reaffirms the established two-tier medical care system. Senior citizens admit that their sickness care is worth less reimbursement than that of younger persons.

From time to time, there appear in some publications lists of free medical services to the aged or discount medical clinics for the aged. These may consist of inadequately trained physicians or paraprofessionals eagerly wishing to bring services to the aged, with some hidden trick to ensure substantial profit. Upon thorough investigation it has been proven that there are no "free" or "discount" quality geriatric medical services. There are costs to the patient, perhaps not in money, but in suffering. If the senior citizens of America accept the idea that this lesser level of care is to their benefit, they are foolish.

However, the aged are apparently willing to encourage, participate in, and develop a two-tier program for their own health care. If the aged campaign for decreased costs in care to start with their program, it will be destructive to them. When they allow themselves to compete with younger patients for the "sickness dollar," and to give the younger patient the advantage of a greater payment for a lesser service, the aged will lose out. Discount care is discounted.

There are geriatric patients who have unquestioned faith in their physicians and who lack sophistication about what is acceptable geriatric care. This patient is cheated because of this ignorance. Again, it is a matter of cost effectiveness and the investment of time. Many physicians reject elderly patients or accept them reluctantly as patients, because the care is time-consuming. Many physicians who see 40 to 60 patients a day cannot maintain this level of productivity with its monetary rewards when seeing elderly people in preference to younger people. To compensate for the time consumed, income is increased per patient by performance of mechanical procedures by office technicians. These various procedures often impress third party payers, who may not reimburse adequately for the time involved, but will overly reimburse for tests.

Some physicians prescribe and then fill a patient's prescription. Some give medication intramuscularly when the same medicine is as effective orally. Some commercial laboratories work out an arrangement with the doctor; for a set fee paid each month to the laboratory, they will do all of the doctor's laboratory work. The physician then charges the patient the regular fee for each test. The more work done, the greater the physician's profit, because his cost remains the same. Additionally, when the nurse draws blood, the patient may be charged for the venopuncture. There is no charge when the patient's blood is drawn at the laboratory. These techniques are all used to exploit the patient (*The Golden Age,* February 1979, p 19).

Sometimes the physical examination may be abused. Patients will claim to have had a "physical," when the doctor has only taken x-rays, has collected blood for chemical examinations, has auscultated the chest and/or taken an electrocardiogram. A complete physical examination consists of thoroughly examining the body from the top of the head to the feet. The physician inspects, palpates, and auscultates all parts of the body and examines all orifices. It is imperative that the patient understand this procedure. Delegating to a less trained assistant the eliciting of the patient's complaints is unfortunate. The entire procedure may be dehumanized by insisting that the patient have an exchange only with a computer.

Dying and Death

Some years ago, Utah modified its Coroner's Law to state that any person dying within the previous 30 days without a physician's attendance would become a coroner's case. This is of serious concern to the aged. When one considers the strong antigovernment ethic in Utah, and the intrusion of the government into "natural" dying, there is an increase in fear and anxiety among the aged ill. Some may equate the coroner with autopsies and may feel that they will be autopsied if they are not seen by their physician regularly, before the expiration of the 30 days: "That's the law!" Therefore, many elderly people will insist upon a monthly visit to ensure that they do not end up on the autopsy table, thus increasing their cost for unnecessary care. Many will deny themselves essentials to pay for this assurance.

Often today one finds a modern refusal to accept the occurrence of natural death. It is an aphorism that all of us are born with a chronic illness called life, and none of us will get out of it alive. Yet, the enthusiasm for scientific treatment and its latest social-political perversions disallow us the right to die naturally; The Angel of Death may be frustrated in his prescribed work.

Admit an elderly patient to the hospital, and unless "DNR" (Do Not Resuscitate) is stated specifically on the chart, all energies are directed at preventing death. Certainly, there are preventable deaths that intrude during an acute illness, yet death is expected as the end in all terminal illnesses.

Modern medical life-support systems in American hospitals enable the energetic and the dedicated to work and to support a person's vegetative functions except those associated with intellectual competency. Too frequently, an aged person, through the expertise of the paramedic, the emergency room personnel, and the professionals in the ICU, is rehabilitated to a healthy vegetable state. *Non compos mentis,* the body is transferred in a state of hibernation to a nursing home.

The elderly should discuss their desires about accepting or rejecting treatment as it pleases them. If their personal physician will not abide by their wishes, they should seek the services of a more compliant physician. If continued hydration and feeding of a patient with a severe stroke, with no possibility of recovery to his premorbid personality, is against the wish of the patient, the person is abused when subjected to further life with a destroyed brain. Appropriate to this is Sophocles' statement: "Death is not the greatest of ills; it is worse to want to die, and not be able to." Or that of Seneca: "Death is a punishment to some, to some a gift, and to many a favor."

Federal Programs

The Red Queen said to Alice: "Now, *here,* you see, it takes all the running *you* can do, to keep in the same place. If you want to get somewhere else, you must run at least twice as fast as that" (Carroll, 1940). Thus it is for the aged who are trying to live up to federal programs. As an example, is Medicare accomplishing that for which it was established? It is obvious that the benefits originally programmed for are gradually disappearing. Congressman Claude Pepper's Select Committee on Aging (U.S. Congress, 1980) estimated that there are 24.3 million older Americans enrolled in Medicare. In addition, three million disabled younger-than-65 persons are covered by Medicare. The average ill senior citizen will have Medicare pay 75% of his hospital bill, 55% of his physician's bill, but none of the cost for drugs, dental care, or eye care.

Medicare will cover less than 3% of nursing home care, and about 3% of home health care expenses. Nursing home care accounts for 25% of the total health care costs of the elderly.

In 1966, when Medicare was enacted, it cost the average American $217 annually for health care. Presently, he is paying $1078, an increase of 395%. Older Americans paid $445 in 1966, and the amount is estimated today at $2500, an increase of 525%. Thus, the costs for the elderly have increased at a greater rate than the costs to the general public.

The cost to the senior citizen to participate in Medicare is increasing also. The premium has gone from $3.00 to $9.00 a month, an increase of 220%. Seniors once paid the first $40 of their hospital bill, they now must pay the first $180 to $204. The amount of money paid by Medicare for services is decreasing. Medicare paid almost 50% of the average senior's health bill in 1969, and today it pays only about 40% of the total. The aged sick are continuing to pay about 50% of their health care costs, the same as in 1965. For the elderly, this sharp reduction in Medicare is psychologically damaging. The aged are denied benefits Congress intended them to have.

Medicare continues to cut back. Hospitalized Medicare patients will be responsible for the first $204. If hospitalized more than 60 days, the patient's share will increase from $45 to $51 a day from the 61st through the 90th day. After 90 days, the patient's share will rise from $90 to $102 a day. For the very rare Medicare patient who is covered by Medicare in a nursing home, the cost will increase. After the 20th day, the cost will rise from $22.50 to $25.50 a day through the 100th day.

It would be unfair to categorize this regression in Medicare payments as a deliberate plan to penalize the aged or to deny them service. Yet, why is there such a lack of understanding? In my testimony before Congressman Claude Pepper's Select Committee on Aging at the time of the 15th Anniversary of Medicare (United States Congress, 1980), I listed five important factors: First, quality geriatric care had never been defined. Medical schools, until the immediate present, have not taught the care of the aged to their students. How could the needs of the aged be filled, when those primarily responsible for satisfying these needs are uninformed?

Second, the rules and regulations developed for Medicare did not come from the thinking, knowledge, experience, or cooperation of geriatricians in private practice. The individuals called on to mandate the administrative regulations were physicians, either bureaucrats or from academic institutions. None were in private practice delivering geriatric service directly to the sick patient.

Third, as a result of the lack of knowledge about quality geriatric care, and the lack of involvement of geriatricians in private practice, there evolved an ignorant Medicare Part A and Medicare B bureaucracy.

The latter tried to develop a program and to service a program about which they were uninformed, an ineptitude that continues to date. Fourth, the mathematical bewilderment associated with the assignment method and its perplexing computations add to the inoperability of parts of Medicare.

Fifth, the fee schedule determined by the Medicare, Part B fiscal agents reflects the historical obtuseness of Blue Shield and its preoccupation with surgery and procedures. Blue Cross-Blue Shield originated as a surgical insurance program. Medicare Part A and Part B are the offspring of the program. I believe that the cause of many malfunctioning government health programs, developed initially with great enthusiasm and optimism, is the ignorance of the program developers.

The Hospital

American physicians overhospitalize, because Americans are deluded by a "cure" mystique surrounding hospitals. If an elderly patient is not improving with the prescribed outpatient treatment, there is pressure to admit the patient to the hospital. It is implied that a hospital has something especially therapeutic to offer. Many people do not know Ivan Illich's (1975) frightening warning that the third most dangerous place in America for the adult is the hospital. (The most dangerous is working underground in a mine; the second most dangerous is working as a steeplejack on high buildings.) According to two studies (McLamb and Huntley, 1967; Schimmel, 1964), 20% of the patients admitted to hospitals are injured in incidents unrelated to their illnesses. Since the aged have the highest admission rate to the hospital, they suffer more than hospitalized younger people.

Geriatric nursing is unpopular in the hospital. Elderly patients suffer from multiple diseases, and frequently during the acute phase of the illness, they are confused, a confusion disturbing to others. For control, many elderly are forcibly restrained; many elderly are overtranquilized; many elderly are neglected to the point of urinary and fecal incontinence; many elderly are fed poorly into a state of acute malnutrition; many elderly are subjected to inadequate turning in bed with the development decubitus ulcers; simply, many elderly are maltreated.

It is a formidable task to get an aged patient out of bed into an easy chair. Eating meals sitting in a chair is not routine in most hospitals. Elderly patients are gotten out of bed, if ever, after meals; it seems never before meals. One essential simple clinical procedure for care of the sick elderly is accurate reporting of their temperature. This easy noninvasive, nonintrusive, and nondangerous determination is often lost in use of complicated, expensive, computerized mechanical determinations.

Dietitians often neglect the aged, the physically incapacitated, the handicapped patients, who wrestle with the packaging of the food service on their trays. Labels are too small to read; cups are sealed with permanent plastic bonding; nutritional philosophies are too narrow to conceive of liberalizing the diet restrictions, so that anorexic, aged sick might approach a meal enthusiastically. The problem of the aged is not the restriction of food but the encouragement to eat. In many hospitals health technicians are often oriented just to treat disease. To the patient's chagrin, the sick are categorized solely, for example, as a hypertensive who needs restriction from salt; as a gall bladder who needs restriction from fat; as a cardiac who needs restriction from cholesterol; or as a diabetic, who needs restriction from sugar. More correctly, and for the patient's well-being, we are helping a person, suffering from loss of appetite, who needs encouragement to eat any and all foods. Restriction is not imperative, but food prodigality is needed.

The expense of the present-day hospital is the result of its capital-intensive, technological advances. Emphasis on mechanics and organ function measurements has sometimes resulted in neglect of the person himself. Patients are restricted to their bedrooms. The surfeit of administrative offices usurps the space for patient's socialization. The vulnerable, aged sick patient, in the state of acute illness with all learned protective reflexes ripe for extinguishing, is prone to easier behavior modification from the social isolation during the illness. This behavior frequently is carried over to life after discharge as an injury to the patient's psyche. Serious enough is the patient's depression associated with the acute illness and hospitalization, without the depression being deepened by the further pathologic effect of the hospital's rigid rules.

Depression deepens when the aged patients, upon discharge, are insecure in their ability to carry on at home. In the more enlightened countries of the world, it is possible to allow patients to demonstrate to themselves their independence (a predischarge competency test). American hospitals need small kitchens, where older persons can demonstrate their ability to cook breakfast. These people should be allowed an opportunity to make their own beds. If they are able to do both, they may go home. Unfortunately, this human concern for the socially discriminated against is not part of the hospital's agenda of geriatric care.

The acute confusional state encountered during the hospitalization of aged patients is not permanent, and it resolves with treatment of the underlying physical illness. Yet, this short interlude of agitation is treated with our modern drugs which restrain the patient. Too many hospitals have rules that do not allow a family to sit with the patient. Or family members may be too busy to invest the time needed in accomplishing the bedside reassurance day and night. Elderly patients are often abused with tie-down restraints. More effective and less traumatic is having a family member sit at the bedside 24 hours a day to aid the emotional needs of the patients by talking with them, by preventing them from pulling out intravenous tubes, by preventing them from getting out of bed and fracturing a hip, by reassuring them—all of which would lessen the need of the impersonal restraining techniques. It serves the family relationship to have the children appreciate the truth that confusional behavior is treatable, and that seriously ill aged patients do get well. It also prevents some of the dreaded complications that are encountered too frequently during the hospitalization of an aged patient. Scientifically we know but we rarely follow in treatment, that heavily tranquilizing aged patients, keeping them immobile with the drug, tied to the side rails, and perspiring heavily, may result in bed sores within less than two hours.

With the nursing shortage in American hospitals, floor nurses are confounded by the demands and multiple needs of the geriatric patient. Often these nurses complain that there is not enough help to care for the older person in the hospital. Many of these same nurses feel incompetent and insecure, because they are untrained in geriatric nursing. The same can be said for the interns and residents, who may dislike care of the aged.

CONCLUSION

The abuse of the aged met by the geriatrician in private practice who renders daily care to these aged people, is not irrelevant. The general public read about the increasing incidents of physical violence directed against the aged. Yet beyond obvious corporal abuse, there are subtle and less obvious destructive atrocities: medical, social, and psychological violence. This cruelty does not arise de novo, as "a result of the times." Historical accounts exist (Fischer, 1977; Achenbaum, 1978) of a perpetual conflict between generations. However one tries to solve the enigma, whether with Freud's teachings, Karl Marx's dialectical materialism, King Saul's and King David's conflict, or King Lear's "senile reaction," it would seem that things are not improving. Modern life has become frustratingly more complicated with the change from the rural to an urban society; with medicine's increased ability to add years to life but not life to years; with the destruction of the extended family; with the loss of importance of the artisan's competency to the machine; all this is confounded with the Master of Business Administration value system of "the bottom line," ie, maximization of profit. Humanism of the human has shriveled.

The question: "Will America's way of life continue with *abuti senectute* (abuse of the aged)?"

BIBLIOGRAPHY

Achenbaum WA: *Old Age in the New Land. Experience since 1970.* Baltimore, Johns Hopkins University Press, 1978.

Brickner PW: *Home Health Care for the Aged.* New York, Appleton-Century-Crofts, 1978.

Carroll L: *The Annotated Alice. Alice's Adventures in Wonderland and Through the Looking Glass.* New York, Bramhall House, 1940.

Devas M: *Geriatric Orthopaedics.* London, Academic Press, 1977.

Fischer DH: *Growing Old in America.* New York, Oxford University Press, 1977.

Illich I: *Medical Nemesis. The Expropriation of Health.* London, Marion Boyars, 1975.

Kassel V: Geriatrics practice: Moving it from the back burner. *Geriatrics* 1979; 34:95–99.

McLamb JT, Huntley RR: The hazards of hospitalization. *South Med J* 1967;60: 469–472.

Pinner FA, Jacobs P, Selznick P: *Old Age and Political Behavior.* Berkeley, University of California Press, 1959, p 14.

Schimmel SM: The hazards of hospitalization. *Ann Intern Med* 1964;60: 100–110.

United States Congress. House Select Committee on Aging. *Medicare: A Fifteen-Year Perspective, Hearing before the Select Committee on Aging,* 96th Congress, 2nd sess., July 30, 1980.

SECTION II
Special Groups of Vulnerable Elderly

Although physiological aging produces changes that increase the vulnerability of the elderly (such as visual and hearing impairments or loss of strength and agility), and social losses and decreased incomes make coping with change for many elderly more difficult, certain groups of elderly are especially vulnerable to victimization. The following six chapters discuss these groups.

Noel A. Cazenave assesses the incidence of elder abuse among black Americans and the association to poverty, households headed by women, neighborhood crime rates, and multigenerational families. The family is discussed as a deterrent to elder abuse, as are social policies for adequate incomes, health care, housing, and supporting services.

The family consequences of caring for a mentally or physically impaired elderly relative are discussed by Jean Luppens and Elizabeth E. Lau who look at the dependency of the elderly and physical and mental conditions that cause it. The authors describe supports and interventions used with impaired aged clients at the Chronic Illness Center in Cleveland, Ohio.

The vulnerability of elderly women to crime and fraud is addressed by Marilyn R. Block. Associated with the vulnerability of elderly women are urban residency, low income, impairments, isolation, and unfamiliarity with financial matters. Community organization efforts that focus on vulnerable older women are discussed.

Joanne L. Steuer's chapter looks at the physical problems likely to lead to disability in elderly persons (eg, stroke, diabetes, arthritis, and injuries) and their ramifications on family members' incomes, life satisfaction, independence, and physical and emotional well-being. Elder abuse may result. The author makes recommendations for needed research, community education, counseling, and community resources to assist family members.

The elderly living in public housing and in neighborhoods with high crime rates are the focus of the chapter by Lynn A. Curtis and Imre R. Kohn. For dealing with neighborhood and environmental problems for the elderly, the authors discuss indigenous neighborhood self-help programs, the benefits of age-segregated housing, environmental design, and opportunities for public surveillance.

Jordan I. Kosberg discusses the special vulnerability of elderly parents to family abuse as a result of the family being a closed system and thought of as a panacea, the failure of elderly parents to report abusive behavior, the cycle of family violence, and intergenerational conflicts. The chapter concludes that family members need to be assessed for appropriateness to care for dependent elderly relatives; protective services legislation are needed in every state; supportive services should be available to the family; and the public should be informed of the possibility of elder abuse so that prevention and treatment will be sought and available.

11 Elder Abuse and Black Americans: Incidence, Correlates, Treatment, and Prevention

Noel A. Cazenave

A cursory analysis of the history and development of social issues in American society reveals a common pattern: Whenever possible, to establish legitimacy of an issue, considerable effort is expended to demonstrate that it has broad, or even universal, relevance.[1] This has been the case with all aspects of family violence, including elder abuse. The point has been persistently made that elder abuse (as was earlier the case with child abuse and spouse abuse) affects individuals from all walks of life: the rich and poor, black and white, the uneducated and the highly educated. Because the problem is thought of as a universal one, it is often assumed that universalistic research and intervention strategies are appropriate. Research focusing on the extent and nature of family violence among different groups works against this legitimization and subsequently is not encouraged. Only after the issue has become firmly

---

[1] Issues concerned with inequality and discrimination against minorities are socially recognized and noteworthy exceptions.

established, sanctioned, and funded is the veil of "selective inattention" (Dexter, 1958) lifted. Then the diversity of distinct populations can be understood and effective intervention strategies implemented to meet their unique needs.

Unfortunately, by the time programs and policies are institutionalized, based on some fanciful notion of a mythical "universal man," it is often discovered that they work effectively for no one. Those who need them most use them least, and the next ten years of research and service efforts are devoted to what went wrong, or what patchwork efforts can be made so the inappropriate theories and practices work.

This pitfall may be avoided in our society's attempts to understand and eliminate the problem of elder abuse. At this stage the relevance of questions raised, as opposed to the definitive answers offered, provides the key through which this can be accomplished. It is the objective of this chapter to explore the limited data available on how family violence is affected by age and race, to review what is known about the black aged and reasons why they may be at special risk and those countervailing forces that may work against such abuse, and finally to make suggestions as to how elder abuse among blacks can best be ameliorated.

INCIDENCE

Family Violence and Race

The relationship between family violence rates and what is broadly thought of as "race" is a perplexing one. The data are inconsistent, and their interpretations can be misleading (Straus, Gelles, and Steinmetz, 1980). In an earlier article concerned with race and family violence rates (Cazenave and Straus, 1979), it was concluded that the existing literature tended to leave the reader with more questions than answers. While it is generally assumed that marital violence is higher for blacks than it is for other groups (Staples, 1976), much of the empirical data on black family violence is based on agency-reported cases of child abuse. Some studies conclude that blacks experience higher rates of child abuse than whites (Gil, 1970). Others have found that blacks have lower rates (Billingsley, 1969), and some found no noteworthy differences (Young, 1963). Family researchers also do not agree on the relationship between race and family violence rates. Some believe that blacks will automatically have higher rates of child abuse, spouse and sibling abuse because of their day-to-day encounters with racial and economic oppression. Others base their theories on research done on black extended family-kin-ties (Hays and Mendel, 1973; Shimkin, Louie, and Frate, 1973; Stack, 1974; Aschenbrenner, 1973; Hill, 1977; Hill and Shackleford, 1978; Jack, 1979) that suggest that strong support networks, especially with regard to children and the elderly, will be a buffer against such violence. Even if empirical data are available, special care must be taken not to confuse the effects of race with income level, employment status, or different patterns of social organization and cultural expectations and values concerning violence.

To provide some answers to this complex issue, Cazenave and Straus (1979) analyzed a subsample of a 1976 survey on violence in 2143 intact American families (see Straus, Gelles, and Steinmetz, 1980). This subsample consisted of 147 black families and 427 white families. Particular attention was placed not only on race, but also on social class and involvements in extended-family-kin networks. The findings showed that no categorical statement can be made as to whether black or white families are more violent. Instead the results are specific for the type of family violence and degree of abuse described. For example, it was found that whereas black husbands were three times as likely as white husbands to have slapped their wives and to have engaged in severe violence (including kicking, biting, hitting with a fist or an object, or the use of a knife or gun) within the last year, black and white parents were equally as likely to have engaged in such abuse against children, and blacks were slightly less likely to report having slapped or spanked a 12-year-old child. Blacks were also less likely to report either sibling abuse or parent abuse within the last year. Finally, whereas income, husband's occupational status, and involvement with family-kin-neighbors were associated with lower rates of family violence for all respondents, their effects were especially dramatic for black families. Thus, ethnically variant patterns of family violence might provide insights in our understanding of elder abuse among black Americans. In later sections of this chapter, a detailed assessment of these findings will show what they suggest for understanding and eliminating elder abuse in black families.

Family Violence: Race and Age

Violence and the black aged is a virtually unexplored research frontier (Cazenave, 1979). What research is available is limited to empirical data contained in a few general reports on elder abuse where prevalence rates by race were included as a minor (generally deemphasized) variable.

The relationship between race and elder abuse incidents is uncertain. None of these studies was based on random or representative samples, and overall the results reflect the particular population served by those who did the reporting. This type of "sampling artifact" is explicitly discussed in the Legal Research and Services to the Elderly (1979) report on elder abuse in Massachusetts. After reporting that 85% of the reported cases were identified as involving white respondents, with only 4% black, 8% other, and 3% race not reported, the authors suggest that these results may simply reflect the nature of the population served by those persons reporting elder abuse cases.

Based on their study of clients of a chronic illness center in Cleveland, Ohio, Lau and Kosberg (1979) found that 26% of the abused persons were black, a finding consistent with their description of the center's client population. Blacks were overrepresented as clients generally, thus blacks should also be overrepresented in actual observed abuse cases. Finally, Block and Sinnott (1979) found from reports of professionals they surveyed that 12% of the abused were black — blacks were proportionally represented consistent with their proportion of the total United States population. Again, however, their study was not based on a representative sample of the total United States population but a survey of professionals assumed to have regular contact with the aged. The racial composition of the clients served by these professionals must be known before conclusions can be drawn as to precisely what that 12% represents.

In brief, based on existing studies of elder abuse, it is not known how the incidence rates for elder abuse are affected by race.

PROPOSITIONAL CORRELATES

Although there are no credible data on the extent or nature of elder abuse among black Americans, some factors associated with elder abuse generally have been identified, and there is an extensive literature on black families which might be helpful in identifying propositions as to possible high risk factors predisposing blacks to elder abuse and countervailing forces which might work against its occurrence.

Steinmetz and Straus' Systems Model

Steinmetz and Straus (1974) suggest that instead of looking at numerous single explanations of family violence, a more comprehensive model can be employed through the use of modern systems theory. Such an approach to elder abuse can be illustrated (Steinmetz and Straus, 1974) through a diagram of the interrelationships of societal level variables, family variables, individual characteristics of family members, and precipitating factors. The systems approach adds a dynamic quality to the analysis of family violence phenomena in that it is possible to illustrate the simultaneous operations of numerous different variables and their interrelationships in one diagram.

Such a model also makes explicit possible intervention points that might ordinarily be overlooked. One can theoretically start anywhere, but all relevant factors must be considered. Another advantage of such a model is that it makes clear how such violence systems — once generated — begin to take on a life of their own. The more a person is physically abused, the more this positive feedback generates more violence in the future. When violence is no longer tolerated, the system must readjust itself. Finally, by treating the system as an open, as opposed to a closed, self-contained entity, this approach emphasizes the dynamic interplay between what happens in families and other subsystems of society, including those social service agencies designed to help them.

Societal Variables

Poverty While family violence cuts across all socioeconomic levels of society and is not the exclusive province of the poor, it must be acknowledged that there is a close relationship between the access that a group has to societal resources and the degree and types of problems encountered by its membership. Cazenave and Straus (1979) demonstrated the relationship between income and family violence rates. Income had an especially dramatic effect in determining rates of marital, parent-to-child, sibling, and child-to-parent violence for black respondents. Their low-income status places many blacks into a high risk group for family violence. The magnitude of this problem can be seen by the fact that collectively the median family income of blacks is only 57% of white American families (United States Bureau of the Census, 1980). Overall, 31% of black Americans live below the poverty level, compared to 9% of whites. Of persons 65 years and older, more than a third of elderly blacks (ie, 36%, compared to 13% for whites) live in poverty (United States Bureau of the Census, 1980).

Households headed by women Abused elders tend to be female (Legal Research and Services for the Elderly, 1979) and research on other forms of family violence shows a strong relationship between income and violence rates. Thus, 42% of black women 65 years or older living in poverty (compared to 16% of white women) might logically suggest that a large portion of these women, because of their (and their families) relative position in this country's opportunity structure, may be high risk cases for the occurrence of elder abuse (United States Bureau of the Census, 1980).

High crime neighborhoods It is also clear that potentially violence-precipitating stresses and strains experienced by poor families are not limited to the home. Poor families generally live in impoverished communities characterized by high rates of interpersonal violence. Elderly blacks are more fearful of criminal assaults within their neighborhoods and are more likely to be the actual victims of such assaults than is the case for white elderly persons (Ragan, 1977). If the black elderly live in a more violent environment, some of this violence may manifest itself in the home in the form of elder abuse.

Family-Kin-Community Organization

Multigenerational households One aspect of black family organization that leads us to expect the potential for relatively high incidence of abuse between the aged and other family members is the number of black multigenerational households. According to United States Census figures (United States Bureau of the Census, 1978), black women 65 years or older "were much more likely to maintain families without a husband (21%) than white women (8%)." This might suggest that their "time at risk" (Straus, Gelles, and Steinmetz, 1980) as potential victims of abuse by family members is greater, and that consequently old black women might experience higher rates of such abuse. However, research is needed before any conclusions can be drawn on the relationship between the large number of black multigenerational households and the occurrence of elder abuse. The nature of these relationships may tell us just as much as their existence does. For example, most of the research on elder abuse (L.R.S.E., 1979; Lau and Kosberg, 1979; Block and Sinnott, 1979) suggest that dependence is a major correlate of abuse. Hill (1971) notes that the black elderly living in multigenerational families tend to have their children living with them while the white elderly tend to live with their children. In a later article Hill (1978) states that "because of their desire to be as self-reliant as possible, black elderly are much more likely to take others into their households rather than permit themselves to be taken into the households of young relatives." Unfortunately, unlike wife abuse there is no evidence that having home ownership and other economic resources will reduce the possibility of the elderly being physically abused. Perhaps the young old who are in good mental and physical health and are heads of multigenerational families may be able to use such resources to prevent maltreatment more than the old old (those 75 and older) — severely impaired persons who are most likely to be the victims of elder abuse.

Such research has implications for all American families since, as Gelfand et al (1978) suggest, with the increased life expectancy of older persons, there is a growing incidence of multigenerational homes

(Cazenave, 1979). Research into the nature of such multigenerational homes is needed since there may be key ethnic differences in family boundary maintenance systems that may affect how elderly members are received and treated.

The impact of non-nuclear family members Cazenave and Straus (1979) found important differences between black and white families regarding the effect of the presence of nonnuclear family members in the home on various forms of family violence. These findings led to the conclusion that "depending on how their presence in the home is interpreted, whether they are considered to be a help, a nuisance, an outsider or what have you, they can, by their mere presence, tend to reduce the amount of family violence, or to create tensions and stresses that might be associated with an acceleration of violence" (*Encore Magazine,* 1980). How the presence of elderly adults in the home is accepted may be just as important a predictor of the potential of elder abuse as their presence per se.

Social isolation and social support systems There is a growing body of literature suggesting that social isolation is a crucial factor associated with severe forms of family violence (Garbarino, 1977; Cazenave and Straus, 1979; Garbarino and Stocking, 1980). Cazenave and Straus (1979) noted that there is considerable evidence to suggest that the amount of social isolation differs by class, residence, and race. For example, Hays and Mendel's study (1973) of 25 black and 25 white families stated that "black families interacted with extended kin more and perceived them as more significant," suggesting that the black extended family-kin system was an important support system which served as a buffer from a racially hostile environment. Shimkin, Louie, and Frate (1973) studied a large black extended family system in the South and concluded that one of its unique functions was the prevention of child abuse and neglect among the black lower classes. Later research by Stack (1974), Aschenbrenner (1973, 1975), Hill and Shackleford (1978), and Jack (1979) documented the role of the black extended family-kin system as an important support system. Cazenave and Straus (1979), looking at how such networks might reduce rates of family violence, found that blacks were more embedded in family-kin-locality networks and that while involvement in such networks was associated with lower rates of marital, child, parent, and sibling violence for both black and white families, the effect was especially dramatic for black families. It was concluded that low income, socially isolated black families constituted a high risk group for the occurrence of family violence. Thus, elder abuse may be most common in the increasing number of poverty-stricken, multigeneraticnal households headed by women, provided that they are socially isolated from support from other kin, neighbors, and friends.

With the increasing number of households headed by women and the rising rate of out-of-wedlock births (more than 50% of all black births in 1976; National Center for Health Statistics, 1978) there may be an erosion of traditional family-kin supports and an increasing problem of elder abuse in such multigenerational households.

In the Cazenave and Straus (1979) study of race, class, and network embeddedness as correlates of family violence it was found that black families were less likely to have been recent migrants to their neighborhoods and that such neighborhood stability was associated with lower rates of family violence, especially for black families. Of course, all neighborhoods are not alike. Some neighborhoods may encourage high rates of interpersonal violence, both in and out of the home, while other neighborhoods might support against the occurrence of such violence.

In his discussion of support systems in different types of neighborhoods Donald Warren (Garbarino and Stocking, 1980) delineated three key dimensions: identification with the neighborhood, interaction within its boundaries, and linkages to the larger community. By evaluating communities as to how many, if any, of these characteristics they possess, Warren identified six neighborhood types. Three of these appear to provide valuable insights for an understanding of elder abuse in predominantly black neighborhoods.

Often black communities are conceptualized as having strong ethnic identity, and being close-knit, self-contained, and independent from the larger, surrounding social environment. It is assumed that despite the difficulties its members face in the racially and economically exploitative "outside," the basic fabric of community life within these parochial communities is essentially healthy. However, considering the reports of urban black elderly persons (eg, Ragan's 1977 study on their fear of crime), many (if not most) do not appear to live under such relatively idyllic circumstances.

In his demographic analysis of elderly blacks, Hill (1978) noted a trend of the black aged moving from rural areas to the central cities of large metropolitan areas while the white elderly moved to the suburbs. Moreover, Bourg (1975) in his study of the elderly in Nashville, found that the black aged were more geographically mobile and less likely to be homeowners. Blacks are more likely to live in transitory neighborhoods, often moving in while white aged move out. Warren (Garbarino and Stocking, 1980) refers to these types of neighborhoods as transitory because, while there are links to outside environments, there is little identification or interaction within the community. In these zones of transition, sociologists have documented almost every type of pathologic behavior. These areas might be expected to have relatively high rates of elder abuse.

The third neighborhood type relevant to the life of many black aged is what Warren referred to as a diffuse neighborhood. In these homogeneous structures there is strong in-group identification but little else. There is little meaningful interaction within the community or transactions with the world outside. For the white aged a diffuse neighborhood might be a socially and geographically isolated suburb. For the black aged it is more likely to be a low income housing project. In both there may exist the social isolation upon which family violence breeds. In many black communities there are the additional burdens of poverty, dirty streets, noise pollution, and high density dwellings.

In brief, there is no one black community. The social and geographic character of where aged black persons live suggests a great deal about the types of problems they may face, including elder abuse; and they also suggest a great deal about its amelioration.

Shared value systems   Related to the discussion of community-ecological factors associated with occurrence of varying rates of elder abuse is the effect of shared value systems which either encourage or discourage such abuse. For example, within black communities it is often said that blacks are more humane in their treatment of their aged than is the case for whites. This is a widely held belief although there is only impressionistic evidence to support it. Wylie (1971) states, "It is generally accepted that black Americans are more inclined than whites to include the elderly in the family structure and to regard the elderly with respect, if not veneration." If this is true we would expect that elder abuse would be a smaller problem among blacks as compared to white Americans. If it is not true, but the folklore about how blacks treat their elderly better persists, these beliefs may work to hinder the recognition of the existence of physical elder abuse within black families, and its amelioration.

One argument used as evidence is the relatively fewer number of black aged who are institutionalized compared to white elderly. When empirical evidence is scrutinized it is obvious that this assumption is severely challenged. For example, Jackson (1977) reports that, "While in 1960, many fewer Southern old black women lived in institutions than the rest of the population (only 1% as compared with 4%), by 1970 the proportion of those over 65 who lived in such group settings was similar to the American population as a whole. In fact, outside the South more were institutionalized (8%)." She also cites a 1968 study by Lopata of black and white widows in Chicago which found that black widows were no more likely to have an enduring kinship structure than white widows.

Empirical research is needed to determine if there are any distinct cultural patterns or values that may serve as countervailing forces against the occurrence of physical elder abuse (eg, another folk value prominent in the socialization of blacks is that "You will never, under any circumstances, hit your mother" *(Encore Magazine,* 1980.) There is no evidence that the black aged are actually treated better than their white counterparts or would be less likely to be victimized by physical abuse.

The issue of the precise effect of shared value systems on the prevalence of elder abuse is further complicated by the suggestion by some sociologists that low income minority communities are characterized by what they refer to as a subculture of violence (Scherer, Abeles, and Fisher, 1975). Individuals growing up in such a subculture learn that violence is normal, expected, and instrumental in achieving certain desired ends and consequently develop favorable attitudes towards its use. Unfortunately, this theory is largely impressionistic, and there is little evidence to suggest that there is a direct causal relationship between proviolence attitudes and the actual occurrence of violence. More attention will have to be paid to the shared value system of black communities to understand the cause of elder abuse and to develop the most effective intervention strategies.

Individual Characteristics

Another way to develop propositions to discover the extent and nature of black elder abuse is to look at research evidence on individual characteristics of abused elders and those who do the abusing. The best available data on the individual characteristics of abused elders show that they tend to be old old (ie, 75 years or older), female, physically or mentally disabled, overly represented among the low income, and to have lived with the abuser who tended to be relatives (Legal Research and Services for the Elderly, 1979).

Age, sex, health, and income   When one considers that the number of black female elderly is increasing faster than is black males (Jackson, 1977), and the low-income status of the black aged already discussed, it is clear that the black aged constitute a potentially high risk group for abuse. In addition to these demographic variables, we also know that black aged persons fit closely the characteristics of abused elders because they are (especially women) more likely to live in multigenerational households (Bourg, 1975), and they are more likely to fit into the category of frail elderly. The evidence about impaired physical condition of black as compared to white elderly is noteworthy. In his study of the elderly in Nashville, Bourg (1975) found that more than twice as many blacks as whites were so physically impaired that they needed to be accompanied to leave their home. Based on their study of blacks, Mexican-Americans, and whites in Los Angeles County, Dowd and Bengston (1978) concluded that "older minority respondents were significantly more likely to report poorer health than white respondents even with the effects of S.E.S., sex, and income held constant."

Alcoholism, drug addiction, and mental health problems   The Legal Research and Services for the Elderly Study (1979) also found that nearly a third of the abusers had problems with alcoholism or drug addiction. Such problems tended to be much more prevalent in low income black communities than in the society at large. Other characteristics of elder abusers including long-term medical complaints, long-term financial problems, history of mental illness, and limited education were also important. All of these characteristics are associated with the amount of stress inherent in such environments and the ability of individuals to manage such stress effectively.

Precipitating Factors

In an attempt to identify specific factors precipitating abuse, the Legal Research and Services for the Elderly survey (1978) "indicated that the abuser was experiencing some form of stress when the abuse occurred." Large numbers of multigenerational households and frail elderly persons combined with the stressful conditions associated with being of low income, black, and living in a stressful environment, may converge to amplify the stressful situations that black Americans may be subjected to in care of frail elderly. Any or a combination of stressors might place the black dependent aged at risk of physical, psychological, emotional or financial abuse.

Overall, when societal, family-kin-community, individual and precipitating factors are considered, it becomes clear that although some countervailing forces may exist against the abuse of the black aged, generally the social conditions under which they live suggest that many black Americans are a potentially high risk population for the occurrence of elder abuse.

TREATMENT AND PREVENTION

Unfortunately the same set of complex factors that may make blacks more (or less) vulnerable to elder abuse may work against setting up effective intervention strategies for its treatment and social policies for its prevention. With reference to child abuse, Gil (1977) makes the important distinction between the amelioration of a social problem and primary prevention. Amelioration refers to what social workers can do within a particular social context to treat a problem. On the other hand, primary prevention involves fundamental changes in the social structure which would eliminate the causes of the problem and its occurrence in the future. In discussing propositional correlates about the extent and nature of the problem of elder abuse, this chapter began with societal level variables and then moved to a discussion of potential abuse precipitating factors. To focus on treatment intervention strategies before discussing policies for primary prevention, it will now reverse this process, and begin with the actual elder abuse incidents.

Elder Abuse Incidents

Thorman (1980) advises that professionals working with abusing families must be positive and nonthreatening if they are to establish the needed rapport to help.[2] It is unlikely that all persons working in areas related to the identification and treatment of elderly abuse possess the sensitivity and skills to enable them to establish a close trusting relationships with clients across racial or socio-economic status boundaries (Day, 1979). After the detection of a suspected case of elder abuse, the most important challenge facing the professional or paraprofessional is the design and implementation of a nonthreatening intervention strategy. Failure at this point might insure the establishment of effective boundary maintenance systems to keep the threatening intruders out, ultimately leading to more isolation and tension and the intensification of abuse encountered by the aged. The importance of nonracist, ethnically sensitive, practitioners who are genuinely concerned with the problems of violence-prone low income black families, as well as their abused elderly members, cannot be overemphasized.

Precipitating Factors and Individual Characteristics

The most common immediate cause of elder abuse appears to be the stress experienced by individuals who must care for the frail elderly without adequate support. Of course, stress has many levels of manifestation and cause. What is clear, however, in the immediate needs of those who care for the frail elderly, is that there has been no systematic training to help individuals to more effectively care for the long-term health care needs of the aged and no assistance for those who are no

---

[2]Thorman (1980) suggests six "dos and don'ts" for social workers attempting to establish rapport with families where child abuse has occurred. They may apply equally to work with family members abusive of the elderly.

longer able to manage such stress in a nonabusive manner. Programs designed to provide support for families responsible for providing long-term custodial care for the aged are sorely needed in black communities. And when we look again at those who are most likely to be abused: the old-old, female, physically and mentally disabled, low income, aged living with relatives, there is evidence that many low income blacks could benefit from stress management-oriented programs to help reduce the potential for elder abuse.

Family-Kin-Community Factors

While there is evidence to suggest that embeddedness in primary networks may be associated with lower rates of family violence (Cazenave and Straus, 1979; Garbarino, 1977; Garbarino and Stocking, 1980), there is also evidence that the types of close-knit network structures common in many black communities may actually work against the use of health and social services. There seems to be an important paradox in the literature about the role of primary networks for lower class blacks. On the one hand, they seem to be the mechanisms that have contributed to black survival in a racist and economically exploitative environment and, on the other hand, they may actually impede the proper use of available helping services. Suchman (1965) found that lower class minority group members tend to have strong in-group identity and parochialism that work against their turning toward outside sources for help during illness. The problem has to do more with the organizational capabilities of different network structures than with attitudes, per se. As Horwitz (1977) states, in distinguishing between the relative merits of open ended and close-knit networks in the use of psychiatric services, "when persons are tied to a number of other people, who are not tied to each other, they have more channels to reach information and influences and they more easily connect to social institutions."

This does not mean that the absence of close-knit primary networks will contribute to the increased use of professional services. Those persons in an anomic environment (ie, with little social support and few resources) would in all probability be faced with the greatest social isolation and the highest incidences of abuse. Such abuse might only be discovered when police and other public agencies are called in to deal with an emergency that has become public.

The presence of family-kin-locality networks provides support, information, and referral services that are not available through other means. For example, while McKinlay (1973) found that women with close-knit networks of kin and friends did delay the use of professional services, when they did use such services it was often after having first consulted with friends and relatives. Thus, social workers may find that such primary network structures can be an important source of help and information for potential clients provided that they and the services they offer are not perceived as outside intrusions.

Leichter and Mitchell (1967) caution that social work generally tends to be geared to working with individuals outside of the family-kin context that is so important in their everyday lives. They warn that until social workers can work with and through relatives and friends many of their intervention strategies will be unsuccessful. This is especially true for elder abuse which thrives on social isolation, is seldom reported by the abused or immediate family members, and can only be effectively treated with the help of those intimately associated with the abused. Many social workers have not only recognized that family-kin-locality network structures must be respected when attempting to administer services to families and individuals who need them, but also realize that these existing natural helping networks can often be incorporated into the intervention strategy. Collins and Pancoast (1976) see these natural helping networks as untapped resources for preventive intervention. Gil (1970) found that blacks respondents reported that they were more willing to become personally involved than whites in case of child abuse in their neighborhood.

In cases where such network structures do not already exist, Collins and Pancoast (1976) suggest the formation of artificial networks. For example, a social worker concerned with the potential of elder abuse in what is perceived as a high-risk neighborhood might attempt to identify a small number of indigenous neighborhood support persons (ie, residents who are already normally called into action when neighborhood members have problems). These persons could regularly visit homes that are burdened with providing long-term custodial care for the aged. Their mere presence might reduce much of the stress and isolation normally associated with elder abuse. They can observe high risk situations and make recommendations as to when additional supportive services are needed (eg, custodial assistance, counseling, training in specific custodial care techniques, financial assistance, or respite care that would provide long-term caretakers with a brief retreat from their stressful duties). They may be able to help more directly when actual cases of abuse are uncovered or are suspected. They can become a friend of the family and help them negotiate what might ordinarily be a traumatic encounter with professional agency workers who intervene on behalf of the elderly. Such community-based strategies may be particularly important where there is strong sentiment against the institutionalization of the aged as even a last resort to dealing with severe and persistent cases of elder abuse.

Beyond "Band-Aid" Approaches: Societal Level Factors

To move past what Straus et al, (1980) refer to "Band-Aid" or "ambulance at the bottom of the cliff" types of solutions to family violence among black Americans will require fundamental changes in the social predicaments in which many black families and many black aged find themselves. Such policies must include provisions for: a guaranteed annual income, low-cost national health insurance, adequate and affordable housing, federal assistance in supportive services for those charged with the long-term custodial care of the frail elderly, tax incentives for relatives who assume such responsibilities, community-based respite care facilities, the expansion of low income home care facilities, federally funded community-based chronic care facilities, and the establishment of family counseling centers to help family members cope with the stress of long-term custodial care.

At present the focus has been limited to mandatory reporting laws and the establishment of a few experimental service programs. As the systems analysis has suggested, a more comprehensive approach would probably be best received and have the greatest payoffs in low-income black communities. "Band-Aid" solutions may not only be ineffective — they may serve to encourage suspicion and retrenchment among those who need it most. If they deal only with the symptoms and not the root causes of elder abuse among black Americans they may serve to increase the hostility that many low income blacks have for externally imposed service functionaries. This may cause more stress, more isolation, and ultimately tend to aggravate the problem rather than to alleviate and eliminate it.

Any effective attempt to eliminate elder abuse among black Americans must involve attacking racism and economic exploitation, respecting and building on the strengths of family-kin-community networks, helping the black aged maintain their health and independence for as long as possible, and the building of better, less stressful environments and circumstances.

CONCLUSION

This chapter has pointed out that just as there is no one cause of elder abuse, there is no one solution. In the development of effective intervention strategies and preventive social policies, one must be sensitive to the precise cause and nature of abuse among different groups of people. Each group's strengths and vulnerabilities will determine how elder abuse is manifested and how it can best be treated and eliminated. The

202

problems faced by the black aged are complex and varied, and do not occur in a vacuum. The solutions, therefore, must be imaginative, diverse, and mindful of the complexity of every level of the social system.

BIBLIOGRAPHY

Aschenbrenner J: Extended families among black Americans. *J Comparative Family Studies* 1973;4:257–268.

Aschenbrenner J: *Life-Lines: Black Families in Chicago.* New York, Holt, Rinehart and Winston, 1975.

Billingsley A: Family functioning in the low-income black community. *Casework* 1969;50:568–572.

Block MR, Sinnott JD: *The Battered Elder Syndrome: An Exploratory Study.* College Park, MD, University of Maryland, 1979.

Bourg CJ: Elderly in a southern metropolitan area. *Gerontologist* 1975; (February)15(1):15–22.

Cazenave NA, Straus MA: Race, class, network embeddedness and family violence: A search for potent support systems. *J Comparative Family Studies* 1979;10: (Autumn):281–300.

Cazenave NA: Family violence and aging blacks: Theoretical perspectives and research possibilities. *J Minority Aging* 1979;4:99–108.

Collins A, Pancoast DL: *Natural Helping Networks: A Strategy for Prevention.* Washington, DC National Association of Social Workers, 1976.

Day D: *The Adoption of Black Children: Counteracting Institutional Discrimination.* Lexington, MA, Lexington Books, 1979.

Dexter LA: A note on selective inattention in social science. *Social Problems* 1958;6 (Fall):176–182.

Dowd JJ, Bengston LL: Aging in minority populations: An examination of the double jeopardy hypothesis. *J Gerontol* 1978;33:427–436.

Encore: The battered elder syndrome: Violence begins at home. 1980;(March): 54–57.

Garbarino J: The human ecology of child maltreatment: A conceptual model for research. *J Marriage Family* 1977;39:721–735.

Garbarino J, Stocking SH: *Protecting Children from Abuse and Neglect.* San Francisco, Jossey-Bass, 1980.

Gelfand DE, Olsen JK, Block MR: Two generations of elderly in the changing American family: Implications for family services. *Family Coordinator* 1978;27:395–411.

Gil DG: *Violence Against Children: Physical Abuse in the United States.* Cambridge, MA, Harvard University Press, 1970.

Gil DG: Child abuse: Levels of manifestation, causal dimensions, and primary prevention. *Victimology* 1977;2(3):186–195.

Hays W, Mendel CH: Extended kinships relations in black and white families. *J Marriage Family* 1973;35:51–57.

Hill RB: *The Strengths of Black Families.* New York, Emerson Hall, 1971.

Hill RB: *Informal Adoption Among Black Families.* Washington, DC, National Urban League, Research Department, 1977.

Hill RB, Shackleford L: The black extended family revisited in Staples R (ed): *The Black Family: Essays and Studies.* ed 2. Belmont, CA, Wadsworth, 1978.

Hill R: A demographic profile of the black elderly. *Aging* 1978;Sept–Oct 287–288:2–9.

Horwitz A: The social networks and pathways to psychiatric treatment. *Social Forces* 1977;56:86–105.

Jack L Jr: *Kinship and Residential Propinquity: A Study of the Black Extended Family in New Orleans.* Unpublished PhD Dissertation. University of Pittsburgh, 1979.

Jackson JJ: Older black women, in Troll LE, Israel J, Israel K (eds): *Looking Ahead: A Women's Guide to the Problems and Joys of Growing Older.* Englewood Cliffs, NJ, Prentice-Hall, 1977.

Lau EE, Kosberg JI: Abuse of the elderly by informal care providers. *Aging* 1979;299–300 (Sept–Oct):10–15.

Legal Research and Services for the Elderly: *Elder Abuse in Massachusetts: A Survey of Professionals and Paraprofessionals.* Boston, MA, LRSE, 1979.

Leichter HJ, Mitchell WE: *Kinship and Casework.* New York, Russell Sage, 1967.

McKinlay JB: Social networks, lay consultation and help-seeking behavior. *Social Forces* 1973;51:275–291.

Ragan PK: Crimes against the elderly: Findings from interviews with blacks, Mexican Americans, and whites, in Rifai MAJ (ed): *Justice and Older Americans.* Lexington, MA, Lexington Books, 1977.

Scherer KR, Abeles RP, Fisher CS: *Human Aggression and Conflict.* Englewood Cliffs, NJ, Prentice-Hall, 1975.

Shimkin DB, Louie GJ, Frate D: The black extended family: A basic rural institution and a mechanism of urban adaptation. Presented at the International Congress of Anthropological and Ethological Sciences. Chicago, IL, 1973.

Stack CB: *All Our Kin: Strategies for Survival in a Black Community.* New York, Harper and Row, 1974.

Staples R: Race and family violence: The internal colonialism perspective, in Gary LE, Brown LP (eds): *Crime and Its Impact on the Black Community.* Washington, DC, Institute for Urban Affairs and Research. Howard University, 1976.

Steinmetz SK, Straus MA (eds): *Violence in the Family.* New York, Harper and Row, 1974.

Straus MA, Gelles RJ, Steinmetz SK: *Behind Closed Doors: Violence in the American Family.* Garden City, NY, Anchor Books, 1980.

Suchman E: Social factors in medical deprivation. *Am J Pub Health* 1965;55:1725–1733.

Thorman G: *Family Violence.* Springfield, IL, Charles C Thomas, 1980.

United States Bureau of the Census: Current Population Reports, Series P-23, No. 85, *Social and Economic Characteristics of the Older Population: 1978.* Washington, DC, Government Printing Office, 1978.

United States Bureau of the Census: Current Population Reports, Series P-60, No. 125, *Money Income and Poverty Status of Families and Persons in the United States: 1979 (Advance Report).* Washington, DC, Government Printing Office, 1980.

United States National Center for Health Statistics: Advance Report, Final Natality Statistics, 1976. *Monthly Vital Statistics Reports* 26 (March 29), 1978.

Wylie FM: Attitudes towards aging and the aged among black Americans: Some historical perspectives. *Aging and Human Development* 1971;2:66–69.

Young LR: *The Behavior Syndromes of Parents Who Neglect and Abuse Their Children.* Doctoral Dissertation. Columbia University School of Social Work, 1963.

12 The Mentally and Physically Impaired Elderly Relative: Consequences for Family Care

Jean Luppens
Elizabeth E. Lau

Much has been written about growing old, for the most part, a grim story. More recent writings (Puner, 1974) show that old age is becoming a better and happier stage of life, for the majority of the population "joie de vivre" is potentially possible.

When considering abuse of the elderly, and more specifically the vulnerability to abuse of the physically and mentally impaired elderly, the focus is on a small segment of the older population. However, it is a population which tends to be confined, whether at home or in an institution, and, thus, "hidden" so that the magnitude of the problem has yet to be defined. We know that a problem exists (Lau and Kosberg, 1979)—a problem serious enough to warrant further exploration and attention.

PHYSICAL IMPAIRMENTS

Older persons become ill more frequently than young people; 86% have chronic health problems, but those who are severely physically and mentally impaired are a small percentage. Only 4% to 5% live in institutions at any one time, although as many as 25% may reside there at some time before they die. As many as 23% of elderly deaths in some communities occur in nursing homes and extended care facilities (Kastenbaum and Candy, 1973; Wershow, 1976). Of those in the community, the percentage of those who are housebound (6% to 7%) and those who are bedbound (2% to 3%) has shown no marked change (Shanas, 1979). Of the total population 65 or older, only 5% have the severe mental limitation associated with chronic organic brain disease but by age 80, the frequency comes closer to 20% (Busse, 1973). Physical disability and chronic conditions are reported as interfering with mobility for 18%; 6% report trouble getting around alone; 7% need some mechanical aid, and 5% were housebound (Facts About Older Americans, 1978). Not all the housebound have mental impairment, nor are all those with serious mental limitation housebound. No specific data are available about persons with both mental and physical impairment. It is clear, however, that both mental and physical impairment increases with age and that, as the older elderly population increases, so will this particularly vulnerable group. The group age 75 to 84 has increased 16.1% between 1970 and 1976 and the group 85 years and over has increased by 39.1%, while the population ages 40 to 64 has grown only 1.9% (Statistical Notes, 1978).

Shanas (1979) indicated that for every person in an institution, there are two in the community requiring extensive care. She pointed out that one in eight over the age of 80 is in an institution, so we can assume that there are another two cared for in the community. Busse (1973) stated that for every elderly person in an institution, there are three living with an adult child, twice as many women as men. It has been documented many times that the elderly have adult children involved with them nearby in their communities (Shanas, 1979; Brody, 1970) and have regular interaction with them and receive varying amounts of assistance. As the old old group increases, however, the strengths and capabilities of these concerned adult children can be expected to diminish as they become elderly themselves. Brody (1970) refers to the rapidly increasing old old in our society and to the fact that the family members on whom they depend are also older. The over-85 group is most vulnerable to the convergence of physical and mental impairments which demand 24 hour supervision and care, and it is often the incapacities or deaths of family members make institutional care necessary for the very old.

This group of elderly, becoming larger and older, who because of mental and physical limitations must depend on some other person to meet the needs of daily living, will be the focus of this chapter.

MENTAL IMPAIRMENTS

The mental disorders of old age are often mistakenly considered a natural part of growing old and therefore untreatable; most are commonly referred to, even by some physicians, as senility. Although some symptoms of various disorders may appear similar, the cause varies and in many cases the conditions are treatable and will improve.

Organic Brain Disease

Organic brain disease is divided into two groups — acute or reversible brain syndrome and chronic or irreversible brain syndrome (Butler and Lewis, 1977). Chronic organic brain syndrome (COBS) is misunderstood and often thought to be caused simply by normal brain cell loss and poor circulation reducing the oxygen available to the brain. It has been shown however, that loss in brain weight up to 20% to 40% does not necessarily correlate with severe memory impairment or other symptoms associated with senility (Sokoloff, 1975). Restriction in blood flow from vascular disease accounts for only 10% to 20% of the cases of COBS (Terry and Wisniewski, 1975). Cerebral degenerative illness accounts for the majority of cases of COBS in the elderly, the most common being Alzheimer's disease, which causes loss of cells in the cerebral cortex and the formation of specific dense masses of cells, but is not related to loss of oxygen supply to the brain (Zarit, 1979).

Diagnosing COBS is complicated because its symptoms may also be the symptoms of other conditions, such as depression or acute brain syndromes. Common symptoms include memory loss, confusion, poor judgment, disorientation, and shallow or labile affect. Differential diagnosis between COBS/acute brain syndromes and depression can often be made by the use of a mental status questionnaire or the face-hand test (Kahn et al, 1960). Persons with acute brain syndromes tend to give symbolic answers rather than right or wrong answers. Acute brain syndromes are largely reversible if they are treated.

> All too often, mentally confused older people are sent home untreated by doctors and hospitals when they are suffering from reversible confusional states — a surprising number of which are due to malnutrition, anemia, alcohol and unrecognized physical ailments including congestive heart failure, infections and even fecal impaction. Sometimes these conditions are drug induced. For example, doctors have created acute brain disorders through the use of tranquilizers. (Butler, 1975)

In some cases once a person is diagnosed as senile, no further assessment is done, and the person's condition is considered untreatable.

Some doctors advocate treating all cases of what appears to be COBS as if it were depression, through supportive relationship and/or with mild antidepressants. Many patients improve, but there is still controversy because depression may be only a part of a person's condition. Whatever the cause, brain syndromes interfere significantly with functioning in meeting one's own needs, increase the level of risk, and may arouse frustrated and angry responses from caregivers. Zarit (1979) suggests five ways to help the caregiver through counseling: (1) provide information about the disorder; (2) give caregiver permission to meet his own needs; (3) respond to the major behavioral problems of the impaired person; (4) arrange for respite or alternative care if the caregiving burden becomes too great; and (5) help the caregiver maximize the affected individual's abilities. If the person has no capable and available family or other caregiver, provision of protective services may enable the person to remain safely in the community. "The person's functioning and well-being are likely to be maintained better at home than in a nursing home" (Zarit, 1979). The less relocation, the less the potential decompensation.

Depression

Depression in the elderly is common and may be chronic or reactive in response to some recent loss, or the retriggering of feelings associated with a past loss where the grief process was incomplete. Depression is frequent, recurring, and often chronic because additional losses occur. Burnside (1973) also includes the following as mental health problems: loneliness caused by confinement, isolation, immobility, meaninglessness, loss of a reason to care, and loss of a reason to live.

There also appears to be a close relation between the presence of significant physical illness and depression in old age. Older persons seem to tolerate the loss of love objects and status better than a loss in physical health. Physical impairment often leads to confinement and isolation. It also disrupts interests and activities which contribute to self-esteem. The impact of illness and the combination of isolation and loss of self-esteem result in depression (Pfeiffer and Busse, 1973).

Schizophrenia

Another common mental illness of the elderly is schizophrenia, a subject not often discussed because many of the most disturbed patients are in hospitals or nursing homes and those in the community are invisible or are assumed to be senile. Those cared for by family may be at risk as they grow older as caregiving parents or siblings also age or die. Some are even pushed into inappropriate caregiving roles when the original family caregivers become mentally or physically impaired and no other family members are available to provide care. A significant number of cases of abuse and neglect have been attributed to this particular reversed caregiving relationship. For example:

> Mr. and Mrs. P raised two sons in a sheltered, isolated and dominated manner. Mr. P committed suicide when son TP was 16. One son left successfully and married. TP joined the army at 18 and was diagnosed as schizophrenic. He came home, and his mother took care of him until she was 75 and broke her hip. Then he cared for her but allowed no medical care, gave her alcohol and some food daily, and threw excrement in the backyard. People complained but he refused any help. His psychiatrist was disinterested. After three years, Mrs. P died. TP cleaned the house, sold it, and moved away.

Within the individuals with both mental and physical impairment, symptoms and characteristics interact, leading to less ability for self-care, greater resistance to receiving help, and increased deterioration and risk.

DEPENDENCIES

The process of aging is accompanied by certain normal dependencies described by Blenkner (1969) as falling into four categories: (1) economic dependency which results from changing from a productive to a consumer status in the economy; (2) physical dependency which arises from diminishing strength, decreasing sensory acuity, slower reflexes, and less energy so that activities of daily living become more and more difficult to perform; (3) mental dependency coming from a decline in the power of mentation which in advanced age forces the old person to rely on others, and (4) social dependency which stems from losses of persons who have been important, the loss of roles, the loss of contemporaneity — all of which move the older person toward isolation and increasing dependency. Dependency in old age can thus be related to loss. The multiple losses confronting older persons have been extensively described (Butler and Lewis, 1973).

Normal dependency in old age is ordinarily exaggerated by the presence of physical and/or mental impairment. The greater impairment the older person suffers, the more dependent he becomes on others. As his dependency increases, so does his vulnerability. He becomes more anxious, and the expression of his anxiety can result in his becoming a prime target for a response such as abuse.

In her discussion of unmet needs and dependencies of the elderly, Blenkner (1969) discusses three types of solutions or partial solutions available: (1) self-solutions, such as restricted consumption, withdrawal, conservation of energy and reminders to jog memory; (2) kinship solutions, that is, greater dependence on family, and (3) societal solutions, social insurances, public housing, services, and supplements. She states:

> Kinship solutions, are sensible and valid solutions up to a point, but if carried too far, they become destructive to both the old and their kin. An excessive burden of care can so overwhelm a family as to actually endanger its members' physical, emotional, and social stability or else result in a complete and irreversible rejection of the old person with all the accompanying guilt and suffering (Blenkner, 1969).

The success of kinship solutions depends on the quality of the relationship and the extent of the dependency.

How much dependency is normal? Our cultural values are unclear. Brody (1979) reaffirms "the psychological truth that interdependence is normal and healthy throughout the life cycle." Clark (1969), however, states: "Only by being independent can an American be truly a person, self-respecting, worthy of concern and the esteem of others." Children are expected to be dependent but to move toward independence and, once that status is achieved, dependence is sanctioned only in times of mourning, illness, or crisis. Old age is a legitimate excuse for dependency only if the dependency terminates within a short time. Those who do not die on time impose strain on others and are defined as a threat to society (Glaser and Strauss, 1968). Being a burden means existing in a social status lacking reciprocity, with nothing of value to provide in exchange for care. Dowd (1975) and Blau (1964) in their discussions of exchange theory recognize that persons who are dependent, who have no other capability to reward and no access to power, use their "humble capacity to comply" as the sole means of rewarding caregivers. Refusal to comply and resisting direction seem a desperate attempt to regain power in a dependent relationship and lead to some of the conflict between caregivers and receivers. Recognition of impending or real dependency arouses feelings of anxiety, guilt and ambivalence in the older adult and a lowering of self-esteem. It also arouses conflicting, and sometimes inappropriate, responses in adult caregiving children. Dependence is associated with disapproval, lessened respect, displeasure and sometimes overt hostility (Kalish, 1967). Kirkpatrick (1955) notes several inappropriate family responses to dependency: (1) parents may resist and struggle to maintain their positions of authority and decision-making rights, even while gradually accepting extensive care from adult children; (2) children may push parents into dependency while still capable; (3)

children may attempt to remain and insist on remaining dependent and subject to parents' authority long after it is appropriate; and (4) the aging parent may choose dependency when it is inappropriate.

Becoming dependent for an extended period of time clearly lowers the status of the elderly person and makes relationships more risky. Having little to offer as reward and behaving in a manner inappropriate for an adult and contrary to expectation diminish the possibility of positive relationships with caregivers who themselves only find socially sanctioned support for the caregiving role for short periods of time. There are some similarities to the child-care role but there is much greater social support for caregiving offered by the parent of a child. Also, a child has never been anything but a child so there are no old relationship expectations to discard, and the child will improve, advance, grow and become independent — impossibilities for the dependent elder.

The elder group defined as mentally and physically impaired often must be dependent to survive. Many have family members able to meet their needs and accept their dependency, but others have family relationships of disharmony, conflict, and even physical and psychological abuse or neglect, perhaps the result of the family's inability to cope with care perceived as too great a burden. Some of these elderly are then in need of protective services.

OLDER PERSONS WITH PROTECTIVE PROBLEMS

The older person in need of protective services is often both mentally and physically impaired. Particularly vulnerable are those elderly who are not institutionalized and 60 years of age or older; mentally incapable; unable to maintain minimum social standards of self-care; unable to meet food, shelter, or warmth needs and unable to manage financial affairs; dangerous to themselves or others as a consequence of mental impairment; lacking relatives or other individuals able and willing to provide assistance.

The protective clients in the Cleveland Protective Services for Old Persons program of the Chronic Illness Center meet the criteria described above in varying degrees. All of the clients are older; they live in the community; mental and physical impairments are usually present; there are more women than men among the population served; some are living alone, others with a spouse or significant other who is either also impaired or unable to cope with problems; all are experiencing a decreased ability to function in daily living. This is a population at risk, and vulnerability to abuse is especially high.

Typically, these protective clients do not seek service — and they are not usually able to respond positively to whatever informal supports may be offered. They are often resistant for a number of reasons. Their energy level is low (organic damage has drained and limited them). Thinking processes are no longer intact. The ability to make judgments is impaired. For many, there is an overwhelming sense of loss of control. The resistance may be a cover-up for desperation. Often the frail older person is trying to hang on to whatever small sphere of control is left. Previous experiences with others who have sought to direct and control him now make it impossible for him to trust anyone who is trying to help.

Loss of function in the impaired older person makes him feel more vulnerable. For example, he finds it more difficult and slower to get around. He no longer has the strength to stand up for any length of time. He knows that he cannot defend himself if it should become necessary. Above all, he is becoming more frustrated with having to recognize the extent of his limitations. Is it any wonder that he becomes anxious? Anxiety manifests itself in many ways. As the older person struggles with the sense of loss, as the impact of a chronic problem which is not going to go away strikes him, more feelings may be expressed. The ill older person is less able to control his emotions. He may cry more, be irritable, or become angry and combative. Unfortunately, his behavior may become less tolerable to those upon whom he depends for assistance.

FAMILY INTERACTIONS

Most mentally and physically impaired elderly have local adult children, sometimes grandchildren and other relatives, and to a large extent they rely on these relatives for the help they require. This group has a need to be dependent on other human beings to some extent. Although frequency of interaction has been documented by Shanas (1979) and many others, only a few studies have addressed the quality of these relationships (Blenkner, 1969, 1965; Brody, 1979; Clark, 1969; Johnson and Bursk, 1977; Kalish, 1967; Robinson and Thurnher, 1979; Streib, 1972).

One study (Johnson and Bursk, 1977) explored the affective quality of relationships that elderly people have with their adult children from the perspective of both persons, and toward understanding the social, psychological, and environmental variables that influence the affective quality. Results indicated that better quality relationships usually existed when the elderly parent was engaged in activities and kept busy. In general, the better perceived relationships were associated with parents who were in better health and independent, and not restricted in choice of daily activities. When the elderly relative was more seriously impaired and when family relationships were already strained, the problem was exacerbated. The study concluded that persons in good health are not as likely to experience problems adjusting to old age. The ill elderly not only seem to experience difficulties in adjustment, but may also experience problems in family relationships. A combination of negative factors including society's attitude toward aging, may result in lowered self-esteem. Poor health can increase the elderly parent's dependency on his adult child with an increase in resentment by the child and increasing frustration by the older person.

Elderly persons who are abused are often persons with both mental and physical impairment who are housebound or limited in ambulation and dependent upon a relative for meeting essential needs. Abuse, whether physical or psychological abuse, severe neglect, or exploitation, is a behavior which occurs in the interaction between caregiver and victim.

Special stresses exist from caring for an impaired relative and are related to the more general problems of expectation, interaction, and behavior of elderly and their caretakers, particularly adult children. All adult children and parents have an array of expectations of the parent-child relationship and of their roles. The role changes and alterations in dependent relationships create sufficient stress, resulting in the occurrence of abusive behavior within some relationships when other factors support such behavior. It is unlikely that problems within the relationship alone are responsible for abuse. Some researchers have indicated that satisfaction and morale regularly decrease between elderly and their children just as dependency and frequency of interaction increase (Robinson and Thurnher, 1979; Simos, 1973; Troll, 1971). Steinman (1979) refers to a family "rejoining" in later life at time of family need, death, illness, increased impairment, or for related reasons. Family relationships often follow an hourglass pattern with frequent intense interaction at the time children are growing up, followed by a period of diminished interaction and then again frequent and intense interaction when elderly parents and adult children rejoin. Long-standing problems and unresolved conflicts from childhood and adolescence may have been dormant for years, only to be reactivated when issues of control, responsibility, and dependence appear in later life. The intensity of some resurrected conflicts, especially when coupled with unclear or overwhelming expectations and responsibility in caring for a mentally or physically impaired person, makes any satisfactory caretaking arrangement difficult. Other new conflicts may also emerge related to recent norm shifts which focus on individual needs, rights, and self-fulfillment.

> Mrs. M (76) lived in a closet-sized room with the shades drawn, in a small bed with side rails. She was withdrawn, contracted, and lived in her own separate world, thinking her contracted leg was her baby. Her

divorced daughter and four teenage grandchildren shared the attractive suburban home where she lived. The household was totally disorganized; the daughter was intelligent, passive, and immobilized. The grandchildren were disinterested. Another daughter did not want Mrs. M, but no one would allow nursing home care because they feared losing the mother's family home. The daughters were poor as children and would not give up what they now had. Nursing home care was finally arranged for when Medicaid no longer required a lien on the house.

Women are usually caregivers for the elderly but today's women are increasingly employed, divorced, or pursuing their own satisfactions. The elder parent's generation grew up supporting the expectation that adult children took care of aging parents. Today's adult children may have witnessed their parents in similar caretaking roles but these adult children have broader options that receive more societal support. Many adults, because of intense emotional conflicts, are badly equipped to undertake extensive responsibility for the mentally or physically impaired parent. Brody (1979) asks the crucial question: "At what point does the expectation of filial responsibility become social irresponsibility?" At one time, giving money to elders, sometimes to the extent that the adult children became impoverished, was considered "good for moral fiber and increases love for needy parents" (Schorr, 1960). Such thinking is no longer considered valid and elders now appear to place higher value on affection and respect.

Blenkner (1965) discussed "filial maturity" as the developmental task of middle age in which the parent comes to be seen as an individual by the adult child who becomes responsible for that parent. Brody (1979) goes on to point out that "if the adult must acquire the capacity to be depended on, the elderly parent must have the capacity to be appropriately dependent and thus to permit such growth." Many parents, impaired or not, are unable to allow such change. This growth cannot be achieved in a vacuum unrelated to the the total family. Filial maturity or filial responsibility cannot be achieved by all adult children or other family caregivers. To assume that a family can care for all mentally or physically impaired is an invalid and dangerous assumption that has led to severe abuse and death of elderly parents. In addition to caregivers lacking the particular qualities of filial maturity, some extremely impaired and dependent elderly are left to the care of adult children who are mentally ill, mentally retarded, alcoholic and — in general — irresponsible. Some of these impaired caregivers only assume the caregiving role when the parent becomes too incapacitated to care for the children. Interference in these distorted family systems without consent of caregiver or client is almost impossible in states without adequate adult protection laws.

Mrs. S, a frail, elderly, nonambulating, and mentally impaired woman was abruptly removed from the hospital by her brain-damaged, alcoholic, verbally abusive daughter who had, until this time, been cared for by her mother. The hospital could not intervene. The daughter repeatedly stated how much she loved her mother but she allowed her to sit in one chair for six weeks, and neighbors and relatives witnessed the mother being beaten. No one would sign a complaint. Workers from the agency would come in and listen to daughter's harangue but were allowed to do very little. When the mother's head had curled so low that she could no longer swallow, her daughter finally permitted hospitalization. This time the agency put great pressure on the hospital and the court to arrange guardianship, and the mother was placed permanently in a nursing home where she improved to a near independent level. The daughter, protesting and proclaiming her ongoing love for her mother, was eventually subjected to probate, declared incompetent, and later placed in the same nursing home as the mother.

SUPPORTS AND INTERVENTIONS

There are many reasons why caregivers find it difficult to cope with some behavior of mentally and physically impaired older persons. The tolerance of debility in elderly dependents by supporters at home was the subject of a study at University College Hospital and Whittington Hospital in London (Sanford, 1975). Most of the problems that caregivers felt unable to cope with centered around future home management. The most frequent problem was that of sleep disturbance in which the care provider was awakened regularly at night by the dependent. This factor generated the most animosity in caregivers. However, no evidence of "granny-battering" was found.

Factors contributing to the feelings of burden by caregivers of elderly persons with senile dementia were studied (Zarit et al, 1980). The level of burden measured was less than expected, considering the complexity of many of the cases studied. (Subjects had considerable cognitive and behavioral impairment, memory problems, restlessness, and neglect of self-care.) It was expected that feelings of burden would relate to the extent of behavior problems, but this was not so. Rather, the extent of burden reported was associated with the social supports available, specifically the number of visitors to the household. The ability of the caregivers to cope with the stress generated by behavior problems may depend on other supports available to them. The potential for abuse might also be considered in relationship to the availability of supports to the caregiver of the impaired elderly person.

The services that the Chronic Illness Center provide to the frail and impaired elderly have been developed within an organizational structure dependent upon the building of support networks for its clients. We know from clinical experience that it is impossible to maintain the more severely impaired older person without essential supports from one or more informal helpers. We are also aware that informal caregivers must receive emotional support and encouragement from formal service providers in addition to any direct services those organizations may provide to the client. Otherwise, the caregivers become so "burned out" that they tend to withdraw from the helping role. Our experience has been substantiated by empirical research (Shanas, 1979; Cantor, 1975; United States Comptroller General's Office, 1977).

The Center's program is recognized for its provision of relatively intense service offered at frequent intervals. (All clients are visited on an average of every ten days. Many are seen weekly, and, during crises, may be seen daily.) Staff visits focus on assessment, counseling, health monitoring, and the provision of concrete services, such as help with shopping, bill paying, and accompaniment to clinics. Homemakers and home health aides may also provide assistance. Even this range of services is not sufficient to maintain the severely impaired in the community. Additional help with meals, transportation, various chores, and checking on must be solicited from informal sources if the more severely impaired are to be maintained. Thus, our approach can be related to Litwak's balance theory (1968) that suggests that effective care requires expertise provided by formally organized services complemented by informal care providers.

Experience has shown that family members and others who may be drawn into the caregiving role are usually not prepared to deal with the kinds of problems presented by the impaired older person. They need help in assuming such a role. The lack of preparation in caregiving may contribute to the potential for abuse of the impaired older person. The ability to tolerate and dispel the types of frustration that can be generated by watching a relative or friend gradually deteriorate or by experiencing the anguish of not being able to make the older person understand may be a deciding factor as to whether or not abuse actually occurs. In other words, a sense of helplessness could trigger such a response. Feeling helpless can be related to not knowing or not being prepared as to what to do.

Since 1976, the Isabella Geriatric Center in New York City has been conducting training programs for families of the mentally impaired elderly (Safford, 1980). The program has included relatives of mentally impaired aged in the community as well as those in nursing homes. Participants ranged in age from age 20 to age 80 and included spouses, siblings, children, grandchildren, nieces, and nephews of mentally impaired aged.

Physical, psychological and social causes of mental impairment were presented as basic knowledge. Behavioral consequences of brain damage in the aged were clarified, practical actions to be taken in providing protective care were described, the absence of satisfactory solutions was recognized, and how to deal with the institutional system of the nursing home and sort out the many problems such a system presents were taught.

The groups shared common problems, talked out the feelings evoked by the behavior of an impaired loved one, discussed community resources, and organized family councils. Participants developed a need to continue with their group on a long-term basis and, as a consequence, a support group was formed which continued to meet for two years.

The training program provided the relatives of the mentally impaired aged knowledge needed for more rational behavior for the needs of the impaired elderly and their own needs. The support group served to help avert unnecessary institutionalization. Various aspects of the experience diffused some of the frustration and anger felt by the caregivers when they found themselves confronted with problems for which they had not been previously prepared.

The experience of the Chronic Illness Center is in keeping with the report of the program benefits at the Isabella Geriatric Center. CIC staff offered leadership and training to support groups of caregivers, and the resulting experiences substantiate the conclusions reached by the New York City program. Such common experiences result in the conclusion that lack of knowledge and understanding of the behavior of the mentally impaired coupled with lack of support networks and significant reference groups for caregivers may contribute to the potential for abuse among impaired older persons.

CONCLUSION

Elderly persons, especially the old old who are mentally and physically impaired, are vulnerable and particularly susceptible to abuse, neglect, or exploitation. The greater the impairment the older person suffers, the more dependent on others he becomes. As his dependency increases so does his vulnerability. Becoming dependent for an extended period of time places the older person in a lower status and increases his risk in relationship. The presence of complex care needs and altered mental functioning may place a heavy burden upon the caregiver.

Society expects family members to assume the caregiving role, but this is not always possible. The family member may himself be impaired—he may be alcoholic or very old or mentally or physically ill. Emotional conflicts, differences in expectations or lack of understanding may exist. Abuse may follow.

To meet the needs that family or others cannot fulfill, the community must respond by providing adequate protective and supportive services backed by effective protective service legislation. Feelings of burden by caregivers have been associated with the availability of social supports. Support networks for clients are inherent in the services provided by the Chronic Illness Center to the frail impaired elderly.

Specific factors precipitating the abuse of the mentally and physically impaired elderly are complex and remain to be defined. The challenge to both research and practice is great.

BIBLIOGRAPHY

Blau PM: *Exchange and Power in Social Life*. New York, Wiley, 1964.

Blenkner M: Social work and the family: Relationships in later life, in Shanas E, Streib G (eds): *Social Structure and the Family: Intergenerational Relationships*. Englewood Cliffs, NJ, Prentice-Hall, 1965.

Blenkner M: The normal dependencies of aging, in Kalish R (ed): *The Dependencies of Old People, Occasional Papers in Gerontology, No. 6*. Ann Arbor, MI, Institute on Gerontology, University of Michigan, 1969.

Brody E: Aged parents and aging children, in Ragan P (ed): *Aging Parents*. Los Angeles, University of Southern California Press, The Percy Andrus Gerontology Center, 1979.

Brody E: The etiquette of filial behavior. *Aging and Human Development*. 1970;1:70–84.

Burnside IM: Mental health in the aged: The nurses' perspective, in *Aging: Prospects and Issues (revised)*. Los Angeles, University of Southern California Press, The Percy Andrus Gerontology Center, 1973.

Busse EW: Mental disorders in later life: Organic brain syndromes, in Busse EW, Pfeiffer E (eds): *Mental Illness in Later Life*. Washington, DC, American Psychiatric Association, 1973.

Butler R: *Why Survive: Being Old in America*. New York, Harper, 1975.

Butler R, Lewis M: *Aging and Mental Health: Positive Psychosocial Approaches*. St. Louis, Mosby, 1973.

Butler RN, Lewis M: *Aging and Mental Health* ed 2. St. Louis, Mosby, 1977.

Cantor M: The Formal and Informal Social Support System of Older New Yorkers. Paper presented at 10th International Congress of Gerontology, Jerusalem, Israel, 1975.

Clark M: Cultural values and dependency in later life, in Kalish RA: (ed): *The Dependencies of Old People, Occasional Papers in Gerontology no. 6*. Ann Arbor, MI, Institute on Gerontology, University of Michigan, 1969.

Dowd JJ: Aging as exchange: A preface to theory. *J Gerontol* 1975;30:585–594.

Glaser BG, Strauss AL: Temporal aspects of dying as a non-scheduled status passage, in Neugarten B (ed): *Middle Age and Aging*. Chicago, University of Chicago Press, 1968.

Johnson ES, Bursk BJ: Relationships between elderly and their adult children. *Gerontologist* 1977;17:90–96.

Kahn RL, Goldfarb A, Pollock M, et al: Brief objective measures for the determination of mental status in the aged. *Am J Psychiatry* 1960;117:326–328.

218

Kalish R: Children and grandfathers: a speculative essay on dependency. *Gerontologist* 1967;7:65–69,79.

Kastenbaum RS, Candy S: The 4% fallacy: A methodological and empirical critique of extended care facility statistics. *Aging and Human Development* 1973;4:15–21.

Kirkpatrick C: *The Family as Process and Institution.* New York, Ronald Press, 1955.

Lau E, Kosberg J: Abuse of the elderly by informal care providers. *Aging* 1979; 299–300:10–15.

Litwak E: Technological innovation and theoretical functions of primary groups and bureaucratic structures. *Am J Sociol* 1968;73:468–481.

Pfeiffer E, Busse EW: Mental disorders in later life — Affective disorders: Paranoid, neurotic, and situational reactions, in Busse EW, Pfeiffer E: *Mental Illness in Later Life.* Washington, DC, American Psychiatric Association, 1973.

Puner M: The promise of age, in *The Good Long Life.* New York, Universe Books, 1974.

Robinson B, Thurnher M: Taking care of aged parents: A family cycle transition. *Gerontologist* 1979;19:6, 586–593.

Safford F: A program for families of the mentally impaired elderly. *Gerontologist* 1980;20:656–660.

Sanford JRA: Tolerance of debility in elderly dependents by supporters at home: Its significance for hospital practice. *Br Med J* 1975;3:471–473.

Schorr A: *Filial Responsibility in the American Family.* Washington, DC, Government Printing Office, 1960.

Shanas E: Social myth as hypothesis: The case of the family relations of old people. *Gerontologist* 1979;19:3–9.

Simos BG: Adult children and their aging parents. *Social Work* 1973;18:78–85.

Sokoloff L: Cerebral circulation and metabolism in the aged, in Gershan S, Raskin A (eds): *Aging, vol 2: Genesis and Treatment of Psychologic Disorders in the Elderly.* New York, Raven, 1975.

Steiman L: Reactivated conflicts with aging parents, in Ragan P (ed): *Aging Parents.* Los Angeles, The Percy Andrus Gerontology Center, University of Southern California Press, 1979.

Streib G: Older families and their troubles: familial and social responses. *Family Co-ordinator* 1972:21:5–19.

Terry RD, Wisniewski MW: Structural and chemical changes of the aged human brain, in Gershon S, Raskin A (eds): *Aging, vol 2: Genesis and Treatment of Psychologic Disorders in the Elderly.* New York, Raven, 1975.

Troll LE: The family in later life: A decade review. in Broderick CB (ed): *A Decade of Family Research and Action.* Minneapolis, MN, National Council on Family Relations, 1971.

United States Comptroller General's Office. Report to Congress. "The Well-Being of Older People in Cleveland, Ohio." Washington, DC, General Accounting Office, 1977.

United States Department of Health, Education and Welfare: Facts about older Americans, 1978. Pub. No. (OHDS) 79-20006, Washington, DC, 1979

United States Department of Health, Education and Welfare: Statistical Notes. Pub. No. (OSDS) 78-20040, Washington, DC, 1978.

Wershow HJ: The four percent fallacy: Some further evidence and policy implications. *Gerontologist* 1976;16:52–55.

Zarit SH: The organic brain syndrome and family relationships, in Ragan P (ed): *Aging Parents*. Los Angeles, The Percy Andrus Gerontology Center, University of Southern California Press, 1979.

Zarit S, Reever K, Bach-Peterson J: Relatives of the impaired elderly: Correlates of feelings of burden. *Gerontologist* 1980;20:649–655.

13 Special Problems and Vulnerability of Elderly Women

Marilyn R. Block

Despite crime and the elderly as an issue requiring close scrutiny, accurate assessments of this problem have been relatively unavailable. It is increasingly apparent, however, that the elderly suffer painful psychological, financial, and physical losses from crime in the United States.

Victimization can be divided into three major categories: personal crimes of violence, where the victim is directly involved in the confrontation; household crimes, which do not involve personal confrontation with the victim; and fraud, which involves nonviolent confrontation in the form of misrepresentation. Victimization patterns are strongly influenced by age, area of residence (urban, suburban, rural), economic status, physical impairment, degree of isolation, and sex. Thus, victimization of the elderly is a distinctive component of the overall crime problem in the United States. The elderly as a group are "undervictimized" by personal crimes of violence and "overvictimized" by household crimes and fraud.

220

Community size is strongly related to victimization. The larger the community, the greater the likelihood of victimization. Thus, urban centers are highly conducive to crime. Individuals of low economic status are more easily and more often victimized than those in higher economic groups.

Physical impairment contributes to victimization. Age-related changes in vision, hearing, strength, coordination, and reaction speed plus fear of sustaining severe injury in a confrontation ensure that an assailant will not be faced with an aggressive reaction; rather these factors render the older victim passive in a crime. Isolation is also a factor. Those who live alone often go out alone, increasing vulnerability to street crime. The isolated individual is at great risk for household crime too, since departure from the home to do errands leaves the home unattended and a more promising target than a busy one.

Elderly women are much more vulnerable to certain types of crime and victimization than elderly men, particularly rape, purse snatching, elder abuse, burglary, and fraud (Table 13-1). Elderly women are also more fearful of crime. However, aggregate figures concerning differences in victimization by sex do not provide a complete picture. The vulnerability of older women to particular crimes is related to the race of

Table 13-1
Type of Victimization of Elderly Victims
by Race and Sex, 1975

Type of Crime	All Women	White Women	Black Women	All Men	White Men	Black Men
Personal Crimes of Violence						
Homicide	50%	25%	25%	50%	25%	25%
Rape	100	70	30	—	—	—
Robbery, armed	34	30	4	66	52	14
Robbery, strong-arm	33	25	8	67	54	13
Robbery, purse snatch	100	90	10	—	—	—
Assault	28	21	7	72	46	26
Elder abuse[a]	78	—	—	22	—	—
Household Crimes						
Burglary	50	38	12	50	37	13
Fraud	66	57	9	34	22	12

From: House of Representatives. Select Committee on Aging. Subcommittee on Housing and Consumer Interests. In search of security: a national perspective on elderly crime victimization, 1977, p 25.
[a]Derived from Block and Sinnott, 1979; Hooyman, 1980; Lau and Kosberg, 1979; Rathbone-McCuan and Voyles, 1980; O'Malley, et al, 1979.

the victim. Older black women are at greater risk of burglary, twice as often the victims of rape, and four times as often the victims of homicide as older white women; older white women are twice as likely to be victims of purse snatching and armed robbery (Table 13-2).

This chapter examines victimization to which older women are most susceptible. It also explains the special problems of older women that render them vulnerable. Finally, it addresses aids against susceptibility to victimization.

Table 13-2
Type of Victimization of Elderly Women by Race — 1975

Type of Victimization	White Women	Black Women
Homicide	0.2%	0.8%
Rape	0.5	1.0
Robbery, armed	7.2	4.1
Robbery, strong-arm	3.4	4.8
Robbery, purse snatch	32.7	16.9
Assault	2.4	3.4
Burglary	50.7	66.9
Fraud	2.9	2.1
	100.0	100.0

From: House of Representatives. Select Committee on Aging. Subcommittee on Housing and Consumer Interests. In search of security: a national perspective on elderly crime victimization, 1977, p 25.

CRIMES OF VIOLENCE

Rape

The reported incidence of rape among older women is considerably less than among younger women (Goldsmith and Goldsmith, 1976). Department of Justice data in Table 13-3 indicate that the incidence of rape occurs at varying rates.

If these data are accurate, rape of older women occurs rarely, even when the likelihood of underreporting is considered. Fallcreek and Hooyman (1980) suggest that underreporting of rape by older women is strongly influenced by: (1) feelings of powerlessness in our youth-oriented society; (2) lack of familiarity and experience with bureaucratic systems, such as law enforcement and criminal justice systems; (3) belief that nothing will be done about the crime; (4) socialization in an era which tended to attribute responsibility to the woman for being raped and consequent reluctance to acknowledge the assault publicly; and (5) fear of reprisal, since older women are disproportionately repeat victims of assault.

Table 13-3
Reported Rape and Attempted Rape by Age — 1974

Age of Victim	Rate per 1000
Adolescent women	
12–15 years	3.6
16–19 years	4.2
Young adult women	
20–24 years	6.4
25–34 years	3.7
Middle-aged women	
35–49 years	.7
50–64 years	1.1
Older women	
65 + years	.7

From: United States Department of Justice, Law Enforcement Assistance Administration, National Criminal Justice Information and Statistics Service. *Sourcebook of Criminal Justice Statistics — 1976.* p 371.

Some of the characteristics of rape are similar for young and old women. Most rapes, regardless of age, occur at night, involve physical force, and are perpetrated by a stranger. But if there are similarities, there are also marked differences. Older women are much more likely to be raped at home, brutally beaten, and raped in conjunction with a theft (Davis and Brody, 1979; Groth, 1978).

Little is known about the impact of rape on the older woman. Although the sexual aspect of the rape is more traumatic psychologically for younger women, the aggressive aspect is more traumatic for older women (Davis and Brody, 1979). This may be because older women usually have at least one chronic ailment, and fear severe injury with incomplete recovery, leading to lessened mobility and independence.

Purse Snatching

Robbery involves the use or threat of force against an individual in order to steal from him (Conklin, 1976). The prospect of physical harm is real and may be more alarming to the victim than the loss of property. Street robberies in general are more often directed toward younger victims, and where the elderly are preyed upon, males are more often victimized than females. One form of robbery, however, perpetrated primarily against older women is that of purse snatching.

Purse snatching is usually perceived as less serious than other forms of robbery since the material loss is usually minimal, the crime is most frequently perpetrated by a juvenile, and weapons are not used. The impact of purse snatching often goes beyond material loss. Many victims are shoved to the ground as the perpetrator grabs the purse, and such falls often result in some degree of physical injury. A small percentage of victims sustain injuries serious enough to require emergency hospitalization. As age increases, so does the likelihood of sustaining a serious injury.

Older women who are poor and who live in deteriorating sections of the city are the most likely victims of purse snatching because they exhibit predictable behavior patterns. They carry cash instead of checks or credit cards, they walk or rely on public transportation instead of driving, and they tend to go out alone instead of in groups. Thus, they are exceedingly vulnerable to being approached from behind at a fast run.

Elder Abuse

Recent explorations (Block and Sinnott, 1979; Douglass, Hickey, and Noël, 1980; Hooyman; 1980; Lau and Kosberg, 1979; O'Malley et al, 1979; Rathbone-McCuan and Voyles, 1980) of victimization of the elderly have identified the phenomenon of elder abuse. This type of victimization is perpetrated predominantly by middle-aged children (usually daughters or daughters-in-law) against their parents. More often than not the victim is an older woman. Elder abuse takes several forms: physical abuse, including direct beatings, lack of food, lack of medical care, and lack of supervision; psychological abuse, including verbal assault, threats, frightening, and isolation; material abuse, including theft or misuse of money or property; and violation of rights, including forced removal from home or forced entry into nursing home (Block and Sinnott, 1979; Lau and Kosberg, 1979). The victim usually resides with the abuser and tends to be moderately to severely impaired. Many cannot perform simple tasks of hygiene; others are incapable of taking medication without help or of preparing a simple meal.

The problem of elder abuse has many dimensions. It is unclear why adult children resort to victimizing their aging parents. The majority of abuse appears to occur for psychological rather than economic reasons. Attacks are usually repetitive, ie, they occur as a consistent pattern rather than as isolated incidents. Psychological abuse is more common than physical abuse. While reported physical and economic forms of abuse are categorized as mild to moderate, reported psychological abuse is generally severe.

In general, abuse victims are vulnerable because of very poor health. The hard work of caring for a relative with increasing disabilities may not be welcomed in family situations where the adult child is nearing retirement age and anticipating a freer, more relaxed life or in situations where job responsibilities reduce time available for caregiving.

HOUSEHOLD CRIME

Burglary is the most frequently perpetrated crime against older women, who often are not able to afford devices that might be a deterrent to burglary, such as deadbolts on doors and pins on windows. Often widowed, they usually live alone, which increases their vulnerability. After age 60 the rate of burglaries decreases; it is lowest for the old-old, and highest for the young-old. Older women are less mobile, less likely to be employed, and more likely to be in the home for extended periods of time than are women between the ages of 60 and 70. The household of the young-old woman, who is more active and more likely to be out of the home, is more vulnerable to forced entry.

FRAUD

Crimes of fraud, bunco, and confidence games are directed primarily toward the senior citizen, and women are much more vulnerable to this type of nonviolent crime than men. The isolation and economic constraints of most older women make them more vulnerable to fraud than older men.

The premise of fraud is to dupe an individual into giving away a large sum of money under the pretext of helping someone or making money quickly. Fraud is widespread because those who have been victimized are embarrassed and afraid to report the crime. They fear they will appear either senile and unable to care for themselves or greedy. It has been estimated that only 20% of fraud victims cooperate with the police. Thus con artists usually walk away from the scene of the crime unscathed. Where the elderly attempt to obtain justice by appearing in court, they make poor witnesses. Limited eyesight, which may preclude positive identification of the con artist, and uncertainty about the exact progression of events allow a defending attorney to disparage testimony. Most convictions for fraud occur when a detective has observed the crime.

Confidence Games

The two most common confidence schemes are the bank examiner and the pigeon drop. In the bank examiner con, the con artist disguises himself as a policeman, FBI agent, or Treasury agent. He calls on an elderly woman and tells her that a number of accounts at her bank, including hers, have recently had numerous large withdrawals, and that a bank employee is suspected of embezzling this money. The victims's anxiety will be high; her total cash assets are probably in that bank account. When the victim is asked whether she is willing to help catch the crooked employee, she is ready to agree. She is told to withdraw all her money and turn it over to the "agent," who will mark it and redeposit it. The victim will not discover the theft of her money until her next trip to the bank, which might be several days after turning the cash over to the "agent."

A related scheme involves hitting the same victim twice. Several weeks after turning the money over to the "bank examiner," the victim will be approached by a man who identifies himself as an IRS agent, who tells the victim he has information on the con artist. He shows her a picture of the con artist whom the victim can identify. She is then told that the con artist has a partner at the bank. The "agent" asks if the victim would be willing to withdraw money, turn it over to the "IRS agent," allow him to mark it and then redeposit it, to catch the partner. Anxious to retrieve the money originally lost, the victim will usually agree. Instead of regaining the stolen money, she ends by losing more.

Unlike the bank examiner scheme, which plays upon the desire to be helpful, the pigeon drop relies on the victim's innate greed. Con women are effective here because older women are the preferred victims, and older women will more readily talk to a strange woman on the street than they will a strange man.

Two con artists are required for the pigeon drop. The first will start a conversation with the intended victim. She will say that she is thinking about moving into the area and encourage the victim to discuss the neighborhood. She will often indicate that she is a young widow with children to support, and she has finally saved enough money for the deposit required on a nice apartment. She will flash a roll of bills to show the victim her deposit money. At this point, the second con artist approaches. She has found an unmarked envelope on the street and wants to know where there is a lost-and-found place in the neighborhood. The first con artist says she is new to the area, but the victim has lived here for many years and can help. Thus, the victim is drawn into the conversation with the second woman. In the course of deciding what to do, the envelope is opened. It contains a large amount of money and a note indicating that the money is from a lottery or off-track betting. The second woman now says that they cannot leave such a large sum in a lost-and-found where anyone could steal it. She works for a lawyer who might know what to do. The first con artist and the victim are told to wait, and the second con artist disappears with the money. She returns to say the lawyer believes it will never be claimed by the people who lost it. They can split it three ways. But the money has to be untouched for 90 days to make it legal. The lawyer wants a guarantee that the money won't be spent before the 90 days. This guarantee should be in the form of "good faith" money which will prove that the three women each have enough to live on for the three-month waiting period. The second con artist says that the lawyer pays her salary, so she doesn't have to prove anything. The first con artist says she has her apartment deposit money, which she shows to the second con artist. The victim goes to the bank to withdraw her money. If the bank insists on giving her a check, the two con artists take her to another branch to cash it. If the bank questions the amount of the withdrawal, she is instructed to tell them that she is purchasing real estate or jewelry. The victim gives the cash to the second con artist who takes it to show the lawyer — and never returns.

Consumer Fraud

One of the most common consumer crimes used to victimize the elderly involves the sale of supplementary health insurance and medical plans. Such plans are sold door-to-door to coerce the victim to buy on impulse.

The victim, often an older woman living alone, purchases the policy on the basis of claims made by the salesman despite the fact that these are unsupported by the printed policy. Women often spend large sums of money on premiums for policies that are virtually worthless in terms of the coverage they provide. The practice flourishes because the victims fail to check the licensing and reputation of the company selling the plan.

Mail order fraud is also used to prey on the elderly. People are encouraged to send money to secure work. Instead of obtaining a job, the victim receives a sheet of instructions on how to look for work. Other forms of mail fraud include phoney puzzle contests, estate searches, chain letter schemes, and pyramid sales schemes. Older women, often with limited skills and desperate to augment a meager income, are particularly vulnerable to this type of fraud.

Older women are also extremely vulnerable to fraudulent home repair, auto repair, and investment schemes. Most women left these matters to their husbands. When such women are alone because of divorce or widowhood, they often do not know whether the cost of a particular service is reasonable or exorbitant.

Another fraud where the elderly are particularly vulnerable involves medical quackery. Promises of quick cures for chronic problems entice them to spend billions of dollars annually. While the economic loss is devastating, of greater concern is the lack of legitimate medical intervention. Because the more serious health problems are the least responsive to treatment, those who turn to medical quacks can probably least afford to relinquish qualified medical services. The result may be a worsening of the problem or death.

FACTORS INCREASING THE
VULNERABILITY OF OLDER WOMEN

The circumstances in which many women find themselves during later life are depicted by the same factors—urban residence, low economic status, physical impairment, and isolation—that strongly influence patterns of victimization. Thus, it is hardly surprising that older women, as a group, are at high risk.

Many older women reside in urban settings, especially in central cities. Few older women are in suburbs or rural areas. Many reside in homes in deteriorating neighborhoods where they are victimized by their adolescent and young adult neighbors. Those who inhabit public housing are often accosted in elevators, stairwells, and hallways by teenagers who know that security precautions in such projects are generally inadequate or nonexistent. The economic status of older women in such housing usually precludes their moving to a better neighborhood. Women constitute 72% of the elderly poor. Low-income individuals exhibit predictable behavior patterns which make them vulnerable to crime. Because the delivery date of social security checks or other forms of income maintenance is readily available information, older women are often robbed immediately after cashing a check.

Older women are likely to acquire some kind of disability which limits their activities. Eighty-five percent of women over the age of 65 have at least one chronic health problem. Their deteriorating physical status renders them vulnerable to crime in two ways. First, their perceived physical weakness suggests them as likely targets for young criminals who might be reluctant to confront stronger, healthier individuals. Second, their fear of long-term disability as a result of criminal confrontation makes older women far less likely to resist the perpetrator of the crime. Most older women are so fearful of losing their independence and mobility from broken bones or other injury that they do not offer even token resistance to an assailant.

Because of differing mortality rates, women often spend a portion of their later years alone. In the ten year span between 1965–1976, there was a 40% increase in the number of women aged 65 and over who live alone (Dovell & Vanhorenbeck, 1979). Almost four times as many older women as older men live alone. This phenomenon is partially the result of increasing numbers of older people who prefer living independently as long as health and income permit. Adult children may also be less able or willing to share their home with an older parent. This trend toward independent living has implications for victimization of older women. Such women are at greater risk for household crime than women who reside with others. And women who live alone often go out alone, thus increasing vulnerability to street crime.

Older women are also easily victimized because of their unfamiliarity with financial matters. Many older women were not expected to participate in financial decisions. After being widowed, they are forced to make decisions about matters in which they have limited or no experience, and are easily duped by unscrupulous salesmen and con artists through consumer fraud and con games.

Where dwindling resources and declining health impel an older woman to move in with a middle-aged child, the threat of victimization is not necessarily eliminated. The stress of caregiving may provoke a formerly loving child to abuse. If the aging parent is in exceptionally poor health, the risk of abuse is higher. If a child is unwilling to care for the aging parent, institutionalization may be the only alternative left to the older woman.

STRATEGIES FOR CHANGE

The continuing trend among law enforcement agencies toward crime prevention and the increasing political activity of local and national organizations representing senior citizens has resulted in new priorities for legislative issues concerning crime and the elderly.

Data from victimization surveys often seriously underestimate the impact of crime on many individuals and communities (Smith, 1979). The physical, psychological, and economic aspects of victimization are devastating for the elderly; even more debilitating is the effect of *fear* of crime.

The findings from a number of recent studies convincingly indicate that fear of crime is a pervasive and onerous problem for older Americans and that women, blacks, and inner-city residents are the groups most profoundly and adversely affected by this fear. Older women have a high rate of fear of crime; according to Clemente and Kleiman (1976), 69% of aged females report fear of crime. Fear diminishes the quality of life for many older women by limiting essential trips for food and medical care and participation in social activities because they are afraid to be on the streets (United States House of Representatives, 1977).

These concerns are presently being dealt with in national programs and federal legislation which support victim assistance, crime prevention, and education programs. Four such legislative efforts deserve particular attention. Community organization efforts will also be discussed.

The Federal Crime Insurance Program (Title VI of the Housing Act of 1970) makes it possible for residents and small businesses to obtain

230

crime insurance coverage which otherwise might not be available or affordable. The federal government, through the Federal Emergency Management Agency (FEMA) acts as insurer. The program was established in response to an insurance industry practice of refusing to insure homes and businesses in high-crime neighborhoods.

The issue of compensation for victims of crimes is particularly critical to low-income groups. The impact of loss of property can be devastating to elderly on low fixed incomes who often are unable to replace their loss. One means of providing compensation is through special crime insurance policies, available at reduced rates to high-risk public housing tenants and central city residents. Insurance premiums might be part of housing subsidies to reduce the financial burden on the elderly poor.

The Crime Control Act of 1976, an amendment to the Omnibus Crime Control and Safe Streets Act of 1968, requires that states provide activities that attempt to prevent crime against the elderly in order to qualify for Law Enforcement Assistance Administration (LEAA) grants. Local communities may use the grants to encourage community and citizen participation in crime prevention.

The Justice System Improvement Act of 1979 reauthorizes and restructures the Department of Justice Assistance program for state and local law enforcement and criminal justice improvement. This act authorizes the Justice Department to retain under its auspices the LEAA and, within the LEAA, the Office of Community Anticrimes Program, which has special priority to fund programs to assist the elderly.

The Public Housing Security Program, of the Housing and Community Development Amendments of 1980, provides support for the continuation of the Public Housing Security Demonstration Program, first authorized in the 1978 Housing Authorizations bill. The goals of the program are to reduce crime and the fear of crime among residents living in and around public housing and to identify the crime-reducing approaches and strategies that are most effective in various types of public housing environments.

Community Organization Efforts

Older women in high-crime areas have been assisted in a variety of ways by community efforts that have evolved out of these federal legislative initiatives. The strategies employed to reduce crime have taken numerous forms. Among the more successful approaches are:

1. Household assessments. Conducted by the police or trained volunteers, security needs such as dead bolts and peepholes

on doors, window locks, and more adequate outside lighting are pointed out. Elderly householders are often assisted in installing security devices, an important consideration for older women who may be unfamiliar with implementing the improvement but cannot afford to have the work done.

2. General educational seminars. Simple instruction is offered on issues related to personal safety. The risk of purse snatching is reduced by teaching older women to carry cash and credit cards in pockets instead of in a purse. Techniques to avoid assault and minimize the risk of burglary are stressed. Seniors are also given information concerning specific types of consumer fraud, medical quackery, and bunco schemes, so they will be less likely to fall prey to these.

3. Media campaigns. Public service radio and television announcements and printed material (brochures, posters, flyers) alert seniors to the more common bunco schemes.

4. Professional training. Various professionals and para-professionals who work with the public are trained to help the elderly avoid victimization. For example, bank personnel are trained to recognize con games and so can offer information regarding the potential for victimization to aging customers.

Other examples of successful crime prevention activities undertaken by individuals and organizations include: group check cashing, utility bill paying, and grocery shopping activities; regularly scheduled discussions between neighborhood residents and local police; public meetings devoted to discussion of crime and victimization; organized residential burglary checks; and cooperative efforts to watch over neighbors' dwellings (Younger, 1976).

IMPLICATIONS

Although community efforts have been quite successful in preventing crime, it is unclear what degree of success has been met in reducing fear of crime. The highly publicized issue of victimization of the elderly and the programs designed to sensitize elders to be cautious about their physical safety and material well-being may exacerbate fear of crime even as actual crime rates are declining.

Fear of crime continues to be a major concern of many older women. If they have not been personally victimized, they often know of friends, relatives, or neighbors who have. Decreasing physical strength compounds this fear, since a minor injury can result in long-term or even permanent physical impairment.

The poorest elderly are more afraid of crime than the more affluent. The poorly educated are more fearful than the more educated. Older adults in poor health are more likely to be afraid than those in better health. And those who have difficulty in getting transportation are more likely to be afraid than those who do not (Eve and Eve, 1981).

Fear of crime will probably be a concern to future cohorts of older women. Today's middle-aged and young women continue to be less well-educated than their male counterparts. They earn 40% less than their male co-workers and, thus, can anticipate poverty in old age more than men. As is true for older women today, limited financial resources will most likely prevent future older women from living outside those areas in cities that are subject to crime.

In an effort to avoid victimization, many older women withdraw from a variety of activities. They become prisoners within their own homes, fearful of walking the streets. It is a growing national tragedy that the quality of life for many older women entails a choice between becoming a victim or a self-imposed prisoner. Unfortunately, the picture is not likely to change in the near future.

BIBLIOGRAPHY

Block MR, Sinnott JD: (eds): *The Battered Elder Syndrome: An Exploratory Study*. College Park, MD, University of Maryland Center on Aging, 1979.

Clemente F, Kleiman MB: Fear of crime among the aged. *Gerontologist* 1976; 16:207–210.

Conklin JE: Robbery, the elderly, and fear: An urban problem in search of a solution, in Goldsmith J and Goldsmith SS (eds): *Crime and the Elderly: Challenge and Response*. Lexington, MA, Lexington Books, 1976.

Davis LJ, Brody EM: *Rape and Older Women: A Guide to Prevention and Protection*. Rockville, MD, National Institute of Mental Health, 1979.

Douglass RL, Hickey T, Noël C: *A Study of Maltreatment of the Elderly and Other Vulnerable Adults*. Ann Arbor, University of Michigan Institute of Gerontology, 1980.

Dovell S, Vanhorenbeck S: *The Impact of Federal Housing Programs on the Elderly*. Library of Congress Report No. 79-176E. Washington, Congressional Research Service, 1979.

Eve RA, Eve SB: *The Effects of Powerlessness, Fear of Social Change, and Social Integration on Fear of Crime among the Elderly*. Paper presented at the 12th International Congress of Gerontology, Hamburg, Germany, July 1981.

Fallcreek S, Hooyman N: *A Neglected Population: Older Women as Victims of Violence*. Paper presented at First World Congress of Victimology, Washington, DC, August 1980.

Goldsmith J, Goldsmith SS: (eds): *Crime and the Elderly: Challenge and Response.* Lexington, MA, Lexington Books, 1976.

Groth A: The older rape victim and her assailant. *J Geriatr Psychiatry* 1978;11: 203–215.

Hooyman N: *Familial Abuse of the Elderly in Seattle, Wa.* Seattle, University of Washington, unpublished paper, 1980.

Lau E, Kosberg J: *Abuse of the Elderly by Informal Care Providers: Practice and Research Issues.* Paper presented at the 31st Annual meeting of the Gerontological Society, Dallas, TX, November, 1979.

O'Malley H, Segars H, Perez R, et al: *Elder Abuse in Massachusetts: A Survey of Professionals and Paraprofessionals.* Boston, Legal Research and Services for the Elderly, 1979.

Rathbone-McCuan E, Voyles B: *Case Detection Issues for Abused Elderly Parents.* Paper presented at the Regional Public Welfare Association Conference, St. Louis, MO, 1980.

Smith RJ: *Crimes Against Persons: Implications for Policy-makers and Practitioners.* Washington: The International Federation on Aging, 1979.

United States Department of Justice. Law Enforcement Assistance Administration. National Criminal Justice Information and Statistics Service. *Sourcebook of Criminal Justice Statistics–1976.* Washington, Government Printing Office, 1977.

United States House of Representatives. Select Committe on Aging. Subcommittee on Housing and Consumer Interests. *In search of security: a national perspective on elderly crime victimization.* Pub. No. 95-87. Report, 95th Cong., 1st Sess., Washington, Government Printing Office, 1977.

Younger EJ: The California experience: Prevention of criminal victimization of the elderly. *Police Chief* 1976;43:13–16.

14 Abuse of the Physically Disabled Elderly

Joanne L. Steuer

Approximately 20 to 24 years have been added to the life span of Americans since 1900 primarily through improved medical care and nutrition in early life. Reductions in mortality at the far end of the life span have not been as dramatic as those in the early years. Nevertheless, white men and women aged 65 years in 1976 could expect to live to age 78.7 and 83.1 respectively while nonwhite men and women could expect to live to 78.8 and 82.6 years of age. The often noted sex difference for mortality rates in late life is growing larger, eg, differences between male and female rates, all favoring female longevity, range from 0.7 years in 1900 for the total population to 4.3 years in 1976. One possible interpretation of this increase is that there is a shift in causes of mortality with infectious and parasitic illnesses and maternal mortality decreasing and chronic degenerative diseases, such as heart disease, malignant neoplasms, and cerebrovascular diseases rising in importance (Siegal, 1980).

Illness and Disability

Of people age 65 years and over, 38% have arthritis, 29% have hearing impairments, 20% have visual impairments, 20% have heart conditions, and 20% have hypertension without heart involvement (Kovar, 1980). Although people aged 65 and over comprise only 11% to 12% of the population, they account for 29% of money spent on personal health care, 15% of all visits to office-based physicians, and 34% of days used in short-stay hospitals (Kovar, 1977). Thus, medical technology has extended the life span by preventing death at the cost of perpetuating chronic illness (Gruenberg, 1980; Kovar, 1980).

Physical illness and physical disability are of course not synonymous. Physical illness can be acute or chronic; treatment can be remedial or palliative; residual can be nonexistent or impede further independent function. Physical disability can also be temporary or chronic, mild or severe, not impede function or be a handicap. The concern here is with persons who are handicapped by their disability and are, therefore, dependent on others for some activities of daily living.

Results from a 1975 national survey indicate that 14% of community residents age 65 and over are restricted in physical mobility, ie, they are either bedfast, housebound, or able to go outside only with difficulty (Shanas, 1980). Twelve percent of Americans age 65 or more have major limitations in their ability to care for themselves. Excluding bedfast persons, capacity for self-care decreases for each five-year age group after age 65, until in the oldest age group (over age 80) 27% of women and 17% of men have difficulty with self-care. In all categories more blacks are restricted than caucasians, and more women than men.

People who cannot function independently must seek help from others, usually their families, to the point that 80% of home health care needs are provided by families (Brody et al, 1978; Shanas, 1979a; Shanas, 1979b; U.S. National Center for Health Statistics, 1978). Thus the presence of a family caring unit is an important predictor of placement for chronically ill and disabled elderly. However, families do not necessarily provide all the help needed, as indicated in one study in which about half of the people who were already receiving care from another person said they needed more help (Branch, 1980). Moreover, family caring units are not necessarily caring social units. Families can be violent and violating environments.

Family Violence

An elderly woman who lived in her daughter's apartment entered an acute care hospital with multiple decubiti. The woman, totally confined to bed, could not care for herself, or even turn herself. The daughter worked all day and could neither afford nor find home day-care help. The daughter said she loved her mother and therefore didn't want to send her to an institution. The decubiti healed, and the patient was discharged to her daughter's home.

A 65-year-old woman with emphysema entered a pulmonary rehabilitation program for training in energy conservation and ambulation. She lived with a son, daughter-in-law, and grandson. Her legs were in severe contractures and the muscles had atrophied. There was no way to straighten her legs to make them weight bearing. She told the hospital staff she had not been out of bed for the previous six months. Her daughter-in-law said she wasn't "strong enough" to get the patient out of bed and it was too late when the son returned home from work. The patient, who was also grossly underweight, stated that her daughter-in-law could not cook. The only meal she ate was dinner which her son cooked. The patient refused to be placed in a skilled nursing facility and was discharged home.

Such case examples abound in the literature on family abuse of the elderly, and cases like the above do not appear exceptional. Although there are few data available on the incidence or prevalence of family abuse of the elderly, one group of researchers estimated there were approximately one million cases of elder abuse in the United States (Block and Sinnott, 1979). This estimate makes elder abuse as common as child abuse. Another study found 9.6% of persons using a home care agency were abused (Lau and Kosberg, 1979). Data from 1977 for Kentucky, which has an Adult Protective Services Act, indicates 55% to 60% of 1037 reported cases concerned adults aged 60 to 90 years (Kentucky Bureau for Social Services, 1980). The little evidence available indicates the physically and mentally disabled are most vulnerable to abuse. Three studies report 75% to 100% of cases of abused elderly had either physical or mental disabilities (Block and Sinnott, 1979; Lau and Kosberg, 1979; Steuer and Austin, 1980).

These data raise the question: Why are the physically ill and disabled elderly particularly vulnerable to family abuse? Are there characteristics of the illness or the old person which cause this phenomenon; are characteristics of the abuser/caretaker more pertinent; are the causes societal? Neglect as well as actual physical or psychological abuse are included in the definition of abusive behavior.

Characteristics of the Disease

A few of the physical events likely to lead to disability in elderly persons and the possible impact of these events and subsequent disability on patient and caretaker are discussed below.

Stroke   A stroke or cerebrovascular accident (CVA) is a "focal neurological deficit lasting more than 24 hours and due to a presumed local disturbance in the blood supply to brain" (Garraway, 1979). Although, in general, the incidence of stroke is decreasing, the chances of having a CVA increases with age so that about three-fourths of CVAs occur in people age 65 or over. Approximately 50% of persons surviving a stroke will either have no disability or be able to compensate, 40% will be disabled enough to require special services, and 10% will require total care (Mossman, 1976; Vallarino and Sherman, 1981).

The first image which comes to mind, when one hears that someone has had a stroke, is paralysis of one side of the body (hemiplegia), the affected side being determined by the laterality of the neurologic lesion. Less dramatic than hemiplegia but equally disabling are cutaneous, proprioceptive (the awareness of the body's positions in space), and visual deficits. Sense of touch, pain, and vibration may be lost in the involved extremity, making the person vulnerable to injury, for example, from hot liquids. Visual impairments may make it difficult for a person to walk without bumping into walls and objects, to control a wheelchair, or even to see food placed in front of her/him. Impaired proprioception means difficulty with so many of the movements we take for granted, such as walking.

"The extent of motor involvement does not indicate the degree of intellectual impairment" (Mossman, 1976) and so-called psychological impairments may cause the most upset for patient and family. Lesions in the left hemisphere can result in expressive or receptive aphasia making communication difficult and frustrating for caretaker and patient. The patient may not be able to say what is wanted or how she/he is feeling. Not only may the caretaker not understand the patient's needs, but also the caregiver and patient may no longer be able to share their lives. The following case is an example:

> Mr. A was the sole caregiver for his wife who had had a stroke. She was unable to walk or to care for her daily needs, and was totally aphasic. Mr. A had no outside help, friends no longer visited, and their children who lived far away could offer no assistance. Since he was unable to leave her alone, Mr. A stayed home to care for her. He would not give himself time off by taking her to a day care center because he thought she would be frightened and that the people there wouldn't understand her. The only time he left the house without her was to do some quick shopping. They previously had shared almost all recreational activities; now there was no recreation.
>
> Mr. A was severely depressed and had developed the habit of drinking a pint or more of whiskey each evening to help him "relax and sleep." He was suicidal and said he would kill his wife first because it wasn't worth living like this for either of them. He said he didn't mind taking care of her but sitting there day after day, evening after evening, not being able to talk was "killing him."

238

This may seem like an extreme reaction to loss, and perhaps it is. It is also, however, an example of how disability can affect a caretaker. Mr. A did not abuse his wife, nor did he commit suicide. He was treated for depression and eventually was able to solve some of his difficulties.

Lesions of the right hemisphere impair visual-spatial relationships and can cause impulsive behavior, poor judgment, impaired foresight and planning, and anxiety. These can occur whether or not the person appears physically intact. Families find it particularly difficult to understand why, when the patient looks all right physically, he cannot be left unsupervised. Such a patient may touch a hot stove, attempt to drive, or, with poor balance, try to walk unaided. Any of these actions can lead to serious injury.

Denial of hemiplegia (anosognosia) is common in persons with right-sided lesions (left hemiplegia). The patient neglects the paralyzed side of the body, and safety instructions tend to be useless since the patient has no concept of the impairment. Dressing can be a problem because the patient may be unable to figure out which piece of clothing goes where.

Two conditions caused by stroke, apactic dementia and emotional lability, can be confused with depression and be upsetting for families and patients. In apactic dementia the patient has abnormal emotional expression, psychomotor retardation, decreased food intake and mobility. The family may urge the patient to eat and be interested in activities; they may be frustrated by their inability to change the patient's mood. Emotional lability means the patient may laugh, or more frequently cry, inappropriately. Emotional lability has a neurologic, not psychologic, cause and can be extremely embarrassing and disconcerting.

Diabetes   More common in women than men, diabetes is caused by insufficient production of insulin. Diabetes is not in itself disabling and can be controlled by diet or medication. The chief hazard of the disease in old persons is the development of arteriosclerosis which causes poor circulation in the legs and feet. This can eventually lead to gangrene infections and amputation. Some patients adjust well to the loss of a foot or a leg, learning to use a wheelchair or, in some cases, a prosthesis. Other patients respond with depression, anxiety, and excess disability. Adjustment to amputation does not appear related to whether or not a prosthesis is fitted (not always possible with elderly patients). Adjustment is probably associated with the patient's coping skills and the supporting environment. Blindness is a second complication of diabetes. Again, adjustment is probably related more to characteristics of the patient and the environment (including significant others) than to the disability itself.

Arthritis   Approximately 38% of Americans over age 65 years have this disease (Kovar, 1977). It is our nation's number one crippling disorder (Arthritis Foundation, 1970). Arthritis means inflammation of a joint, but the term is used to denote almost 100 different conditions, all of which cause joint pain, but not all involve inflammation. Inflammation is, however, one of the primary causes of joint damage. Two of the most common forms of this disease are osteoarthritis and rheumatoid arthritis.

Osteoarthritis is the most common form, and according to the Arthritis Foundation, everyone, if she/he lives long enough, will develop the disease. The disorder is usually mild, is rarely crippling, and tends to be localized in a single joint. The cause of osteoarthritis is not known, but is thought to be related to "wear and tear," with body parts simply wearing out as the person ages.

The cause of rheumatoid arthritis, the most dangerous and disabling form, is unknown. It is a chronic, inflammatory, and progressive type of arthritis which can affect not only the joints but connective tissue. The patient may tire easily, have fever, decreased appetite and be anemic. Joints can be destroyed by the disease, and terrible distortions of body parts (eg, the hands) may occur.

A person with severe arthritis may be unable to handle kitchen tools, cook, or even walk unaided. Unless one notices the twisted hands of an arthritic person, it may be difficult to understand why that person cannot take care of her/himself. Pain may be severe and, of course, cannot be seen. It can, however, be depressing and it can cause the afflicted person to be cranky and irritable.

Injuries Epidemiologists now call accidents injuries or injury events. Injury rates are lower for old than young people, but in 1976 were the sixth and seventh leading causes of death in persons age 65 and age 75 and over respectively (National Center for Health Statistics, 1978). Seventy-five percent of injuries in the elderly are accounted for by falls, fire and contact with hot substances, and car crashes (Hogue, 1980).

Falls, which may be caused by transient ischemic attacks, medical and alcohol impairment, or osteoporosis, can result in broken bones, particularly broken hips. In turn, a broken hip and subsequent surgery to set or replace the hip can leave an elderly person unable to walk and thus permanently disabled. Some old people who do regain function become so afraid of falling that they will not walk. Then physical therapy is an excellent intervention.

Injury from fire and contact with hot substances is thought to be caused by impaired physical function, such as that associated with arthritis or stroke. The elderly may be unable to manipulate kitchen equipment or extricate themselves from a hot surface. In some cases of stroke, the person may have no sensation in the affected arm and therefore be unaware of being burned. The forgetfulness associated with senile dementia is another possible cause of this type of injury.

Whether injury from car crashes of the elderly is due to perceptual difficulties or medical conditions is unknown (Hogue, 1980). Well known, however, is the elderly's need for more illumination, decreased glare sensitivity, and increased length of time for adaptation to darkness (Fozard et al, 1977). Other than injury, a possible outcome of a car crash is that the old person will stop driving. In urban and rural areas without adequate public transportation not being able to drive is a handicap. Though not physical, this can increase an old person's dependency and demands on the family support system.

Characteristics of the Person

It may be that there is "considerably less correlation between the nature and extent of physical injury or illness and one's adaptive response than between certain psychosocial determinants of the individual and his coping pattern, adaptive or otherwise" (Kiely, 1980). Age, sex, intelligence, education, vocation and socioeconomic level are all factors which may contribute to a person's response to illness (Verwoerdt, 1976). The most frequently cited example is that a woman would find a disfiguring disorder more threatening, while a man would find it more difficult to cope with physical disablement. Whether or not this is true is unknown, but it fits our sex role stereotypes. It also points out that to understand an individual's reaction to disability, we must understand what the handicap means to the individual. In this author's experience both men and women find the inability to communicate or to walk independently the most frightening disabilities.

Both "stage" theory and copying styles are used to explain a person's reaction to disability. Each theory, though valuable, provides only a partial understanding of the process. Stage theorists account for movement from the moment of crisis to the final resolution which may or may not be adaptive (summarized in Power and Dell Orto, 1980). Stage theorists do not take individual characteristics of the person into account but do provide a framework for understanding the changes from shock to depression, grief, shame, embarrassment, and anxiety so frequently associated with loss of a body part or function.

Coping strategists, on the other hand, attend to characteristics of the individual. Coping devices are considered to be long-enduring methods of dealing with stress or threat and include perceptions, thinking, feeling, and overt behavior. These modes of behavior may be destructive or adaptive depending on the circumstances.

Both stage theorists and coping strategists have given much attention to denial as a response to devastating life circumstances (Kiely, 1976; Power and Dell Orto, 1980; Verwoerdt, 1976). Life after sudden disablement will never be the same again, and denial may provide an effective strategy for not dealing with that fact. Denial may also curb anxiety, but unfortunately, at the same time, this particular defense can impede the patient's participation in self-care and the rehabilitation process.

Since the focus of these two theories is on the individual, neither accounts for the effect of the patient's emotional reaction on the caregiver, or vice versa. It is difficult for any family to cope with a depressed person, and perhaps even more difficult when the depressed individual is also physically disabled. Depressed people are frequently angry, demanding, and negative while at the same time helpless and hopeless. One concept which considers the patient-caregiver interaction is that of the "sick role." Verwoerdt (1976) thought personality types may be predictive of response to illness; for example, the dependent personality may welcome the "sick role" as a way of gratifying dependency needs, while other personality types, such as the overly self-reliant and emotionally distant, may use illness to gain warmth and affection (Verwoerdt, 1976). Rehabilitation has been directed toward helping the disabled person give up the "sick role" and to function with as much autonomy as possible, particularly in the work world (Gellman, 1973). Perhaps, because of the emphasis on vocational counseling, the role of the family in the rehabilitation process has been relatively neglected, despite the implication of the concept of "sick role" — any role implies the presence of a cast of characters which for many disabled persons means the presence of family members.

Families in Stress

Wawzonek (1974), discussing disability, thought it unlikely to find a "sick" patient in a "well" family. Although the antecedents of abuse of the elderly have not been investigated, it is equally unlikely, when such data are available, that an abused old person will be found in a "healthy" family. Despite the importance of the family as a support system, families of the disabled have been relatively neglected by the medical and psychology professions. There are, however, some data on what these families find most stressful.

Fengler and Goodrich (1979) found that two-thirds of the men participating in a sheltered workshop would have been institutionalized if their wives had not been willing and able to care for them. The authors, comparing wives with low and high life satisfaction, found women with low scores had less support from children and friends, were less likely to have their husbands as confidants, and tended to see family income as inadequate. These wives were also more likely than high scorers to be working full time, as well as caring for their husbands.

Adams et al (1979), who studied the effect of an illness crisis in an elderly person on responsible family members, found caregiving caused deleterious changes in the homemaking, recreational, and vocational activities of the caregiver. Major hardships identified concerned the care and assistance of the disabled patient, conflict within the family, confinement due to the care of the patient, and adjustment to the emotional changes of the patient. For children with elderly parents, the most stressful situation was when caretaking was considered confining, ie, it caused a disruption of the child's life-style or the cancellation of expectations for the future (Robinson and Thurner, 1979).

Dementia is not categorized as a physical illness, but physical disability is often an accompaniment. Therefore, the results of the next study are applicable. Among families caring for dementia patients, sense of burden was not significantly related to degree of the patient's impairment or to length of the illness. Burden was, however, strongly related to the number of family visits received in the caregiver's home (Zarit et al, 1980).

Sanford (1975) reviewed 50 cases in which patients were referred from a caretaker's home to a geriatric unit. Caregivers were asked to identify the types of problems which, if alleviated, would enable the caregiver to accept the patient at home again. Eight percent refused under any condition to continue as a caregiver, while 92% of the respondents could identify such problems. Sleep disturbances and the inability to walk independently to and from the toilet were the problems most frequently given as requiring alleviation. According to the author, respondents seemed to tolerate restrictions of social functioning well but this conclusion may be suspect as patients with the above problems would require virtually full-time care and supervision. Thus, the caregiver would be constrained.

Caregivers' feelings of isolation and patient denial of disability appear to be associated with loss of functional capability after discharge from a hospital. Labeling this phenomenon the Jekyll and Hyde syndrome suggests that physical illness per se does not account for inconsistencies in patient function, but rather that deterioration is a product of an unhealthy patient-caregiver interaction (Boyd and Woodman, 1978).

Just as degree of disability does not appear related to the living situation, it seems that it is also not associated with the degree of distress experienced by informal caregivers. Certain types of disability or inconsistencies in behavior may be stressful. Consistently, however, burden and low life satisfaction appear to be related to small or nonexistent support systems. Families caring for disabled elderly members may become isolated (Fengler and Goodrich, 1979; Lezak, 1978) whether through choice, the withdrawal of family and friends, or both. While not concluding that isolation alone is sufficient cause to induce abusive behavior, the above studies present some clues for prevention and perhaps even interventions.

Social Issues

> As the mainstay of family support systems, it is the daughters who have taken widowed mothers into their homes, have run errands, and have provided custodial care. Devoted though sons may be, it is clear that the major responsibility for psychological sustenance and physical maintenance of the aged has fallen traditionally to female members of the family (Treas, 1977, p. 488).

Thus in all available studies of caregiving, the majority of participants are women. Women tend to outlive their husbands, both because of greater longevity and the practice of marrying men older than themselves, and as widows they may require help from their daughters. Only one-third of women over age 65 live with their spouses, compared with three-fourths of men in this same age group (Siegal, 1978). Elderly men, therefore, often have a younger spouse to continue caring for them. Between the daughters and wives, family caretaking of the disabled elderly appears to become a "woman's issue."

Equally obscured by such terms as *family,* or *informal caregiver,* is that abuse of the elderly is a "woman's problem." Reports of elder abuse show that the majority of abused are women. This is not particularly surprising, since women are more likely than men to require family aid and women of all ages are more vulnerable than men to physical, social, and psychological abuse. What is surprising, however, is that the majority of abusers are women. Why do women, the traditional care providers, become victimizers? Does the victim identify with the aggressor and act in a similar fashion? Abusing middle-aged children may be re-enacting abusive behavior learned from parents (McCuan, 1978).

When a parent moves into an adult child's home, often old and unresolved family conflicts related to the child's battle for independence may be reactivated. Reactivated conflicts are usually described in terms of differences in life-styles, values or religious practices. New conflicts, based on the dependency of the parent on the child, may also arise (Steinman, 1979). New and old conflicts, if unresolved, might provide the breeding ground for abuse to develop, though whether this would happen in a family without a tradition of violence is unknown. The role reversal involved in becoming a parent's parent can frustrate the middle-aged child's financial and emotional goals (Steinmetz, 1978b). Middle age is usually thought of as a time of lessened financial burden since children have or are about to leave home, and a couple can expect to have time and money for themselves. Suddenly there is a new (old) dependent person in the home who requires attention, affection, and possibly financial support. For such middle-aged couples the future may appear to be destroyed by this new responsibility. It takes enormous amounts of time to care for physically dependent people. For example, Newman (1976 cf Treas, 1977) found that at least two-fifths of the children taking care of a resident parent worked the equivalent of a full-time job. For the single child, usually a maiden aunt, such a situation may force the child to give up her current life-style, including social relationships, entertainment, and even work to provide the necessary care.

One wonders how to extrapolate further from the theory of violence as learned behavior to account for wives who abuse. Is it that abusing wives were previously abused by their husbands? As in all relationships, the duration of a marriage is not a measure of its quality. Perhaps in already stressed marriages, the additional strain of caring for a mate who no longer can care for his own daily needs can cause long smoldering hostility to surface. Physical dependency may be considered an opportunity to get even for long-felt injustices. Even in warm and supportive marital relationships, disablement means the younger or healthier spouse (usually the wife) has lost the long-known partner and the expected future. Shared personal activities are probably curtailed, and the physical and emotional requirements of continuous care added. These new stresses, along with the loss of other family supports, may lead to frustration, resentment, and ultimately abuse (Lezak, 1978).

Among young siblings violence is not uncommon (Steinmetz, 1978a), and dislike between siblings can continue into old age. In such a situation abuse could be an exacerbation of a previously unpleasant relationship in which the now disabled sibling is no longer able to maintain the balance of power.

Another way of viewing the problem is to see relationships as concerned with power. The elderly as a group, and old women in particular, have diminished social and economic power with which to make power exchanges with younger persons (Dowd, 1975). Perhaps lack of social power is one cause of elder abuse. It is certainly considered as such in instances of child and wife abuse. Yet this apparent lack of social power is difficult to reconcile with results from personality studies which indicate that women become more domineering, instrumental, and aggressive with age. These characteristics, generally not exhibited in the public sector, are usually vented within the family. These "may revive . . . archaic fears of the 'bad mother' as expressed in the persona of the witch" (Gutmann, 1977). Social scientists are not comfortable with concepts drawn from the murkier realms of folklore and psychoanalysis, but bad mother and witch can be translated into a more acceptable term, perceived power. Perhaps the discrepancy between the perceived emotional and actual social, physical power of older disabled women is a cause of abuse in some families. It is likely that any useful analysis will account for both aspects of power relations.

Recommendations

In-depth studies of abusing families should be conducted. Caregiver stress seems to be related to lack of family supports and to constraint, not to degree of disability. Socioeconomic class does not appear to be associated with abuse, but perceived financial stress could be relevant (Block and Sinnott, 1979; Steuer and Austin, 1980). Personal power relationships need to be investigated, particularly mother-daughter relationships.

In-depth studies of abusing families could help denote commonalities and guidelines for intervention. However, until such information is available, suggestions for prevention of abuse and intervention, once abuse has taken place, can still be made. At the primary prevention level, dissemination of information about community resources might be helpful. Our social service system is a morass in which it is easy to get lost and difficult to find information. The media, including newspapers, radio, and television could be used to inform the public about eligibility for financial aid, and how and where to go to receive such aid. Information about the availability of community home health care, such as visiting nurse associations and homemaker chore services, day care centers and other special programs for the disabled elderly and their families should also be publicized, as should the costs or methods of obtaining third-party payment for these services. Family education in caring for an aging parent is needed and could be part of adult education curriculum. Educational programs could also be broadcast on public service radio and television stations.

Counseling should be available during the time a family is making decisions regarding care for a disabled elderly person. Families endure enormous social pressure to care for their own, and the professional's role should be to aid the family to make an intelligent decision based, not on social values or guilt but, on what they want or are able to do. For example, when both members of a two-adult household work all day, who will be at home to feed the old person, or to take her to the toilet? How will the family's life-style have to change to accommodate the new household member? Such issues need careful evaluation and the family may need support. Education of families in the care of a disabled person is also needed. A family should have the opportunity of rehearsing care requiring special skill, such as transferring the patient from bed to chair.

On the societal level, more facilities for day care, home help, or intermittent hospitalization permitting the caretaker to have time out are needed. These programs might reduce the frustration and burnout which may lead to abuse.

Physicians, psychologists, social workers, nurses — all persons having contact with families with a disabled old person — should be aware that all families are not harmonious and abuse of the aged does occur. Early warning signs of hostility, abuse, or neglect should be heeded and at-risk families identified.

Once an at-risk family has been identified, professional counseling should be available to help work out conflicts and hostile feelings. Intervention may include convincing a family to use community resources, such as day care programs, and aiding the primary caretaker to understand that she/he should have time away from the disabled person. Behavioral techniques for managing difficult patients should also be taught. Counseling may also be directed at resolving guilt associated with wanting a life of one's own, with not wanting the burden of parenting a parent, or with placing a parent, spouse or sibling in institutional care.

Once abuse has occurred, intervention on both a social and legal level is necessary. Counseling services should be mandatory and families monitored. If the abuse does not stop, legal action should be possible. At the present time the first agency to be contacted is often the Department of Public Social Services (DPSS). In states without adult protection laws the DPSS usually can only manipulate financial aid if the family is receiving public funds. Under the Criminal Code of some states, caretakers could be prosecuted for assault and battery or possibly for imprisonment; but charges must be brought, investigation is unlikely, and evidence is difficult to accumulate. Sometimes legal action can only be taken when a person is gravely disabled or a danger to themselves, or when a person's life is in danger from action by others. Then a person can be institutionalized, for a very brief period of time or conservatorship could be sought. This latter solution is a drastic measure and often not wanted by either the old person or the caretakers. Legal action is probably the intervention of last resort, but rehabilitation programs and adult protection laws are needed. Such programs and laws, when formulated, must take into account the issue of standards, the desires of the old person and the caretaker, and the right to privacy of the family and the individual.

Summary

Two of the major hazards of old age are poor health and an increased risk of disablement, such that the elderly account for a disproportionately high rate of usage of medical services. Moreover, approximately 14% of elderly community residents are restricted in physical mobility. Ill health and disability often mean an old person can no longer function independently but must turn to other people, most frequently a family member, for assistance in ordinary activities of daily living. Most families provide care for their aging members, but not all families are caring, and violence occurs within some families. Violence means physical, financial, or psychological abuse, as well as a more insidious type of abuse, neglect.

Estimates of elder abuse range from approximately 5% of the aging population to just under 10% of persons receiving home health care. Although the causes of abuse are unknown, it is unlikely that illness or the residual of illness are causes. More probable is that the cause will be found in characteristics of the person, the family caregiver, and the social structure.

An individual's perception of the meaning of a disability is a primary factor in determining her/his response to loss of function. This perception in turn is probably affected by such personal characteristics as age, sex, intelligence, vocation, and socioeconomic level. Both stage theory and coping styles are used to explain a person's response to disablement, each theory providing only a partial explanation of the process. But theory tends to reduce the emotional impact of disability on the reader and to make the increased dependence, vulnerability, and possible ensuing depression seem distant. Moreover, neither stage nor coping theory do anything to account for the interaction of the disabled person's response with that of the caregiver, even though it is known that it is extremely difficult to live with a depressed person who is often angry, demanding, and negative while at the same time experiencing feelings of helplessness and hopelessness.

Family caregivers find it difficult to cope with inconsistencies in patients' behaviors and with certain types of physical dysfunction. Over time caregivers tend to lose their support systems, perhaps because caretaking is extremely confining and time consuming or perhaps because less involved people do not want to be confronted with severe disability. Whatever the reason, small or nonexistent support systems appear to increase feelings of burden and distress in the caregiver, making the difficult task more difficult.

As with much of the literature on elderly persons, this discussion of disability, caregiving, and elder abuse disguises an important issue. Most

248

caregivers are women. Moreover, in studies of elder abuse most of the victims are women as are the majority of the victimizers. It thus appears that elder abuse is a "women's issue."

Several nonexclusive hypotheses are suggested concerning cause of abuse. One is that violent behavior is learned within the family and perpetrated within and across generations. A second hypothesis is that violence develops when power relationships change within the family structure and when unresolved hostilities or social circumstances provide the necessary fertilization. Another hypothesis is that family violence is bred by the place women, and particularly old women, have within our social structure. It is likely that no single cause will be found, but causation will be found in the complex cross product of patient and caregiver characteristics and personal and social environments.

Clearly, in-depth studies of abusing families are needed to provide guidelines for intervention at the primary, secondary, and tertiary levels. At the primary prevention level there is a need for provision of information and education. Counseling should be available at crisis points, such as at a time when a family is deciding how to best care for a disabled elderly person. Education in special skills, such as transferring a patient from a bed to a chair, should also be provided. More facilities for day care, home help, or intermittent hospitalization are needed. Professional intervention should also be possible when early warning signs of hostility or verbal abuse are identified. Finally, when abuse has actually occurred, both social and legal interventions are necessary. Counseling services should be mandatory and families monitored. If abuse does not cease, legal action should be possible and for this, laws protecting the disabled elderly are needed. Such laws must not be solely the products or thoughts of legislators and mental health workers but must also account for the wishes and privileges of the caregiver and the disabled old person.

BIBLIOGRAPHY

Adams M, Caston MA, Danis BG: A neglected dimension in home care of disabled elderly persons: Effect on responsible family members. Presented at the 32nd Annual Meeting of the Gerontological Society, Washington, DC, 1979.

The Arthritis Foundation: *Arthritis—The Basic Facts.* New York, The Arthritis Foundation, 1970.

Block MR, Sinnott JD: Methodology and results, in Block MR, Sinnott JD (eds): *The Battered Elder Syndrome: An Exploratory Study.* College Park, MD, University of Maryland Center on Aging, 1979.

Boyd RV, Woodman JA: The Jekyll-and-Hyde syndrome: An example of disturbed relations affecting the elderly. *Lancet* 1978;2(8091):671–672.

Branch LG: Functional abilities of the elderly: An update on the Massachusetts health care panel study, in Haynes SG, Feinleib M (eds): *Second Conference on the Epidemiology of Aging*. Bethesda, MD, National Institute of Health, 1980.

Brody SF, Poulshock SW, Masciocchi CF: The family caring unit: A major consideration in the long-term support system. *Gerontologist* 1978;18:556–561.

Dowd JJ: Aging as exchange: A preface to theory. *J Gerontol* 1975;30:585–594.

Fengler AP, Goodrich N: Wives of elderly disabled men: The hidden patients. *Gerontologist* 1979;19:175–183.

Fozard JL, Wolf E, Bell B, et al: Visual perception and communication, in Birren JE, Schaie KW (eds): *Handbook of the Psychology of Aging*. New York, Van Nostrand Reinhold, 1977.

Garraway WM, Whisnant JP, Furlan AJ, et al: The declining incidence of stroke. *New Engl J Med* 1979;300:449–452.

Gellman W: Fundamentals of rehabilitation, in Garrett JF, Levine ES (eds): *Rehabilitation Practices with the Physically Disabled*. New York, Columbia University Press, 1973.

Gutmann D: The cross-cultural perspective: Notes towards a comparative psychology of aging, in Birren JE, Schaie KW (eds): *The Psychology of Aging*. New York, Van Nostrand Reinhold, 1977.

Gruenberg EM: Discussion of MG Kovar. Morbidity and health care utilization, in Haynes SG, Feinleib M (eds): *Second Conference on the Epidemiology of Aging*. Bethesda, MD, US Department of Health and Human Services, DHEW Pub. #80-969, 1980.

Hogue CC: Epidemiology of injury in older age, in Haynes SG, Feinleib M (eds): *Second Conference on The Epidemiology of Aging*. Bethesda, MD, United States Department of Health and Human Services, NIH Pub #80-969, 1980.

Kentucky Bureau for Social Services. *Protective Services Report,* 1980 (unpublished).

Kiely WF: Coping with severe illness, in Power PW, Dell Orto AE (eds): *Role of the Family in the Rehabilitation of the Physically Disabled*. Baltimore, University Park Press, 1980.

Kovar, MG: Health and health care of the elderly. *Publ Health Rep* 1977;92:9–19.

Kovar MG: Morbidity and health care utilization, in Haynes SG, Feinleib M (eds): *Second Conference on The Epidemiology of Aging*. Bethesda, MD, United States Department of Health and Human Services, NIH Pub #80-969, 1980.

Lau EE, Kosberg JI: *Abuse of the elderly by informal care providers: Practice and research issues*. Presented at the 31st Annual Meeting of the Gerontological Society, Dallas, TX, 1978.

Lezak MF: Living with the characterologically altered brain injured patient. *J Clin Psychiatry* 1978;41:261–268.

McCuan ER: Intergenerational family violence and neglect: The aged as a victim of reactivated and reversed patterns, in *Proceedings of the 11th International Congress of Gerontology*. Tokyo, Scimed Publications, 1978.

Mossman PL: *A Problem Oriented Approach to Stroke*. Springfield, IL, Charles C Thomas, 1976.

National Center for Health Statistics. Home care for persons 55 and over — United States July 1966–June 1968. *Vital and Health Statistics,* Series No. 10, No. 73, DHEW Pub. HSM72-1062, Washington DC, Public Health Service, 1972.

National Center for Health Statistics: Advance report — final mortality statistics,

1976. *Monthly Vital Statistics Report.* Vol. 26, No. 12, Supp. 2. Washington DC, Public Health Service, 1978.

Newman S: *Housing Adjustments of Older People. A Report from the Second Phase.* Ann Arbor, MI, Institute of Social Research, 1976.

Power PW, Dell Orto AE: Impact of disability/illness on the adult, in Power PW, Dell Orto AE (eds): *Role of the Family in Rehabilitation of the Physically Disabled.* Baltimore, University Park Press, 1980.

Robinson B, Thurner M: Taking care of aged parent: A family cycle transition. *Gerontologist* 1979;19:586–593.

Sanford JRA: Tolerance of debility in elderly dependents by supporters at home: Its significance for hospital practice. *Br Med J* 1975;3:471–473.

Shanas E: Social myth as hypothesis: The case of family relations of old people. *Gerontologist* 1979a;19:3–9.

Shanas E: The family as a social support system in old age. *Gerontologist* 1979b; 19:169–174.

Shanas E: Self-assessment of physical function: White and black elderly of the United States, in Haynes SG, Feinleib M (eds): *Second Conference on the Epidemiology of Aging.* Bethesda, MD, National Institute of Health, 1980.

Siegal JS: *Demographic Aspects of Aging and the Older Population in the United States. Current Population Reports: Special Studies,* Series P-23, No. 59, Washington, DC, Government Printing Office, 1978.

Siegal JS: Recent and prospective demographic trends for the elderly population and some implications for health care, in Haynes SG, Feinleib M (eds): *Second Conference on the Epidemiology of Aging.* Bethesda, MD, National Institute of Health, 1980.

Steinman LA: Reactivated conflicts with aging parents, in Regan PK (ed): *Aging Parents.* Los Angeles, Andrus Gerontology Center, University of Southern California, 1979.

Steinmetz SK: Overlooked aspects of family violence: Battered husbands, battered siblings, and battered elderly. Testimony prepared for the Committee on Science and Technology, U.S. House of Representatives, February 15, 1978a (mimeo).

Steinmetz SK: Battered parents. *Society* 1978b;15:54–55.

Steuer J, Austin E: Family abuse of the elderly. *J Am Geriat Soc* 1980;28: 372–376.

Treas J: Family support systems for the aged: Some social and demographic considerations. *Gerontologist* 1977;17:486–491.

Vallarino R, Sherman FT: Stroke, fractured hip, amputation, pressure sores, and incontinence: Principles of rehabilitation, in Libow LS, Sherman FT (eds): *The Core of Geriatric Medicine. A Guide for Students and Practitioners.* St. Louis, Mosby, 1981.

Verwoerdt A: *Clinical Geropsychiatry.* Baltimore, MD, Williams & Wilkins Company, 1976.

Wawzonek SJ: The role of the family in disability. *Am Arch Rehabil Ther* 1974; 22:49–57.

Zarit SH, Reever KE, Bach-Peterson J: Relatives of the impaired elderly: Correlates of feelings of burden. *Gerontologist* 1980;20:649–655.

15 Policy Responses to Problems Faced by Elderly in Public Housing

Lynn A. Curtis
Imre R. Kohn

In this chapter we will discuss some significant policy responses that can be applied to the multiple problems faced by the elderly in public housing.

The overriding statistical fact about crime and the elderly appears to be an enigma. National victimization surveys show that the over 65 age group is among the least victimized, yet fear of crime is their most serious personal problem — ahead of critical issues like health, income, and housing (Louis Harris and Associates, 1975; Select Committee on Aging, 1977; and United States Department of Justice, 1975 and 1977). How can this be explained? Part of the reason relates to problems in measuring victimization, but there also are reasons for understanding a bona fide perception of fear greatly exceeding reality, particularly among the older residents in public housing. The chief reason is that elderly persons often are more vulnerable than other population groups. They are aware of this, and the invitation to crime this gives the criminal. Physically, the activities of older Americans become more restricted with chronic diseases

and reduced sensory input. Socially, they become less active, often finding themselves among neighbors who may only relate to them as
predators relate to prey. Economically, they grow poorer, unable to
work and forced to live on incomes that buy less each year. Psychologically, they experience a diminished sense of personal influence over what
happens around them.

The problems of increased vulnerability are made worse in ill-suited
environments. Lawton (1975a, 1975b) has discussed the adverse consequences to elderly residents in low quality, badly located housing projects. This, plus inadequate and poorly designed facilities, greatly restricts
the older resident's mobility, range of activities, and personal sense of
freedom. For many, any excursion to the outside world is filled with
risks. For example, the elderly often have to use public transportation,
and bus stops and train stations provide excellent opportunities for offenders because of the anonymous character of waiting areas and limited
surveillance. Frequently, the offender has committed assault or larceny
and escaped before the victim is aware of it. An old woman, who is accidentally knocked to the sidewalk by a child who does not look where he
is running, might not immediately realize that the young man apparently
coming to her aid actually intends to take her purse. Too often elderly
victims do not fully recover from such injuries and personal losses (Conklin, 1976; Harris, 1978). This can have an impact on the amount of fear,
however deferred, generated by a given amount of actual crime. It is
understandable why several studies have found that the elderly are fearful of leaving their homes during the day as well as at night. (Cunningham, 1976; National Council on Aging, 1975).

Beyond the basic reality of vulnerability, there are other reasons to
explain why fear among elderly citizens is so magnified. The elderly may
be more likely than the younger population to discuss crimes, and the
mass media may sensationalize crimes against the elderly more than
crimes against younger persons. The elderly may have fewer friends than
younger persons, thus lowering their perceived ability to recuperate.
Finally, the elderly may be less involved in the neighborhoods they live
in. This could increase the number of neighbors they consider as
strangers and weaken their social support network (Yin, 1980).

In considering the kind of lives that older public housing residents
must lead in many places, one feels impotent to redress the effects of
fear. Fear becomes a pervading characteristic of one's life, lending a tone
or a quality inhibiting in the extreme. The growing sense of helplessness
becomes a tragic accompaniment of the last half of the twentieth
century's elderly in America. Crime, then, is more profound in its effects
on the elderly, quite different from its effects on the young, who are more
resilient, more adaptive and more able to cope with a similar challenge.

Policy

There is much that can be done. There are programs that make sense — we are not starting from scratch and there is evidence of what works. They make sense politically too: a constituency of 25 million voters can be expected to respond positively if their number one concern is diminished.

We need a broad policy focused toward the managers of buildings with elderly residents and, more importantly, the elderly themselves, as they are organized into citizen groups. We need facts on the incidence of crime and policy implications spelled out to senior citizens in a clear-cut way. Television and radio can play an important part, because the elderly make up a sizable proportion of viewers and listeners. Specialized programs for the elderly, like "Over Easy," can devote time to this topic, as can special news programs. Awareness of the facts cannot eliminate fear entirely, a usually well-justified fear. But fear should correspond to reality, within limits.

There appears to be hope because of residents public housing for the elderly have shown that, with the right kind of programs, untapped inner resources can be called on to, in Rosenthal's (1975) term, help the elderly "reclaim their turf."

**Indigenous Neighborhood
Self-Help Programs**

Senior citizens involved in neighborhood self-help efforts are less fearful than those who are not (Cohn et al, 1978). Successful anti-crime, self-help demonstration programs have been developed over the last few years. One example is the Senior Citizen Action Network (SCAN) in New York, where in addition to tenant patrols in buildings, SCAN organizers have helped set up block-watch programs and encouraged senior volunteers to walk the streets as part of block patrols. Lobby patrol members stay in touch via walkie-talkies with street patrollers, and relay emergency reports to the local precinct through a special CB channel. Other services, often initiated through tenant meetings in apartment lobbies, are the installation of free locks and the implementation of an Operation Identification program. If an elderly victim needs help, such as replacing lost identification and credit cards, a referral is made to a social service worker in a local senior citizen center. Five part-time aides, four of them senior citizens, help make these referrals work. If a victim is in need of money, the SCAN office can make an emergency gift.

Many experiments like SCAN have been targeted solely on the elderly to learn what is most effective for them, and to insure that services reach an elderly population that traditionally has been underserved by social and criminal justice programs. Experiments have uncovered a great deal about those approached and about services which are most beneficial in alleviating the stresses that crime imposes on older persons. Special kinds of outreach, education, and counseling developed for the senior population now can be passed on to others.

The most important lesson is a renewed understanding of the need to involve senior citizens not just as recipients of services but as the leaders and workers in a community effort against crime (Eisenhower Foundation, 1982). Older workers can be trained to fill many needed positions: as neighborhood organizers, to bring residents together to plan and carry out a local anticrime campaign; as community advocates, to promote the involvement of local officials and agencies in more effective anticrime policies and programs; as crime prevention specialists, to provide information and education to residents on how to reduce their chances of becoming victims; and as victim counselors, to act as back-up agents for the police and courts in providing emergency assistance and referrals for their neighbors who are crime victims.

The elderly also can participate as partners in a community organization involving both young and old, working together to prevent crime. Is is not yet known whether seniors working alone are more or less effective than seniors working with others. The effectiveness may vary according to the community. Nonetheless, the underlying notion of neighborhood self-help has grown in recent years while traditional, more expensive, and professionally oriented anticrime programs have often not turned back rising crime.

Although there must be more evaluation of what works and why, and although there have been failures, examples of successful age-integrated neighborhood anticrime programs are available, such as some of the 39 sites in the HUD Interagency Urban Initiatives Anticrime Program, some of the 175 sites in the LEAA Community Anticrime Program, and certain local efforts which arose with little, if any, federal funding. Illustrations are Philadelphia's House of Umoja; Ponce, Puerto Rico's Center for Orientation and Services; St. Louis's Carr Square Resident Association; and Seattle's National Exemplary Burglary Prevention Project (Eisenhower Foundation, 1981). In addition to success against crime and fear at relatively lower cost, many of these and other programs have increased the stake of minority groups in the community — by hiring minority directors, placing minorities in key staff positions, and empowering minority residents (Eisenhower Foundation, 1982).

Age-integrated neighborhood programs need to organize residents into block watches, patrols and escort services and to combine these efforts with the broader objectives of local neighborhood organizations. Such programs also need to use neighborhood structures, such as family and church, more effectively in mediating between the individual and larger institutions, such as government agencies. Among the potential benefits of such organizations, in addition to improving public safety and working more closely with the police and criminal justice agencies, are the identification of natural neighborhood leaders — whatever their ages — and community members who can raise funds from block grants, other local, state and federal sources, and the private sector. These organizations can pursue money-making ways to rechannel work from illegal markets to legal markets. For example, neighborhood youth can be employed as helpers (with elderly citizens), rather than as recipients of help from outsiders, and the organization can locate jobs for youth in the private sector.

Although federal efforts along these lines are being lessened, private sector ventures (like the Eisenhower Foundation for the Prevention of Violence) are establishing new programs, sensitive to senior citizens, that emphasize capacity-building and self-help, thus increasing the ability of local citizens to act collectively, rather than individually, and creating a permanent capability to fight crime among citizens of all ages. The potential hardly has been tapped for neighborhood anticrime efforts which incorporate protection of local businesses into an overall safety plan. There is a need to find corporations with local outlets, work with them on ways to involve citizens in neighborhoods where such outlets are located, identify such neighborhoods where community organizations are operating, and institute demonstrations in some of these places. The skills of senior citizens with business backgrounds could be invaluable to such work.

Based on past efforts attempting to involve the private sector in the solution of urban problems, such partnerships should be formed on mutual self-interest rather than on less practical motives. A quid pro quo needs to be developed: community organizations can involve citizens through patrols, block watches and the other kinds of indigenous anticrime efforts used to protect residences and individuals, and these devices can be extended to protect businesses, as well. The businesses, in turn, can financially assist the community organizations. Such support, for example, might cover stipends for community residents (including elderly needing extra money), persons who patrol the neighborhood, work with police, and keep their eyes and ears open. The self-interests of both the business and the community must be met (Eisenhower Foundation, 1982).

Age Segregation

Whether a neigborhood anticrime program is run solely by elderly citizens or by all age groups, it embraces geographic areas with potential elderly victims who live alone, elderly victims who live with others, and households without elderly persons at all. However, a conscious effort also can be made to link neighborhoood programs to a policy of age segregation, or to use age segregation as the prime means of preventing crime, even if no neighborhood group is operating.

Age segregation as an anticrime tool commonly is proposed within subsidized housing (United States Department of Housing and Urban Development, 1980). Arguments are based on observations that the elderly and families with children do not mix comfortably, and where they are mixed, the elderly are highly victimized. It has been found that each life-style (age) group operates best in certain types of buildings, and the provision of security in a building with a single life-style (age) group is easier because the self-identified security needs of residents are similar, as is their tolerance for the security mechanisms and services provided.

The argument against housing uniform age and life-style groups together is twofold. First, by removing the elderly from areas with children and youth, important elements of surveillance and informal social control are lost. Second, the interaction of old and young can have the effect of deterring antisocial behavior due to caring attitudes that may develop between members of each group. Elderly people also can be role models for youth, a view long held by gerontologists. The question is not whether elderly persons who want to live by themselves should be allowed to do so, but rather whether elderly residents who do not fear victimization by youth should be allowed to reside in buildings that are primarily occupied by families with children.

Evidence suggests that elderly residents of public projects may prefer age segregation. For example, when elderly residents in three projects were asked how safe they felt in their buildings, a marked difference was found between those living in age-segregated buildings and those at age-integrated sites. In age-segregated projects, 2% of the elderly said they were fearful of being in their buildings during the day. Approximately 15% expressed having similar fears at night. In the totally age-integrated project, however, 31% of the respondents were fearful during the day, and 72% were afraid of being criminally victimized at night. When asked whether they felt there was so much crime in their project that they wished they could move, no respondents residing in the age-segregated settings expressed a desire to move. In contrast, 42% of the elderly tenants in age-integrated buildings wished to move. The study concluded that, whether in high-rise or low-rise buildings, age-segregated public housing offers a social environment in which residents share information about one another. In so doing, they often come to define their territorial boundaries, are able to identify outsiders, and participate in the basic regulation of their own security. According to the study, not only does age segregation appear to offer a more secure environment for the elderly, but it seems simultaneously to reduce some of the social isolation and anonymity often associated with public housing (United States Department of Housing and Urban Development, 1980).

As a result of this study and others, almost two million older persons now live in subsidized housing designed for them. Although age segregation induces a fortress mentality, it appears to reduce crime and fear. Accordingly, even though we believe that people-based self-help approaches have more long-run potential than architectural solutions, age segregation appears to have a role, especially if it can be combined with indigenous community sharing.

Environmental Design

Other forms of environmental design besides age segregation also have potential. Table 15-1 summarizes various environmental design strategies that can be used with elderly and other citizens in support of people-based programs that encourage shared self-help. Assembled through past anticrime programs employing environmental design (especially the United States Department of Housing and Urban Development's Interagency, Urban Initiatives Anti-Crime Program in Public Housing), these strategies range from simple lock installations to comprehensive community rebuilding projects, all aimed at reducing crime and fear and improving the quality of life for the population. The appropriateness of particular strategies for particular housing developments depends on the kinds of criminal targets (persons and things) that are present, the level of risk and effort involved for the potential offender, and the potential payoff to the offender.

The array of environmental design options can be divided into six general categories: target hardening, access control, formal surveillance, natural surveillance, activity and program support, and territorial reinforcement. Target hardening is illustrated by door locks and security screens that bar entry or at least force the offender to exert a greater effort. In contrast, access control includes barriers that discourage unwanted intrusion through the use of symbolic or psychological "walls." While these strategies may present a physical obstacle for the offender, they are really intended to strengthen social control protective mechanisms by establishing points of legitimate access, such as separate lobby entries for visitors. As a physical obstacle, the lobby may be easily

Table 15-1
Environmental Design Strategies and Examples

Strategy	Example
Target Hardening Obstacles placed in the way of the potential offender to bar entry	Provide secure doors and locks for semi-public interior spaces (laundry rooms, mail rooms) where intruders hide.
	Install window security screens.
Access Control Barriers created to discourage unwarranted intrusion through the use of symbolic or psychological "walls"	Create separate entries for visitors.
	Fence off private and semi-private outdoor areas (playgrounds, sitting areas).
	Erect barriers to impede undetected access to area through adjoining vacant lots.
	Redesign or close streets to control vehicular traffic.
	Station doormen at building entries.
	Conduct premise security surveys.
	Develop building security codes.
Formal Surveillance	
	Install electronic surveillance equipment, such as CCTV.
	Install card readers at entries.
	Establish block-watch associations.
	Establish local police precincts in vacated stores.
	Provide security training programs for residents.
Natural Surveillance Control achieved over who uses space and what happens as a by-product of normal and routine activities.	Use transparent materials for entrances, lobbies, stairwells, laundry rooms.
	Reduce the number of families sharing a building entry.
	Locate building entries so that they are visible from active social areas.
	Upgrade street lighting.
	Design and locate bus shelters that are clearly visible and easily watched.
	Install buzzer-reply intercom systems.
	Arrange for adults or teenagers to watch children playing outdoors.
	Arrange with neighbors to provide surveillance during vacations.

Table 15-1 (continued)

Strategy	Example
Activity and Program Support New facilities created where programs are established to forestall the development of offender prevention awareness and increase community involvement.	Establish a message center. Create a resident anti-crime center. Develop outdoor social gathering areas for passive activities (picnics). Create spaces and facilities for social service outreach programs. Instruct children how to recognize and report emergencies. Create semi-public gardens to be maintained by resident volunteers. Establish resident patrols. Improve police-community relations through citizen education programs and police involvement in community affairs. Initiate property identification projects. Hire residents to maintain property. Sponsor escort programs for children and elderly. Establish zoning ordinances that prevent land uses incompatible with security objectives.
Territorial Reinforcement Fostering a stronger sense of "turf" and related protective behavior.	Initiate paint-up and fix-up programs with resident volunteers. Use construction and landscape to reinforce the transition from public to private spaces (planters, low walls). Provide amenities that encourage and support resident use. Reinforce territorial identity through color coding, signs. Sponsor yard improvement contest where individual families receive prizes. Sponsor special events for special age and interest groups to promote group identity. Create paraprofessional security jobs for local residents. Develop positive neighborhood image by having residents meet with developers and real estate agents to familiarize them with desirable environmental qualities.

penetrated by the offender, but a separate entry increases the risk to the offender because it is easier for residents and management to distinguish between persons with legitimate reasons for being there from those whose presence is questionable.

Formal surveillance tactics refer to spaces developed and equipment provided for official surveillance activities (eg, elderly block watches with walkie-talkies with access to police). Natural surveillance, on the other hand, refers to physical design elements that increase resident awareness of environmental happenings as a by-product of normal and routine activities. This is exemplified by locating bus shelters close to on-site active outdoor social areas and designing shelters so that users are visible from all directions.

Activity and program support strategies, similar to formal surveillance, focus on spatial and facility requirements for specific anti-crime programs. The juxtaposition of program activities with informal activities can effectively increase opportunities for natural surveillance and access control. A common example is to locate a program office next to the mail delivery area.

Whereas program and activity support is concerned with on-site program facilities and the kind of environmental props that will enhance the value of the community to the resident, territorial reinforcement deals directly with the question of what can be done physically to increase "turf" feelings and related protective behavior. These strategies aid the resident's natural territorial inclination by clarifying through physical design what spaces belong to whom, as for example, construction and landscape materials (low walls, planters) to reinforce the transition from public to private spaces.

Territorial reinforcement is really an umbrella concept, embodying all the other principles. If the other strategies are to succeed, potential offenders must see that intrusion will elicit territorial responses. For example, natural surveillance operates to increase the likelihood that intrusion will be observed by individuals who care but are not officially responsible for regulating the use and treatment of spaces. If people observe inappropriate behavior but do nothing about it, the most elegant natural surveillance techniques are useless.

The elderly are satisfying clients because they are so responsive to environmental modifications. Their vigilance goes beyond taking advantage of surveillance opportunities created for them — whether in the form of transparent barriers in lobbies or closed circuit television monitors — to exercising their territorial prerogatives to intercede or seek help when people or property are threatened. In no other age group is the link between observing and acting upon so well established. This is important because a major problem in public housing today is that criminals assess risk of apprehension not in terms of how easily their offense will be seen but in terms of the likelihood (usually low) that bystanders will act.

CONCLUSIONS

We have discussed the reality of fear of crime in the lives of the elderly, the discrepancy between the incidence of crime and the extent of fear derived from it, the profound significance of crime on senior citizens, the involvement of older persons and their neighbors in containing crime, and age segregation and environmental design.

The elements for a significant contribution to solving and ameliorating the impact of crime all are present. The job now remains to weave these elements into a coherent national policy. Here, the private sector, especially foundations and membership organizations, can play a critical integrating role.

BIBLIOGRAPHY

Cohn E, Kidder L, Harvey J: Crime prevention vs victimization prevention: The psychology of two different reactions. *Victimology* 1978;3:285–296.

Conklin J: Robbery, the elderly and fear: An urban problem in search of a solution, in Goldsmith J, Goldsmith S (eds): *Crime and the Elderly: Challenge and Response.* Lexington, MA, Heath, 1976.

Cunningham C: Patterns and effects of crime against the aging: The Kansas Study, in Goldsmith J, Goldsmith S (eds): *Crime and the Elderly: Challenge and Response.* Lexington, MA, Heath, 1978.

Eisenhower Foundation for the Prevention of Violence, *First Annual Report,* Washington, DC, 1982.

Harris C: *Fact Book on Aging: A Profile of America's Older Population.* Washington, DC, National Council on Aging, 1978.

Harris, L and Associates: *Myth and Reality of Aging in America.* Washington, DC, National Council on Aging, 1975.

Lawton MP: *Planning and Managing Housing for the Elderly.* New York, Wiley, 1975a.

Lawton MP: Competence, environmental press and the adaptation of older people, in Windley P, Byerts T, Ernest F (eds): *Theory Development in Environment and Aging.* Washington, DC, The Gerontological Society, 1975b.

National Council on Aging: *The Myth and Reality of Aging in America.* Washington, DC, 1975.

Rosenthal SJ: An approach to neighborhood security. *Ekistics,* 1975, February.

United States Congress Select Committee on Aging: *In Search of Security: A National Perspective on Elderly Crime Victimization.* Washington, DC, Government Printing Office, 1977.

United States Department of Housing and Urban Development: *First Annual Report: Urban Initiatives Anti-Crime Program.* Washington, DC, Government Printing Office, 1980.

United States Department of Justice: *Criminal Victimization Surveys in 13 American Cities.* Washington, DC, Government Printing Office, 1975.

United States Department of Justice: *Sourcebook of Criminal Justice Statistics.* Washington, DC, Government Printing Office, 1976.

United States Department of Justice: *Public Opinion About Crime: The Attitude of Victims and Non-Victims in Selected Cities.* Washington, DC, Government Printing Office, 1977a.

United States Department of Justice: *Criminal Victimization in the United States.* Washington, DC, Government Printing Office, 1977b.

Yin PP: Fear of crime among the elderly: Some issues and suggestions. *Social Problems* 1980;27:492–504.

16 The Special Vulnerability of Elderly Parents

Jordan I. Kosberg

There is growing awareness of the existence of crime against the elderly. Most studies in this area have focused upon victimization of the elderly on the street and in the home by strangers who prey upon the vulnerability of the elderly (Goldsmith and Goldsmith, 1978; Sparks, 1978; Malinchak and Wright, 1978). Less empirical work has been done on the abuse or maltreatment of the elderly by their families. It is the family that has been viewed as the "last line of defense" in the care of the elderly. The existence of children can keep the elderly out of institutional settings (Atchley, 1978). Much has been said about the need for a family allowance to permit families to care for their elderly relatives. Adult foster care homes have been stressed as a way of recreating a family unit for the care of the elderly. Family members have been turned to by professionals in the community for care and as legal guardians. The existence of abuse of the elderly by their families conflicts with these efforts to emphasize and turn to the family as an effective informal care system for the elderly.

It appears that only a small proportion of the elderly are abused by family members: a spouse, a sibling, or a grown child (the focus of this chapter). For example, Block and Sinnott (1979) found that 42% of abusing relatives were children and 19% were grandchildren. Lau and Kosberg (1979), in their study of elder abuse, found that of 49 abusers of elderly persons, about 39% were children and 12% were grandchildren. In a survey of abuse of the elderly in Massachusetts, O'Malley et al (1979) found that 39% of the abusers were sons and daughters.

This chapter will discuss reasons for the special vulnerability of elderly parents to abusive behavior by children and grandchildren, explanations that are complex and varied (Kosberg, 1980). Each case is unique and can be related to the characteristics of the elderly parent, the abusing relative(s), the family network, community support systems, and societal norms and values. It is necessary both to focus on, and seek to change, factors that cause parental abuse.

Reasons for General Vulnerability

Elderly individuals are susceptible to criminal and abusive behavior. The following discussion gives reasons why elderly persons are vulnerable, and emphasizes the losses and negative attributes of the elderly — a most heterogeneous group of individuals.

There is a great likelihood that the elderly will be singled out as a victim because they live in neighborhoods of high crime and are "in closer proximity to the groups most likely to victimize them — the unemployed, teenage dropouts" (Goldsmith and Tomas, 1974). The elderly live in high crime areas because low incomes require movement to low rental areas of a city, and there is reluctance to leave a neighborhood (and home) of many years, even when the neighborhood has greatly changed. The economic, social, and psychological meaning of the dwelling may be more important than the extent of crime or incongruity of population in the neighborhood.

The elderly are likely to live alone, especially elderly women. Combining this with living in an area of high crime increases vulnerability and the probability of isolation (anticipation of crime and fear to leave one's dwelling) or the actual commission of crime.

"Older people have diminished physical strength and stamina; hence, they are less able to defend themselves or to escape from threatening situations" (Goldsmith and Tomas, 1974). They are likely to suffer from physical disabilities and have impairments affecting hearing, sight, touch, and mobility, with lessened ability to resist crimes, whether the aggressor is a stranger or a relative.

Given a low income, the elderly are especially vulnerable to fraudulent promises and quick wealth schemes (Butler, 1975). Poor health conditions, with little if any hope for improvement, can make an elderly person vulnerable to health care quackery or schemes to evoke anxiety about health or economic security. Expensive or excessive health insurance, funeral arrangements, cemetery plots, and health devices are a few of many gambits. In addition, loneliness makes an elderly person vulnerable to an overly friendly and solicitous clerk, salesman, or stranger. Many elderly have had their savings stolen by a variety of confidence games and unscrupulous salesmen.

Many elderly persons rely on walking or on public transportation to get around in the community, thus are more visible and vulnerable. Walking to and from public transportation, waiting at stops, getting on or off a bus or subway, and being in crowds have ramifications for accidents and victimization.

"The dates of receipt of mail of monthly pension and benefit checks (and hence the dates when older people are most likely to have cash on their person or in their dwelling) are widely known" (Goldsmith and Tomas, 1974). Such knowledge results in mail boxes being broken into and checks stolen, robberies, and purse snatchings—crimes that are especially common near banks, shopping malls, and grocery stores.

The perception of the elderly as worthless can result in aimless and senseless crimes against them. Often one reads about muggings, beatings, and killings with no apparent motive; the only conclusion can be that the crime was based upon thrills or the seeking out of a defenseless or (perceived) valueless individual. If an elderly person is also considered a deviant (ie, an alcoholic, a drifter, handicapped, or mentally ill) there is a greater likelihood of becoming a victim. Katz (1980) suggests that bias against the handicapped and aged can result in abusive situations.

Abuse and Elderly Parents

There are specific issues related to the abuse and maltreatment of elderly parents and the visibility of the problem. Although responsibility for one's elderly parents has its roots in religious and cultural norms of behavior, with urbanization and industrialization social change has resulted in individualism or emphasis upon the needs of the nuclear family. Even though reciprocal relationships are found to exist between elderly parents and their middle-aged children (Schorr, 1980), the increasing level of impairments and losses of the parents (social, psychological, physical, and economic) is proportionately related to dependency on the family and often results in family pressures. Abusive behavior can be one consequence of such pressures. Such pressures may exist whether or not the elderly parent resides with the child or in his own dwelling.

The Family as a Closed System

The family is viewed to be the major social unit in society and is almost sacrosanct. There has generally been little interference with the family by outsiders and, indeed, individuals may see their family as a symbolic island in a world of formal and impersonal day-to-day relationships. Outsiders, even professionals, are reluctant to intervene in family problems of child and spouse abuse. Experience with elder abuse has found that both the elderly abused relative and the abusing child have not admitted the existence of a problem nor permitted the involvement of a professional to provide necessary intervention (Lau and Kosberg, 1979). Accordingly, the parent becomes more vulnerable when the problem is defined as a family affair and to be solved — if at all — by the family. This view can be shared by the abused, abuser, other family members, and the helping professions.

Elder abuse by grown children occurs within the home and is hidden from outsiders. The interaction of family members within the home is beyond public scrutiny, increasing the vulnerability of the elderly parent to abusive behavior. As Straus (1979) states:

> The rules of our society make what goes on in the family a private affair. This aspect of the family system insulates the family from both the social controls and assistance in coping with conflicts. Moreover, even after violence occurs the rule of family privacy is so strong that it prevents the victims from seeking help. That is why Erin Pizzey's book on wifebeating is called *Scream Quietly or the Neighbors Will Hear* (1974).

Even when detection of elder abuse occurs, in many states there are no mechanisms for legal access into the home by professional care providers. Protective services legislation would permit entry into the home to investigate alleged abuse and maltreatment of elderly persons.

The Family as a Panacea

The family, in general, and children, specifically, have been used as a panacea in care of the elderly by legal, social service, and health care systems. Judges turn to family members as guardians for confused and incompetent elderly. Social workers often engage the family in the solution to a problem of dependency. Health care professionals believe that a good discharge plan for elderly patients is if they go to the home of grown children. While in most cases the family may recognize its responsibility for caring for an elderly relative, in some cases grown children are ill-suited, ill-prepared, and undesiring to care for an ill, perhaps confused, dependent elderly relative. A child's motivation to provide care may be for the wrong reasons, such as economic exploitation. Children may be embarrassed to refuse a request to care for an elderly parent. In the eagerness to find an easy and inexpensive solution to care for an elderly person, those making referrals or legal guardians may turn too quickly to family members without assessing the appropriateness of the family or pressures on the family to be caused by having to care for an elderly relative.

Often there is an assumption regarding family responsibility for elderly parents in racial or ethnic cultures. Such assumptions pertain not only to the idea that "they care for their own elderly," but that such care is adequate and loving. Historically, such minority groups did mandate responsibility for elderly parents; often they continue. As an example, Johnson (1980) found that for Italian Americans the "family system retains an impressive capacity to function as a support system to the elderly." However, assimilation and acculturation have had an impact on traditional norms. The break-up of ethnic enclaves, the achievement of middle-class status and values, the high rate of mobility in American society may mean that the care of the elderly parent by children of racial or ethnic backgrounds will approximate the care by the larger society. There is probably no difference in rates of abuse between white and non-white populations, which has become more an issue of socioeconomic level and education.

Failure to Report Abusive Behavior

The problem of detecting adult abuse is exacerbated by the perception of the family unit and the invisibility of events. Elderly parents are also apparently reluctant to report abuse, maltreatment or exploitation by grown children. In the study of abuse by Lau and Kosberg (1979), it was found that one-third of the elderly, judged to have been abused, denied this. An additional one-fourth had resigned themselves to their plight. It is not difficult to understand why elderly parents would be unlikely to report maltreatment by children or grandchildren. First, the parent may believe the problem is a family affair and should remain within its domain. The elderly parent may be embarrassed or ashamed at the lack of respect and the abusive behavior of a child. There may be a fear of reprisals by the abusing child, or fearful anticipation that reporting the abusive behavior (to either persons outside the family or to other family members) may result in legal or criminal action against the abusing child. An elderly parent may feel guilty for being dependent causing family tensions and pressures (eg, economic, psychological, or physical space). Accordingly, the parent may feel he is the culprit.

Cycle of Family Violence

Parents may not report abusive behavior by children because they believe they are being "paid back" for their use of physical means in bringing up their children. There is anecdotal information (if not empirical) that children who were abused by their parents are likely to abuse their parents. This cycle may be a manifestation of learned behavior by children, although the abusive treatment (both by parents toward young children and by grown children toward elderly parents) may be of a pathologic nature. Also, violence in the home is a normal response to stress and tension in some families. "An individual who was raised by parents who used physical force to train children and who grew up in a violent household has had as a role model the use of force and violence as a means of problem solving" (Gelles, 1973). A "culture of violence" (or use of physical means) is characteristic of behavior patterns in working or lower class families or in certain cultural backgrounds (Blumberg, 1964). The vulnerability of dependent elderly parents within such families is great.

Intergenerational Problems

Discrepancies in values and standards of behavior between generations can result in tensions and conflict. Conflicts between elderly parents and middle-aged children can be long-standing personality conflicts and bickering worsened by the passing of time (Farrar, 1955). Intergenerational conflict is more likely to occur when family members, individually or collectively, have difficulty coping or when an elderly parent is suffering from a chronic disease (Maddox, 1975). Having to care for the needs of one's own family members and one's own aging, coupled with the need to care for an increasingly dependent elderly parent, may result in great pressure to a grown child. "The middle-aged individual often has the burden of caring for his own children, himself, and his aged parents at a time when he begins to experience the first evidence of his own aging as indicated by fatigue or decrease in stamina and change in appearance" (Goldfarb, 1965).

Cavan (1956) has suggested that there are three probable causes for conflict between the old and middle aged. First, a rural-to-urban transition has resulted in grown children holding urban values while parents still have rural outlooks. Second, a change in upbringing from foreign to American culture results in older parents retaining precepts and customs of the foreign culture which can be rejected by their Americanized children. Third, the upward social mobility by children with more education, higher paying occupations, and greater assimilation into higher social classes may result in resentment toward or embarrassment of their more "common" parents.

Costs to the Family

Pressures resulting from care of an elderly parent can turn into hostility, frustration, confusion, and potentially abusive behavior. Insufficient attention has been given to the costs to a family of having to care for an aged relative (whether or not living with the child). The most apparent cost is economic, resulting directly from needed care and treatment for the elderly parent or from confinement of a member of the family (most often daughter—married or unmarried—or daughter-in-law) who may not be able to leave to seek supplemental family income or pursue a career because of the dependent elderly parent. Additionally, the economic burden may result in the family being less able to afford other things such as another car or a vacation.

Social and psychological costs are caused by infringement on the life-style of the family. These costs affect family privacy, mobility, independence, and flexibility. Horowitz and Shindel (1980) in investigating the consequences of such care stated that although there were positive aspects of caregiving, negative aspects were: restrictions on personal time, freedom, use of leisure time; changes in future plans (vacation, relocation, or retirement); and giving up social activities and financial expenses. One-third of the respondents in their study reported deterioration of their own physical health and one-half reported an increase in depression and anxiety.

While abuse can result from the resentment or pressures from caring for an elderly parent, abusive behavior can also result from the frustration and guilt from either not wanting to provide such assistance or not being able to provide needed care and attention. Tuzil (1978) has described the feelings of guilt and panic experienced by adult children when they discover they are unable or unwilling to care for an elderly parent.

Individual and Family Characteristics

Because an elderly person has a grown child to take care of him does not guarantee that humane and loving care will be provided. A grown child could be schizophrenic, retarded, an alcoholic, a drug abuser, or have a criminal or deviant life style. Some parents had cared for deviant or impaired children for many years. "As aged parents weaken and (themselves) need care, these adult children become abusing and neglecting caregivers because of an inability to make appropriate judgments and perceptions" (Lau and Kosberg, 1979). Further, there is an increasing likelihood that the children of the elderly may, themselves, be elderly and possibly confused and impaired. Such children might be unaware of their behavior or its effects on their parents.

A child may wish to appropriate financial resources, possessions, and property of a parent by theft, coercion, or deception. Some grown children have either tried to institutionalize (or commit) a parent inappropriately or sought to expedite the death of a parent, to receive an inheritance more quickly.

Empirical research findings have identified family characteristics associated with child and spouse abuse and family conflict. It is suspected that similar associations will be found for adult abuse, as well. Gelles (1973) found an association between abusive behavior and unemployment and low social class. Gil (1971) found an association between low socioeconomic status and child abuse. Gelles (1973) also found an association between unwanted pregnancy and child abuse. Could unwanted responsibility for an aged parent also be associated with abuse?

Lystad (1975) has studied family violence and concluded that with increased isolation of the nuclear family, and an increase in the number of one-parent families, who are constantly on call, stresses and tensions build up. Similarly, Garbarino (1977) believes there is greater likelihood of child abuse if the family is isolated from support systems in the neighborhood and community. Caplan and Killiea (1976) have discussed family support systems as being formal or informal, and related to the extent of personal relationships, the characteristics of the neighborhood, and existence of social services.

Role Definitions

A final area for explaining the special vulnerability of elderly parents is related to a failure to redefine family roles, rights, and responsibilities, vis á vis the elderly dependent parent. Such failure with the passing of years can result in either hostility (Blenkner, 1965) or overt violence (Glasser and Glasser, 1962). Rejecting the notion of role-reversal, Blenkner (1965) discussed the need for children to successfully perform a "filial role" for being depended upon and dependable for the care of an aged relative. Garbarino (1977) discussed caregiver incompetence as having three causes: (1) no opportunity for rehearsing the role; (2) lack of knowledge and unrealistic expectations; and (3) inability to reorder priorities regarding gratification of needs.

PROGRAM AND POLICY RAMIFICATIONS

The message of this chapter is that grown children of abused and maltreated elderly may be as much a cause of the problem as a solution. Abusive and exploitive behavior may be a result of deviant, criminal, or hostile children. It may also be a result of subtle pressures and tensions, or unresolved or undefined roles. Regardless of the cause, efforts are needed to safeguard elderly parents, especially the more dependent and invisible. Suggestions for prevention and treatment of the problem of the vulnerable elderly parent follow.

Family Assessment

Inasmuch as children and other family members may be abusers of elderly relatives, there is a great need to assess suitability of family members who are being considered to be entrusted with the care of an elderly, dependent parent. Designating a relative a guardian, placing an elderly client with a child, or discharging an elderly patient to the family without adequate assessment may be viewed as a panacea by service providers but may result in great problems for the elderly person. An alcoholic, mentally ill, senile, or deviant child is probably an inappropriate care provider for a dependent and elderly person, even a parent.

There must also be an assessment of the family constellation to be involved in care, including a determination of the number, location, availability, and suitability of family members. Abusive behavior is often a result of family tensions and strains from having to care for an elderly relative. Accordingly, then, the costs to the family (economic, social, and psychological) must be assessed before entrusting care of an elderly parent to family members.

Needed Legislation

Legislation is needed on many levels. In June, 1980, a bill was introduced to the United States House of Representatives for aid of programs for the prevention, identification, and treatment of adult abuse, neglect, and exploitation, and the establishment of a National Center for

Adult Abusers (H.R. 7551). Consideration should be given to legislation that would make financial assistance available to families who wish to care for their aged relatives. Among other policies might be a family allowance plan, tax supports and benefits, and direct financial assistance. Recently, there has been discussion of family tax credits for the day care costs of children. Could there not be a comparable tax credit for adult day care as well?

The economic benefits from such legislation could be of vital importance to a family; on the other hand, might such legislation be viewed as a mandate for family responsibility and coerce (however subtly) a family to care for an elderly parent? Family members may be motivated to care for an elderly relative for inappropriate reasons (such as economic benefits) and the quality of care might be suspect. Two final questions which need to be addressed in legislation pertain to (1) the adequacy of the benefit or credit, vis á vis the actual costs for care to the family, and (2) the guarantee that an allowance to the family will be used for care.

Supportive and Protective Services

Care of an elderly parent may require continuous attention. Especially if the needs of the elderly person are great or family members few, the demands from the provision of such intense care need to be relieved (or abusive behavior may result). Communities need to provide supportive services to families, such as adult day care, day hospitals, transportation, friendly visitors, respite care, homemaker and home health aides, and chore services. In addition, there is need for family social services. Oktay and Palley (1980) indicate that such services should be available as a part of any national policy on the family. Communities vary considerably in the existence of formal supportive services, and the effectiveness of such services is related not only to existence, but also to community awareness and accessibility. In their study of service needs of those who care for elderly in New York City, Mellor and Getzel (1980) concluded that few of the care providers were receiving formal services to assist in the care of the elderly.

Adult protective services legislation is needed in all states to ensure an effective mechanism for surveillance of dependent elderly and entry into a setting where there is adversity. In 1980, 25 states had some type of protective services legislation (Salend, Satz, and Pynoos, 1981; United States Select Committee on Aging, 1981). Common to most of the legislation is the reporting (sometimes mandatory) of suspected abusive behavior toward an elderly person, legal entry into a home or facility, service provision, and legal intervention. Such legislation seems necessary for safeguarding the dependent elderly, given the sanctity of the family and home from outside scrutiny.

Public Acknowledgment of the Problem

Although abuse of the elderly parent is judged to be relatively infrequent, it is suspected that the problem will grow. Inflation, increased longevity and multigenerational families, earlier retirement, higher divorce rates and more remarriages, and multiple grandchildren, grandparents, and step-parents are among the forces causing change in family systems. Not only is there a failure to define role responsibilities adequately, but also roles are getting increasingly complex.

The problem of abuse of elderly parents needs to be acknowledged. Grown children and family members facing tensions from having to care for elderly parents must not see problems as personal or moral inadequacies but must realize that these same problems are faced by many other families. Such a realization should result in a realistic desire to assess their capability for care, seek alternative plans if it is apparent that the costs are too great, and seek professional counseling and guidance in a tension-filled situation.

The elderly parent, too, should realize that abusive or exploitive behavior by grown children is not to be endured in silence or to be denied, nor should they feel responsible for the behavior of grown children. The abusive behavior of their children may be more a reflection of pressures and tensions than of personal flaws or limitations. Help should be sought, by both the parent and the family member.

Human service workers need to be sensitive to the potential vulnerability of elderly parents to abusive behavior. Rathbone-McCuan (1980) stated that failure to explore the problem and intervene is "an abdication of professional responsibility." The family should not be viewed as a panacea, but must be assessed as to its ability to give care. Individual and family counseling should be more available where there is tension. Professional staff should be trained to identify and intervene in adult abuse, and to work with the abused and abusers.

CONCLUSION

Family responsibility should not be mandated nor should it be the sole alternative in the care of the elderly. Societal values must change and resources developed for the care of the dependent elderly (ie, housing, community service systems) independent of the family and for the assistance of those families who desire to care for their elderly relatives.

Rheinstein (1965) has raised the important issue of family motivation for the care of the elderly.

> What indeed motivates an adult son or daughter to support, or to take care of, an aged father or mother? Is it love pure and simple, unselfish concern about a beloved human being near to the heart? Or is it concern about what the neighbors might say or think, or is it unthinking habit or compliance with an unquestioned tradition, or obedience to a duty felt in conscience, or the fear of God, or the fear of the court, ... ?

We cannot guarantee appropriate motivations, but we, as a society, can preclude coercion of the family into unwanted responsibility or excessive responsibility for elderly dependent parents. We can also provide financial and social service support to permit a child and family to carry out their wishes to care for an elderly loved one. In doing so, society minimizes the opportunity for abuse and maltreatment of the elderly parent, thereby assisting the family and the parent.

BIBLIOGRAPHY

Atchley RC: *The Social Forces in Later Years,* ed 3, Belmont, CA, Wadsworth, 1980.

Blenkner M: Social work and family relationships in later life with some thoughts on filial maturity, in Shanas E, Streib GF (eds): *Social Structure and the Family: Generational Relations.* Englewood Cliffs, NJ, Prentice-Hall, 1965, pp 46–59.

Block M, Sinnott J (eds): *The Battered Elder Syndrome: An Exploratory Study.* College Park, MD, University of Maryland Center on Aging, 1979.

Blumberg M: When parents hit out. *Twentieth Century* 1964;Winter,173:39–44.

Butler RN: *Why Survive: Being Old in America.* New York, Harper & Row, 1975.

Caplan G, Killiea M: *Support Systems and Mutual Help.* New York, Grune & Stratton, 1976.

Cavan R: Family tensions between the old and the middle aged. *Marriage and Family Living* 1956;18:323–327.

Farrar M: Mother-daughter conflicts extended into later life. *Social Casework* 1955;36:202–207.

Garbarino J: The human ecology of child maltreatment: A conceptual model for research. *J Marriage Family* 1977;39:721–735.

Gelles G: Child abuse as psychopathology: A sociological critique and reformulation. *Am J Orthopsychiatry* 1973;43:611–621.

Gil D: Violence against children. *J Marriage Family* 1971;33:637–648.

Glasser P, Glasser L: Role reversal and conflict between aged parents and their children. *Marriage and Family Living* 1962;24:46–51.

Goldfarb AI: Psychodynamics and the three-generation family, in Shanas E, Streib GF (eds): *Social Structure and the Family: Generational Relations.* Englewood Cliffs, NJ, Prentice-Hall, 1965, pp 10–45.

Goldsmith J, Goldsmith S: *Overview of Crimes Against the Elderly,* testimony before United States House Select Committee on Aging, January 31, 1978.

Goldsmith J, Tomas N: Crimes against the elderly: A continuing national crisis. *Aging* 236–237, June–July, 1974, pp 10–13.

Horowitz A, Shindel L: *The Impact of Caring for an Elderly Relative.* Paper presented at 33rd Annual Scientific Meeting of the Gerontological Society, San Diego, CA, November, 1980.

H.R. 7551, A Bill Submitted to the 96th Congress, 2nd Session, June 11, 1980.

Johnson C: *Family Support Systems of Elderly Italian Americans.* Paper presented at 33rd Annual Scientific Meeting of the Gerontological Society, San Diego, CA, November, 1980.

Katz, K: Elder abuse. *J Family Law* 1979–1980;18:695–722.

Lau E, Kosberg J: Abuse of the elderly by informal care providers. *Aging* 299–300 September–October, 1979, 10–15.

Lystad M: Violence at home: A review of the literature. *Am J Orthopsychiatry* 1975;45:328–345.

Maddox G: Families as context and resource in chronic illness, in Sherwood S (ed): *Issues in Long Term Care.* New York, Holstead, 1975.

Malinchak A, Wright D: The scope of elderly victimization. *Aging,* March 1978: 10–16.

Mellor J, Getzel G: *Stress and Service Needs of Those Who Care for the Aged.* Paper presented at the 33rd Annual Scientific Meeting of the Gerontological Society, San Diego, CA, November, 1980.

Oktay J, Palley H: A national family policy for the chronically ill elderly. *The Social Welfare Forum,* Washington, DC, National Conference on Social Welfare, 1980, pp 104–120.

O'Malley H, et al: *Elder Abuse in Massachusetts: A Survey of Professionals and Paraprofessionals,* Boston, MA, Legal Research and Services for the Elderly, 1979.

Pizzey E: *Scream Quietly or the Neighbors Will Hear.* Baltimore, MD, Penguin Books, 1974.

Rathbone-McCuan E: Elderly victims of family violence and neglect. *Social Casework* 1980;May,61(4):296–304.

Rheinstein M: Motivation of intergenerational behavior by norms of law, in Shanas E, Streib GF (eds): *Social Structure and the Family: Generational Relations.* Englewood Cliffs, NJ, Prentice-Hall, 1965, 241–266.

Salend E, Satz M, Pynoos J: Mandatory Reporting Legislation for Adult Abuse. UCLA/USC Long-term Care Gerontology Center, March, 1981.

Schorr A: . . . Thy Father and Thy Mother—A Second Look At Filial Responsibility and Family Policy, Washington—DC: Social Security Administration (Publication No. 13-11953), 1980.

Sparks R: *Crimes Against the Elderly: Problems and Perspectives.* Testimony before the United States House Select Committee on Aging, January 31, 1978.

Straus M: *A Sociological Perspective on Causes of Family Violence.* Paper presented at American Association for the Advancement of Science Conference, Houston, TX, 1979.

Tuzil T: The aging role in helping children and their aged parents. *Social Casework* 1978; May,59(5):302–305.

United States House of Representatives, Select Committee on Aging: *Elder Abuse (An Examination of a Hidden Problem).* Washington, DC, Government Printing Office, 1981.

The following chapters present information on actual or possible interventions which focus on the victimization of the elderly. Legislation should be enacted and enforced to safeguard the rights of the elderly. Trained professionals are needed to provide treatment and counseling for the elderly and their families. Community education is needed to publicize the existence of abuse and maltreatment of the elderly, to make appeals for the victimized to seek assistance, and to create community sensitivity and a demand for action. Advocates are needed to ensure that this occurs.

The pros and cons of protective services for the elderly are discussed by John J. Regan. The author provides an historical review of involuntary intervention and guardianship and discusses principles for protective services legislation reform and current efforts for such reform. Jacqueline C. Walker describes the historical development of protective services for the elderly in Connecticut and the experience of the program. Case examples are provided to illustrate the impact of the protective services program for victims of abuse, neglect, abandonment, and exploitation.

Paul Nathanson provides an overview of legal issues and services related to elderly persons in general, and frail and impaired elderly in particular. Public legal services are compared to private ones, and neighborhood dispute resolution is described as a potentially significant development for the elderly as an alternative to traditional courts.

Victoria Holt Jaycox and Lawrence J. Center have written about a comprehensive response to violent crimes against the elderly, and they describe the concept of crime prevention. The victim assistance concept is described and discussed in combination with crime prevention. The authors describe the creation of new resources to support anticrime services. The use of consumer advocates to ensure the quality of nursing home care is discussed by Peter A. Stathopoulas. The author describes the goals, structure, and activities of Consumer Advocates for Better Care in North Central Massachusetts and makes recommendations based upon the experiences of this advocacy effort.

The application of a task-centered approach for families of abused elderly relatives is discussed by Eloise Rathbone-McCuan, Barbara Voyles, and Ann Travis. After background information is presented, the authors describe the task-centered model, apply it to cases involving the abuse of elderly relatives, and present a case to illustrate the use of the model. Nancy R. Hooyman discusses community interventions in the solution of elder abuse and the importance of strengthening family support systems for the elderly. The chapter also identifies community systems for the detection of elder abuse and needed intervention. Several examples of community efforts are presented.

Elizabeth Reynolds and Sheila Stanton's chapter focuses on the special responsibility of nurses in hospitals to detect elder abuse. They see the role of the nurse to include that of an advocate for geriatric patients and to be involved in discharge planning and patient education. The authors report on a survey of experiences with abuse by nurses who work in hospital emergency departments and discuss needed curriculum. Kenneth Solomon, MD, describes types of treatment with elderly patients and their families which include crisis intervention (pharmacologic and psychotherapeutic) and long-term intervention. The chapter also presents information on the education of medical students and others preparing for careers in the health field working with geriatric populations.

The final chapter is coauthored by Congresswoman Mary Rose Oakar and Carol Ann Miller who discuss federal legislation to protect the elderly. The chapter reviews child abuse legislation and domestic violence bills, and summarizes recent Congressional hearings on elder abuse. Federal legislation related to abuse of the elderly is discussed, as are needed policies to provide assistance and alternatives to families who care for elderly relatives.

17 Protective Services for the Elderly: Benefit or Threat

John J. Regan

The plight of the neglected, abused, and exploited elder person has spurred many state legislatures over the past decade to enact adult protective services acts. "Protective services" is traditionally defined as a system of preventive, supportive, and surrogate services for adults living in the community to enable them to maintain independent living to avoid abuse and exploitation.

Services programs have two main characteristics: the coordinated delivery of services to adults at risk, and the actual or potential legal authority to provide substitute decision-making for the client. The services element consists of a wide variety of health, housing, and social services, such as homemakers, house repair, periodic visitors, special transportation, visiting nurses, and hot meals. These services are not just help given randomly by agencies ignorant of one another's efforts toward a particular client. Instead, coordination is provided by a caseworker-manager, who is responsible for assessing an individual's need and arranging for the requisite services from the appropriate agencies.

The second component of a protective services program, authority to intervene on behalf of the client, directly involves the legal system and will be the focus of this chapter. Ordinarily, the client has the right voluntarily to delegate such powers to agents of his own choice. If, however, he refuses assistance but intervention appears necessary, the legal system provides several mechanisms for authorizing involuntary assistance, including civil commitment, guardianship, court orders for protective services and protective placement, and emergency commitment or treatment orders. Emergency medical care may also be rendered to an unconscious patient on the basis of a legal presumption that the patient would consent to such treatment if able to make a decision.

Historical Development of
Involuntary Intervention

The origins of legal authority for involuntary intervention lie in the principle established in English law 700 years ago that the king, as father of the country (parens patriae), was responsible for protection and care of the person and property of the mentally ill. The king exercised this power through the chancellor, who was authorized, on petition, to conduct an inquiry whether the subject was an "idiot" (one born with "no understanding") or a "lunatic" (one who had been born with understanding but had lost the use of reason), and also was the owner of assets likely to be dissipated. If, as a result of the inquiry, the person was found by a jury of peers to be a lunatic, the chancellor would commit him to the care of a friend, who would receive an allowance from the assets to pay costs of services and care. Responsibility for managing the assets typically was assigned to another person, the ward's heir. The heir had to account to the court of chancery, to the incompetent (if recovered), or to the incompetent's caretaker, according to a gradually evolving set of customs, rules, and standards.

It is noteworthy that the chancellor opened an inquiry only if the alleged incompetent had assets sufficient to bear the expense, since the purpose was only to insure the proper administration of the incompetent's property and thereby safeguard the king's income. The law made no provision for care or custody of the poor; they were left to their own resources or to the good will of others.

In colonial America, the same policy prevailed. Persons lacking both assets and family drifted at the mercy of fortune, singly or in company with others. Instead of providing for their needs, the ethic of the period, which equated labor with virtue, produced laws that compelled them to work. Those who could not work were obliged to beg.

The violent mentally ill were given more public attention than those who were merely helpless. People deemed too dangerous to be at large were confined by law, in what was to become the civil commitment process, for the duration of the dangerous condition. In the company of criminals and paupers, the insane were shut up in a public jail, workhouse, poor house, or a private cage, pen, or strong room. Such confinement increased during the second quarter of the 18th century as the population increased. Newly formed communities dealt more impersonally with the unfortunate than did rural areas.

The scandalous treatment of the mentally disordered inspired a movement in the latter half of the 18th century that ultimately produced state mental hospitals. Procedures for committing a person to these institutions were frighteningly simple. A few words scribbled by a physician on a piece of paper, as "Jas Sproul is a proper person for the Pennsylvania Hospital," were all that were necessary. By contrast, to declare that same person incompetent to administer property required a petition to the court for a writ, adequate notice, jury trial, or appointment of a guardian.

As the number of state hospitals multiplied, so did the need for laws defining commitment procedures that were humane and just. The confinement of Josiah Oakes, in particular, excited public attention in 1843 and led to widely followed guidelines for the detention of mental patients. Oakes, an elderly and ordinarily stable man, had become engaged to a young woman of unsavory character a few days after the death of his wife. His family had him committed to the Massachusetts asylum on the allegation that he suffered from hallucinations and displayed unsoundness of mind in conducting his business affairs. In ordering his release, the Massachusetts court declared:

> The right to restrain an insane person of his liberty is found in that great law of humanity, which makes it necessary to confine those whose going at large would be dangerous to themselves or others . . . . And the necessity which creates the law, creates the limitation of the law. The question must then arise in each particular case whether a patient's own safety, or that of others, requires that he should be restrained for a certain time, and whether restraint is necessary for his restoration, or will be conducive thereto. The restraint can continue as long as the necessity continues. This is the limitation, and the proper limitation.[1]

This decision signaled a subtle but significant expansion of the law's authority to intervene in the lives of the mentally disabled. No longer was the state intervening merely as parens patriae to protect the incompetent and their property. Instead, the state was bringing to bear its police power to protect society from persons whose presence in the community was thought to be a danger to others.

The next major step in this legal evolution came late in the 19th century, when medical figures like Dr. Benjamin Rush and Dr. Isaac Ray, in combination with pioneers in social work like Mrs. E. W. P. Packard and Dorothea Dix, led a popular movement to aid the mentally disabled. The stream of state legislation that followed still constitutes much of the basic legal pattern in effect today.

Until the close of the 1960s, civil commitment to a state mental hospital became the standard method for providing involuntary care and treatment for mentally disabled, including the elderly, who lacked family willing and able to care for them in the community. State law governing civil commitment was often poorly drafted and loosely administered, making it easy to institutionalize the elderly person who showed symptoms of mental illness. The statutory criteria for identifying persons needing confinement were vague and circular. The court procedures for reaching this determination did not adequately protect the constitutional rights of the patient.

Once inside the hospital, an elderly person often reacted to the trauma of institutionalization by simply dying. Others experienced psychological trauma. The loss of familiar objects, well-learned patterns of daily living, and environmental clues produced a sense of defeat and uselessness, which, in turn, aggravated the symptoms of brain syndrome which may have been the basis for commitment in the first place. The hospital, for its part, segregated elderly patients in geriatric wards where the patient's life was structured into an extended act of dying rather than one of active physical or psychiatric treatment. The state mental hospital became the end of the road for the elderly.

In the late 1960s, many states, motivated both by changes in the philosophy of treatment and by the expectation of large fiscal savings, began to discharge large numbers of these patients into nursing homes and the community at large. At the same time, persons whose problems were primarily physical, social, or economic, and who did not specifically require acute institutional care, were no longer admitted to the hospital. These same states, however, often failed to provide alternative institutional settings or community services to these persons. As a result, thousands of elderly who may need limited assistance in daily living have been cast adrift with little more than a Supplemental Security Income check.

As a result of recent studies,[2] a second group of elderly who need community-based intervention services, the abused elderly, must be added to this population of adults-at-risk. As discussed elsewhere in this book, a significant number of older people living with their families or other caretakers who are subject to physical and psychological abuse has been identified. To meet the needs of both groups, state protective services programs have developed rapidly throughout the 1970s, using a variety of intervention mechanisms, of which guardianship is in the forefront.

Guardianship

The process for appointment of a guardian begins when an "interested person" files a petition with the appropriate court asking that a particular person be declared incompetent and a guardian appointed. Notice of a hearing on the petition is then sent to the alleged incompetent and sometimes his relatives. At the hearing, the alleged incompetent is entitled to be present and to produce evidence and witnesses to dispute the allegations of the petitioner and the evidence against him or her. The person may be represented by counsel if he or she chooses, and in some states the court, in its own discretion, may appoint counsel.

The typical statutory definition describes an incompetent as one who, by reason of mental illness, drunkenness, drug addiction, or old age is incapable of caring for himself and/or providing for his family or is liable to dissipate his property or become the victim of designing persons. Thus, in declaring a person incompetent, a court is making two findings: (1) that the person suffers from a condition affecting mental capacity; and (2) that certain functional disabilities result from this condition, such as inability to do business, manage property or make personal care decisions. Legal incompetency, however, is not the same as mental illness; rather, it is one possible consequence of that condition.

If the person is declared incompetent, the court will appoint a guardian of the person or a guardian of the estate (sometimes known as a conservator). The former is authorized to act as the legal representative of the ward. In this capacity, he may make medical care decisions, decide where the ward resides, sue or be sued on behalf of the ward, and void contracts entered into before the guardianship began. The guardian of the estate is the ward's property manager, and is responsible for preventing waste and providing for the ward's needs. He assumes possession, use, and control of the ward's property, although title may remain in the ward's name. He usually must render a periodic accounting to the court and must obtain court permission for certain activities, particularly those affecting the disposition of real property.

The practical reality of guardianship laws in many states, however, makes them inappropriate and even repressive instruments for assisting neglected or abused elderly as part of a protective services program. The statutory criteria for identifying the incompetent person, the procedures for appointing guardians, and the legal and economic consequences of a guardianship are open to criticism.

First, in their effort to determine whether a person is incompetent, courts overemphasize mental incapacity while ignoring the need for evidence of functional disability. This distortion arises out of overreliance on the "medical model" of mental illness and on psychiatric testimony.

According to this medical model, behavioral variances are analogous to disease in the physical body, implying that there is a distinct discontinuity in the continuum of behavioral differences that can be objectively discerned, measured, and labeled pathologic. Thus, a psychiatrist may testify that, in his opinion, the person's behavior is symptomatic of a particular type of mental illness. This opinion, which is relevant only to the first finding a court must make, nevertheless may be transformed by the judge or the psychiatrist himself into a legal conclusion that the person is incompetent and, therefore, needs a guardian. What is overlooked in this process is that the psychiatrist's own diagnosis may include value-laden judgments about the person's behavior and that little, if any, attention has been paid to the actual functional abilities of the proposed ward.

Furthermore, the term *old age* may be used as a synonym for the term *senility,* although it obviously is not. It is easy to label a few behavioral aberrations sometimes associated with old age, such as forgetfulness or careless habits, as chronic brain syndrome and again jump to the conclusion that the person is incompetent and therefore in need of a guardian.

Another difficulty is that the court proceedings for appointing a guardian are often characterized by unseemly informality. Notice of the filing of a guardianship petition may be defective in the short period allowed for response, in the uninformative type of notice provided, or even in complete waiver of any notice requirement in certain circumstances. At the hearing the alleged incompetent is seldom present, particularly when a doctor's affidavit stating that appearance in court might produce a harmful effect on the person is submitted to the court. Representation of the proposed ward by counsel seldom occurs, and when it does, it may be of a perfunctory nature. Jury trials are not permitted in some states, while in those that permit them, such trials rarely happen. The result of this procedural informality is that persons may be deprived of significant personal rights with little or no opportunity for a meaningful challenge.

Finally, the consequences of the appointment of a guardian are drastic. The person found to be incompetent is thereby rendered virtually incapable of performing an act bearing legal consequences. He will be limited in his ability to execute documents, initiate litigation, participate in business and professional activities, and exercise political rights and privileges. The guardian may assume complete control and even title to the ward's property and decide where the ward will reside. It is this all-or-nothing character of the guardian's control that makes guardianship a poor instrument for assisting many elderly who experience only a partial and gradual deterioration in functional capacity. Many elderly persons require assistance only with certain recurring duties, such as paying bills, or with certain transactions, such as selling a house. They need a flexible guardianship tailored to their individual capacity that allows them to retain control over other decisions which they are capable of making without such assistance.

Another unwelcome effect of a guardianship is its high cost. Persons with modest assets may find them rapidly depleted to pay for a conservator's statutory fee. On the other hand, the poor or those living on small fixed incomes may be deprived of any form of guardianship assistance because of the lack of financial incentives for others to assume such duties.

These deficiencies indicate that a guardianship obtained in a state where traditional guardianship law is still in force is a poor instrument for use in a protective services program serving neglected and abused adults. The easy, uncontrolled intervention fostered by such laws may result in more oppression to the client than the neglect or abuse that initially brought the client to the agency's attention.

If traditional guardianship has been a heavy-handed procedure for authorizing involuntary intervention in the lives of neglected and abused adults, it has been utterly useless for dealing with crisis situations where swift action is needed. The major alternatives, however — emergency civil commitment to a mental health facility and the common law principle of implied consent to emergency medical treatment — are no better. The chronic deterioration of mental faculties and physical health associated with serious neglect or abuse does not fit neatly into any of these categories.

Principles for Reform

Despite these difficulties, many protective services advocates believe that involuntary intervention is essential to their programs. The primary task, as they see it, is to correct the faults and fill the gaps in traditional guardianship law and thus permit intervention in appropriate cases.

Two fundamental principles lie at the heart of this reform movement. First, client consent for protective services is essential. No service, be it hospitalization, guardianship, placement in a treatment center or nursing home, or home services, should be imposed on an individual who is mentally competent and refuses to accept such assistance. Only when a person is found by a court to be mentally disabled (in the case of civil commitment) or incapable of giving consent (in cases of guardianship, protective services, or placement) should involuntary intervention be authorized. The one exception is the rendering of short-term institutional services when a person will suffer immediate and irreparable physical injury or death without such services, and even here court authorization should be sought within a matter of hours.

Second, only the least needed restriction on a person's liberty and other civil rights should be permitted. This principle has been evolving in a number of recent court decisions and makes eminent constitutional sense. Concretely, it means that states must establish treatment alternatives for those who would otherwise be committed to state mental hospitals. These alternatives might include, in the words of one federal court:

> Voluntary or court-ordered outpatient treatment, day treatment in a hospital, night treatment in a hospital, placement in the custody of a friend or relative, placement in a nursing home, referral to a community mental health clinic, and home health aide services.[3]

For those persons whose disability requires surrogate services rather than mere treatment, the state may even be obliged to provide a spectrum of guardianship arrangements graduated according to the ward's functional disabilities. Thus, besides the traditional guardianship or conservatorship law which transfers complete jurisdiction over the ward's property or person, or both, to the court-appointed manager, a state would be obliged to establish less drastic forms of surrogate services. The device for achieving this goal would be to require that a court, in finding that a person needed such services, also specify the precise nature of the person's disability and confer only such powers on the manager as are necessary to fill the gap in self-determination created by the disability. The massive transfer of powers over a ward currently authorized under many state laws would have to give way to a case-by-case process of matching powers to needs.

These advocates have proposed a number of specific guidelines for legislative reform:

1. The criteria for determining incompetency should be revised to emphasize specific functional disabilities resulting from a variety of disorders, rather than to stress proof of mental disorder alone.

2. Guardianship proceedings should be made adversarial. Stronger requirements for notice to the client of an impending guardianship hearing and for the person's presence at the hearing should be developed. Counsel for the client, private or appointed, should be mandatory, and other traditional elements of due process — the right to present evidence, to confront and cross-examine adverse witnesses, and to a decision based on the evidence — should be made explicit.

3. Courts should be authorized to appoint limited guardians, ie, to delegate to the guardian only as much power over the ward as is needed to compensate for the ward's functional disability.

4. To assist the court in determining the type and degree of intervention needed in each case, a professional screening team should be

established. This group would conduct an assessment of the physical, mental, and social needs of the proposed ward, and present the court its recommendation concerning the least restrictive course of intervention, care, or treatment consistent with the client's welfare.

5. Where possible, the client's wishes concerning the choice of a guardian should be followed. Private social agencies should be empowered to act as guardians in appropriate circumstances.

6. Guardianships should be reviewed periodically by the court. Guardians should be required to submit annual reports describing the present personal status of the ward, the guardian's plan for preserving and maintaining the future well-being of the protected person, and the need for continuation or discontinuation of the guardianship. If the guardian did not justify continued intervention, the guardianship would cease.

7. Specific statutory provisions for emergency intervention should be enacted based on the previously listed due process standards.

Progress of the Reform Movement

In the protective services legislation of the 1970s these principles and guidelines have encountered a mixed reception. In one group of about 40 jurisdictions, the state has authorized its social services agency to provide protective services but has made no serious attempt to overhaul its guardianship law, with a few exceptions. These exceptions include states which have adopted the Uniform Probate Code to replace older guardianship statutes, but which typically have made no effort to address the problem of intervention in a protective services setting.

A second group consisting of 11 states has enacted integrated protective services/intervention systems. A few of these states have revised their guardianship laws as part of their new protective services legislation. Most of these states have bypassed their guardianship laws and instead created a new court proceeding to authorize intervention. This new proceeding may lead, depending on the jurisdiction, to orders for protective services, protective placement, or emergency services, all of which are to be implemented by a public social services agency.

The recent protective services legislation in Maryland and Alabama is illustrative of the wide variation in approach taken by these 11 states. Involuntary intervention in a protective services setting can occur in Maryland either by court appointment of a guardian of the person or by an emergency court order creating a temporary guardianship. The key provision in the state's adult protective services act is a drastically revised law concerning guardianship of the person.

Any person, including a governmental agency, may petition a court to appoint such guardian for a disabled person, who is defined as one lacking "sufficient understanding or capacity to make or communicate responsible decisions concerning his person, including provisions for health care, food, clothing, or shelter, because of any mental disability, senility, other mental weakness, disease, habitual drunkenness, or addiction to drugs."[4] After notice, the court must hold a hearing, at which the person is entitled to be present, to be represented by counsel, including appointed counsel if indigent, and to secure and present independent medical evidence. Waiver of the right to attend the hearing, or incapacity to be present, may not be presumed from nonappearance but must be determined on the basis of factual information supplied to the court.

The court may then select a guardian from a priority list of possible guardians. Preference is given to a guardian designated by the person, but if no other person is available or willing to serve, the director of the local department of social services or the state director on aging, if the disabled person is 65 years of age or older, may be appointed. The court may then grant the guardianship those powers necessary to provide for the demonstrated need of the disabled person. The guardianship of the person may not manage the estate, nor may the person's residence be changed without special court approval. Transfer to a mental health facility is specifically prohibited except through regular civil commitment proceedings.

The Maryland act also provides a complementary special court procedure for dealing with emergencies.[5] On petition, after 24 hours notice to the person, the court must hold a hearing within 48 hours, and if it determines the person is disabled and an emergency exists, the court appoints a temporary guardian of the person for 72 hours and provides the guardian with only those powers needed to eliminate the emergency. The order may be extended for an additional 72 hours, but if the need for services continues thereafter, a regular guardianship proceeding must be commenced while the temporary guardianship continues.

In Alabama, an adult in need of protective services is defined as a

person 18 years of age or older whose behavior indicates that he is mentally incapable of adequately caring for himself and his interests without serious consequences to himself or others, or who, because of physical or mental impairment, is unable to protect himself from abuse, neglect or exploitation by others, and who has no guardian or relative or other appropriate person able, willing and available to assume the kind and degree of protection and supervision required under the circumstances.[6]

A court may order protective services when such a person is in need of care and protection because of danger to his health or safety, but is unwilling to accept the services. The intervention is apparently intended to be less formal than a guardianship. None of the court procedures is specified, no guardian is appointed, and the authorization given to the department of pensions and security for provision of protective services is of indefinite duration.

In emergencies involving a person whose health or safety is in immediate danger; who is unable, because of physical or mental disabilities, to provide for his basic needs for shelter, food, clothing, or health care; and who is either incapable of giving consent or does not consent, the court may order on an ex parte basis the placement of the person in a foster home or nursing home.[7] Thereafter, within ten days, the person and certain others are informed of the court's action and the person's whereabouts. Only then does the person receive a hearing on his need for protective placement and on the appropriateness of the present placement and arrangements for future care.

Protective placement may also be ordered in nonemergency cases when a court determines that a person is unable to provide for his own protection from abuse, neglect, or exploitation.[8] Procedures here are more formal, in that a guardian ad litem must be appointed to represent the person if he is not represented by counsel, a jury trial is required, and a comprehensive evaluation of the person has been made. The court is directed to give preference in its determination to the least restrictive alternative considered proper and to choose noninstitutional care where possible. Placement may be made to nursing home, personal care facility, or a foster care home, but not to a mental health facility. A guardian may also be appointed in accordance with ordinary state guardianship procedures, but the department is disqualified from serving as guardian.

While the Maryland legislation is representative of the best of the new adult protective services acts, the Alabama statute and others in this group of 11 states are no better than the old system. The client often has little procedural protection in the court hearing to determine whether the protective services order is to be issued. If the agency is then successful in obtaining the requested order, there are few limits placed on its power over the client. Virtually any kind of social or health service may be imposed for an indefinite period. The agency need not file periodic reports about the client's status or conditions, nor is it required to seek renewal of the order. Even an agency decision to change the residence of the client to a hospital or nursing home is largely unreviewed.

The new criteria for identifying candidates for protective services also present problems. Neglect and abuse are often defined in broad terms, allowing courts and agencies too much leeway to disapprove a client's behavior and impose on that person their own views about a proper lifestyle. Further, a few states now permit involuntary intervention when the basis for the client's alleged incapacity is purely physical rather than mental. Both trends may infringe on the client's right of self-determination.

Finally, the new legislation's use of public guardianship causes deep concern. There may be a conflict of interest between an agency's fiduciary responsibility as guardian to serve the best interests of the client and its limited fiscal authority as a public body to provide the particular services needed by that client. Moreover, the delegation of day-to-day guardianship duties to a variety of caseworkers within an agency to an individual with a heavy case load may depersonalize guardianship and negate any real personal fiduciary role. Finally, special oversight of a public agency that has assumed complete power over a citizen's personal life is of critical importance. Yet, on all counts, most of these 11 states, and indeed, most of the 34 in the nation that have public guardians have failed to address these issues.

Both involuntary protective services and public guardianships raise important questions about the limits of governmental power when exercised for benevolent purposes, but in a paternalistic way. How secure can we be in the court determinations that individual clients are incompetent and therefore not allowed to make their own decisions to neglect themselves or even to suffer abuse or exploitation from others? Is the court process leading to this determination really fair since it is so one-sided in favor of the petitioner? Do guardians really make better decisions than their wards? Is placement in an institution really a great improvement over the previous environment in the eyes of the client or perhaps only of the caseworker? Are public agencies really capable of the heavy burden of personalized interest in a ward which the responsibility of guardianship demands?

The record of the past decade of protective services legislation does not inspire confidence that satisfactory answers to these questions have been found. Protective services, especially when provided by a public agency, may be becoming a mechanism leading to total dominion over elderly clients by public agencies. Too much emphasis may have been placed on involuntary intervention, while the development of methods for providing strictly voluntary services, even to mentally disabled clients, has been overlooked. Social services agencies may instead need to find innovative ways through creative casework to win client confidence and thus the client's consent to the recommended services. These efforts may then lead to a decrease in the incidence of uncooperative clients and a consequent decline in the need for involuntary intervention.

While agencies are developing voluntary service programs, state legislative action will also be necessary. Legislatures could revitalize mechanisms for persons needing assistance to appoint their own agents. It has also been proposed that probate law be revised to permit creation of a living will, ie, a document which would allow individuals to direct the management of their property in case of future incompetence.[9] At the same time, reform of state guardianship, protective services, and public guardianship laws to eliminate their substantive and procedural defects should be pressed vigorously.

The weakness of current state intervention laws and their inappropriateness for many cases of neglected, abused, and exploited adults does not mean that these clients are to be abandoned by helping agencies. The full range of voluntary services will still be available. Legal remedies for deterring or incapacitating the abuser or exploiter should be vigorously pursued. Involuntary intervention, however, should be the last resort. Doing good for the adult at risk may mean not just providing help when needed, but also knowing the limits of one's power to help.

FOOTNOTES

[1]*Matter of Josiah Oakes:* 8 Law Rep. 123 (Mass. 1845–46).
[2]Block MR, Sinnott JD (eds): *The Battered Elder Syndrome,* College Park, Maryland, University of Maryland Center on Aging, 1979; O'Rourke M: *Elder Abuse: The State of The Art,* National Conference on Abuse of Older Persons. Boston, Massachusetts, Legal Research and Services for the Elderly, 1981.
[3]*Lessard v. Schmidt,* 349 F.Supp. 1078 (E.D. Wis. 1972), vacated and for a more specific injunctive order, 414 U.S. 473 (1974), amended opinion, 379 F.Supp. 1376 (1974).
[4]Md. Est. and Trusts Code Ann. §13-705(b) (Supp. 1981).
[5]Md. Ann. Code art. 88A, §109(b); Md. Est. and Trusts Code Ann. §13-709 (Supp. 1981).
[6]Ala. Code §38-9-2(1) (Supp. 1981).
[7]Ala. Code §38-9-5 (Supp. 1981).
[8]Ala. Code §38-9-6(c) (Supp. 1981).
[9]Alexander G: *Premature Probate: A Different Perspective on Guardianship for the Elderly,* 31 Stanford Law Review 1008 (1979).

18 Protective Services for the Elderly: Connecticut's Experience

Jacqueline C. Walker

In July 1977, Connecticut passed two significant pieces of legislation. The first established a Nursing Home Ombudsman Office in the Department on Aging.[1] The second established a reporting law for protection of the elderly.[2] Both acts were innovations in the United States and have proved to be important adjuncts to the other responsibilities of Connecticut's Department on Aging.

From October 1975 until July 1977, the department had attempted to develop an ombudsman/advocacy program for nursing home residents under an Administration on Aging discretionary grant of $18,000. The same grant was available to every state in the union. The small amount of funding made it difficult to develop a viable, statewide, advocacy program that would adequately respond to complaints and problems concerning care and treatment of nursing home patients. Therefore, after consultation with Connecticut's Commissioner on Aging and the program's advisory committee, it was decided to write legislation which would establish an Ombudsman Office within the

Department on Aging which would be funded by the state. Both the Ombudsman and Elderly Protective Services laws were passed through the efforts of the Governor's Blue Ribbon Committee to Investigate the Nursing Home Industry in Connecticut. Those bills, along with others relating to the care provided in and the ownership and management of nursing homes, were submitted as a package and concerned themselves, primarily, with the life-style and well-being of Connecticut's elderly citizens.

The Ombudsman Office

The Ombudsman Office consists of a State Ombudsman and five Regional Ombudsmen. The Regional Ombudsmen recruit and train volunteer patients' advocates to work in nursing homes and homes for the aged throughout the state. The State and Regional Ombudsmen are appointed by the Commissioner on Aging. In Connecticut, the Ombudsmen are women, each of whom has had extensive experience dealing with the frail elderly in some capacity, although their education and experience vary considerably.

The State Ombudsman is a registered nurse with a Master of Social Work degree. She has worked in a nursing home and helped develop a home care program designed to keep the elderly out of nursing homes by providing home care services. Three of the Ombudsmen have masters degrees, one in education, one in urban planning, and one in geriatric counseling. The other two have bachelors degrees in psychology and sociology, respectively. The volunteer advocates, of which there are presently about 90, vary tremendously in background and experience. Some are retired professionals such as pharmacists, psychologists, nurses, and social workers. Others have had only a high school education. Advocates are recruited through radio and television public service announcements and newspaper advertisements. The Regional Ombudsmen screen the advocates for the following requirements: (1) They must not have preconceived ideas about nursing homes; (2) they must not be affiliated with a nursing home in any way; and (3) if they have a relative in a nursing home, they will not be assigned to that facility.

After a two-day training program, the volunteer advocates are assigned to one or more nursing homes that they must visit at least once a week. Any problem found is brought to the attention of the administrator where, hopefully, it is resolved. Confidentiality is maintained concerning complainants' and complainees' names. The advocates attend monthly follow-up training sessions to keep abreast of new regulations and policies concerning nursing homes.

The responsibilities of the Regional Ombudsmen are twofold: (1) to receive and investigate complaints concerning residents in long-term care facilities, and (2) to receive and investigate reports of abuse, neglect, abandonment, and exploitation of any person 60 years or older in the state.

This chapter is concerned with the second responsibility.

Why Protective Services for the Elderly?

During the last several years, there has been increased emphasis and concern on the part of the media, research centers, social service agencies, and state and federal governments, concerning elderly abuse and neglect. In Connecticut, that concern came to light during meetings of the Governor's Blue Ribbon Committee. The members of that committee's task force on "Alternatives to Long-Term Care" expressed their belief that there were probably many elderly citizens who, through no fault of their own, were suffering from neglect and abuse of some kind. The task force felt that many elderly people could probably extricate themselves from such problems, but others, for either mental or physical reasons, would be unable to obtain the necessary ancillary help. At that time, approximately 400,000 elderly persons 60 years or older lived in Connecticut. Somewhat arbitrarily, it surmised that 1% (4000 persons) might find themselves in a neglectful or abusing situation during the year. The assumption was made that of those 4000 elderly persons, 75% would be able to overcome the problems through the help of family, friends, adequate finances, and knowledge of available community services. Twenty-five percent (approximately 1000 persons) would be unable to handle serious personal disasters, according to rough calculations.

The task force members attempted to gather as much information as possible from social service agencies, police, and hospitals, but to no avail. There were no statistics available anywhere concerning volume and frequency of abused elderly clients. Unfortunately, unless a law mandates that agencies report such incidences, there is no incentive to keep records of such cases.

Those on the task force were undaunted, however, and were determined to fight for the establishment of an elderly protective services law even though using "gut feelings" as a basis for their endeavors. Persistence triumphed in the end, and our new bill passed the legislature.

As it turned out, calculations were quite accurate, also, for during the first year the Ombudsman Office received and investigated 700 referrals. (The program did not get into full swing until June 1977, because of the wait for the regulations to be approved.)

How Elderly Protective Services Work

Under Connecticut's elderly protective services law, the State Departments on Aging and Human Resources work together to provide help to persons 60 years or older who are victims of abuse, neglect, abandonment or exploitation.

A wide range of professionals and paraprofessionals, whose work brings them into contact with the elderly, are mandated to report cases of abuse and neglect to the State Ombudsman or one of the five Regional Ombudsmen within five calendar days of the time the abuse is discovered. Failure to report such a situation may result in a fine of not more than $500. Legal immunity from any civil or criminal liability related to a mandatory report is provided to those who report in good faith, except for cases of perjury. There are a number of provisions tailored to protect the rights of the elderly persons who may need protective services. Two important ones are as follows:

1. Elderly persons must give their consent before services are arranged for them.
2. If it is felt that an elderly person lacks the capacity to give consent for state intervention, a petition for custody of the person may be filed in probate court. The elderly person must be represented by an attorney during those proceedings.[3]

A temporary conservator may be appointed by the appropriate probate judge if there is a certificate signed by two physicians, licensed to practice medicine in Connecticut, stating that they have examined the client and found her/him to be incapable and that irreparable injury to the mental or physical health or financial or legal affairs of the respondent will result if no conservator is appointed immediately. A temporary conservatorship is valid for no more than 30 days.[4]

For example, in one case, the State Ombudsman was called by the owner of a rooming house because one of the boarders, an 80-year-old woman, was very ill and not responding coherently. On arrival at the home, the Ombudsman found a frail, feverish, dehydrated woman in bed. The woman was incoherent in her response to questions and refused to go to the hospital. The Ombudsman notified the local health director (physician) and the client's own physician. The health director arrived, examined the woman, and concurred that there was need of hospitalization. Both physicians signed the required certificate indicating imminent danger to health. The Ombudsman submitted the certificate to the probate judge who immediately appointed the selectman as emergency conservator. The client was taken to the hospital by ambulance where she subsequently died of a severe urinary tract infection.

The Regional Ombudsman, responsible for the town in which the abuse occurs, must make an immediate, personal investigation of the situation. The Ombudsman obtains all available information from the client, family, friends, and referrant after which she determines whether the case is valid. If the situation meets the appropriate criteria, the Ombudsman refers her assessment of the client and recommendations for action to the protective service unit in the closest district office of Human Resources. The protective services worker then visits the client and arranges for the provision of necessary services that will alleviate the problems. The effort is, always, to keep the client in his home rather than to institutionalize.

The Ombudsman Office maintains a statewide file on all clients and receives 10-day, 45-day and subsequent 90-day reports on each individual case from the protective services worker. There are six district offices of Human Resources, each housing an elderly protective services unit consisting of a supervisor and at least one worker.

Even though many of the workers had had previous experience dealing with adult or elderly problems, intensive, three-day training sessions were held for all personnel, including Ombudsmen, at the University of Connecticut School of Social Work. The sessions covered such topics as interviewing techniques, the aging process, methods of determining competency, conservatorship, and a precise review of the law and its legal ramifications.

Initially, all mandatory reporters were sent a flyer informing them of their responsibility under the new law as well as the names of the Regional Ombudsmen and the towns in their regions. Mandatory report forms were included in the mailing. The Department on Aging and the Department of Human Resources held public meetings throughout the state to discuss the new program more fully with those persons who would be involved.

Because the program would be involved with conservatorships (guardianships), the administrator of the probate court system, met with the local probate judges to review the new conservatorship law. Finally, both departments appointed an advisory committee to the program which continues to meet on a quarterly basis.

Types of Abuse

It is not known whether elderly abuse is a relatively new phenomenon or whether it previously has simply been unrecognized. The extended family of the past offered many opportunities for abuse, inasmuch as three, sometimes four, generations lived under the same roof. Life-styles were different from those of today, however, in that the majority of grown children, when married, settled down in the same town in which they and their spouses had been reared. This provided much needed support for aging parents and relatives. The majority of women did not work outside the home which meant that help was always available either in the same household where the elders lived or close by.

Today, society is entirely different. Young people are extremely mobile, often ending up far from family and friends. Living accommodations are no longer large rambling dwellings, capable of housing more than one family, but efficiency apartments, condominiums or houses, barely large enough for a small family. Many wives and mothers work full-time, thus prohibiting an older, dependent parent from moving in and being cared for unless outside help is brought in. Finally, the population is living longer, bringing along increased physical and mental infirmities.

Connecticut's law delineates four categories of abuse which are reportable to the Ombudsman office. Following are the definitions of those four categories and case examples from files:

Abuse   Abuse includes but is not limited to the willful infliction of physical pain, injury or mental anguish or the willful deprivation, by a caretaker, of services which are necessary to maintain physical and mental health.

Case 1.   A woman, aged 79, was referred by a hospital emergency room for injuries sustained in a beating from her husband. Bruises were noted on head, hands and back. The husband had been drinking for the past few years and abused his wife when intoxicated. The husband threatened the client with a butcher knife, and she was sent to a battered women's shelter overnight. Homemaker services were brought into the home; counseling was arranged for husband and client. The husband began alcohol treatment at a center. The case continues to be monitored by a protective services worker.

Neglect   Neglect refers to an elderly person who is either living alone and not able to provide for himself the services necessary to maintain physical and mental health or is not receiving necessary services from the responsible caretaker.

Case 2.   A man, aged 71, was referred by the city housing authority for self-neglect. The client lived in an apartment which had been condemned as unfit for human habitation. Because of debris and rubbish in the apartment, the fire department had labeled it a fire and safety hazard. The client collected garbage, junk, and debris and, as a result, there was nowhere to walk, sit, or sleep. The bathtub and sink were overflowing with garbage and the refrigerator was filled with rotten, rancid food. Arrangements were made for temporary housing while the

298

apartment was being exterminated and cleaned by chore services. During the clean-up, $15,000 was found in the walls, floor, and ceiling. The client has returned to the apartment and is being monitored by protective services. A homemaker comes in twice a week. Money and valuables are kept in a safety deposit box at the bank. The client is cooperating in the entire attempt.

Abandonment   Abandonment refers to the desertion or willful forsaking of an aged person by a caretaker or the forgoing of duties and obligations owed an elderly person by a caretaker or other person.

Case 3.   The hospital emergency room reported that a woman, aged 84, was brought in by her son and daughter-in-law, after which they left the hospital. The Ombudsman found the client to be frail with a cardiac problem, a severe leg ulcer, and mild hypertension. The client was fairly alert and oriented to place. In attempting to call the son's home it was learned that the phone had been disconnected. The client had been abandoned. After a short hospitalization, the client was placed in local home for the aged. The protective services worker continues to counsel her and the client has become quite active, participating in outings and going out on her own.

Exploitation   Exploitation refers to the act or process of taking advantage of an elderly person by another person or caretaker whether for monetary, personal, or other benefits, or gain or profit.

Case 4.   An administrator of a home for the aged reported that a woman resident, aged 85, whom she felt was incompetent, was being exploited by daughter, who had power of attorney.

The Ombudsman visited the client who was not oriented to place, did not know her name, and could not speak coherently. During the Ombudsman's visit, the daughter arrived and attempted to have her mother sign over the mother's house to the daughter. The Ombudsman refused to allow this. The Ombudsman notified the probate court and requested that a conservator be appointed for the client and that the conservator not be the daughter. The Ombudsman learned that the daughter was attempting to sell the house and keep the money for herself. The probate hearing was held with many testifying as to the incompetency of the client and the motives of the daughter. The court appointed a close friend of the client as conservator. The house was sold, and the money from the sale is now being used to care for the client.

Program Experience

Many facts have emerged from the Ombudsmen experience that play a key role in abuse, neglect, abandonment, and exploitation of the elderly.

1. Abuse, of the four types mentioned, occurs in rural, suburban and urban settings.
2. Abuse occurs in all economic groups.
3. The majority of (abused) clients are women.
4. The majority of clients are 80 years or older.
5. The majority of abusers are family members.
6. Advanced age, alcoholism, and psychiatric problems appear to influence the family members's handling of an older person.

As of June 1981, the Ombudsman Office has investigated more than 3600 cases of abuse, neglect, abandonment, and exploitation of the elderly. By far the largest number of cases have involved neglect, either by self or by the caretaker. The caretaker is, most frequently, a family member, either a grown child or spouse.

According to the State Ombudsman's statistics, the greatest number of cases involve clients from urban areas, the smallest number are from rural areas, and the remainder from suburban areas. These percentages do not correspond with the actual percentages of elderly persons living in those areas. The greatest number of elderly, in Connecticut, live in suburban areas, the next largest in urban, and the smallest percentage in rural areas. The discrepancies may be due to two factors: (1) some towns may not be reporting cases or may not know about the program; and (2) those elderly living in urban areas may be experiencing more problems than those residents of suburban areas. Although the largest number of cases involve clients in the lower socioeconomic groups, many reports are received of abuse, neglect, and exploitation of elderly in the middle and upper-middle class.

That the majority of clients are women is no surprise, especially when this statistic is coupled with the fact that the largest proportion of clients are 80 years or older. Women live longer than men and, therefore, problems become more severe as women become older and more fragile.

The latest national census (1980 United States Census) indicates that a great many older citizens reside with a family member. Therefore, again, it comes as no surprise to discover that most neglectful caretakers are family members. It is important to remember, however, that many cases involve self-neglect, where older people have simply reached a point, both mentally and physically, when they are no longer capable and do not realize that they are neglecting themselves. Age, alcoholism and psychiatric problems must be considered when assessing the abusing caretaker.

It is not unusual to find a 65- to 70-year-old son or daughter attempting to care for an 85- to 90-year-old parent. In many instances, the 65-year-old caretaker cannot manage his/her own needs and is, therefore, frustrated over having to carry the additional burden of an elderly parent. Frequently, this frustration results in physical acting out against the older person.

During the past year, the Ombudsman Office carried out a small study (unpublished results) on elderly abuse using 22 case studies. In 10 of those cases, the abuser was between 60 and 70 years old. In another, the abuser, the husband, was over 80. In many instances where abuse and neglect are present, as soon as the burden or responsibility is removed from the caretaker (abuser) and ancillary services are introduced, the abuse and neglect stop. The caretaker simply needs relief from the pressures of providing continuous, uninterrupted care.

Case 1.   Mr. and Mrs. X, in their 80s, live in a middle class suburb. During the past year, Mrs. X suffered a fractured hip and has been confined to a wheelchair since then. Until that time, the couple had been managing well. The Ombudsman received a report from the visiting nurse, that she suspected that Mr. X was physically abusing his wife. Upon arriving at the home, the Ombudsman noted some welts and bruises on Mrs. X's hands and arms. Mr. X confessed that he, on occasion, would hit the client with his cane. He admitted that he was having difficulty caring for his wife and that he would become angry when she asked for assistance. The protective services worker arranged to have a homemaker and home health aide come in at regular intervals to care for the client, the meals, and the house. Arrangements were also made to transport the husband to the senior center during the week so that he might enjoy the company of others his own age. On the instigation of those services, the abuse immediately stopped, and the animosity between the husband and client lessened.

It is felt, however, that many caretakers abuse, neglect, and exploit older persons for other reasons such as money, property or assets. Deprivation of food, verbal abuse, and physical beating and threats are weapons used to force an older person to sign over property, bankbooks, or social security checks.

Case 2.   The Ombudsman received a complaint from a social worker at the State Department of Social Services that an 84-year-old female client was being abused by a family member. The Ombudsman visited the client at her residence and observed her chained in a chair. The Ombudsman noted that the client appeared to have a black eye and a bruise on her face. The Ombudsman spoke with the client's daughter-in-law, who denied injuring the client. The only information she offered was that there was no bathroom in the house and that she bathed her mother-in-law in a tin tub because she was incontinent. When the Ombudsman attempted to speak with the client, however, the only verbal response was cursing. The Ombudsman notified the police who, upon arrival at the house, authorized an ambulance to remove the client and transport her to the hospital for examination.

The first floor of the residence consisted of a small kitchen and living room area, heated by a wood stove. Attached to the living room was an eight foot square bedroom used by the client. The bedroom was heated by a 110 volt electric space heater. The Ombudsman observed that the bedroom held an iron crib-type bed next to a very cold wall. The mattress was old and filthy, covered with a torn piece of plastic. Several bare wires hung from the ceiling of the client's bedroom. On the ceiling and floors were roaches and other unidentifiable insects. The effluvium caused by the stool and urine of more than 20 dogs and cats permeated the entire house. The grandson stated that the dogs and several cats were always inside. He also stated that, frequently, he had to physically excite his grandmother, an effort initiated to keep her breathing properly.

Although the house was nothing but a shack, the property on which it stood — owned by the client — was prime development property and worth a great deal of money. The Ombudsman learned later that the client's son and daughter-in-law were attempting to force the client to sign over her social security check and property to them. Both son and daughter-in-law were arrested and the grandson was picked up by the Department of Children and Youth Services and placed in a foster home.

Many times the Ombudsmen have discovered elderly clients, suffering from senile dementia, who have unknowingly signed away their homes or property to a relative. In some instances, a younger relative may ask the older person to change her bank account to a joint one, alleging that it would be easier for him to sign checks and purchase goods. Once accomplished, the relative closes out the account and leaves the state.

Case Resolution and Monitoring of Clients

The reporting of protective services clients and the investigation carried out by the Ombudsmen are only part of the program's requirements. Another important aspect deals with the arrangement of services and monitoring of the client's progress by the protective services worker. Many services are used by the protective services worker: homemakers, home health aides, visiting nurses, physicians, ambulance, hospitalization; meals on wheels, chore service, friendly visitors, companions; counseling on alcohol, mental health and family problems; conservatorships; and police intervention. In more severe cases, admission to a nursing home or commitment to a mental hospital may be needed.

In cases where a client refuses assistance and where the Ombudsman has judged the client to be incapable of making such a decision, the case is referred anyway. The protective services worker then obtains a psychiatric evaluation in those cases in which the client is deemed to be a danger to himself or others.

CONCLUSION

Connecticut is proud of its innovative law dealing with the abused elderly. It is believed that such programs are needed throughout the country. Whether or not elderly abuse is on the upswing is a guess, but judging from Connecticut's three-year experience, many older people are living in drastic situations that require intervention for their survival.

FOOTNOTES

[1] Ct. Ss. 17-135 a et seq. Public Act 77-575, An Act Establishing an Ombudsman Office.
[2] Ct. Ss. 46 a et seq. Public Act 77-613, An Act Adopting a Reporting Law for Protection of the Elderly.
[3] Ct. Ss. 45-70c(b)(2), Appointment of Conservators.
[4] Ct. Ss. 45-72, Appointment of Temporary Conservators.

19 An Overview of Legal Issues, Services, and Resources

Paul Nathanson

Other portions of this book have discussed problems faced by abused older people. This chapter discusses legal services and neighborhood dispute resolution as a possible approach to solving some of these problems, since many of the problems of elderly abuse relate to the law or can be solved by the law.

Perhaps more than any other group the elderly rely upon complex public and private institutions for their daily subsistence. Therefore, their legal problems frequently relate to the policies and actions of governmental agencies and private corporations, both of which are often bureaucratic mazes that even younger persons find difficult to understand.

Superimposed on the lives of low income and frail elderly is an array of complex statutory, regulatory, and decisional law. Their shelter may be provided or secured under federal and state public and subsidized housing laws, relocation laws, environmental protection laws, and zoning laws. Their health is often dependent on Medicare, Medicaid, laws regulating nursing homes, and laws relating to the advertisement of prescription drugs. Their nutrition is often secured by the food stamp program and nutrition programs established by other federal laws. The source of their income may be Social Security, Supplemental Security Income (SSI), civil service or railroad retirement programs, or private pensions. Their personal freedom and control of property are subject to the vagueness of the law of guardianship, conservatorship, involuntary commitment, and other types of protective services intervention.

Since they enter into contracts, own property, and have family relations, the elderly have the same legal concerns as the rest of the population. The elderly, particularly low income, minority, and frail elderly, often confront legal problems peculiar to their age and status; their age may give rise to increased difficulty in seeking or using available legal services.

The frail or vulnerable elderly are especially in need of advocacy and legal services assistance. All of their basic needs for income, housing, health care, and nutrition are exacerbated by their special condition, which makes it more difficult for them to use even the relatively meager legal and advocacy assistance available.

The legal problems of older people often relate to their complicated additional relationships with doctors, nurses, social workers, family, and institutions. Each one of these complex relationships has a dominant and inferior side to the relationship, and many legal problems may evolve.

OVERVIEW OF LEGAL PROBLEMS

Elderly Population in General

As discussed, many elderly persons are dependent on government programs for support, and frequently encounter problems in obtaining and maintaining these benefits. Thus, they may need assistance in avoiding delay in initial eligibility determinations and appeals, appealing eligibility denials, finding missing payment checks, suspensions, reductions or recoupment of benefits. In this context, legal advocates can act to humanize the government bureaucracies and computers that handle the basic needs of many elderly individuals. On a broader basis, legal advocates are currently bringing challenges on constitutional and statutory grounds to various unfair procedures of SSI, Medicare, Social Security, Civil Service, and Medicaid programs.

Veterans' benefits include an entire system of income, health, and housing programs that have received little attention from legal services and other advocates. Legislative efforts are currently underway in a bill to provide for judicial review of veterans' benefit claims and to remove the $10 attorney fee limitation. This should afford an opening wedge to examine the Veterans Administration and its programs more closely.

A frequently encountered issue in Medicaid litigation relates to the issue of "deeming," which is concerned with the required transfer of (for purposes of eligibility determinations) income from a noninstitutionalized spouse to an institutionalized Medicaid recipient, causing the noninstitutionalized spouse severe financial problems.

The Age Discrimination Act of 1975 prohibits age discrimination in programs and activities receiving federal financial assistance — especially including Title XX of the Social Security Act, the Community Mental Health Centers Act, and community mental health centers authorized by Title III of the Public Health Service Act. Thus, this legislation prohibits discrimination on the basis of age in the allocation and use of resources provided under many federal programs. This area is just beginning to receive attention and should be especially significant for many frail and abused elderly. Such individuals are shunted away from community mental health centers and perhaps other community crisis intervention centers solely because of an assumption about their advanced age — that they are useless to the community.

The elderly are consumers just like the rest of the population. But because of their special health and other needs they tend to be involved to a large extent with hearing aid overcharges, door-to-door salesmen who can easily pressure them, mail order purchases, prescription drugs, various consumer financing arrangements, funeral expenses, utility problems, eye glasses, and dentures.

The elderly often have problems dealing with insurance companies with respect to life, property, and health insurance. They may encounter discrimination in obtaining insurance and in obtaining benefits. Of special concern is the subject of Medicare supplemental health insurance. Many policies are sold as a way to cover gaps in Medicare coverage; yet, the elderly often purchase unneeded or overly expensive policies.

The area of wills and estate planning is extremely important for older persons — whether they are poor or rich, healthy or frail. A particularly important activity in estate planning is to work creatively with various government benefit program eligibility guidelines which affect the elderly, so as to qualify older people for benefits under the complex resources and income tests that are required in all the need-based programs.

Frail Elderly

The handicapped, weak, and institutionalized elderly are especially reliant on government benefits for their daily needs; they are subject to special guardianship and conservatorship laws which may take away or limit their civil rights; they may, in addition, be dependent on doctors, lawyers, social workers, board and care homes, nursing homes, hospitals, and other institutions for basic needs and protections. Because of their particular weak and vulnerable status, the frail elderly often cannot reach even the limited available legal assistance. Thus, special outreach efforts (including the use of trained lay advocates, special mobile vans, telephone hotlines, special visits to churches, nutrition sites, and nursing homes) must be an integral part of the overall legal assistance effort.

Those vulnerable elderly who are already in institutions may need legal assistance: to be deinstitutionalized if they are in an inappropriate care setting; to protect their basic rights vis-à-vis the institution, physicians, other patients, and perhaps other family members; to receive their basic benefits and entitlements under appropriate government and nongovernmental programs; to assert and protect their rights under all other laws such as those pertaining to probate, landlord-tenant, or domestic relations; as a class, to receive more humane treatment from the care institutions upon which they are reliant. Vulnerable older persons are in need of legal assistance to avoid unnecessary and inappropriate institutionalization and to receive appropriate protective services assistance with guardianship and conservatorship proceedings and with the designing of special appropriate and least restrictive alternatives to institutionalization.

Due process safeguards (eg, notice, presence of the alleged incompetent at the proceedings, appointment of a lawyer, and trial by jury) do not presently exist in many state guardian and conservator statutes, and broad litigative and legislative efforts in this regard are important. Unnecessary legal guardianship might be prevented and the least restrictive alternative employed by proper advice concerning the use of powers of attorney or the representative payee system under Social Security and SSI. The entire question of least restrictive places and means of care is currently being litigated and reform legislation being proposed. Many states and local governments are now establishing so-called public guardians to provide guardianship services for poor people. It is unclear how well these new institutions are working, and individuals may need legal assistance to deal with these evolving bureacracies.

Since many frail elderly reside in nursing homes, legal efforts in this area are proving useful. A primary area of attention has been cases challenging and responding to nursing homes' and states' demands for the involuntary transfer of their elderly residents. (Involuntary transfer is caused by decertification of facilities, by utilization review decisions, and by facilities' unilateral decisions to terminate their participation in

Medicaid or to reduce their Medicaid populations.) Involuntary transfer may result in transfer trauma, a phenomenon that causes increased mortality and morbidity for involuntarily transferred elderly nursing home residents. Affirmative litigation seeks to stop illegal transfer (such as that resulting from discrimination against Medicaid recipients), to secure residents' due process rights, and to require states to develop adequate transfer plans for those instances where transfer cannot be avoided.

A second area of nursing home litigation concerns discrimination against Medicaid recipients and some states' efforts to increase access to nursing home care for poor people. Recent suits by the nursing home industry have challenged a state law that requires nursing homes participating in Medicaid to agree not to charge their private-paying residents any more than the Medicaid rates, and challenged New Jersey regulations that require all facilities to accept and provide care for a reasonable number of Medicaid-eligible people as a condition of state licensure.

Litigation is also beginning to deal with the quality of care in nursing homes. Some advocates are considering the tactic of filing a receivership action to upgrade a grossly deficient facility and bring it into compliance with federal and state law, instead of waiting for decertification to become final and transfer to be demanded. A second strategy for improving quality of care invokes state consumer protection laws, which are generally liberal and authorize expansive remedies.

Federal legislative efforts have centered around strengthening patients' bill of rights regulations and providing the Attorney General of the United States power to bring suit against a nursing home if the civil rights of a resident have been violated.

LEGAL SERVICES AS A POSSIBLE SOLUTION

Legal Services Defined

The term *legal services,* as used regarding the special legal problems of the elderly, includes a wide range of services. Legal services may include the services of lawyers, paralegal persons, nursing home ombudsmen, and various other community workers and advisors. Of course, a lawyer (actually a member of the bar of the state where he or she is practicing law) could legally perform all of the functions which any of the above individuals could perform, but the actual practice of law as defined in each state would be legally limited only to members of the bar, ie, lawyers.

The various tasks which are performed under legal services include: (1) Broad litigative (test cases and class actions) and legislative law reform. These are primarily handled by lawyers. (2) Crisis intervention and other individual legal confrontations. These are also matters where attorneys are usually involved, but often—especially in publicly funded legal services programs—they receive extensive support of paralegals, law students, and other community workers. These are often cases involving actual litigation in court. (3) A very significant range of services can be, and often has been, provided by nonlawyers. Thus, nonlawyers are involved in representing individuals in government benefit application and appeal processes, nursing home resident advocacy, preventive law counseling, and legal check-ups. For example, especially significant for abused elders, community workers can provide assistance in protective services contexts. They may be particularly helpful in examining problems of abuse and exploitation by making referrals to legal services programs, other law projects, district attorneys, police, and other officials, and by finding appropriate alternative care situations.

To understand the nature and potential of legal services, it it important to reemphasize a broad distinction in types of services. Thus, there is individual advocacy (ie, with an individual's government benefit or protective services situation, or with a consumer, housing, income, or legal problem), and there is systemic legal advocacy for broader problems. This latter type of legal problem results in legislative change and/or class action or test case litigation. The accumulation of numerous individual complaints (whether they are, for example, about a certain type of individual practice in a nursing home or family abuse of elders) often results in the attempt at systemic change by legal advocates.

What Services Are Presently Available?

The public bar 1. The Legal Services Corporation, presently funded at about $300 million, provides general legal aid services to the nation's poor. It has approximately 1000 offices located in all major cities and rural areas of the country, and is funded directly by Congress.

Although this network of legal aid programs provides legal services to the elderly, two special caveats are important: (1) the services are not focused specifically on any age group, and (2) the near poor cannot avail themselves of free legal services from the Legal Services Corporation since its programs apply an income and resource means test for eligibility of potential clients.

In addition, since these programs are usually located in downtown offices and clients are expected to come to the office, those elderly clients and others who are institutionalized or home-bound or have no transportation find it difficult to use these services even if they would otherwise qualify.[1]

A final limitation relates to the Reagan administration. President Reagan has traditionally been an opponent of legal services to the poor, and his history as governor in California indicates that he may well attempt to cut back on the services provided by the Legal Services Corporation, rather than expand them. As of this writing, President Reagan is threatening to veto legislation continuing the Legal Services Corporation, even though congressional appropriations are likely to incorporate a substantial cutback in funding.

2. The Administration on Aging within the Department of Health and Human Services, under the Older Americans Act, has in recent years placed special emphasis on the provision of legal services to the institutionalized and noninstitutionalized elderly. The programs under this act are all focused on older individuals over the age of 60, and no particular income or resources means test is applied to individuals.

Through the special emphasis provided by Congress under the Older Americans Act, several hundred programs of special legal aid for the elderly have been started throughout the country. It has been estimated that $13 million were spent in 1980 to serve 400,000 older individuals under the Older Americans Act.[2] Often these programs are part of an existing Legal Services Corporation program, or they may stand alone. Because they have a special concern with older individuals, their outreach efforts and understanding of special needs of the institutionalized elderly can be assumed to be greater than those of legal aid programs.

To provide support to the existing legal aid for elderly programs, the Administration on Aging has put in place its Older Americans Advocacy Assistance Program. A major part of this effort is the bi-regional advocacy centers, which provide training, materials, and resources to existing programs. Whether this advocacy assistance support network will continue under the Reagan administration is an open question. The Reagan administration has announced its intention to cut back this support system.

A significant part of the advocacy assistance effort under the Older Americans Act is the Nursing Home Ombudsman Program. Under this program each state agency on aging has on its staff a nursing home ombudsman. The ombudsman is charged with providing information and expanding access to nursing homes for community groups and others interested in helping preserve the rights of individuals in nursing homes. The focus is related to legal services advocacy, and in many instances statewide class actions or legislative change have been initiated by the nursing home ombudsmen.

The major problem with these programs under the Older Americans Act is that they are funded by Congress, and with the recent fiscal conservatism and present political viewpoint of the administration, expansion is not likely. Although the programs are, in many instances, providing excellent services, there are too few of them and they are underfunded.

3. There are, in the public sector, numerous additional resources, their availability depending on the local situation. In some communities, church groups may provide legal services to the elderly. In others, the attorney general or the county attorney may provide services by setting up special (usually consumer) programs; sometimes private foundations have funded legal services to the elderly projects. Several law schools have begun projects which provide legal assistance to the elderly in their communities.

However, the main point is that the public sector and its present resources are not enough to provide the needed services, and with the economic outlook of the 1980s, the public sector may be contracting rather than expanding services.

The private bar   These various public legal services resources notwithstanding, the problem of providing adequate legal representation to the elderly cannot be solved without full and effective participation by the private bar. With respect to pro bono (free) efforts of the private bar, it should be noted that the American Bar Association has established a Commission on Legal Problems of the Elderly. This Commission is presently involved in an activation of the private bar project which is to set up numerous pro bono panels of retired and other attorneys providing free and low cost special legal services to the elderly. This project entails setting up lawyer referral services, pro bono programs, and continuing education training for members of the bar so that they will be sensitized to the special legal problems of the elderly, and perhaps try to provide such services free or for greatly reduced fees.[3]

Although members of the private bar may provide some services on a pro bono basis, their participation as private attorneys will be largely on a compensatory basis. Any effort to increase the availability of legal services for the aged from the private bar, therefore, must identify services which can be provided on a fee-generating basis, and develop methods for providing these services at a cost that the elderly can bear.

A major impediment to adequate legal representation for the elderly is that many elderly people do not have adequate funds to hire an attorney. It is thus important to review mechanisms by which someone other than the elderly client pays the attorney's fee.

As has been noted elsewhere,[4] there are numerous government benefit programs (including Social Security, SSI) which provide for a fee to be paid to the attorney. Even though this fee is taken out of past benefits awarded to the individual claimant, it enables many people to get legal assistance they could not otherwise afford.

There is a $10 attorney fee limitation on a private attorney representing an individual in a veteran's benefit claim. The impact of this is to keep private attorneys (unless they are willing to work for nothing) from handling cases of veterans. The challenges to the system which might result with normal private attorney involvement cannot be expected here.[5] Some have argued that attorney's fees should be provided by the losing party in litigation, as is often done in legal systems of other countries.[6]

However, the primary method by which attorneys receive their fees, especially in the kinds of cases that might result from abuse of the elderly (primarily the area of personal injury, either by friends, family, or institution) is the contingent fee mechanism. This is a system by which the attorney, after assessing that he has a chance of winning the case and recovering a substantial amount of damages, decides that he will take a percentage of the recovery (usually 25 to 35%) as his fee. Thus, the attorney is taking the chance that the case will prove victorious for his client; if it is not, both client and attorney have invested their time and effort to no avail.

The major problem here is that the largest part of the damages recovery is often for loss of future earnings. Thus, unless an older individual is still in the work force and has an actuarially long life expectancy, it is unlikely that he or she will be losing future earnings, no matter how drastic the abuse and personal injury he or she has suffered. The result is that the possible damages award will be limited to medical expenses incurred and perhaps some amount for pain and suffering. This possibility may have an impact on the size of the damages award and, therefore, the size of the attorney's contingent fee. Thus it becomes unlikely that an attorney will even take the case.

The result of this inability to receive the assistance of attorneys may be that various oppressive and injurious social institutions (many of which have special impact upon the elderly) will not receive appropriate judicial review and reform because they are never brought into the courtroom. Thus, the policing effort, carried out over public institutions by lawyers and the judicial system, does not ever become activated. Judge Frank M. Johnson, Jr, a major voice in judicial review of inequalities in prisons and mental institutions, stated:

> The economic poverty of the aged, racial minorities, and women who are solely responsible for small children often is compounded by accompanying deprivations of fundamental legal rights. During my more than 20 years on the federal bench I have repeatedly observed the effects of

the exclusion of poor people from our courts. The barbaric conditions in our prisons and mental institutions, which only recently were brought to light, existed for years without redress largely because the victims of these conditions were too poor and too powerless to bring their situations to public attention. Further, the law itself too often reflects the interests only of those who have the means to participate in its formulation. Thus, for example, the law governing relationships between landlord and tenant, or between parties to a consumer sales contract, generally favors the landlord and the seller. Finally, rights that are cognizable by the courts are meaningless unless the procedures for asserting those rights are within the reach of all citizens regardless of their financial means.[7]

Until some change in the American system of providing fees to attorneys in the abuse cases is formulated, it may be that abuse and abusing institutions will not be reformed.

NEIGHBORHOOD DISPUTE RESOLUTION

There is a potentially significant development now taking place across the country relating to the concept of neighborhood dispute resolution as an alternative to traditional courts. These projects may have particular impact for the elderly.[8] They should be studied by persons interested in preventing elderly abuse and victimization.

In general, neighborhood justice centers (often also called mediations centers or alternative dispute resolution programs) are usually informal, nonjudicial, and community-based. They attempt to solve personal disputes between people who have a continuing relationship. The techniques used may include counseling, mediation (where a third party facilitates a resolution reached by the parties themselves), or arbitration (where the third party may actually formulate the solution and may enforce it with sanctions). The programs may be limited in the types of cases they take (eg, criminal or civil), may be sponsored by various groups or agencies (eg, police, prosecutors, or community organizations), and may have various types of funding and eligibility criteria.[9]

By 1980, there were over 100 mediation programs operating or planned across the country.[10] The Law Enforcement Assistance Administration has funded several pilot projects in Atlanta, Kansas City, and Los Angeles. The American Bar Association has set up committees to look at neighborhood justice. The Chief Justice of the United States Supreme Court has extolled its virtues, and Congress enacted the Dispute Resolution Act (P.L. 96-190), but legislation has yet to receive an appropriation. In addition, various private foundations are now funding pilot projects and information clearinghouse efforts are underway.

In many ways, the neighborhood justice programs offer a possibility for keeping traditional ethnic and neighborhood values intact, instead of replacing them with the sometimes cumbersome and not always appropriate Anglo-American legal standards. Although several studies[11] have shown that the elderly are not a particular focus of most of these programs across the country, their potential, especially with respect to abused or institutionalized elderly, should be examined.

There are various reasons for looking at the dispute resolution concept as it may affect the elderly: (1) The formal court process often takes years to reach a resolution, and it may be particularly financially or physically stressful to older people. (2) Courts and prosecutors are reluctant to deal with what may appear to them as unimportant personal and neighborhood disputes, but disputes that start out insignificantly may become so irritating to the participants that they may end up as major disputes causing great social disruption. (3) Costs of attorney's fees and fees for other expert witnesses are a barrier to elderly and near-poor disputants. (4) The adversary system used in the court is based on findings of guilt and innocence, right and wrong, winners and losers, and this is often a difficult situation for anyone, especially older people who must live with each other and community members. (5) Legal principles and procedures may be particularly complex and intimidating. (6) Finally, courts are designed to deal with problems that occur once, do not recur, and do not arise among people who must relate to each other on a continuing basis.[12]

An attempt should be made to try to see if the concept of neighborhood justice centers can be applied to the problem of abuse of older people; in family, criminal, and institutional contexts. Some dispute resolution no doubt already goes on in informal ways. Thus, social workers, clergy, lawyers, family members and others often provide this service for people with whom they come in contact.

A dispute resolution mechanism might be set up in areas of high concentration of older people such as mobile home parks, senior citizens housing, nursing homes, and board and care homes. In addition, if the program were tied in some formal part of the justice system, such as the district attorney's office or the court system, it might aid individuals who otherwise would have no mechanism for the resolution of their disputes. Then the disputes that arise between individuals who live as neighbors might well be resolved. Especially useful assistance might come with respect to victimization of older people by criminals. Victims may be reluctant to go into court and be witnesses, and the informal process may be more desirable. However, it is also possible that confrontation with the criminal — especially if a violent or offensive crime was involved — would be unacceptable to many elderly and nonelderly.

The application of this process to protective services should be explored. Here individuals could be brought in who are concerned with the care of the individual (physician, social worker, nurse, family, or lawyer) and in a mediation process work out the least restrictive and most efficient protective mechanism for the older person.

Several warnings should be heeded with respect to the informal process.[13] Disputants might not receive the full procedural and privacy protections afforded in court; the informal dispute resolution process probably will not address broad social problems as perhaps might occur in litigative or legislative efforts; the process may begin informally, but after various funding and regulatory requirements are met and human nature acts in its customary way, a new "informal" yet stultifying bureaucracy may arise.

CONCLUSION

The law, and those providing services under it, is and can be a significant force in the lives of abused older people, both as it relates specifically to their abuse, frailty, or institutionalization and as it relates to the normal legal affairs of those who are abused, frail, or institutionalized. Although the law cannot create basic human feelings of caring and decency toward our elders where these are lacking, it can provide some basic protections, and it may help to provide a tone of humanity which ultimately may exist without the threat of legal sanctions.

Acknowledgment is hereby gratefully given for much of the raw materials of this chapter to numerous documents, grant applications, court pleadings and legal memoranda prepared by the author and staff of The National Senior Citizens Law Center in Los Angeles, California.

FOOTNOTES

[1]See Legal Services Corporation, "Study on the Special Difficulties of Access and Special Unmet Legal Problems of the Elderly and Handicapped" (1980).

[2]Information obtained from AOA Legal Services Offices, H.H.S. Washington, DC, as of June, 1980.

[3]For a complete review of the private bar efforts in this regard, see American Bar Association, Young Lawyers Division, "The Law and Aging Resource Guide" (1981).

[4]Nathanson, P: "Legal Services for the Nation's Elderly," 27 *Ariz L Rev* 275(1975).

[5]*Ibid.*

[6] See E. G. Ehrenzweig, "Reimbursement of Counsel Fees and the Great Society." 54 *Cal L Rev* 792(1966); Nussbaum, "Attorney's Fees in Public Interest Litigations," 48 *NYU L Rev* 301(1973).

[7] Johnson, "The Legal Profession and Social Change," 28 *Ala L Rev* 1 (1976).

[8] See Richard Hofrichter, *Neighborhood Justice and the Elderly: Policy Issues, Report for Criminal Justice and the Elderly Program of National Council of Senior Citizens* (1980); Paul Nathanson and David Berman, *Helping the Elderly Cope with Legal Conflict: Alternative Dispute Resolution,* Report for Andrus Foundation by Florence Heller Graduate School for Advanced Studies in Social Welfare (1980).

[9] See generally Daniel McGillis and Joan Millen, Neighborhood Justice Centers, Government Printing Office, 1977; Paul Worhhaftig, Citizen Dispute Resolution: A Blue Chip Investment in Community Growth, Pretrial Services Annual Journal (1978).

[10] Hofrichter, supra note 8 at p 18.

[11] Hofrichter supra note 8 and Nathanson supra note 8.

[12] See generally Hofrichter supra note 8 and Nathanson note.

[13] See Hofrichter supra note 8 and Nathanson supra note 8.

20 A Comprehensive Response to Violent Crimes Against Older Persons

Victoria Holt Jaycox
Lawrence J. Center

Once again, reported crime is on the increase in this country—despite the record expenditure of almost $26 billion to combat it at every level of government (Hindelang, Gottfredson, and Flanagan, 1980). Current crime control efforts have provided little or no relief to senior citizens who are the group most adversely affected by crime and the poison of fear that spreads from it (United States Congress, 1977). For the past four years, the Criminal Justice and the Elderly Program at the National Council of Senior Citizens has worked with people across the country to develop public service programs that can reduce the incidence of victimization and the suffering that goes along with it.[1] But

[1]The Criminal Justice and the Elderly Program, housed in the legal arm of the National Council of Senior Citizens, Legal Research and Services for the Elderly, was set up in 1977 to play the central role in a $4.7 million program to demonstrate model anticrime services for the elderly in six major cities. It has received funding from the Law Enforcement Assisance Administration, the Community Services Administration, the Department of Housing and Urban Development, the Administration on Aging, and the Ford and Edna McConnell Clark Foundations.

these programs are too few to reach the average elderly person, much less those seniors most in need—the isolated elderly and those living in our center cities (Davis and Brody, 1979).

Further, where much needed community crime prevention services have been established, they are rarely linked with the network of social services available to the aging, or with services to victims of crime, such as emergency counseling, compensation, or restitution, or with community mental health services (Jaycox, 1978b). And some of these remedial programs still treat the elderly whom they serve as helpless clients rather than as the potential force for organizing and service delivery which they are.

To understand the need for new and better anticrime programs for the elderly, it is important to understand how serious are the effects of crime on senior citizens. Many older Americans live in a state of insecurity, exposed to the economic, emotional, and physical harm that crime and other misfortunes can bring. Statisitcs showing that the elderly are less victimized than other age groups are misleading—since millions of older persons have purchased their safety at the price of a shrunken and fearful life-style and lost mobility and freedom (Cunningham, 1978; Bishop and Klecka, 1978). Crime is of special concern to older persons living in our inner cities, where their victimization rates are two to five times the rate for the elderly nationally (Jaycox, 1978a). For all of these reasons, national polls show that seniors often rank crime as their most serious problem, even ahead of poor health and insufficient income (Harris, 1976).

Lack of understanding about the serious nature of the problem of crime against older persons is one possible cause for the sporadic and narrow nature of these programs. Another reason may be the belief that little of practical good can be done to mitigate the effects of crime and fear of crime on older persons.

Our review of a wide range of pilot anticrime programs, sponsored by government at all levels, offers evidence that this is not so. Experimental programs across the nation have addressed crime-related needs of seniors and have proven their effectiveness. These projects have usually been of one or two types: crime prevention and victim assistance.

In this chapter, an introduction is provided to the range of crime prevention and victim assistance services which have proved useful for seniors, the rationale for combining crime prevention with victim assistance, and recent trends in these areas.

This report was prepared under Cooperative Agreement number 90-AT-0024/01 between the Administration on Aging, Office of Human Development Services, Department of Health and Human Services and the National Council of Senior Citizens. Points of view or opinions are those of the authors and do not necessarily reflect the policies or positions of the United States Government.

THE CRIME PREVENTION CONCEPT

In the past, the term *crime prevention* has referred to many kinds of strategies aimed at controlling criminal activity. Examples include: the use of standardized sentences and punishments as deterrents to criminal action, various treatments to rehabilitate the offender, and changing the social environment that spawns criminals. This last approach encompasses many programs aimed at improving social conditions thought to breed crime, job training and placement, rehabilitation and diversion of first offenders, remedial education, drug abuse treatment, and recreational activities. In recognition of the need for these efforts, a Presidential Commission, in a comprehensive report on crime, concluded:

> Crime flourishes where the conditions of life are worst and therefore the foundation of a national strategy against crime is an unremitting national effort for social justice. Reducing poverty, discrimination, ignorance, disease and urban blight, and the anger, cynicism or despair those conditions can inspire, is one great step toward reducing crime. (United States President's Commission on Law Enforcement and Administration of Justice, 1967).

Such efforts to root out the causes of crime are important; at the same time, they are also expensive and demand extensive skill on the part of planners and administrators. Their impact is difficult to measure, partly because it may not be immediate.

Crime prevention, as discussed in this chapter, is more limited. It is geared to private citizens, and to their own capacity to control what happens to them. This approach to crime prevention does not require knowledge of the causes of crime, the characteristics of offenders and their susceptibility to rehabilitation, or the workings of the criminal justice system. It only requires an understanding of the elements of crime and application of simple practical methods to address them.

The elements of crime are:

- Desire or motivation on the part of the offender;
- The skills needed to commit the crime; and
- The opportunity.

Trying to reduce criminal desire has proven very difficult. Certainly no one can be inoculated against criminal intent and, in recent years, programs aimed at doing so through rehabilitating offenders have come under greater scrutiny and criticism as recidivism rates rise.

It is also very difficult to attack crime by reducing criminal skills. Research has shown that most criminals — especialy those who victimize the elderly through muggings, purse snatchings, and burglaries — are not professionals. Usually they are learning from each other and through trial and error. Access to the tools of a criminal's trade cannot be inhibited when such tools are as commonplace as a blunt object, a kitchen knife, or a credit card.

The most practical short-term approach to crime prevention is opportunity reduction; it is also the approach most accessible to potential victims. One of the originators of the idea of crime prevention training states:

> Potential victims can reduce their vulnerability to criminal attack by taking proper security precautions. It is not necessary to identify the criminal, to take any action to directly affect his motivation or his access to skills and tools. What is necessary is that potential victims reduce criminal opportunity by understanding criminal attack methods and taking precautions against them. (National Crime Prevention Institute, 1978.)

Crime prevention techniques are based on two assumptions: criminal opportunities can be identified and many stranger-to-stranger personal and property crimes are committed by amateurs. When older persons can learn to identify criminal opportunities in their environment and assess their risk, they can then take simple precautions to divert the criminal's behavior. This will not make them immune to crime, which will always exist. However, the practice of crime prevention measures in the home and on the street can reduce crime and deter many people from victimizing older persons.

Components of Comprehensive Crime Prevention Programs for the Elderly

Crime prevention has the best chance of succeeding when a number of strategies are implemented together in a community by citizens, the police, and policymakers. Too often crime prevention efforts are fragmented, with the result that an older woman, for example, who takes great care to avoid risks when she is on the street, may come home to discover her apartment burglarized because her neighbor left the lobby door open or she did not have an adequate lock.

Comprehensive crime prevention for the elderly cannot deal solely with older citizens and the police as the only involved parties; rather, it should involve citizens of all ages, legislators and policymakers, and a range of local agencies, like the housing authority, the area agency on aging, and all social service and community agencies which deal with older persons. The activities included in a comprehensive crime prevention program should be targeted to the specific crime problems in a defined geographic area. While these activities can be carried out by either individuals or groups, the most effective programs rely on both.

Individual crime prevention activities that can help older persons include:

1. Residential security surveys: These are home inspections by trained staff, police or others, to determine the security status of a home, to identify particular security risks, to recommend needed protective measures, and to suggest burglary prevention behavior. While it is usually the responsibility of the citizen to implement recommended changes, people working with older persons, often on low fixed incomes, have found it important to suggest sources of free or discount help to purchase and install new hardware. Otherwise, older clients unable to afford security changes may become more fearful.

2. Property-marking programs: This tactic, often referred to as Operation Identification or Operation ID, is frequently available through the local law enforcement agency. It involves the permanent marking of people's property so that it can be easily identified and more easily returned if stolen and recovered. Participants in these programs usually mount a decal on their home indicating their property has been marked, as a deterrent for burglars.

3. Improved residential security hardware and precautions: While security surveys may produce hardware upgrading recommendations, citizens can make such changes on their own. While many elderly cannot afford expensive new locks, they can take measures such as "pinning" windows and sliding doors, cutting down shrubbery, leaving lights on, and, most importantly, using the locks that they have.

4. Increased precaution on the street: The best defense against street crime is cautious behavior. Usually senior citizen crime prevention programs advise clients to take steps such as: being aware of their appearance and environment; being alert to their surroundings; being accompanied on local errands; carrying no purse and little cash; avoiding potentially dangerous places; and appearing purposeful and confident whenever on the street.

In recent years, police and others traditionally burdened with the responsibilities of preventing crime have recognized the importance of cooperative citizen efforts as a supplement to their actions. These citizen efforts are based on the belief that increased neighborhood cohesion produces a safer neighborhood. Because elderly persons are often home during the day, they are prime participants in collective crime prevention programs. And because they are frequently more fearful of crime than anyone else in the neighborhood, these security-building programs can be most beneficial to them.

Collective crime prevention strategies include:

1. Block clubs: Block clubs serve to increase citizen awareness by encouraging street surveillance and close communication by neighbors. This approach has been working because citizens have a clear interest in keeping crime out of their immediate surroundings and it is easier to get people together within a small radius. Familiarity about one's neighbors is also greater, so that suspicious people or behavior is easily recognized.

2. Neighborhood Watch: These programs often cover areas larger than the single block, but are based on the same concept as block clubs. Neighbors are urged to be watchful for unusual activities and quickly report them to the police. Activities often include the exchange of names and telephone numbers among neighbors as well as the establishment of regular communications between the group and the beat patrol officers.

3. Citizen street patrols: These patrols, usually manned by local volunteers, are intended to deter crime and, where possible, stop crimes in progress by notifying authorities quickly. Citizens patrol on foot or in cars, sometimes using citizen band radios.

4. Building patrols: The main purpose of these patrols is to protect a building and the surrounding grounds. They are often operated by tenant organizations which recruit volunteers to patrol hallways, lobbies, and other common areas. The objective is deterring unwanted strangers from entering the building or committing crimes around the building.

5. Whistle or airhorn programs: These programs, often called "Blow the Whistle on Crime," consist of the distribution of whistles or freon airhorns to residents of a small area and training them in how to use them. Citizens are urged to use the whistles or airhorns when they are victimized, observe a crime, or hear someone else blowing them. Those who hear the noise are supposed to call the police. The underlying assumptions of this program are that significant noise will deter criminals and alert neighbors who can help.

6. Telephone assurance programs: This strategy can be especially helpful to elderly citizens, many of whom are somewhat immobile. It includes local volunteers, working from a roster of clients, calling people regularly to check on their health and safety. The telephone contacts are also tools for providing crime prevention information to clients and for recruiting participants for block club and Neighborhood Watch programs.

7. Escort service: This program is also particularly valuable for older citizens, since it reduces their isolation and their vulnerability to crime. Volunteers escort neighbors — elderly or others in need — to and from necessary destinations such as banks, supermarkets, social service agencies, and doctors' offices.

8. Case monitoring: In this strategy, groups of senior citizens go to court to observe proceedings in cases involving older victims. Its primary

goal is to put the criminal justice system under public scrutiny, reserving the participants' right to publicly criticize officials who appear insensitive to legitimate concerns of older citizens. It also serves to educate citizens about the system, provides peer support for elderly victims and witnesses in the courtroom, and gives senior citizens an opportunity to be advocates for specific changes they believe are needed in the courts.

9. Environmental design: This approach aims at redesigning the physical appearance of a neighborhood or building to enhance its residential character, increase use of public space by residents, and deter strangers from entering. Techniques include erecting fences, closing off streets, planting shrubbery, and installing lighting.

A network of programs has arisen in recent years to address crime prevention needs. This network has been of particular value to senior citizens because the relatively low rate of crime committed against older persons masks the serious impact of crime on this age group. Elderly people who are victimized suffer from economic, psychological, or physical harm which can affect them for considerable periods of time. Moreover, there is considerable clinical evidence that the crime itself can cause older persons to develop even greater fear and further inhibit their life-styles (*Criminal Justice and the Elderly Newsletter,* 1978).

THE VICTIM ASSISTANCE CONCEPT

Crime has traditionally been a major domestic issue in the United States for both policymakers and citizens. Since the inauguration of the Law Enforcement Assistance Administration (LEAA) in the United States Department of Justice in the late 1960s, billions of dollars have been spent on components of the criminal justice system in an attempt to reduce crime and its impact. A great part of this money has been devoted to the individual needs and rights of the criminal offender. Little or no attention has been paid until recently to the victims of crime, who have a great many needs and very few rights within the American criminal justice system (Chelimsky, 1981). A recent publication of the American Bar Association stated that the average crime victim's experience will probably include some, if not all, of the following:

- Official indifference concerning matters of little relevance to the "case," but of grave importance to the victim, such as retrieval of stolen property and advice about victim compensation;
- Insensitive, adverse questioning by police and other law enforcement officials who may harbor a "guilty victim"

syndrome — a feeling that the victim is responsible for his
or her victimization;

- Perfunctory, summary, and insensitive interviewing by
prosecutors who also may feel that the person has some-
how "asked" to be victimized;
- Poorly coordinated, conflicting, repetitive, and usually
unexplained summonses;
- Uncomfortable and insecure accommodations at the
police station or in the courthouse, often involving proximity to defendants, associates of defendants, or adverse
witnesses;
- Lack of clear, lay explanations of proceedings and decisions during and after the case;
- Fear resulting from real or imagined intimidating threats
and acts by defendants, or, in the case of defense witnesses, by police, prosecutors, or other persons with an
adverse interest; and
- Lack of special services for special classes of crime victims, such as the elderly, abused children, and sexually
assaulted persons. (American Bar Association, 1980)

Grass-roots programs at the local level in the early 1970s were the
first sign that people were devoting some attention to crime victims.
These programs, which grew out of the women's movement and similar
citizen activities, focus on the crime victim as a person in distress. Programs which are primarily concerned with helping people recover from
their crime-induced stress usually offer counseling and social services,
and may lobby for sensitive handling of victims by social agencies and
criminal justice professionals. The most common examples of this approach to victim assistance are the rape crisis centers and family abuse
centers which have been established across the country.

The second and probably larger group of victim service programs
also grew out of a concern for people who had been victimized, but has
been based on another equally strong concern: the improved management of criminal cases in the court system. The most common type of
program in this category are prosecutors' victim/witness assistance units,
which try to make witnesses' experiences as painless as possible and
reduce the bad side effects of the system's typical delays. The theory is
that better treatment for witnesses will not only benefit them but also the
system because their increased cooperation will lead to fewer case
dismissals and increased conviction rates (Stein, 1980).

While both crisis-oriented and witness-oriented services are helpful
to crime victims in general, the more important of the two in terms of

numbers of victims helped is the crisis service provided to victims after a crime has been reported to the police. The great majority of victims never see their complaints result in an arrest. Since only a very small percentage of arrests results in an actual prosecution, even the best of the courthouse-based victim services is of no use to most victims.

Additionally, recent research suggests that the greatest impact of crime on older victims is on their physical and psychological well-being. This would suggest that rapid victim assistance services, delivered as soon as possible, are a high priority for older victims (Jaycox, 1980).

The earliest counseling and victim-oriented programs were based in public and private agencies outside the criminal justice system. These included mental health centers, hospitals, and United Way-type organizations. Lately there has been a trend for law enforcement agencies to sponsor such services, partly to respond more fully to the frustrations their officers face daily and partly to serve some of their own investigatory needs. Police are finding that a victim who has had an opportunity to ventilate his emotions to a trained crisis worker makes a much better witness than one who is still agitated, shocked, or withdrawn (Stein and Ahrens, 1980).

In recent years, many states have also demonstrated a commitment to crime victims by enacting different kinds of victim compensation laws. In general, these programs provide awards to injured victims of violent crime to compensate them for unreimbursed losses of wages or medical expenses. At the beginning of 1980, 28 such state programs were in operation. While many of these programs are hampered by administrative difficulties and restrictive statutes (see the following section on "Trends"), they represent a recognition that the crime victim deserves help. Some states have also established statewide victim assistance networks.

These networks have in many cases been funded by LEAA, the agency that has generally led federal efforts to improve the plight of crime victims. It has funded victim/witness reception centers, witness telephone alert programs, victim counseling services and property return programs. A great number of these programs are located in a prosecutor's office and are focused on the needs of witnesses and of the court system (Cronin and Bourque, 1980).

The LEAA has also funded several projects in the past few years specifically for elderly crime victims. Funding for these projects was grounded in the recognition of the serious role crime plays in the elderly's quality of life, inducing fear, restricted life-styles, and often long-lasting and severe psychological after effects. Soon, other agencies such as the Administration on Aging and the Community Services Administration also began sponsoring victim assistance programs for the elderly.

The main objectives of victim assistance for older crime victims are:

- To assist them in recovering from the psychological and emotional impact of victimization;
- To help them obtain whatever benefits are available to them as compensation for losses caused by crime; and
- To provide, directly and through referrals, services which they need to recover from victimization and to participate fully in the criminal justice process.

Victim assistance, whether performed by an assigned case worker or a concerned friend, also serves another important purpose. It can be a means of identifying senior citizens, most notably the isolated elderly, who need a variety of social services, some of which may be unrelated to a victimization. These may include services concerning housing, social security, transportation, medical problems, homemaking, or nutrition. In any of these cases, the person talking to the crime victim can try to see that the need is met by referring the victim to the social service agency or that senior citizen organization that provides the appropriate service.

Often the most valuable service that can be provided to crime victims is an empathetic, understanding ear. Victims need emotional support as soon after the victimization as possible. Simply to be told they did nothing wrong, that someone is sorry it happened, and that help is available can be of great comfort (Center, in press). Even if friends or relatives do not have the time or skill to provide some of the services listed above, they can make contact with local agencies that do have the resources to help elderly crime victims. Such referrals can do much to ease the extreme stress felt by many victims of crime. Thus in actuality, we can all help crime victims if equipped with a set of very basic skills.

Components of Comprehensive Victim Assistance Programs for the Elderly

Victim assistance programs that serve the elderly must accomplish several functions if they are to do an effective job. They are: victim identification; victim contact; assessment of victim needs; provision of direct service; making referrals; and following up victims' cases.

In performing victim assistance, the critical agency for coordination is the local law enforcement agency, since it is the primary source of the identity of crime victims. Thus, law enforcement officials have to be convinced of the value of victim assistance work. Only after that task is accomplished can the police be approached about cooperating with a victim services program (Stein and Ahrens, 1980).

Unfortunately, many elderly crime victims do not report their victimizations to the police. However, they will tell one or more people about the crime, and these people can also refer them to a victim services project. They include friends or relatives of victims; staff of social service agencies; doctors, clinics, or hospitals; and staff at senior citizen centers, nutrition programs, retirement centers, housing projects, or apartment buildings. Victim identification should, therefore, include a publicity effort aimed at all of these people. Once contacted, victim services can be provided either directly or by referral. Those services most often provided to older victims are advocacy, counseling, transportation, and home security assistance.

Advocacy means acting on behalf of someone in support of his or her needs. Often elderly citizens are unable to cope with bureaucracies and need help in obtaining the services and attention to which they are entitled; helpful advocates can direct them through the maze of social service referrals and intervene when necessary to see that their needs are being met.

Counseling (often called crisis intervention when performed on an emergency basis) is the process by which someone helps a crime victim sort out his feelings in order to accept the experience and return to a precrisis state of mind. Counseling need not be done by professionals trained in the art of counseling, the most important attributes to bring to it are courtesy, empathy, interest, and involvement.

Transportation is a relatively easy direct service to be provided to elderly crime victims. Many need to visit doctors, lawyers, the police, court, or social service agencies as a result of their victimizations. Often they must rely on public transportation, which can be slow and/or unreliable.

Home security assistance is especially needed by elderly burglary victims, who are often as traumatized as victims of personal crimes. This may range from the boarding up of a broken window, to the installation of new doors, locks, or hardware. Once accomplished, the security provides great relief to the victims.

Other assistance that can be provided through a program's direct service component, or through the efforts of concerned citizens, includes the provision of emergency food or shelter; assistance in replacing lost documents; help in filing medical or legal claims (eg, for insurance or victims' compensation); or help in communicating with representatives of the criminal justice system.

The provision of victim services by referral requires some knowledge on the part of the person making the referral, whether it is a social worker from a victim assistance project or a concerned neighbor. While the former may have time to develop relationships at local agencies and examine their effectiveness, the latter can make referrals if he has a resource directory or simply the telephone number of a local information and referral agency.

The follow-up component of victim assistance programs serves as both a check and reinforcement of the victim's recovery from the effects of victimization. The objective of this component is to assist victims in becoming self-sufficient or at the very least to cope at a level matching that before the crime. Rather than make victims dependent on them for future support, programs usually concentrate on connecting victims with the local senior citizens support network, eg, senior centers and clubs, nutrition sites, and local government services. Friends and relatives, though they are not associated with victim assistance programs, can also make efforts to tie elderly victims into the senior support network. It requires only a little time for research and some telephone calls (Center, in press).

COMBINING CRIME PREVENTION AND VICTIM ASSISTANCE

A brief examination of the crime prevention and victim assistance movements sheds light on their different purposes. The former aims for better personal security and stronger neighborhood ties, while the latter seeks courtesy and compassion for those who have been victimized. Though both are tied to criminal justice, they have developed independently, and their roles are geared in great part to the needs of their clients. One deals with the concerns of potential crime victims, while the other focuses on the needs of actual crime victims.

However, for the older person who has a serious fear of crime, who is vulnerable to serious physical and emotional consequences of victimization, and who is often not sufficiently adept at using the social service system, a merger of those two movements is appropriate. Such a joining would address all the main crime-related concerns of older Americans.

Moreover, a combining of crime prevention and victim assistance services can make both more effective. For example, victim assistance program workers often discover that victims have been hurt partially due to their own carelessness. They provide more complete service if they weave crime prevention advice into their counseling services. Many victims are eager to get suggestions on how to make themselves less vulnerable in the future. However, such advice has to be given delicately and at the right time so that victims' feelings of self-blame are not reinforced.

Similarly, crime prevention workers are better able to get their points across if they are armed with victim assistance skills. Older persons who have been victimized can be cynical of crime prevention advice, disrupting a crime prevention education session, a block meeting, or even refusing an offer of a home security check. A knowledge of victim assistance skills can be used to get a group to be supportive of its victimized members or simply to be helpful to the victim themselves (Stein, 1979).

Special Programs for the Elderly

Increasing recognition of the tumultuous consequences which crime and fear of crime have on older people has resulted in a number of programs across the country to combat that problem. One major effort is the National Elderly Victimization Prevention and Assistance Program. This joint effort of several government agencies and the National Council of Senior Citizens included seven demonstration projects in six major cities. To respond to the distress and fear that victimization inflicts on the elderly, these comprehensive projects offered both victim assistance and crime prevention services.

All the projects provided victim assistance to elderly persons whose names they received from local police and social service agencies. Staff contacted victims immediately, assessing their needs. Case workers then tried to secure whatever help the elderly persons required, either directly or by referral. Services provided included counseling, transportation, home care, medical aid, replacement of lost documents, emergency food and clothing, temporary shelter, and legal aid.

Crime prevention strategies included educational sessions for groups of seniors, the organization of block clubs, and home services. These included home security surveys, assistance in upgrading the quality of security hardware, engraving of valuables with personal identification numbers, and individualized suggestions on how to avoid being victimized (Center, in press).

Other similar programs have been established that also take direct aim at the crime problems of older people. For example, a national training program for police officers was developed by the American Association of Retired Persons. In this program, law enforcement personnel are sensitized to the older person's needs and feelings, taught how to interact with seniors in diverse crime-related situations, and how to make use of senior volunteers (National Retired Teachers Association-American Association of Retired Persons, 1980).

A number of local projects have been implemented in both urban and rural areas of the country, sponsored by aging programs, law enforcement agencies, and community activist organizations. There are successful programs in Las Vegas, Nevada, where both crime prevention and victim assistance services are a major focus of the local RSVP; Detroit, Michigan, where a network of senior center staff provides crime prevention information and assistance on a continuing basis; and Tucson, Arizona, where the Pima County District Attorney's Office operates both a witness and a victim assistance component, with staff members and volunteers riding with detectives on night shifts, and next-day follow-up work with victims who cannot be seen immediately (*Criminal Justice and the Elderly Newsletter,* 1980; Lowenberg, 1980). These projects are an indication of a growing trend toward recognizing, and working against, the adverse effects that crime has on so many of our nation's older people.

TRENDS IN CRIME PREVENTION AND VICTIM ASSISTANCE FOR THE ELDERLY

The fields of crime prevention and victim assistance for seniors are always changing as new issues arise, new problems develop, and more effective ways of delivering services to older persons are discovered. Those who wish to become involved in helping the elderly face crime-related problems, whether they are area agency staff members or concerned friends, should remain aware of developments so they can provide appropriate assistance or referrals as needed.

One encouraging development is the institutionalization of crime prevention and victim assistance services by making them available through regular elderly service providers. The states of Pennsylvania, Florida, and Michigan are all trying variations of this concept. Training is being given to homemakers, senior centers staff, visiting nurses, and others so they can effectively respond to the crime-related concerns of the elderly people with whom they come in contact. This could involve a senior center worker giving counseling to a small group of people who have been frightened by the mugging of one of their friends; a homemaker aide giving empathetic counseling and then making a referral for a woman who has just been robbed; or a visiting social worker checking the hardware, doors, and windows in an older man's home after he has heard about a local burglary. Because crime can be a survival issue for older people, it is appropriate that service providers who deal with them on a daily basis become knowledgeable about it and able to help.

Another positive step is the emergence of peer counselors in anticrime programs for the elderly. This is important both for those seniors who seek assistance and for their colleagues who wish to play a part in lessening the crime problems their age group faces.

All demonstration programs associated with the National Elderly Victimization Prevention and Assistance Program have used senior aides for both victim assistance and crime prevention activities. With adequate training, these workers proved to be real assets because of the relationships of trust they were able to establish with their peers.

An extension of this concept is being used by the Victim Assistance Program for Older Adults (VAOA) in the city of Tampa and Hillsborough County, Florida. The core of that program is its staff of 26 neighborhood workers, generally nonprofessionals, all over age 55, who work on an hourly basis for a victim assistance program administered by a mental health center. They are all trained in Florida state law affecting the elderly, crisis intervention counseling, and the services available from local social service agencies. Each day these workers are assigned new victim assistance cases in their neighborhoods. They interview senior victims, counsel them, and make referrals for more intensive counseling and other services when needed. In its first year, nearly 75% of those victims contacted wanted help from VAOA. Most victims needed crime prevention education and crisis intervention counseling. The program made a major impression on the state's Bureau of Criminal Justice Assistance which has promoted it as a model for other areas. This peer-oriented approach offers several advantages: (1) agencies can provide the service through volunteers or community aides at low cost; (2) the decentralized neighborhood approach works well for both the clients and the workers; and (3) older persons who want to become active in community work are helping their peers in a very important way (*Criminal Justice and the Elderly Newsletter,* 1979).

Another trend in the field of victim assistance concerning older Americans is the increasing attention being paid to elderly crime victims by several of the 28 state victim compensation programs. Lately, a number of national and state policymakers have pointed out that the ambitious goals of these programs have not always been realized. Only a very small portion of deserving victims receives compensation awards. The failure to compensate more victims is primarily due to the inherent limitations in the laws and program characteristics such as lack of public awareness, award denial conditions, and lack of linkages with more comprehensive victim assistance programs. The requirements and complexities inherent in many victim compensation programs affect all victims, especially the infirm, the poor, the inarticulate, and the socially isolated. A great number of elderly victims are incuded in these categories. Without personal intervention, few of these victims learn of the programs, have enough information to understand whether they are eligible for benefits, or have sufficient skills to meet the requirements necessary to receive compensation awards.

Policymakers, program officials, and private citizens interested in improving elderly victims' chances of receiving compensation for losses they suffer are lobbying for a number of changes in existing programs. These include greater publicizing of state programs, including using law enforcement officers as referral agents; removal of financial hardship tests, which deter many older victims from applying because they are reluctant to list their assets or apply for charity; and the removal of minimum loss provisions, since for many older people the loss of a relatively small amount of money represents not an inconvenience but a critical shortage of food, medicine, or rent monies.

Other policy changes being pushed by older persons' advocates are the establishment of effective pre-award provisions for deserving emergency cases, of special importance to older victims living on small, fixed incomes who cannot wait the 10 to 20 months needed for processing their claim. There should also be compensation to replace or repair damaged or stolen property essential to an older person's physical or psychological health, like glasses, hearing aids, a door lock or a telephone, and the development of full service programs in which counseling and social services provision are combined with efforts to secure compensation for victims (Criminal Justice and the Elderly, 1979; Hofrichter, 1979).

The movement toward recognizing the special needs of older crime victims has been led by the states of New York, New Jersey, and California. Both New York and New Jersey have established special units to deal with the claims of elderly victims.

CREATING NEW RESOURCES IN SUPPORT OF ANTICRIME SERVICES

Many of the recent pilot programs set up to deal with older persons' fears and losses resulting from crime have been the result of funding from federal agencies, most importantly the LEAA, the Administration on Aging, the Community Services Administration, the Department of Housing and Urban Development and ACTION. But clearly, for at least the next few years, we cannot look to the federal government to play the kind of leadership role in this area that it has played in the past. Furthermore, the demise of LEAA at the end of fiscal year 1981 makes it doubtful that criminal justice agencies, whose innovations in recent years were largely underwritten by LEAA, will remain in the forefront in this field. A realistic look at the prospects for expanding crime prevention and victim assistance services for seniors could easily conclude that, given the

332

current atmosphere of budgetary austerity at all levels of government, progress would not seem to lie in mounting new programs under any kind of funding scheme.

On the other hand, it has been shown that people who work with the elderly on a daily basis — nutrition workers, visiting nurses, senior center staff and the like — can be taught to recognize and deal with the problems of crime and fear of crime experienced by their clients. Thus, this community of elderly-serving agencies could become an extraordinary resource for continued reform, if it is effectively mobilized.

A second, relatively neglected source of potential growth for anti-crime services is senior citizens themselves. As in the case of other kinds of problems confronting the elderly, seniors are not just asking for more. They are asking, instead, to be trained and used as volunteers in crime prevention and victim assistance activities; to help, for example, to organize their neighborhoods, or to assist their peers in recovering from a victimization (*The Police Chief*, 1977).

In our dealings with programs across the country, we have found that among the most promising are those which have developed within them a corps of trained, reliable, productive older volunteers. The capacity of such volunteers to expand the services of existing programs at low cost, while at the same time gaining a great deal in return for those who do the volunteering, is clear. Seniors who have enlisted in the war on crime have found that their feelings of impotence and vulnerability about crime have changed, and that they can be an effective force to reduce crime and its impact for themselves as well as for their neighbors.

BIBLIOGRAPHY

American Bar Association, Section on Criminal Justice. *Bar Leadership on Victim Witness Assistance.* Washington, DC, ABA, 1980.
Bishop G, Klecka WR: *Victimization and Fear of Crime among the Elderly Living in High-Crime Urban Neighborhoods.* Presented at the annual meeting of the Academy of Criminal Justice Sciences. New Orleans, March 8-10, 1978.
Center L: *Anti-Crime Programs for the Elderly: A Guide to Program Activities.* Washington, DC, Government Printing Office (in press).
Chelimsky E: Serving victims: Agency incentives and individual needs, in Salasin SE (ed): *Evaluating Victim Services.* Beverly Hills, CA, Sage, 1981.
Criminal Justice and the Elderly, The National Council of Senior Citizens. *Victim Compensation and the Elderly: Policy and Administrative Issues.* A report to the Select Committee on Aging, U.S. House of Representatives, Comm. Pub. No. 96-179. Washington, DC, Government Printing Office, 1979.
Criminal Justice and the Elderly Newsletter. Stein JH (ed). Fall, 1978; Fall, 1979; Winter, 1979-80; Summer, 1980.
Cronin RC, Bourque BB: *National Evaluation Program Phase I Assessment of*

Victim/Witness Assistance Projects, Summary Report. Washington, DC, American Institutes for Research, 1980.

Cunningham CL: The pattern and effect of crime against the elderly American. *Research into Crimes Against the Elderly, Part II*. Joint Hearings before the Select Committee on Aging and the Committee on Science and Technology, U.S. House of Representatives, Comm. Pub. No. 95-123. Washington, DC, Government Printing Office, 1978.

Davis LJ, Brody EM: *Rape and Older Women: A Guide to Prevention and Protection*. Washington, DC, Government Printing Office, 1979.

Harris L, and Associates: *The Myth and Reality of Aging in America*. Washington, DC, National Council on Aging, 1976.

Hindelang MJ, Gottfredson MR, Flanagan TJ: *Sourcebook of Criminal Justice Statistics*. Washington, DC, Department of Justice, Bureau of Justice Statistics, 1980.

Hofrichter R: *Victim Compensation and the Elderly: The Programs in Practice — A Follow-Up Report*. Washington, DC, Criminal Justice and the Elderly, 1979.

Jaycox VH: The elderly's fear of crime: Rational or irrational? *Victimology* 1978a;3:329-334.

Jaycox VH: Prepared statement. *Research into Crimes Against the Elderly, Part II*. Joint hearings before the Select Committee on Aging and the Committee on Science and Technology, United States House of Representatives, Comm. Pub. No. 95-123. Washington, DC, Government Printing Office, 1978b.

Jaycox VH: Using anti-crime services to reach elderly women in need. Presented at the Second Annual Women in Crisis Conference, Washington, DC, June 5-8, 1980.

Lowenberg DA: Your clients will be there next year. Will you? in Viano EC (ed): *Victim/Witness Programs: Human Services of the 80s*. Washington, DC, Visage Press, 1980.

National Crime Prevention Institute. *Crime Prevention and the Elderly: Special Information Package*. Louisville, KY, NCPI, 1978.

National Retired Teachers Association-American Association of Retired Persons. *Law Enforcement and Older Persons*. Revised Edition. Washington, DC, NRTA-AARP, 1980.

New CJE counselor, Dr. Martin Symonds, in Stein JH (ed): *Criminal Justice and the Elderly Newsletter*. Washington, DC, Fall 1978.

The Police Chief 1977;44:2, February.

Stein JH, Ahrens JH: *How to Win Law Enforcement Support for Victim Services Projects*. Washington, DC, Criminal Justice and the Elderly, 1980.

Stein JH; *Anti-Crime Programs for the Elderly: Combining Community Crime Prevention and Victim Services*. Washington, DC, Criminal Justice and the Elderly, 1979.

Stein JH: Perspectives on the Victims' Movement: 1972-1980. Presented at the 1980 Annual Meeting of the Network of Consultants on Knowledge Transfer, Princeton University, March 19-21, 1980.

United States Congress, House Subcommittee on Housing and Consumer Interests, Select Committee on Aging. *Elderly Crime Victimization (Crime Prevention Programs)*, Hearing, March 29, 1976. Washington, DC, Government Printing Office, 1976.

United States Congress, House Subcommittee on Housing and Consumer Interests, Select Committee on Aging. *In Search of Security: A National*

334

Perspective on Elderly Crime Victimization. Comm. Pub. No. 95-87. Washington, DC, Government Printing Office, 1977.

United States Department of Justice, Law Enforcement Assistance Administration, National Criminal Justice Information and Statistics Services. *Criminal Victimization in the United States: 1975, A National Crime Survey Report.* No. SD-NCS-N-7. Washington, DC, Government Printing Office, 1977.

United States President's Commission on Law Enforcement and Administration of Justice. *Challenge of Crime in a Free Society.* Washington, DC, Government Printing Office, 1967.

21 Consumer Advocacy and Abuse of Elders in Nursing Homes

Peter A. Stathopoulos

The majority of the elderly in our society live in the community, either by themselves or with their families. Recent sociological studies indicate that the elderly want to remain as independent as they can for as long as possible (Shanas, 1979). Yet, over the past 50 years, there has been continuous growth of several types of long-term care facilities for the elderly unable to care for themselves. This appears directly related to the fact that the American population not only is growing older, but also is living longer. However, with advancing age, Stotsky (1968) contends, the incidence of physical illness and disability has increased. As a result, the nursing home* has become the major institution for the care of persons with a variety of physical and mental handicaps. Unlike its predecessor, the boarding home, it is both a health care facility and a hotel.

The enactment of the Social Security Act in 1935, with its provision

---

*Nursing home refers to a continuum of long-term care that includes skilled nursing facilities (SNF), intermediate nursing facilities (INF), and rest homes (RH).

for direct payments to the aged for living accommodations, encouraged boarding homes to spring up in every part of the country. Gradually the use of nursing and medical personnel in these homes transformed them from strictly residential to health-care facilities. In 1939, there were 1200 such nursing facilities with approximately 25,000 residents. Federal assistance in the early 1950s for the construction and renovation of proprietary nursing homes, and the passage of the Kerr-Mills Act (Medicaid) in 1960, stimulated nursing home industry growth. A report of the Department of Health, Education and Welfare (HEW) (1975) indicates that between 1967 and 1974 the number of beds increased from about 600,000 to roughly 1,200,000. This expansion of nursing home beds made possible a decrease of patients in mental hospitals. A survey in 1974 by the National Center for Health Statistics (HEW) showed that since 1969 there had been a 48% increase in the number of nursing home patients with mental illness.

The pressure on general hospitals to reduce costs has also contributed to the growth of nursing homes to provide convalescent care for patients unable to return to their homes. Thus the nursing home serves a variety of populations and fulfills diverse functions in our society. With the complex demands placed on nursing homes, how well are they meeting the needs of their clientele?

Some of these functions are not complementary, nor can the needs of diverse subgroups be easily fulfilled under the same roof. Garbarino and Smyer (1980) have criticized the public policy approach which sets one program against another for competition for funds, and the lack of a comprehensive and integrated plan to empower families to provide service to difficult members. They express concern that the deinstitutionalization movement may undermine rather than strengthen the family as caregivers. Nursing homes should fulfill the needs of their residents and patients and provide high quality care. The needs of nursing home residents include mainly food and shelter, medical care, privacy, independence, and intimacy.

The nursing home, like every other institution, meets the social needs of its residents only partially. There is a loss of privacy in exchange for the legitimate surveillance necessary to assure security. Good nursing home care focuses on the strengths of the resident and takes into account the social-psychological needs and values of the older person. Admission to a nursing home signifies a major change in an individual's life and often represents discontinuation of previous life roles. Like every other institution, nursing homes become efficient by making certain tasks routine. Yet such routine, as Jellinek and Tennstedt (1980) observed, often leads to dependency, withdrawal, physical and mental deterioration. They also note the high risk of induced chronicity, due to lack of opportunities in nursing homes for patients to exercise their various functional capabilities.

A seven-year study of the United States Senate (Moss Report) has amply documented a variety of abuses in the nursing home industry. Of 23,000 nursing homes, more than half are below standard. Only 5% are good, and a few are exceptional (*Boston Globe,* 4/25/76). Such an assessment is certainly disappointing. What are the reasons? To understand this situation, one must consider the political and economic contexts within which the industry operates, the role of government as financier and regulator of the industry, and the lobbying power of the industry that effectively blocks any major reform, despite almost daily newspaper accounts of patient abuse and maltreatment, financial swindles, kickbacks, and fraud.

Without going into details, it appears that the main issues in nursing homes are:

1. Although the nursing homes industry receives three-fourths of its income from the government, it is considered a private enterprise; thus, the industry is not accountable to the public, even though it is heavily tax-supported.

2. The industry is highly profitable. According to Carnoy and Weiss (1973), in 1969 the industry grossed $2.8 billion, up 20% from 1968 and 529% from 1960. Responsible for this phenomenal expansion was the advent of Medicaid and Medicare which guarantee costs, plus a reasonable profit to the owner, usually 13%.

3. The industry has organized itself into very powerful constituencies—state and federal associations—that organize conventions, publish monthly journals, and conduct extensive public relations campaigns, such as Nursing Home Week in Massachusetts. All the costs of these events are partially or fully included when the daily rates for reimbursement are established. Thus, the daily rates of care include extensive advertising costs.

4. Financing mechanisms, flat rate or cost plus profits, do not offer any incentives for better patient care, better food, more skilled staff, or less medication. On the contrary, poor care is inadvertently encouraged by current funding methods.

5. There is increasing regulation, so much that in many instances federal regulations cancel out state regulations, and vice versa, a condition that the industry uses to blame "the government" for its deficiencies rather than itself. With the political power of the industry, even when regulations exist, they are not enforced. As Mendelson (1974) pointed out, "The problem is not lack of regulations but the will to enforce them."

6. Most nursing homes rely heavily for the delivery of services on untrained and inadequate staff. Mendelson and Hapgood (1974)

estimates that 80% to 90% of patient care in nursing homes is given by nurses' aides and orderlies. These employees have very little formal training, little understanding of the needs of the elderly, and insufficient supervisory support from the institution to deal with the demands of their jobs. Despite the industry's protests that it is overregulated, there is no requirement for formal training to become a nurses' aide in a nursing home. Dissatisfaction with working conditions and low pay is common and has led to mobilization of workers for unionization.

The majority of workers in nursing homes are trying to do a good job, often under great pressure, with little or no training, limited financial incentive, and no job security or further career opportunity. Widespread understaffing also contributes to the pressures that often lead to abuse and neglect of patients. To blame the staff only for elder abuse would be not only unfair, but also too simplistic an approach.

NURSING HOME REFORM STRATEGIES

Proposed remedies for reform vary with the perspectives and self-interests of the reformers. This section will present mainly the strategy advanced by advocates of consumerism. A brief statement on other reform strategies is included to suggest the possible array of alternatives.

Free Market Strategy

The industry blames its inadequacies on government through over-regulation, delays in payments, and low reimbursement rates, and suggests that more money and less regulation will be sufficient motives for the owners to provide quality care, as the free market should operate.

Unionization

Employees and labor organizations argue that low wages, especially for nurses' aides and orderlies, cause high turnover and low morale. They contend that unionization of the workers, along with support from relatives of nursing home residents, will lead to improvement of care. The title of a recent article (*Service Employee,* 1980) captures this view: "Working Together to Improve Conditions in Nursing Homes." The reporter states: "Workers are afraid to report abuses. Residents are scared to complain. Relatives are fearful of pointing to problems. None of this is happening in a dictatorship." Unionization is proposed as the preferred strategy for reform.

Consumerism

Consumerism is part of a broad tradition of citizen participation and advocacy in program planning and social reform, exemplified in model cities or community mental health programs. Yin et al (1975) have identified the following critical objectives of participation: (1) to improve program effectiveness by making services more accountable to consumers; and, (2) to increase consumer control by developing a degree of power over social programs. Similarly, Fauri (1973) states that citizen involvement, and more specifically consumer participation, has been viewed as providing program planners and government officials information on "what consumers actually want and need and may provide a feedback mechanism for consumers to indicate whether program output is actually meeting these wants and needs."

Consumer advocates perceive themselves as citizens who have a more direct interest in the welfare of nursing home residents than the citizen-at-large. To emphasize the nature of their involvement, these groups call themselves advocates. It is not mere involvement or participation as volunteers, friendly visitors, or members of the board of nursing homes — their focus is advocacy on behalf of the client. *Advocacy* (Random House Dictionary of the English Language, 1969) is the "act of pleading for, supporting, or recommending: active espousal." In consumer advocacy for nursing homes, advocacy activities are designed to enable special interest groups to acquire and use power effectively to modify undesirable conditions. According to Berger (1976), "the advocate is one who attempts to influence persons or groups who have control over the situation with which the client group is dissatisfied in order to make decision-makers more responsive to client needs."

The rallying point for nursing home advocacy has been the dissatisfaction with the power imbalance between the nursing home industry, on the one hand, and the consumers (residents or their relatives and families), on the other.

The main premise is that advocacy in conjunction with other initiatives is critical in efforts to improve the quality of care. Through consumer advocacy, the industry must be made more accountable to the public, since it is largely financed through government funding. Maggie Kuhn, a proponent of this view, stated: "Those who are responsible for managing institutions and the government officials who are regulating them must be held accountable to the patients and to the consumers in the community" (Horn and Griesel, 1977).

What chances do consumers have to bring about significant improvements in nursing home care, including elimination of abuses of all types? Nationally the picture is disappointing. The nursing home industry has been effective in lobbying for its interests in Washington as well as in the states. Representatives of the consumers' groups stated succinctly why consumers cannot win the battle. "The industry is a big money business. Like any business, they have lobbyists. They are good, and they have a great deal of influence. We are just outgunned" (*Chicago Tribune,* July 24, 1980).

Although the federal and state picture is disappointing, there have been efforts of successful advocacy at the local level in dealing with elderly abuse and neglect (Stathopoulos, 1980). The work of a consumers' group in the North Central Massachusetts area will be discussed below.

CONSUMER ADVOCATES FOR BETTER CARE: A CASE STUDY

The Setting

North Central Massachusetts contains a population of approximately 200,000 spread over rural, suburban, and urban areas, including 22 cities and towns. The twin cities of Fitchburg and Leominster have approximately 80,000 people, with the remaining towns ranging in population from 2000 to 13,500.

As a result of depressed economic conditions, Fitchburg is losing population, especially young adults. Consequently, the elderly are becoming an increasing percentage of the total population. The percentage of people over 65 years of age in Fitchburg (1970 census) is 12.5, with another 10% between 55 and 64 years of age. Most of the elderly live in poorer neighborhoods and in crowded or substandard housing conditions. Approximately 30% of the families in Fitchburg and Leominster living below the federal poverty line are heads of households who are over 65 years old.

There are 39 nursing homes in the area with a total capacity of approximately 2020 beds. The Consumer Advocates have expanded their work from nursing to rest homes. The group currently visits 22 area homes with a capacity of 1420 beds in nursing homes plus 600 in rest homes.

Historically, nursing homes have been located in spacious houses built for well-to-do families during the 19th century, in what is now the central section of each city. Typically, these homes are wooden structures with exquisite interior wood-carved decorations. As conditions in the central city neighborhoods have deteriorated, these homes have gone through a sequence of uses, being sold again and again and eventually becoming boarding houses. With the advent of Medicaid and the requirements for licensing, many of these facilities were upgraded to qualify for payment. Recently, as fire safety and other building code regulations require extensive structural changes, these homes are gradually but slowly converted to rest homes.

Thus, smaller homes are disappearing. The trend here, like elsewhere, is toward large facilities, so large "that people think of (them) almost as hospitals" (*Boston Globe,* April 25, 1976). The small homes, in most cases, are run as family businesses, providing a very homelike atmosphere. The larger and more recently built homes are owned by corporations, either local or national chains. What has happened in this area, in size, type, and ownership of nursing homes, is similar to what is occurring throughout the country: larger homes and concentration of homes in fewer corporations with ever-increasing control of the market. This oligopoly is at the root of the power imbalance between the industry, on the one hand, and consumers and government, on the other.

Goals

The consumer advocacy group has two major goals: first, to improve the quality of care in the local nursing homes, and second, to alter the power equilibrium in favor of the consumers of nursing home services at local and national levels. To achieve these goals, the group has engaged in several activities, the focus of which varies, depending on the goal pursued and the strategy adopted. The target of advocacy may be the local nursing home, the state legislature, or some part of the federal government (Figure 21-1).

Structure

The Consumer Advocates for Better Care began as a small nonincorporated citizen group under the aegis of the area Community Mental Health Center. Gradually, it has moved to incorporation as an independent organization with its own board of directors, staff, and citizen advocates. Some of the key principles in the organization's development have been:

1. Advocacy activities should focus on local area homes. Over the years the group's experience has shown that, especially for citizen advocates, interest can be maintained when the advocates deal with specific, concrete issues affecting people from their own communities rather than with general national issues. This also makes visiting easy.

2. The organization is dominated by elderly consumers. While membership is open to all ages, most of its past and current members are elderly. All of its 14 paid advocates are between the ages of 62 to 76. These

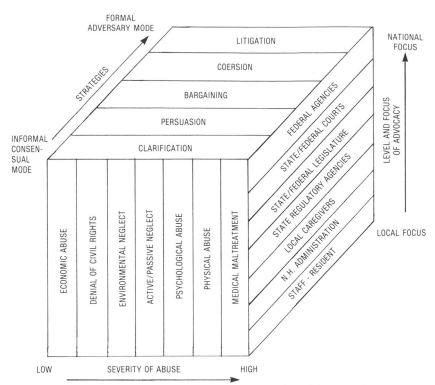

Figure 21-1 Type of elder abuse, focus and strategies of intervention.

advocates are paid near minimum hourly wages. Their main incentive, however, is their commitment to help fellow elderly persons. One must observe them in action to appreciate their enthusiasm. This element facilitates the development of a trusting relationship with residents, and often inspires overworked and underpaid staff to provide the best care possible.

The ten-member board of directors includes two attorneys who do legal advocacy work, two lay members who visit area nursing homes for advocacy, and officers of the organization. Some members of the board have had relatives placed in nursing homes. To protect the autonomy of the group from the influence of area nursing home owners, administrators, and staff, the constitution excludes from membership any person with pecuniary or other direct involvement with nursing homes or the health industry.

3. Multiple sources of support and funding must be developed to ensure program independence. The group receives funds from four organizations to pay its advocates. Thus, a cut-off from any one organization will not drastically cripple the group's ability to continue its advocacy program. A federal grant from the Administration on Aging

(AOA) covers the salary of the secretary-receptionist and the executive director, who, in addition to other duties, operates a hotline for people to register complaints and/or request information about conditions in area nursing homes. A local council on aging and the area United Way program provide funding used to cover travel expenses, while the area mental health center and the Department of Mental Health have subsidized the organization's rent, telephone, and other expenses.

In addition to the above sources of financial support, the group relies on support from other organizations. The Legal Aid Society represents clients regarding eligibility for various benefits, grievances, personal needs, allowances, preparation of testimonies, and other legislative activities.

4. Effective consumer advocacy requires ongoing training. Consumer advocates have generally been citizens with much interest and commitment to serve the elderly, but seldom with legal or other specific training. Learning takes place through seminars conducted by outside speakers, participation in workshops, and conferences in nearby colleges, but more significantly through sharing experiences with each other during regularly scheduled meetings. To meet their needs for understanding the scope and nature of their role, a training program has been devised that covers the following topics: aging process, residents' rights and responsibilities, Medicare-Medicaid eligibility and regulations, nursing home facility regulations, role and function of state regulatory agencies, and the network of community agencies working with the elderly.

5. Linkages and coordination mechanisms with other community agencies must be developed. Obviously, a small organization such as the Consumer Advocates cannot deal with abuses of nursing homes without support from the broader community. Thus, the group works with other agencies such as the Mental Health Center, Legal Aid, and Homecare Corporation, on issues of common interest. For instance, the executive director chairs an area-wide committee which consists of elderly citizens, Silver-haired Legislators, and social agency directors. This committee presents to area legislators issues of critical concern to the elderly and recommends legislative action.

6. Linkages at the state and national levels must be developed. The realization that the effectiveness of consumer advocacy at the local level is problematic in the long run without corresponding efforts at the state and national levels has led the group to increased involvement in coalition building at the state and federal levels. At these levels far reaching policies are developed and, therefore, consumer representation and input are critical in altering the power balance between the nursing home industry and consumers. The group is one of the founding members of the National Coalition for Nursing Home Reform.

MAJOR OBJECTIVES AND ACTIVITIES OF
CONSUMER ADVOCATES FOR BETTER CARE

Monitoring of Quality of Care

The first major objective is to monitor the quality of care provided by area nursing homes. This involves a number of activities by the advocates. Advocates visit each of the area's nursing and rest homes daily for periods ranging from one to four hours. Advocates have the right to make unannounced visits. They visit on different days and at different times, including weekends, so as to observe more accurately what is happening at each home. The frequent and regular visitation by the advocates with detailed documentation of irregularities or abuses provides the public, state, and federal agencies with information on which to act. Access to such information is the best weapon against unacceptable policies and practices. As Garvin and Burger (1968) stated: "The greatest ally of the disreputable home is secrecy. The only protection of the aged and their families is information."

However, the advocates have learned from experience that before they begin going into a home it is best to meet with the administrator and the executive director of the home to explain the role and function of the group, the nature of its activities, and the procedures used for the solicitation, verification, and resolution of complaints. Such an initial meeting helps to clarify and in a way to alert the administrator that the advocates will continually monitor the services rendered by the home. It is especially made clear that the advocates are not just friendly visitors, although friendly visiting with the residents is a major part of their work. Advocates also make it clear that the resolution of complaints follows an established procedure, with every effort being made to resolve the complaint within the home. No complaints are brought to agencies outside the home without the administrator's knowledge. Such an approach helps in the development of trust and a climate of mutual willingness to resolve problems at the local level.

The advocate's primary purpose for being at the home is to receive complaints from individual clients, verify, and try to resolve them. However, the group maintains a telephone hot line where residents, relatives, employees, and visitors of nursing homes can register complaints anonymously or by identifying themselves. Once a complaint has been registered about mistreatment of a specific resident, or unacceptable conditions in a home, advocates take steps to verify the situation and then correct it. Whenever advocates become aware of a complaint or problem that a resident wishes to have a response to, they complete a form with pertinent data about the complaint, where it took place, what action was taken, and the outcome. Compilation of these complaints on a monthly basis gives an aggregate picture of the volume, types of complaints registered, and number of complaints resolved. These aggregate data are critical for presenting evidence at hearings in support of bills, regulations, and court decisions affecting consumer rights and quality of care in nursing homes.

Problem Resolution Efforts of the Organization

The following are specific examples of types of abuse and examples of problem resolution.

Financial abuse   A variety of abuses occurs frequently in this category. Some of the complaints involve loss of small amounts of money. In some instances it may be simply a question of misplacement, and the staff must take time to locate the funds. However, there are more serious abuses that advocates become aware of. For example, in one nursing home the administrator asked residents to sign their social security checks without their seeing the amount of the check. The advocates testified in court against this administrator, who subsequently lost his bid to qualify for buying the home when it was placed in receivership. The group had collected detailed evidence over a two-year period about the administrator's lack of cooperation with the advocates, his abuse of residents' rights to receive unopened mail, and their right to sign social security checks and handle their personal needs accounts. Two of the advocates were court witnesses during the trial in which the court ruled not to accept the administrator's bid to purchase the home.

In another example of economic abuse, the advocates became aware from four residents about widespread misuse of the personal needs allowance in one home. However, no one was willing to make a formal complaint. It took several months of support from the advocates and reassurance that the residents would be protected as much as possible by the Consumer Advocates from any retaliation before two residents signed a complaint. Then the Attorney General's Office became involved and reviewed the entire accounting practices of the home. The daily presence of the advocates at the home is probably the single key factor in development of the trust and courage necessary to take such a risk.

Denial of civil rights   The advocates deal constantly with violation of the right to privacy of residents to be examined privately by nurses, physicians, and other caregivers. Curtains should surely be pulled to allow for minimal privacy. The advocates also see to it that residents have an opportunity to vote in municipal, state, and federal elections. Advocates also deal with establishing eligibility in Medicaid. Each new or prospective resident in each of the area's homes is oriented as to his/her rights as aresident of the facility, which includes the right to be a member of the residents' council and to receive visitors (including advocates).

Another reported violation of residents' rights is their removal from private and semiprivate rooms to three- or four-bed wards in order to accommodate private-paying residents. Current regulations require at least a 24-hour written notice of transfer to another room, along with a medical justification for such a transfer. Such violation is subject to action by the Attorney General's Office. However, no action can be taken unless the residents who were transferred are willing to sign a complaint. In one recent episode, the affected residents have not been able to act for fear of retaliation, and in this instance the Consumer Advocates have no right to proceed. However, an advocate is visiting the residents daily, documenting the negative impact of the transfer on them. Such documentation is often used by the group when legislative action is needed. This case also illustrates a serious problem facing all caregivers working with situations of abuse; that is, the limited actions one can take without the consent of the abused client. Fear of retaliation is invariably the predominant motive for the victim's unwillingness to take action.

Neglect Complaints of neglect are numerous and involve individual clients in every home. Some of the incidents are indicative of passive or inadvertent (at best) neglect. For example, advocates report situations where aides or orderlies make the beds while talking to each other, completely neglecting to acknowledge and include a resident in the conversation. An example of this passive neglect involves a resident in a wheelchair in a hallway as the nursing staff passed on the way to a staff meeting. The man sat there waiting hopefully for a word, a nod, a touch, or some acknowledgment, yet none of the staff took the time to greet him. It was the advocate who noticed him and spent enough time with him so that he felt like a human being in need of acceptance and respect. When the advocate confronted with staff with their behavior, they admitted how easy it is in the rush of their "duties" and forget the patients' needs.

Advocates deal with other forms of active neglect. There are many complaints about the food being cold, tasteless, medically contraindicated and, in one or two instances, spoiled. To deal with such complaints, the advocates visit homes at lunch and supper time to determine whether the weekly menu is followed and to ask for explanations if it is not. As a result of continuous surveillance and visitation, food is almost always served in adequate quantities and hot, and residents eat in the dining room instead of being served in their beds.

Advocates have received complaints about failure of professional caregivers to provide required services. A recent complaint involved a speech therapist who saw a resident for one-quarter hour when the prescribed treatment was for one-half hour. This was brought to the attention of the nursing supervisor, who intervened and corrected the situation.

Advocates also participate actively in social programs for residents, by encouraging them to get out of bed, to put their clothes on, and to participate in social activities. Residents' reasons for resistance to socialization are varied and sometimes very unsuspected. Here is an example of male chauvinism. A male resident, ex-mental patient, was placed in a rest home. He was the only male among female residents and nurses. For two years no one had heard him talk so it was believed that "Joe" was mute. A male advocate was assigned to that home, and naturally the advocate sought out the man on his visits to the home. After several months of acquaintance, Joe, while splitting wood, asked the advocate a question. The advocate could not believe what he heard until Joe asked the question again more loudly. "But aren't you mute?" the startled advocate asked. "No," Joe answered, "but who wants to be bothered with endless talk from all those women." It took months of acceptance and companionship with the advocate for Joe to trust him and speak up. Humorous as the story may sound, it is surely a sad commentary on the lack of sensitivity of professionals in placing a single male resident in an all-female environment. Men, like women, have a need for companionship and identification with members of their own sex.

Environmental neglect   Some of the common complaints that advocates deal with include the presence of unpleasant odors, lack of soap and toilet paper, or dirty carpets. A rest home which the advocates began visiting last year had ceilings that were peeling, walls that needed paint, and neither curtains in the windows nor any form of decoration in the rooms. The owners initially used as an excuse for the condition of the facility the fact that most of the residents were former mental patients who could not keep the place clean. With constant, but tactful, pressure and suggestions from the advocates for six months, all these deficiencies have been corrected.

Psychological abuse   Some of these complaints involve threats to individual clients, as well as groups of clients. As a result of deinstitutionalization, ex-mental patients, as well as retarded clients, have been placed in many of the area's homes. The advocates have been receiving numerous complaints about staff abusing such residents by calling them "nuts," "retards," and other derogatory terms. Here again, the residents are afraid to lodge a complaint or give consent for action by the advocates. Their therapists and other caregivers to whom they report this abusive behavior are equally reluctant to identify specific homes and abused clients and no action can be taken. The fear and threat of expulsion makes it difficult for clients to come forth and formally report such abuses.

Physical abuse   This abuse is infrequently documented. Realizing how difficult it is for the victims to report it, the advocates are trained to watch for signs of abuse. They observe the face and hands of the residents in their daily visits. When they notice signs of suspected abuse, they ask questions of staff and patients. Sometimes the response was that the residents fell. Then the advocates asked to see the patient's chart. (This constant surveillance should act as a deterrent to physical abuse, but not necessarily eliminate it.)

That these types of abuse exist in nursing homes is not a secret. Like most types of abuse, whether it is child, wife, or parent abuse, in homes or in institutions, there are serious difficulties in documentation and evidence. Complaints are usually made only after a good, trusting relationship has been developed by the residents and advocates. In one case four residents came forth and made a complaint. Any single resident is much more willing to take a risk and report abuse if other residents are prepared to act also.

Maltreatment Among the numerous forms of abuse with life-threatening or potentially serious impact on the well-being of the residents, one is widespread — overmedication. In many instances complaints about overmedication have resulted in review of the prescribed medication by physicians. Often such review has led to a change or a drastic reduction, with corresponding alleviation of undesirable side effects. However, in a few cases, more complicated situations have developed, as in the following case:

A former mental patient was placed in a nursing home. According to policy and the contract between the Department of Mental Health and the nursing home, the Department of Mental Health is responsible for psychiatric follow-up for at least the first year. During that period, if the patient's condition warrants hospitalization, the patient should be admitted. However, with widespread efforts to keep former mental patients out of the hospital, admission to psychiatric hospitals is difficult. The consumer advocates were involved in this case at the request of the nursing home administrator who felt that the client, in spite of a large dosage of psychotropic medication, was unmanageable in the nursing home and his behavior interfered with the rights of other residents in the facility. More specifically, the physician began treatment with 5 mg Thorazine and increased the dose until the patient reached a condition of coma. The consumer advocate's intervention resulted in a visit by an official from the Department of Mental Health the following day. The client was promptly admitted for inpatient services at the local state hospital.

In another case, the consumer advocates became involved with the transfer of a resident from a nursing home to the local general hospital. This 96-year-old resident had developed gangrene at the heels, spreading to her upper legs and reaching her spine. She subsequently died after four months of hospitalization. Her family had refused to give consent for amputation of the legs. The consumer advocate has begun a preliminary investigation to take the case to court for maltreatment. An attorney who is a member of the board is donating his time. However, the consumer advocates are financially unable to undertake such a case. There is a fee for obtaining a copy of the medical record, and a high hourly fee for a state-appointed physician to review the record for evidence of maltreatment, before the case can go to court. Such expenses are beyond the budget of this and similar consumer advocacy organizations.

These two cases of maltreatment are extreme and the exception rather than the rule in medical abuse. They are discussed because they point out some of the strengths and limitations of consumer advocacy given the legal and financial constraints within which these organizations operate.

Community Involvement

Another major objective is to promote local community involvement with nursing homes and to foster interest in the needs and issues of concern to nursing home residents. The success of consumer advocacy depends in the long run on how much the local communities become interested in the needs of elderly residents. Nursing homes are only one part of a network of services in the community, and successful advocacy has to involve community caregivers. The organization also needs visibility, credibility, and legitimacy from various constituencies to carry on its mission. Visibility and credibility are important if prospective nursing home residents, their families, and other community agencies are to use the information and referral services of the organization in their search for nursing homes. Visibility also helps members of the community know where to complain about abuses in nursing homes. Legitimacy is important if the organization is to be effective and also to obtain funds to continue its work. The Consumer Advocates cooperate with other caregivers in their efforts to serve residents. An example of this is found in the discharge of nursing home residents into aggregate housing.

Community agencies which are involved in collaborative, consultative arrangements with nursing homes are limited in their role as advocates for changes in local homes. They often channel their inside information to the advocates, who in turn can raise questions about a specific client or prevailing conditions in a facility. Such examples include observation of adherence to a prescribed or recommended diet for a client or follow-up of recommendations by consultants.

In one facility a former mental patient was assigned the distribution of psychotropic drugs, an illegal assignment, since only licensed personnel can dispense medication. This was especially serious because this client had been diagnosed as suicidal. Also, there had been complaints from other clients that they were not always given their medication by the designated dispenser. The personnel from the mental health center made several efforts to persuade the administrator-owner to stop this practice without success. At that time, the Consumer Advocates were notified of the situation and agreed to intervene if the practice continued after a final attempt by the mental health staff. During that final attempt, the owner was told that the advocates knew of the situation and planned on taking action. Immediately, he assigned a nurse to give the medication. Administrators take the work of the Advocates seriously, and other agencies in the community use the Consumer Advocates in pursuit of quality of care and elimination of abuse.

The Consumer Advocates are also involved in cases of elder abuse in the community, especially when the only realistic solution is placement in a nursing home. To educate community caregivers about the needs and rights of nursing home residents, the group has developed a video slide show, which the executive director of the Consumer Advocates shows in speaking engagements in nursing homes, local colleges, community groups, and social agencies to sensitize community caregivers about the conditions in nursing homes and the significance of community involvement for increasing nursing home accountability and quality of care.

In its efforts to enhance the community's awareness of the needs of residents in nursing homes, the Consumer Advocates publish an educational newsletter. The newsletter is distributed free to nursing home residents, staff, and the population at large through the mailing list of its supporters. Thus, this quarterly newsletter reaches approximately 2000 families in the area. In addition, local television stations have presented the work of the Consumer Advocates in an attempt to sensitize the public about the needs of residents in nursing homes. As an indication of its acknowledged success in dealing with consumer issues, the group has been awarded contracts from the Department of Elder Affairs to organize and train advocate groups in other parts of Massachusetts.

Efforts to Influence Public Policy Formulation

The last major objective is to influence public policy at the state and federal levels. Although the greatest volume of activity occurs in the local area, the long-term effectiveness and impact of the Consumer Advocates will be determined at the state and federal levels, where critical, far-reaching decisions are made affecting the quality of services in nursing homes. With the strong and influential lobby of the industry, Consumer Advocates realized early that a National Coalition for Nursing Home Reform, expressing and representing the consumer interest, was needed. Indeed, the Consumer Advocates was one of the few groups throughout the country that took part in the establishment of such a coalition. Over the years the group has been actively involved in the work of the Coalition, and its executive director is vice president of the Coalition.

The Consumer Advocates, through its extensive documentation of prevailing undesirable conditions in nursing homes, has repeatedly taken an active role in the development of public policy. As early as 1977, through formal testimony and informal discussions, it influenced the development of the Massachusetts Attorney's Office regulations on nursing homes. Notable victories included the regulations granting community groups the right of access to nursing homes, as well as the development of procedures safeguarding arbitrary transfer of residents by nursing homes. More recently, the executive director testified in support of the Massachusetts Nursing Home Patient Abuse Law. The information presented in this testimony and on similar occasions is detailed, specific about residents or facilities, and persuasive.

Currently there are two bills in the Massachusetts Legislature, one dealing with provisions for the transfer of residents because they are on Medicaid, and the other with provisions for the appointment of a receiver to operate a nursing home in certain emergency situations. The detailed documentation that the advocates have collected over the past year will be of immense value in demonstrating the need for the passage of these bills. Similarly, monthly reports which the Consumer Advocates submit to the Massachusetts Department of Elder Affairs and the Area Agency on Aging amply document the type and volume of abuses in local homes. Such evidence also places a burden on these agencies to act on their own for the improvement of nursing homes.

CONCLUSION

This chapter discussed the activities and strategies of a consumer advocacy organization in North Central Massachusetts to deal with elder abuse in nursing homes. Review of the limited literature indicates that elder abuse is a serious social problem. It is also clear that abusive behavior, whether within families or institutions, is complicated. Approaches to intervention have ethical, legal, psychological, and social dimensions.

The experience of the Consumer Advocates indicates that the right of consent is critical in the difficulty of documentation and intervention. Unless the victim is willing to make a formal complaint, almost no action can be taken. What emerges, however, from the experience of the Consumer Advocates is that given certain conditions, such consent is more likely to be obtained:

First, the development of trust between the victim and other witnesses of abuse, such as other residents, staff, and the advocates is essential. The advocate must gain the victim's trust for being reliable, trustworthy, and effective. One key concern to overcome is the fear that the victim will be left to the mercy of the abuser. Most residents want to be assured that they will not be abandoned by the advocates after they take action. They want to be visited regularly and frequently. This is in contrast to the Ombudsman program of the Department of Elder Affairs and the inspectors of the various state Departments of Public Health, who visit homes for inspection periodically and irregularly. Residents cannot count on support from an unknown state official who most likely will not be back the next day to deal with the anger and possible retaliation that the victim may face. Thus, the second condition is the regular and frequent visitation of the advocates. The third condition for consent, is the willingness of more than one resident to take action. To the extent that the advocate can encourage and facilitate collective action, it is easier for the victim to make a formal complaint.

The experience of the Advocates also indicates that legal interventions and the recently enacted laws of mandatory reporting of abuse (although important) will not alone contribute substantially to the reduction of the problem. The barriers to documentation and consent, as indicated above, are more psychological than legal. What laws and regulations do is to give consumer advocates some clout. In institutions, as opposed to families, it is possible to document some types of abuse or neglect because of existing regulations permitting access of the Consumer Advocates to the facilities. Such documentation is critical when the focus changes from case to issue advocacy, and from local to state and national levels of policy formulation.

The extent of abuse and neglect in nursing homes is still a debated matter. According to a survey by Melrose (1974), the best measure of the prevalence of abuse and dissatisfaction with conditions in nursing homes is the percentage of residents or consumers who want to complain rather than the percentage of registered complaints.

Much more systematic research is needed. Also it is important to specify the prevalence of abuse by category. An impression from the review of the work of the Consumer Advocates is that the vast majority of documented and undocumented abuse or neglect is of a less severe nature, such as gross appropriation of personal funds, passive neglect, and verbal abuse. The more severe forms of life-threatening abuse are limited. Review of the situation shows that resolution of most complaints received by the Consumer Advocates seldom goes beyond the nursing home administrator. Most of the complaints are settled in an informal manner, using clarification and persuasion strategies. The continuous presence of advocates in each facility is important in the development of a positive relationship with the residents as well as with the staff, so that, when complaints exist, the staff is apt to respond positively to the advocates in most instances. There are also situations when the staff, especially nurses' aides, see the advocates as allies to whom they report questionable practices of administrators and owners, or other professionals. On a few occasions, even administrators seek the support of the advocates in their efforts to deal with community and state agencies unresponsive to the needs of their residents.

Consumer advocacy for the needs of abused elders in nursing homes eventually leads to the realization that elder abuse does not always start or end in the nursing home. Elder abuse in institutions is one part in the continuum of abuse in our society. Public policy which supports institutionalization of the elderly to the exclusion of other forms of care in the community is in many instances at the root of elder abuse in institutions. Programs such as day care or respite care have often been suggested as mechanisms to alleviate family stress which leads to parent abuse and the removal of elderly from the family by placement in institutions.

So far, the areas of success in dealing with institutional abuse through consumer advocacy have been presented. Some limitations of advocacy must be noted. Some of these refer to the limits imposed by legislation. For instance, VISTA volunteers who work as advocates are not allowed to engage in lobbying activities for more than 20% of their time. The organization, as a nonprofit entity, is limited by its charter from becoming involved in partisan and other political activities. In addition to the above legal restrictions, the organization's program and political independence is threatened as it depends more and more on state and federal funding for its activities. Advocacy involves political risks, and therefore the interests of the organization in survival may displace the original focus from advocacy to service. Thus, the more the organization becomes another agency, it has a stake in maintaining the status quo and probably losing its effectiveness as a force for change and as advocate for the needs of the individual client. Despite these potential barriers to effective advocacy, this case study supports the view that the presence of consumer groups at the local level can deal effectively at both the local and the national level for the improvement of the quality of care and the prevention of resident abuse in nursing homes.

BIBLIOGRAPHY

Berger M: An orienting perspective on advocacy. in Kerschner PA (ed): *Advocacy and Age.* Los Angeles, The University of Southern California Press, 1976.

354

Boston Globe, April 25, 1976.

Carnoy J, Weis M: *A House Divided: Radical Perspectives on Social Problems.* Boston, Little Brown, 1973.

Chicago Tribune: "Watchdogs outgunned by industry lobbyists," July 24, 1980.

Fauri DP: *Consumer Participation in the Planning and Administration of Public Social Programs.* PhD Dissertation, Syracuse University, 1973.

Garbarino J, Smyer MA: *A Continuum of Care for the Family.* Paper presented to the 33rd Annual Scientific Meeting of the Gerontological Society, San Diego, California, Nov. 21–25, 1980.

Garvin RM, Burger RE: *Where They Go to Die: The Tragedy of America's Aged.* New York, Delacorte, 1968.

Horn L, Griesel E: *Nursing Homes.* Boston, Beacon Press, 1977.

Jellinek T, Tennstedt S: Prevention of chronicity in the nursing home. *Psychiatr Ann* 1980;10:338–343.

Melrose GJ: Would you call this a home? Maine Nursing Homes: A Consumer's Perspective. Public Interest Research Group, Augusta, ME, 1974.

Mendelson M: *Tender Loving Greed.* New York, Alfred A. Knopf, 1974.

Mendelson MA, Hapgood D: The political economy of nursing homes. *Ann Am Acad Polit Soc Sci* 1974;415:95–103.

National Health Survey, Series 13, No. 29, Vital and Health Statistics: *Profile of Chronic Illness in Nursing Homes—National Nursing Home Survey. August 1973–April 1974.* Hyattsville, MD, DHEW Pub # (PHS)78-1780, December 1974.

Nursing Home Care in the United States: Failure in Public Policy. Introductory report prepared by the subcommittee on long-term care of the United States Senate Special Committee on Aging. November 1974, Report No. 93-1420.

Service Employee, Providence, RI. Oct. 10, 1980;40(3):9.

Shanas E: The family as a social support in old age. *Gerontologist* 1979;19(2):169–174.

Stathopoulos P: Consumer advocacy: A strategy to improve services in nursing homes. *Generations* 1980;4(1)28–29.

Stotsky B: *The Elderly Patient.* New York, Grune and Stratton, 1968.

United States Public Health Service, *Health in the United States: A Chartbook,* Washington, DC, 1975.

Yin K, Lucas WA, Stanton PL, Spindler JA: *Citizen Organizations: Increasing Client Control Over Services.* Santa Monica, Rand Corporation, 1973.

22 Family Intervention: The Task-Centered Approach

Eloise Rathbone-McCuan
Ann Travis
Barbara Voyles

As the problems of abuse and victimization of the elderly become more widely recognized and more frequently reported, practitioners are questioning the efficacy of traditional intervention approaches and are exploring possible alternatives. This chapter discusses provision of services to the elderly, the caregiver, and the larger family group as an alternative to casework services provided only to the aged person. There has been intervention into intrafamily victimization (violent or nonviolent) but there have been barriers to applying it in elder abuse. For example, many clinicians define family members as part of the problem, but do not directly include them in the intervention plan. Some workers assigned to elder victimization cases have little familiarity with or training in family-oriented intervention as compared to individual-oriented. Also, many agencies providing services to this group of elders do not encourage innovative intervention approaches.

The Task-Centered Model appears to be helpful to the aged client and their significant others. The field research undertaken in clinical gerontology at the George Warren Brown School of Social Work involved, in part, the application of the Task-Centered Model with elderly clients of an adult protective service unit in St. Louis, in connection with a larger project to develop a clinical gerontology component in masters-level social work training (Fortune and Rathbone-McCuan, 1981). The authors will summarize the observations of those involved in the work on elder abuse intervention.

FAMILY-ORIENTED INTERVENTION AND CLINICAL GERONTOLOGY

In discussing some issues involved in a family-oriented approach to clinical gerontology that could be applied to a range of counseling situations with older families, numerous family therapy frameworks could be explored. Our discussion is limited to three approaches. The Contextual Family Therapy Model is a long-term approach that lends itself to the treatment of multigenerational families where intrapsychic factors may be associated with elder victimization. The Problem-Centered Systems Family Therapy and the Task-Centered Model are short-term and action-oriented and may be useful in crisis counseling.

With the emergence of interest in social gerontology during the 1960s and early 1970s came recognition of the relation between the elderly and their families. The sociological and social psychological research done during the 1960s (Troll, 1971) and 1970s produced much information on older families (Streib and Beck, 1980). Despite advances, the gaps in this research are still similar. Among the neglected areas are better analysis of the crisis-promoting aspects of caregiving and studies on the effectiveness of clinical intervention with older families.

Herr and Weakland (1978), in summarizing some writing on the elderly and their families, concluded that including families of the elderly in the search for solutions to the problems of aging is necessary. Saying that families are an important component of clinical intervention does not provide the practitioner with empirical knowledge to decide when to apply individual, group, or family-oriented interventions; how to combine clinical counseling into agencies not designated as responsible for long-term family counseling; and on what basis which to select a framework for intervention. These issues are relevant to stressful caregiving situations, and become even more complex when elder victimization is involved.

Evaluating empirical knowledge for guiding practitioner intervention into problems of family-related elder victimization is frustrating. The nonintervention-oriented research produced by the social sciences and the youth-oriented studies of family therapy are not directly applicable to the elder abuse situation, and have been overlooked for their potential adaptation and modification for problems related to caregiving, including aged abuse and neglect. The way to develop better knowledge for intervention is to explore how to adapt family-oriented approaches.

The Contextual Family Therapy Model

The writings of Brody (1966) and Brody and Spark (1966 and 1970) were notable exceptions to the meager body of information available to practitioners before the surge of research about the family and the aged. Their work reflected the combined perspectives of clinical social work practice with the aged and family therapy developments at the Eastern Pennsylvania Psychiatric Institute since its founding in 1957 under the leadership of Boszormenyi-Nagy (Broderick and Schrader, 1980). The conceptual roots of this work were grounded in psychoanalytic psychology with existential and experimental dimensions. In the early 1960s the approach moved from the nuclear family to an intergenerational family system. This work produced a framework for applying the ethics of transgenerational relationships as therapeutic leverages (Boszormenyi-Nagy and Spark, 1973; Boszormenyi-Nagy, 1976). The original framework has been revised and expanded into a framework known as Contextual Family Therapy (Boszormenyi-Nagy and Ulrich, 1980). This framework has yet to be empirically tested for intervention with the aged and their families, but some of its premises are relevant to family counseling and therapy, as for example, the following:

1. Influences of the multiple generations of family members are recognized and would be appropriate for dealing with problems of victimization where revenge on the part of the younger generation (adult child) or the aged spouse (elderly wife) is a cause for abuse or neglect.

2. Issues of transgenerational loyalty may put the adult caregiver into an impossible situation trying to balance what is perceived as indebtedness to an aged parent, desire to fulfill personal needs, and care for dependent children.

3. Acts of concrete and symbolic exploitation of the elder by another family member are recognized.

As a long-term psychoanalytically oriented therapy, contextual family therapy merits additional exploration and investigation in clinical gerontology. It could be applied in private counseling where clients are able to bear the cost of extended therapy, but its viability as a short-term approach is not clear. Training is essential for successful application, and most clinicians who apply the model have extensive clinical training in its application. It would be a valuable area of advanced training for clinical gerontologists who plan to specialize in multigenerational family therapy.

Problem-Centered Systems Family
Therapy and the Task-Centered Models

Other family therapists and clinical researchers have contributed frameworks appropriate for application in clinical gerontology. For example, the Problem-Centered Systems Family Therapy Model grew out of research and clinical work in the Departments of Psychiatry at McGill and McMaster Universities in Canada (Epstein and Bishop, 1980, 1981). The focus of therapy is on specific family problems. The problems are either instrumental or affective and are identified during assessment which is the first stage of the four-stage model (there are multiple steps in each stage). Active collaboration of the family is vital, and a contract is developed for the length of therapy — between 6 to 12 sessions distributed over a period established by the type of problem. The initial schedule of time set forth in the contract is adhered to, and lengthening therapy is not advocated. Assessment, an essential part, includes orienting the family to what to expect from therapy, getting information, describing the problem, and clarifying and agreeing on the problem. Contracting (the second stage) involves orientation, outlining options, negotiating expectations, and signing contracts. Treatment (the third stage) involves orientation, clarifying priorities, setting tasks, and task evaluation, with emphasis on the importance of ending the therapy; the fourth stage of closure requires orientation, summary of treatment, long-term goals, and follow-up.

To a far greater extent than the Contextual Family Therapy Model, the Problem-Centered Systems Family Therapy Model is anchored in systematic evaluation for both intervention benefits and model-related training outcomes. The model was developed exclusively for application with families. The developers to this approach have not explored how it could be applied to older families, but there is no reason why it should not be appropriate for field tests.

The Task-Centered Model was developed at the School of Social Service Administration at the University of Chicago (Reid and Epstein, 1972), and has been continuously applied, evaluated, and adapted for use with families (Reid, 1977; 1978; and Reid, in press, Gibbons et al, 1978; Tolson, 1977). The model deals with problems of living that are faced by families, and the types of problems are categorized in the following ways: interpersonal conflict, dissatisfaction in social relations, problems with formal organizations, difficulty in role performance, problems in social transition, reactive emotional distress, and inadequate income. In conjunction with numerous efforts to apply the model to families, there has been an evolution of the Task-Centered Model as a framework for counseling the elderly (Cormican, 1977), working with aged persons in residential settings (Dierking et al, 1980), and in case management functions in an adult protective service unit for elderly and handicapped clients (Wanless and Rooney, 1981). These clinical field trials have contributed much to its application in physical and mental health problems of the elderly in building a foundation for clinical gerontology training (Fortune and Rathbone-McCuan, 1981). As one component, the Task-Centered Model has been applied to aged and their families in an adult protective service unit where there are serious problems of daily living that victimize the aged and/or their caregiving family. In the majority of cases where the Task-Centered Model was applied, stress- and isolation-related problems suggest a potential for future violence and abuse if help to families is unavailable. Therefore, its application was preventive but the elders were still at risk from the circumstances of daily living.

ISSUES RELEVANT TO THE APPLICATION OF THE TASK-CENTERED MODEL

Characteristics of human service provision to the elderly (Harbert and Ginsberg, 1979) and to the aged and their families (Silverstone and Hyman, 1976) correspond with the basic features of the Task-Centered Model: (1) defining resources appropriate to the client, (2) allowing for choice and participation of the client, (3) maintenance of the client in the community, (4) emphasis on the client's positive potential for problem solving, and (5) restoration. The Task-Centered Model has broad application. Its basic features are summarized by Epstein (1977):

> Task-centered practice is a set of procedures for alleviating explicit target problems perceived by clients. In instances when clients are involuntary participants, there are procedures for a preliminary sequence to elicit problems and negotiate goals with referring agencies. Processes relied on to alleviate target problems are specific goals, client's commitment to selected and agreed-on tasks [tasks are actions which have a reasonably good chance to alleviate target problems and are divided into tasks to be performed by the client and worker], interventions aimed at overcoming obstacles to task achievement, and a service contract containing time limits. Types of interventions to produce problem reduction include: problem exploration, task selection and task-planning, task reviews, rehearsals for task action, anticipation and analysis of

obstacles or barriers, procurement of concrete resources, encouragement and reinforcement, direction, advice, a rationale for work on tasks, enhancing client awareness of his own and others' actions, and obtaining cooperation from significant others to support task work.

The Task-Centered Model is a goal-directed strategy that involves multiple steps: specifying target problems, developing goals and contracts (including time limits), planning and achieving tasks, terminating, and — if necessary — extending and monitoring. The model is a multiple-planned, short approach to practice that includes psychodynamic forms of brief treatment and crisis intervention (Reid, 1978). The approach does not emphasize past history; it lessens the problems of ambiguity, uncertainty of goals, and lack of clarity that have plagued other therapeutic systems. The client is a partner in formulating a plan of intervention, of importance to older persons who generally do not feel in control of their lives. The contract is a key element in the process of Task-Centered interventions.

To train a clinical gerontologist to apply the Task-Centered Model with cases of victimization of the elderly requires that they have received in depth preparation and have skills to apply the model first to individual elderly clients. Applying it to the family unit requires additional preparation, students must have: (1) knowledge about the aged and the family; (2) some preparation in family-oriented intervention; and (3) understanding of intrafamily victimization of the elderly. There are common conditions of stress and isolation within the daily life of the elderly and those who provide care to them without adequate supports. Conditions of isolation of the abused and the abuser are caused in part by lack of resources (Rathbone-McCuan and Hashimi, 1982). Basic needs are nutrition, transportation, homemaker health services, and primarily, economic resources. Isolation is also caused by the abuser or abused's lack of social skills or opportunities to practice problem solving. These dimensions of elder victimization may become translated into target problems by either the elderly or the caregiver. The Task-Centered approach can quickly identify problem areas, link clients appropriately to resources, and facilitate teaching new skills.

Just as isolation produces unique individual and caregiver problems, the Task-Centered Model produces unique and individualized solutions for the individual and larger family unit. It is not an intervention framework that depersonalizes the aged or caregivers by the worker, even though it is a short-term intervention. Rather, the approach supports these individuals by individualizing each client's needs and dividing tasks to solve these problems. Sometimes practitioners without training in gerontology using the Task-Centered Model superimpose their definition of problems into the counseling situation and address too many problems simultaneously. These are counter-productive actions, given the complexity of needs and resources among many elder abuse victims. It is wiser to focus on what can be done practically and see the possibility for change as within immediate reach, not so far in the future. Since a significant proportion of the problems that produce vulnerability among the aged are the result of present circumstances, both the aged person and the caregiver are likely to accept help more readily if they see it is connected to their immediate situation. Basing intervention on target problems defined by clients is an important strength of the Task-Centered Model in social service intervention with the victimized elder and family.

A FAMILY VIEW OF VICTIMIZATION ISSUES

Caregiving to the eldest members of a family system is one of the functions of contemporary family life that has implications for its social, psychological, and biological development as well as its economic maintenance and stability. If there are problems related to caregiving functions that have an impact on the well-being of the family members the situation should be assessed. Some of the problems families experience are related to a lack of basic resources such as food, money, transportation, and shelter. Without basic resources, caregiving is difficult if not impossible and will cause stress. The developmental cycle of a family is important to consider because each member is at a particular stage and experiencing important transitions, and each stage is related to the development of the entire family. Assessing individual and family development requires understanding of both normal and abnormal development. The caregiving functions of a family may be hindered by a crisis that disrupts the balance of family functioning. Epstein and Bishop (1980) note that a multidimensional assessment of the family is valuable. An assessment that focuses on only one dimension, such as communication, without considering problem-solving skills, family roles, behavioral control and other aspects of family structure, organization, and interaction would produce an incomplete analysis.

If the victimizing family is isolated from resources needed for daily living a basic task area can be seen (a three-generational family unit where the major bread winner is unemployed and scarce dollars must be divided between expensive medication for grandmother and clothes for young children to attend school). In situations where the middle generation (middle-aged couple) is caught among and between different life cycle transitions, dealing with the multiple demands of caregiving that compete with their marital dyad, decision-making about their own future could involve both individual and family developmental task areas. An abuse- or neglect-catalyzing event may be a recent discharge from a medical or psychiatric institution putting other members of the family in a crisis position because the facility "dumped" the aged person onto the family with no supportive resources.

The complexity of these task areas points to why the worker should assess the caregiving family's situation as well as that of the elderly person or single/primary caretaking family member. How is the caretaker currently finding her situation? Is a network of support available from other family members or friends and neighbors? Are other living arrangements desirable, at least temporarily? Is the caretaker able to leave the home once in a while? What could be done to insure personal security? What immediate supports does the caretaker need for a crisis? Much can be learned by observing the condition of the home, the interaction of the caregiving family and aged person, and the tension of the client and family during an in-office interview. On the other hand, the assessment process is complex, requiring practitioner skill. Unfortunately, many practitioners are faced with having to complete an assessment without benefit of adequate training, readily available consultation, or a standardized interview procedure. The lack of training may leave a worker feeling uncomfortable with gathering data from the family; no consultation may leave the worker without additional opinions upon which to plan intervention; and no schedule for guiding the interview may generate only fragmentary information. An excessively strained family group with problems that overlap into multiple areas of need and dysfunction may be as much victims as they are making a victim of the elder. Assigning priorities to interventions directed toward the elder, the caretaker, and other parts of the family system are facilitated by the application of the Task-Centered Model and the Problem-Centered Systems Family Therapy Model.

If the practitioner must make a decision to intervene with some part of the family system and rely on other clinical resources to provide therapy with the larger family unit, priority should be devoted to the caregiver and the elder. That is the only feasible alternative for many clinicians attached to protective service units. Time limitations and other agency regulations restrict the practitioner's role in counseling the larger family group. If the caretaker(s) is included in the service provision, it is useful to let her know that caring for an aged person is often difficult and that the conditions being faced are not unique. That awareness may not resolve target problems, but it may reduce some of the frustration accumulated from the perception that nobody shares his fate of the burden of caring for an invalid. The caretaker needs to be assured that the worker is interested in helping her as a person who is burdened. Both the

Task-Centered Model and the Problem-Centered System Family Therapy Model emphasize the importance of explaining the parameters of the intervention and the value of the clients' definitions of their problems and needs.

Sometimes the process of explaining the steps of an intervention approach and the joint responsibility shared between the worker and caregiver (specified in the contract) can be used for establishing recognition of the worker's concern. Assessment is a part of the intervention, and its completion should be an activity that is acceptable to the family. The first interview in which a contract is mentioned and possibly formed is a good point to reinforce assessment and insure that it begins as a supportive rather than confrontive process. Reviewing what might be planned or discussed as target problems and actions can help to promote confidence.

Following assessment, at least three factors seem to influence whether or not intervention assists the caretaker: (1) the worker's ability to maintain concern for the caregiver as a person; (2) the worker's knowledge of formal and informal resources that can benefit the caretaker and ability to refer the person to a supportive opportunity for help; and (3) the support the worker receives from the agency. A worker needs to think carefully before making an ambiguous commitment of support or help to the caretaker. Promises unfulfilled can lead to more problems, (the caretaker acts abusively toward the older person, cuts off access of the worker to the elder, or simply becomes more hopeless and untrusting of any offer of respite or support).

Both the elderly person and the caregiver referred to protective services are clients who face crisis situations, often having been passed over by other agencies or passed among service settings. Hooyman (1980) indicates the need to develop a responsive system with all appropriate resources coordinated. As most communities lack a system of services, clients seeking service may have been offered little in the way of supportive resources that help resolve day-to-day problems. Without a range of diverse services, easily coordinated, both practitioners and clients are handicapped. Resolution of target problems is often difficult if supports for needs cannot be mobilized. It is difficult to overcome conditions of nonexistent and fragmented resources, but practitioners may need to assume tasks related to closing the gaps between clients and resources. The isolation of the client and caregiver may be reflected in the lack of opportunity these individuals have to be socially involved in community life. It may also be reflected in alienation from service agencies or an alienated feeling resulting from their perceptions of no alternatives to the current situation. For example, the aged person may fear decision-making independent of the caregiver because he has been powerless for an extended period of time and/or fears retaliation from the caregiver if boundaries of the caregiver's authority are crossed. The caregiver(s) may perceive the functions of care provision to the aged person as so confining and restrictive that hope of finding some acceptable alternative has faded, and thus hopelessness leads to immobilization to take active steps to relieve their own burdens. Since these conditions are typical, they are the focus of target problems or dealt with as barriers to accomplishing specific tasks to change or reduce the stresses of the caregiving environment.

THE MODEL DISCUSSED IN A SERVICE CONTEXT

This section will summarize some of the relevant practice observations gathered during a field trial conducted at the Adult Protective Service Unit of the Missouri Division on Aging. Using the family as a focus of intervention is appropriate even though difficult in some cases. Both the aged person and the caregiver may be at risk. The elder is vulnerable to neglect, abuse, or exploitation, and the caregiver is subject to stress, isolation, and burdens of care. Systematic application of the Task-Centered Model can help both individuals as well as the larger family group.

The Clients Who Need Help

The cases encountered in settings such as Adult Protective Service Units are often elderly persons with cognitive impairments. Their caregiving family members may have functional limitations, such as minimal to moderate developmental disabilities or psychological impairments (including histories of chronic and acute psychiatric illness).

Protective service workers typically encounter such conditions as lack of resources, resistance, or fear of the older person or the caregiver. Even simple questions from the worker such as "Could you tell me if you have some financial resources to help with your move?" or "What alternatives do you have as far as someone else in your family to talk to about what you should do?" can open the discussion into areas that do not seem directly focused on completing the important tasks. Yet, sometimes disjointed and emotionally charged conversations can provide the practitioner with crucial information about the extent to which other people might be appropriately or inappropriately asked to play a role. One case recording noted a wandering and seeming aimless monologue on the part of an elderly woman regarding her loss of an old antique doll collection. At first the worker thought that she was totally disoriented, but at the end of the conversation the worker gathered enough information to suspect that multiple family members had engaged in financial exploitation and mismanagement of the client's funds. Before that conversation, the worker had been about to ask these relatives to assume greater money management functions for the elderly relative.

An important element of clinical gerontology is having acceptance of the elderly person's right to define her own needs. This position is central to the Task-Centered Model. Thus, the model reinforces an important aspect of counseling with elders. Even among elderly clients with some cognitive dysfunctions, conversations with the practitioner may have special meaning since elders may experience few opportunities to talk with a caring person about past or present issues important to them. The building of a feeling of trust in the solution-oriented relationship; the worker's reinforcement of interest in past successes of the elder or the caregiver; identifying present strengths and talking about them can all be helpful in breaking impasses that are hard to anticipate before they emerge in the process of intervention. These are important and appropriate actions whether the worker is involved with the elderly, caregiver, or a larger group of family members.

Some of the older protective service clients do not have families or maintain a relationship with only the caregiver. For example, the elderly never-married woman who outlived all of her extended family members or the retarded male grown old and out of contact with other family through institutionalization and uprootedness represent the isolated non-family affiliated. However, a significant proportion of the clients have living family members, often living nearby. Given the existence of family members and their potential connections to the elder, many cases are inappropriately conceptualized if only the elder or the dyad relationship between elder and caregiver is considered as the focus. A conceptualization of the entire family system might be more appropriate because it focuses on the various parts of the family as interrelated, it helps to understand the system, and it clarifies the structure and organization of the family members in relation to their behavior and circumstances. Developing an intervention plan for a family group (including short-term family counseling on long-term family therapy) may be facilitated by conceptualizing the family as a system. The application of the Task-Centered Model to families can incorporate a systems approach to the family.

Comments About the Model's Application

There are many important elements to consider in applying the Task-Centered Model to elder victimization. The adaptations for counseling the elderly suggested by Fortune and Rathbone-McCuan (1981) are appropriate for work with victimized elders. Also, Epstein's adaptations of the Task-Centered Model for involuntary clients (1977) are also useful when intervention is a legal requirement.

Travis (1981) summarized her observation regarding the application of the Task-Centered Model in a setting where the field trial was conducted:

> Given the diverse caseload, the intervention model must have relevance to either very rapid intervention approximating crisis intervention and/or address problems that are ongoing and chronic. My experience suggests that the Task-Centered Model could be used by many different helpers (police and home health staff). Elder and caregivers may need to learn new skills, especially if they wish to continue to live together and/or be interdependent. I would apply more care-giving skills training as a specific intervention for caregivers and self-management training for elders, if time and resources were available. Given the type of target problems, education and retraining has both preventive and interventive value.

High degrees of apprehension may require more active input from the practitioner as to the details of problems specification (Epstein, 1977) in regard to what, how often, when, where, with whom, content, antecedents, and consequences. The initial step of problem identification and the next steps of task formulation and possible task modification may need to be scaled down into manageable units for the level of function of either the elderly person, the caregiver, or both. The discussion of what is happening may require emphasis to be placed on what will happen to the elderly person within a very short period of time if, for example, medical attention is not provided by a professional. The consequences of delaying treatment may be best understood by the caregiver if the practitioner states it clearly and simply. The worker must be able to give information to the aged person and caregiver in a way that is understandable but does not superimpose the worker's perspective onto the client's definition of the problem. Also, as denial and misunderstandings of conditions are frequent, the practitioner must be careful not to add to the distortions and confusions.

At times, the caregiver's confusion about how often a medical treatment is required by the elderly individual is the primary reason for neglect or poor care. A practitioner may find it necessary to state clearly the exact frequency of treating a wound and design some time-of-dressing schedule or arrange to have someone look in on the elder and caregiver during the period when care is required. When an aged person or a caregiver is to complete a task of making a contact with an agency for resources, the worker may have to assume active and direct responsibility for tasks related to linkage of the client and family to needed resources. In some practice settings it is sufficient merely to inform the caregiver about where to go for the service, but in the majority of these cases information given without aid to link the clients to service is not sufficient. At least in the early stages of intervention the worker may need to facilitate the "where to go" and "whom to see" by actually going with the caregiver and/or elderly client to the Social Security Office, the public health clinic, or other agencies (Weissman, 1977).

One of the other typical characteristics of the protective service cases handled by the unit is the resistance or refusal of the elderly person and/or caregiver to receive services. The worker, performing service contacts without the power of attorney or the authority and security of a police escort to enter the home, is familiar with the hostile and suspicious nature of those who need help and crisis intervention. Client cooperation is an essential ingredient for the application of the Task-Centered Model. This point needs to be carefully considered since many of these clients and their caregivers are not cooperative. Reid and Epstein (1972) feel that the client should acknowledge and perceive the problem and be able to solve it with his skills or resources; also the problem should be specific and limited. However, these observations suggest the optimal conditions of cooperation and agreement and are not that common during the initial steps of intervention. There have been some occasions when the elderly person and the caregiver would or could not agree to perform tasks despite the fact that problem statements had been agreed upon by all. In one situation the worker clarified and reinforced what tasks she would perform relevant to the target problems. The assurance that the worker will perform tasks in the midst of little client cooperation does not always serve as a positive motivator for clients to begin to take responsibility for tasks; however, for some people, seeing the worker complete a task that she has promised to do gives some confidence leading to cooperation.

The authors have been concerned about the widely held professional perspective that elderly may not be motivated to change and that other people besides the aged person know best what should be done to solve problems. In some of the cases resistant behavior seemed to reflect the older person's unwillingness to accept the worker's definition of what was wrong and what needed to be changed. When the client (individual or family) does not agree with the worker, to comply unwillingly is to run the risk of losing independence. If elders and caregivers have little control over their environment, a worker's challenge of their personal perceptions about problems and needs can be a threat, so help is rejected.

AN INTERVENTION ILLUSTRATION
FROM THE FIELD

The application of the Task-Centered Model to families where adult abuse is operating, or where a potential problem exists, is highly experimental. Information available from several cases has been combined to illustrate the intervention process. The format of the presentation follows Epstein's (1977) document prepared to guide Task-Centered intervention in circumstances where legislative mandates for social service provision are not clear. In the unit where the model was applied, new legislation has been passed to insure that services are provided to elders who are abused, neglected, or exploited, but the specific guidelines for intervention have not been set forth in detailed agency policy. Thus, decisions about where, when, and how to include the larger family unit in the intervention plan is still open to the clinical judgment of the practitioner. The case demonstrates how the worker attempted to maintain a balance in the needs of the elder, the caregiver, and other key family members within the context of a family intervention plan.

Before Task-Centered Intervention

Mildred, an 84-year-old white woman, was referred by a public health nurse to the adult protective services unit. The nurse reported that she had noticed bruises on the old woman and indicated that she had overheard the caretaking daughter verbally abuse the mother while she was performing a home visit. The old woman was living with her daughter, Lucy, a 55-year-old divorced mother of two grown children, both married daughters, one with children. The granddaughters had been close to the grandmother, making visits to her home and keeping an eye on her while Lucy went out to shop. Mildred had breast cancer several years ago, had arteriosclerosis, and was recovering from a recent minor operation. She wandered and was confused, at times being very uncooperative when assisted in activities of daily living. The mother and daughter both lived on a trust fund left by the mother's husband; Lucy once received disability insurance but at that time had no income. Mildred received Social Security of $120 per month. Her daughter did not work and had been drinking but would not talk to family about that behavior, she seemed strained and frustrated by her mother's condition. She had few if any social contacts at the time of referral, even though she had previously enjoyed playing poker with a group of friends at her former job.

Task-Centered Intervention

Application   Worker visited home and explored need for service with Mildred and Lucy. Mildred was confused about the information given by worker so Lucy made a formal request on behalf of her mother and herself.

Clients' Target Problems	1.	Mildred wanted to see her granddaughters (she could not articulate other problems even though she gave evidence of other concerns).
	2.	Lucy wanted to be rid of the burden of the mother.
	3.	Lucy wanted some life of her own and friends.

| Mandated Problems | State Agency: | Must determine if abuse exists, filing appropriate case information (legal mandate). |
| | Local Unit: | Potential danger of neglect/abuse, daughter isolated, stressed, and potentially explosive toward mother when drinking too much (practitioner assessment). |

| Client Priorities | 1. | Mildred wanted to see greatgrandchild. |
| | 2. | Lucy wanted out of current caregiving situation. |

| Negotiation Strategy | 1. | Worker had conference with supervisor to explain that abuse could not be documented, crisis family intervention could prevent abuse. |
| | 2. | Supervisor checked with regional district case consultant and got permission for investigation to remain ongoing for additional intervention. |

Assessment
It was the agency's evaluation that Mildred needed to have more care than available through public health nurse visitation and should be considered a priority for either institutional care or an equivalent alternative (in this case the agency did not have any legal authority to intervene unless the assessment had produced evidence of neglect or abuse; this family was a voluntary client). Mildred wanted more contact with grandchildren, and Lucy wanted to be free of her mother. Lucy's emotional responses did not indicate long-standing psychological problems, but were becoming serious to the point of a potential breakdown or other crisis. Lucy did not seem to know how to organize social alternatives to reduce her isolation. Financial circumstances were very limited, mother would need assistance in covering cost of nursing home or day care as trust fund was not large enough to cover cost, but would initially disqualify her from receiving Medicaid. Granddaughters appeared very concerned, but frightened.

They had not visited mother and grandmother for a while because they were afraid they would make the situation worse by fighting with their mother, whom they cared about. Married daughter without children had extra time on her hands as she had quit job hoping to get pregnant.

Contract	Made written contract with Lucy. A verbal contract was used with Mildred.
Target Problems	Mildred lacked adequate supportive care. Lucy had no economic independence. Lucy lacked contacts with friends.
Time Limit	9 weeks

Major Intervention

1. Mildred was informed about some places she could get care, and granddaughters offered to take grandmother to visit several and have her spend more time with them and the great-grandchildren.
2. Specific tasks were planned for Lucy to seek employment, not to drink in her home when caring for her mother, to think about her drinking behavior, and make efforts to contact old friends.

Clients' Response

1. Mildred was upset about being pushed out of her home, but then decided she'd look at facilities because she could then visit her grandchildren.
2. Lucy declared disgust with herself for drinking, decided that she would do whatever necessary not to be a middle-aged woman in the gutter.

Practitioner's Tasks

1. Set up counseling session for Lucy at Vocational Bureau.
2. Make contacts with several programs and nursing homes that might be appropriate for Mildred, giving information to granddaughter.
3. Check to make sure that a senior volunteer would be available to spend time with Mildred while Lucy was out of the home for job interviews.
4. Provide necessary updated information about case and advocating against additional efforts to press neglect charges against Lucy.

Obstacles to Task Achievement

Obstacles	*Intervention*
1. Lucy's anger at the attitude of the worker at the Vocational Bureau.	1. Exploration of what happened, support, role playing, and assistance to develop a job resume for the next meeting at Bureau.
2. Mildred's not wanting anyone to come into her home as a sitter.	2. Childless granddaughter met with worker to discuss having her grandmother visit her home for a week while her husband went on a fishing trip.
3. Lucy having a fight with Mildred over financial situation.	3. Worker meeting with Lucy to talk about financial circumstances and the possibility of Lucy not needing to rely on mother's income with regular employment.
4. Lucy's threat not to go to job interview arranged by her friend who could help her get a job.	4. Getting Lucy invited to a group session for reentry middle-aged women through Displaced Homemakers Program.

Outcome of the Intervention

Lucy was able to find employment where she could receive a good salary for work that she liked and could renew a former friendship. Through the job she was able to deal with both of her target problems, ie, attain economic independence and make contacts with friends. Her participation in the Displaced Homemaker support group produced new social opportunities for close interpersonal sharing with other women in midlife who were in circumstances comparable to hers. She found an inexpensive living arrangement by sharing an apartment with a woman in her support group, and this was pleasant as well as inexpensive. The group home placement for Mildred resolved the target problem to obtain more supportive care. She maintained her pride and dignity in that setting because she was active but also secure. The brief placement was interrupted by Mildred's illness and hospitalization which could not be controlled. The granddaughter became pregnant while Mildred was hospitalized, so she did not work and had extra time and a desire to remain close to her grandmother. When Mildred faced discharge from the hospital, Lucy became fearful that she would again be burdened by the care of her mother. She was able to share this feeling with her daughters who told Lucy that they would handle finding a good nursing home for Mildred. Once Mildred was settled in the nursing home, Lucy was able to maintain some contact with her mother by visiting the nursing home. Lucy and her daughters related better because the tensions between Lucy and Mildred were reduced. Both daughters welcomed the opportunity to be free of the pressure of divided loyalties.

The overall intervention taking place over nine weeks followed the Task-Centered Model and was successful because the target problems for Mildred and Lucy were resolved. The intervention did not superimpose an inappropriate definition of abuse into this family's circumstances or label the coping behavior of the caretaker as pathological. If Lucy did abuse Mildred, it was not an act repeated during the intervention period.

Problem-solving efforts proceeded while clarification of the potential abuse was explored. The worker's interaction with the family provided an opportunity to observe the caregiving situation very closely. Assessment indicated that all three task areas were involved in the dyad relationship of Mildred and Lucy. The problems in the relationship had an impact on the granddaughters. The report of potential abuse was handled in a manner appropriate to meet the agency's mandated requirements, but the worker and her agency supervisor took advantage of the service flexibility and instituted family-oriented treatment.

The case illustration shows how the Task-Centered Model can be adapted to meet the needs of a vulnerable elderly client within a family systems approach. Unlike some family therapies, many sessions did not involve all members, but the focus on the family group was still present. All three generations of women were interconnected, and their collective involvement in the treatment plan facilitated resolution of multiple problems. The feedback given to the worker by Lucy during the last session (also attended by the granddaughters) indicated that she felt she had been able to complete a successful job interview because she had had the role-playing experience and resume planning assistance from the worker. The support of the group she joined was important. She appreciated not being labeled an alcoholic, but needed to be confronted about her behavior and its consequences. The worker believed Lucy would remain much involved with the support group, and might be able to use her own experience to help others. Both granddaughters were more comfortable with their mother and felt less helpless to participate in family decision making.

Selecting no more than three target problems of concern to family members helped them to mobilize what resources they could command within themselves or their environment. Mildred's situation was handled in a manner that met her original target problem, that which involved relationships with her granddaughters. Services facilitated her move into a setting where she could receive care and remain supported by family members who could carry some responsibility without being dangerously burdened.

CONCLUSION

The chapter discussed how family-oriented intervention and the Task-Centered Model (including its adaptations from an individual to a family and an adult to elderly client perspective) can be integrated into the context of adult protective services. As a framework for intervention, it has potential as a cost-efficient, sensitive, and individualized approach to difficult and time-consuming caseloads. This approach can be used to provide crisis intervention and also prevent further breakdown of family functioning.

The family system is important to the aged and adaptations of family therapy frameworks must be explored. Systematic investigation of the outcomes for elder-victimizing families should be pursued through field trials; the service experience should be viewed as a first step. The Task-Centered Model cannot be systematically applied unless workers receive training, but this could be offered through in-service workshops and continuing education sessions. To date, such training has not been provided to many full-time protective service unit staff. Perhaps its value must be further demonstrated by professional practitioners in health, mental health, and social service agencies knowledgeable about elder abuse, family therapy, and the Task-Centered Model.

Many of the elements of generic supportive services to the elderly can be applied to the needs of abused, exploited, and neglected aged. Many of the problems discussed in the first section of this book translate into specific problems in daily living. For example, fear is common to many aged whether or not they are victims of actual crimes or whether they reside in the community or institutions. Fear was a common problem among the elders serviced. It was often handled within the context of other target problems. The various special groups of vulnerable elderly of concern in this text are representative of the elderly clients who are referred to public agencies. Applying the Task-Centered Model is feasible for those cases even though some additional or different modifications may be required.

Clinical intervention with the aged and their family should not occur isolated from program and legislative innovations. Such resources as ombudsman programs, nursing home advocates, hotlines, caregiver self-help groups, and fraud prevention programs are resources which the clinician needs to help the elder and his family. The Task-Centered Model gives the practitioner a framework for introducing these into the intervention plan while also maintaining therapeutic and behavioral change priorities.

Special acknowledgment is given to Anne E. Fortune for her research and training contributions in the larger project described in the chapter, and to Laura Epstein and William Reid for having continued to build the Task-Centered Model in an empirical, clinical tradition relevant to the future of clinical gerontology.

BIBLIOGRAPHY

Boszormenyi-Nagy I: Behavior change through family change, in Barton A (ed): *What Makes Behavior Change Possible.* New York, Brunner/Mazel, 1976.

Boszormenyi-Nagy I, Spark G: *Invisible Loyalties: Reciprocity in Intergenerational Family Therapy.* New York, Harper & Row, 1973.

Boszormenyi-Nagy I, Ulrich DN: Contextual family therapy, in Gurman AS, Kniskern DP (eds): *Handbook of Family Therapy.* New York, Brunner/Mazel, 1980.

Broderick CB, Schrader SS: The history of professional marriage and family therapy, in Gurman AS, Kniskern DP (eds): *Handbook of Family Therapy.* New York, Brunner/Mazel, 1980.

Brody E: The aging family. *Gerontologist* 1966;6:201–206.

Brody E, Spark GM: Institutionalization of the elderly: A family crisis. *Family Process* 1966;5:76–90.

Cormican J: Task-centered model for work with the aged. *Social Casework* 1977; 58:490–494.

Dierking B, Brown M, Fortune AE: Task centered treatment in a residential facility for the elderly: A clinical trial. *J Gerontol Soc Work* 1980;2:225–240.

Epstein L: *How to Provide Social Services with Task-Centered Methods.* Report of the task-centered service project, vol 1. Chicago, School of Social Service Administration, University of Chicago, 1977.

Epstein NB, Bishop DS: Problem-centered systems therapy of the family, in Gurman AS, Kniskern DP (eds): *Handbook of Family Therapy.* New York, Brunner/Mazel, 1980.

Epstein NB, Bishop DS: Problem-centered system therapy of the family. *J Marital Family Ther* 1981;7:23–31.

Fortune AE, Rathbone-McCuan E: Education in gerontological social work: Application of the task-centered model. *J Ed Soc Work* 1981;17:98–105.

Gibbons JS, Butler J, Urwin P, Gibbons JL: Evaluation of a social work service for self-poisoning patients. *Br J Psychiatry* 1978;133:111–118.

Harbert AS, Ginsberg LH: *Human Services for Older Adults: Concepts and Skills.* Belmont; Wadsworth, 1979.

Herr JH, Weakland JH: The family as a group, in Burnside IM (ed): *Working with the Elderly Groups Processes and Techniques.* North Scituate, MA, Duxbury, 1978.

Hooyman NR: Elderly Abuse and Neglect: Community Interventions. (Unpublished paper, 1980.)

Rathbone-McCuan E, Hashimi J: *Isolated Elders: Health and Social Intervention.* Rockville, MD, Aspen Systems Corporation, 1982.

Reid WJ: Process and outcome in the treatment of family problems, in Reid WJ, Epstein L (eds): *Task-Centered Practice.* New York, Columbia University Press, 1977.

Reid WJ: *The Task-Centered System.* New York, Columbia University Press, 1978.

Reid WJ: Family treatment with a task-centered framework, in Tolson E, Reid WJ (eds): *Models of Family Treatment.* New York, Columbia University Press, in press.

Reid WJ, Epstein L: *Task-Centered Casework.* New York, Columbia University Press, 1972.

Silverstone B, Hyman HK: *You and Your Aging Parent.* New York, Pantheon, 1976.

Spark GM, Brody EM: The aged are family members. *Family Process* 1970;9: 195–210.

Streib GF, Beck RW: Older families: A decade review. *J Marriage Family* 1980; 42:937–956.

Tolson ER: Alleviating marital communication problems, in Reid WJ, Epstein LL (eds): *Task-Centered Practice.* New York, Columbia University Press, 1977.

Travis AL: Practice Suggestions for Applying the Model of Task-Centered Intervention with Adult Protective Service Cases in a Public Service Agency. (Unpublished paper, 1981).

Troll L: The family of later life: A decade review. *J Marriage Family* 1971;33: 263–290.

Wanless M, Rooney RH: A Model for Caseload Management based on Task-Centered Casework. (Unpublished paper, 1981).

Weissman A: In the steel industry, in Reid WJ, Epstein L (eds): *Task-Centered Practice.* New York, Columbia University Press, 1977.

23 Elderly Abuse and Neglect: Community Interventions

Nancy R. Hooyman

Much of the research on elderly abuse has focused on the legal and practice issues involved in the detection and reporting of abuse. Increasing only the case-finding and reporting mechanisms will not solve the various societal and family conditions underlying abuse. Once abuse is reported and detected, the only alternatives for many older people may be institutionalization or remaining in the abusive situation. Community-based policies and practices need to be developed that can have a positive impact both on the family caretakers and on the older victim and can also be cost effective. This chapter will define ways to use existing community resources creatively and effectively in both the prevention of abuse and in intervention with abusers and victims.

In periods of scarce economic resources, it can be difficult to think creatively about mobilizing community resources for intervention and prevention. Despite this gloomy picture, there are numerous ways to use the most valuable and least expensive resources available — the informal support systems of family, friends, neighbors, peers, and local community organizations. Informal personal networks are defined as a series of linkages along which information and services flow to and from the anchor person and his exchange relationships. These services may be economic, social, or emotional. What distinguishes informal social networks from traditional social service delivery systems is that exchanges are not formalized, but instead employ people's caring about each other and their natural helping tendencies to respond to day-to-day needs, ranging from household chores to crises requiring immediate attention.

The role of the family in providing care to older relatives, the stresses of such caregiving, and the vulnerability that this creates for family members is first addressed. The importance of social supports for physical and mental well-being of both the caregiver and the older person is discussed. With what is known about the importance of social supports, how can this knowledge be used to provide more supports to family caregivers as a preventive measure and to expand the social networks of vulnerable elderly to detect and intervene in high-risk situations? Many projects for the prevention of child abuse and mental illness have used informal or natural helping networks and can serve as prototypes for efforts to prevent elder abuse (Caplan and Killilea, 1976; Collins and Pancoast, 1976; Froland et al, 1979; Garbarino and Stocking, 1980). Components of these projects that may be adaptable to the aging network, particularly to adult protective services, are identified.

THE IMPORTANCE OF NATURAL HELPERS

Natural helpers are individuals (eg, friends, neighbors, relatives) to whom people turn in difficult times because of the concern, interest, and innate understanding they possess. The natural helper is not paid for her/his services and is characterized by the equality and mutual exchange s/he brings to the act of helping. In working with families to prevent abuse, a number of natural helping resources must be considered: their primary group helpers or other family members and close friends; informal caregivers, such as neighbors; people with similar problems, such as other family caregivers; and community gatekeepers, such as postal workers, grocery clerks, public utilities workers, apartment house managers, and local merchants. These helpers can provide the following kinds of social support: (1) emotionally sustaining help, such as contact with a trusted party during stressful periods; (2) problem-solving behavior, such as providing new information or direct assistance; (3) indirect forms of assistance, such as simple availability; and (4) advocacy (Garbarino and Stocking, 1980). Families may be more likely to turn to these natural networks for information and skills since they are more accessible and more likely to be trusted than the formal service delivery system.

Admittedly, natural helpers may not exist in every network and some families are not involved in supportive networks. Likewise, strengthening or building informal social networks should be just one part of a comprehensive strategy against abuse. Nevertheless, networks and central figures have been found in a variety of social settings, and few elderly are totally socially isolated (Wagner, 1980). Informal supports may have been rejected by an older person, but may still be functional. Few people are totally alienated and isolated. Even if neighbors do not have daily contact with an older person and/or their family, they may nevertheless know or suspect what is going on. Therefore, an approach based on identifying and strengthening natural networks is a viable one. Professional intervention by home-health nurses, adult protective service workers, outreach workers, and mental health workers, would focus on reducing the disruptiveness of caregiving by expanding or mobilizing the skills and resources of the part of the social network not already viewed by the family as a support resource. Such an approach can affect a large number of families with a minimum of effort and without increasing the family's dependence on formal services.

THE FAMILY AS CAREGIVER

With the increasing attention to elder abuse, caution must be exercised that documentation of cases of abuse not be used to create a backlash against families as caregivers. The importance of the family in providing care has been extensively documented in the gerontological literature (Brody et al, 1978; Lebowitz, 1978; Treas, 1977; Robinson and Thurnher, 1979). Only recently recognized are the burdens of such caregiving (Gross-Andrew and Zimmer, 1978; Mellor and Getzel, 1980; Zarit et al, 1980). These strains are likely to increase in the next few decades, along with the growing number of very old elderly—those who most need intensive in-home care—and with the growth in the number of middle-aged women in the labor force. Middle-aged women have traditionally been the caregivers, but now they are confronted with multiple responsibilities and conflicts of time and loyalties. Brody (1980) has noted that for many middle-aged women, the empty nest is being refilled by the frail elderly. In addition, family caretakers may be facing their own midlife developmental challenges and awareness of their own aging, issues that are further intensified for them by their interaction with their elderly parents.

Family caregivers face a number of burdens: financial, emotional, and instrumental or those that are associated with the daily routine tasks of caregiving. Research on family caregiving indicates that the greatest strain is emotional, feeling alone and burdened by sacrifices (Cantor, 1980; Horowitz, 1980). Caregivers tend to make considerable personal sacrifices (eg, giving up free time for themselves, socializing with friends, and vacations) and restrict their lives to the essentials (Cantor, 1980). Accordingly, caregivers have had to make numerous changes in their daily routines and income and have experienced increased interpersonal conflict with other family members (Lebowitz, 1978).

Such sacrifice appears to be more tolerable to a spouse than to children; both Horowitz (1980) and Myllyluoma and Soldo (1980) found that dissatisfaction and conflict with care is more likely when a child is the caregiver than a spouse, in part because of the inequality of power in the parent-child caregiving relationship. The exchange of resources between adult children and an aging parent is often unequal, especially when the demands of daily care strain the relation beyond repair, making emotional exchanges difficult. As the distribution of power and resources shifts, the adult child may be unable to cope with the dependency needs of an aged relative, who is culturally defined as roleless and noncontributing. An additional burden in caring for an elderly parent is that one generally cannot look forward to increasing independence and consequently reduced daily physical demands, as when caring for children. Hickey (1979) suggests that when adult children are unwilling or unable to accept their parents' dependencies, they are more likely to view their parents as vulnerable. Myllyluoma and Soldo (1980) found that families providing home care to older widowed female relatives are the most vulnerable to disruption.

Given these stresses, how can caregivers carry such heavy loads without negative effects on themselves and their families? In his work on explanations of family maltreatment, Kosberg (1980) suggests that such negative consequences may be inevitable. According to Kosberg, no one is immune to the possibility of being an abuser, given a major discrepancy between the needs of the caregiver and the needs of the elderly family member. Kosberg contends that abuse results from incompetence in the role of caregiver, resulting from the interaction of social stress and a relatively low level of skill as caregiver. Hickey (1979) also suggests that 70% of abuse and neglect cases may result from the older person not making her needs known and the family not being able to bear the burden of care.

Most families probably have limited skills for providing continuous care to an older person. In our society, cultural guidelines or specific norms for behavior are lacking in intergenerational relationships. It is not very clear in our society whether families of older people are to feed, clothe, and take care of them on a 24-hour basis, in contrast to expectations regarding the care of young children. The media and a variety of handbooks all advise young parents about what to expect in caring for children, but such information is generally lacking for adult children attempting to care for elderly parents. Most families have few opportunities to rehearse the role of caregiver; they may hold unrealistic expectations for themselves and for their older parents, which serve to increase the stress they experience. To prevent misunderstandings and conflicts, families need information about the aging process, more awareness of their own values and resources, and knowledge of community resources.

At the same time that most families are lacking skills and experience in caregiving, they may be isolated from potential support systems that could reduce their stress. In his work on networks and mental health, Caplan (1974) found that the outcome of an individual's response during difficult times was influenced not only by the degree of stress and the individual's ego strength, but also by the quality of emotional support provided by his natural network. Research on family caregivers indicates that the most vulnerable caregivers are those who do not have a support network (Cantor, 1980; Horowitz, 1980; Zimmer et al, 1977). The level of stress is related not only to the extent of disability and amount of care needed by the older person, but also to whether the caregiver receives help and support from others. In several programs for support of families, such as the Natural Support Program in New York City, families most frequently requested housekeeping services. While they did not initially recognize emotional support as a need, when they experienced it within a group, they found this supportive component to be the most helpful part (Zimmer, 1980). Yet, families often do not turn for help and emotional support, if at all, until the stages of crisis and burnout. Work on child abuse indicates that the more one needs emotional support, the less likely one is to have the personal resources to reach out and obtain it (Garbarino and Stocking, 1980).

The research on family caregiving points to the importance of strengthening the resources and social supports available to families. Trying to maintain the family caring unit is a necessary first step, because the living alternatives for older people are limited and generally negative. An appropriate preventive approach, thus, appears to be to strengthen family support systems or, where none exist, to develop alternative supportive networks. Admittedly, pathologic family situations exist, where abuse has been the historic norm and where alcoholism, drug addiction, or mental illness are part of the cause of abuse. In such cases, the need is not for support of the caregivers, but for detection of the problem and the development of community care alternatives, so that the older person can be removed from a dangerous situation. More research on family dynamics underlying abuse is needed; however, the research on stress to the family of caregiving is sufficient to point to the importance of reducing such stress.

STRATEGIES TO STRENGTHEN FAMILY SUPPORTS

Having emphasized the importance of informal social supports, what specific things can be done? Professionals must first determine what is already occurring that can serve to increase the personal social resources for the family caregiver. The professional locates natural helpers, people who have influence and credibility with the family, and works intensively with them. Natural helping efforts can be strengthened by providing information, consultation (eg, advice, support, and reassurance), or skills training; linking isolated persons with natural helpers; facilitating referrals to formal services; and advocacy. It is essential that the natural helpers feel that the professionals will stand behind them, especially if they fear any retaliation from the family.

In addition to support and information, families also need relief from their nearly constant caregiving responsibilities. Respite care and assistance with daily household chores and with personal care are essential. All of these needs can be met by professional intervention that focuses on strengthening social supports for families.

Demonstration programs throughout the country, for example, have provided these components of education, emotional support, help with tasks, and respite for families. While none of these programs was explicitly designed to prevent abuse, they did aim to reduce the stress of caregiving and undoubtedly minimized the risk of abuse and neglect. The Natural Support Program, sponsored by the Community Service Society in New York City, provides cash grants plus service planning for the family. The family, not the service providers, defines the service need and thus acts as a case manager. The program provides respite care, counseling to the caregiver, assistance in systems negotiation and groups for education, skills training, and emotional support of the caregivers. Two types of groups are offered: community-wide informational meetings and small informal discussion groups. For 64% of the participants, the program's major benefit has been the support and mutual aid provided by the small group meeting (Mellor and Getzel, 1980). A similar type of program, the Family/Friends Support Project of the Ebenezer Society in Minneapolis, Minnesota, provides monetary reimbursement for some daily help, emergency backup for care, training on how to give care, and aid from a mutual support group (Gray et al, 1980).

Another model for education and support is the multigenerational family group, such as the group "As Parents Grow Older," developed through Child and Family Services in Ann Arbor, Michigan (Silverman et al, 1977). Focusing on content, feelings, and interaction, these groups provide information about aging and community resources as well as mutual problem solving and support. Participants frequently cited the following positive outcomes: increased ability to communicate with their older relative, increased ability to cope with and deal with the situation, and recognition of needs and responsibility to one's self in the setting of realistic limits (Silverman, 1979).

Such educational programs could be offered through neighborhood centers, senior centers, family agencies, mental health centers, and religious institutions for relatively small expenditures of funds. For example, Silverman's intergenerational model of support groups cost $1200 to replicate twice in the first year, $600 in the second year. Seed money for such groups is estimated as $500 to $600 (Silverman, 1979). Volunteers from original groups could also be trained to begin and help new groups at relatively low cost. The framework for providing such support to families probably already exists in most communities; for example, many family service agencies have either groups or training sessions available to families; support groups for caregivers of patients with particular chronic illness (eg, Alzheimer's disease, stroke) are being developed, but support efforts have not been implemented within a wide variety of service settings (eg, day centers, hospitals, or senior centers); nor have such group efforts been specifically conceptualized as a way both to detect and prevent abuse and neglect.

Components of programs to prevent child abuse may be transferable to the aging network. For example, in a Maryland program, three local family physicians were used to reach parents at-risk of child abuse by convening a randomly selected parent group from their practices. Random selection and an emphasis on primary prevention were important, so that no stigma was attached to attending the meetings. The physicians drew upon their existing relationships with the families to solicit participation. Through the group, the physicians and their staff provided information and problem-solving skills and encouraged the formation of social ties that parents used between and after meetings (Garbarino, 1980). Physicians frequently encounter abused elderly and their families, but do not take any action. Strategies need to be developed to mobilize medical staff who are familiar with high-risk families to intervene in potentially abusive situations.

Another transferable example from child welfare is the pairing of volunteers, who are parents, with families at high-risk of child abuse to provide support, information, and relief from caregiving to the abusive parents. It should be equally possible to train volunteers to work with family caregivers of the elderly who are at high-risk. Most cities have developed Parents Anonymous groups to prevent child abuse and teach child-rearing skills. Childrens' Anonymous groups could be established to teach parent-caring skills and provide support to adult children. Natural helping networks that already exist could be employed or, where needed, alternative support networks for family caregivers could be built as one means to prevent abuse. These networks can then provide family caregivers with respite, education about caregiving, emotional support for their efforts, and help with daily caregiving tasks.

STRATEGIES FOR DETECTION AND INTERVENTION

Where abuse is occurring, however, preventive, educational, and support strategies are probably not appropriate. Then community mechanisms to detect abuse and to intervene are needed.

Research on elderly abuse indicates that the elderly victim is unlikely to seek help, because of isolation, shame, feelings of powerlessness, or fear of reprisals. In addition to reluctance to report abuse by a family member, a number of reasons may keep an older victim from using any available community resources in order to change their situation. These barriers include lack of information about service availability, service inaccessibility, the bureaucratic red tape within the service delivery system, impersonalization of services, and service fragmentation. In both the Michigan and Maryland studies, help had been sought by either the victim or abuser in the majority of cases, yet these help-seeking efforts were generally not successful. Interventions need to be developed that make it easier for older victims to let it be known that they are being abused, to obtain necessary services if they choose to attempt to leave the abusive situation, and then to provide them with support for their decision. Again, service providers could use natural helping networks to inform victims of needed services, to report abuse, to provide the follow-up to ensure that help is obtained. Information could also be disseminated through informal networks as a way to increase community awareness about the problem of elderly abuse; as community education and awareness increase, an atmosphere more conducive to the reporting of abuse is likely to be created.

Natural helping systems not now fully utilized that could provide information and support to victims are gatekeepers, role-related helpers, or informal services provided by businesses and community organizations. These are people in visible "crossroads" positions who have access to valuable resources and interact with the elderly on a regular, predictable basis. They include postal carriers, cab drivers, local merchants, doctor's office receptionists, beauticians, bank tellers, bus drivers, pharmacists, and ministers. Because of their visible positions, they are likely to be turned to for help, to know and keep an eye on others' actions, and to offer both emotional support, practical aid, and information. In a study in two California cities, such gatekeepers were found to provide companionship, advice, physical assistance, financial aid, transportation, and health care (Robinson and Regnier, 1980).

Since these informal caregivers already serve a valuable information and referral function, their frontline contributions could be strengthened by providing more information and skills training to them. For example, Southern California Rapid Transit bus drivers were trained regarding the sensory and motor losses of aging (Robinson and Regnier, 1980). A gatekeeper project in Philadelphia provided training in crisis intervention as well as consultation and support to individual gatekeepers (Collins and Pancoast, 1976). In an effort to reach isolated elderly, the Community Mental Health Center in Spokane, Washington trains fuel oil dealers, meter readers, fire department staff, taxi drivers, and postal carriers to watch for situations and symptoms that indicate an older person's needs for services. One out of five of their referrals comes from these gatekeepers (*Information and Assistance Program, Elderly Services,* 1980). Training programs specifically about signs of abuse, available services, and reporting procedures could be implemented in communities or neighborhoods known to have a high incidence of elderly abuse or family strains. As it is now, gatekeepers may suspect abuse and neglect, but may not know what to do. In all these efforts, professionals would need to convey to the gatekeepers that "it's okay to be suspicious" and to reward their reporting and other forms of involvement.

Other family members and neighbors also may report abuse; their reluctance may stem from ignorance about the reporting procedures, fear, or adherence to cultural norms that prohibit intruding into other people's privacy. When responsibility for taking action is diffused throughout the community, neighbors and friends probably need social support from each other or from a third party before they can define a high-risk situation as one requiring action and can mobilize themselves to act. Friends, neighbors, and other family members already have the potential support mechanisms, but need training, consultation, and information about signs of abuse and reporting procedures. Such information could be disseminated through the community's informal channels. An obvious resource for strengthening such informal ties is the elderly who are already natural helpers within the neighborhood. Because of their proximity, neighbors can provide immediate assistance to an older person, can checkup on well-being, and can provide day-to-day support. In all these situations, professionals would need to provide backup to neighbors and friends, because it may be very difficult for them, both personally and with regard to their safety, to report cases of abuse.

Programs throughout the country have used elderly neighbors as outreach workers who can go into homes and visually assess problems (Neighborhood Outreach Programs, San Diego; Toseland et al, 1979), as peer counselors in the homes (Turner Geriatric Clinic, University of Michigan, 1979), and as providers of light housekeeping, shopping, meal preparation, and transportation (Area Agency Programs in Alabama, Virginia, and Arkansas). O'Brien and Whitelaw (1978) have advocated a Neighborhood Care program that would include respite care, neighborhood aides, and neighborhood elder-sitting pools. A neighborhood block home for the elderly, similar to block houses for children, could be identified as a place where neighbors could turn for assistance. Neighborhood aides would routinely canvass the neighborhood, report problems, visit homebound elderly, and provide a link to community services. They would informally watch over the neighborhood and meet the needs of their elderly neighbors as they arise. Neighborhood watch programs that have been developed for crime prevention and safety could be adopted for the detection of abuse.

There are already a wide variety of informal support systems that could be trained for detecting abuse. A senior center in Eugene, Oregon, keeps files on all those in a neighborhood known to help their elderly neighbors and uses this information to locate someone to provide help when needed. These block workers serve as a liaison between the senior center and more isolated elderly (Chapman, 1980). In San Antonio, the elderly in an Hispanic neighborhood organized into task forces to provide friendly visiting, home repair, and help in dealing with agencies (Chapman, 1980). In the Senior Block Information Service in San Francisco, elderly volunteers get to know all the residents on their block. While distributing a monthly newsletter, they engage in conversation and consequently can often provide information and referrals for help in problem solving (Ruffini and Todd, 1979). In Iowa's Project-Be-My-Guest, women from local churches reach out to friends, neighbors, and relatives and go with them to the area agency to explain available services and to increase their awareness of programs (Select Committee on Aging, 1979). Comparable informal networks already exist in most communities. Telephone check-ups, neighborhood house watches, friendly visiting, postal alerts, and "buddy systems" have been instituted for other purposes in a variety of settings. Such networks need to be deliberately expanded through training and consultation for the purpose of detecting high-risk situations and for providing support to victims of abuse and neglect. For example, managers of senior centers or nutrition sites could be trained regarding the perception of abuse and where to report it.

The mutual help model also has the potential both to encourage neighbors to take action when they suspect abuse and to support the victims who attempt to leave an abusive situation. The mutual help model emphasizes reciprocity, exchange of services, and watching out for each other. The rationale of the Benton, Illinois, Mutual Help Model and the Miami, Florida, Neighborhood Family is that money cannot buy community spirit nor the willingness of neighbors to help each other out (Erhlich, 1979; Ross, 1978). These programs draw upon research that shows older people are more likely to bring problems to significant others who are neighborhood-bound rather than to formal agencies (Kahana and Felton, 1977). They are staffed by professionals familiar with consultation techniques and neighborhood workers well acquainted with local networks and cultural patterns. In the Neighborhood Family, neighbors were able to identify physical and emotional changes, quickly pinpoint people needing service, and use peer pressure to encourage individuals to seek help. Both of these models, building upon natural neighborhood ties, could be expanded to watch for signs of abuse and neglect.

Likewise, mutual help groups could also serve a monitoring function to protect the victim from reprisals after the abuse has been reported. Neighbors and friends could set up a system to check several times a day, either through personal visiting or telephone reassurance, that the abuser has not retaliated against the victim. Professionals could work with this natural support network to make sure the home is monitored.

Another example of the mutual help model is the Widow-to-Widow Program, which brings people together through a shared problem rather than their geographic location. For victims who leave an abusive situation, comparable support groups would be essential. Perhaps shelters for battered women could expand their groups of primarily younger women to be cross-generational or could develop groups specifically for older women. Intergenerational support groups would recognize the rich resources that older women could share with younger women. As Wagner (1980) has noted, even those elderly who may be categorized as "frail" or at-risk have a variety of resources upon which to draw. Multiple forms of support for the decision to leave an abusive situation may be especially important for older women who may have been abused for years, first by a spouse and then by adult children. As one step in developing such multiple supports, shelters need to assess the extent to which their structure and service philosophy are compatible with older women's needs.

Some professionals may resist this approach because they do not view lay people as having the expertise to intervene; indeed, strengthening natural helping networks can be threatening to professionalism and rules of confidentiality. However, in a time of tight professional resources, it may be necessary to think of modifying the rules of confidentiality in order to reduce the pain experienced by a client. In making decisions about confidentiality, professionals need to assess whether rules of confidentiality are benefiting the client or the professional bureaucracies.

This approach should not be viewed as an abdication of government or professional responsibility. Policies are needed that support natural helpers and self-help efforts without weakening public responsibility. Likewise, natural helpers should not be involved with victims or families in clinical assessments or in a long-term treatment capacity. What is being advocated is a partnership between professionals and natural helpers that draws upon each group's strengths. Professionals, thus, need to recognize and identify the unique role that natural helpers can play, and be prepared to provide them with necessary resources and backup so that they are not hurt by their involvement.

An appropriate professional role, then, is to provide information, consultation, and support to elderly neighbors, community gatekeepers, and mutual help groups to strengthen natural networks for the detection and intervention of abuse. Such a role requires flexibility and creativity on the part of the professional. Interventions must be carefully planned so as not to weaken or replace natural supports. In any such intervention, professionals must take account of the family and victim's culture and of cultural differences in the giving of care.

For professionals to work effectively with natural helpers, changes in the formal service delivery system are needed that will obviously require spending public dollars. Training and information dissemination to service providers must take place through the domestic violence, mental health, and aging networks. These providers must then transmit this information to the natural helping networks. Providers need training in detecting signs of abuse, using appropriate treatment interventions, and supporting the positive efforts of informal natural networks. Strides have been made in providing training to police and community service officers in the areas of spouse and child abuse; such efforts can be modified and expanded to deal with elder abuse. Service providers also need training in how to work effectively with the natural helping systems (Collins and Pancoast, 1976).

CONCLUSION

The approach suggested in this chapter is not new to the fields of child welfare, mental health, or aging. What is unique is considering natural helping networks as a means to prevent and detect abuse. An appropriate professional intervention thus becomes the training and supporting of informal support systems so that these informal systems can work more effectively with formal systems. Our society has begun developing the expertise and resources to prevent and detect child and spouse abuse. Using natural helpers is one way that we can make similar gains in the area of elderly abuse.

BIBLIOGRAPHY

Brody E: *Women in the Middle and Family Help to Older People.* Presented at the 33rd Annual Meeting of the Gerontological Society, San Diego, CA, November 1980.

Brody S, Poulschock W, Maschiocchi C: The family caring unit: A major consideration in the long-term support system. *Gerontologist* 1978;18(6): 556–561.

Caplan G: *Support Systems in Community Mental Health.* New York, Behavioral Publications, 1974.

Caplan G, Killilea M: *Support Systems and Mutual Help: Multidisciplinary Exploration.* New York, Grune and Stratton, 1976.

Cantor M: *Caring for the Frail Elderly: Impact on Family, Friends, and Neighbors.* Presented at the Annual Meeting of the Gerontological Society, San Diego, CA, November 1980.

Chapman N: *Working with the Informal Helping System: A Way of Supporting Families of the Elderly.* Presented at the Workshop on Family Support Systems for the Elderly, Western Gerontological Association, San Diego, CA, March 1980.

Collins A, Pancoast D: *Natural Helping Networks: A Strategy for Prevention.* New York, NASW, 1976.

Ehrlich P: Service delivery for the community elderly: The mutual help model. *J Gerontol Social Work,* 1979;2(2):125–137.

Froland C, Pancoast D, Chapman N, et al: *Professional Partnerships with Informal Helpers: Emerging Forms.* Presented at the Annual Convention of the American Psychological Association, New York, September, 1979.

Garbarino J, Stocking S: *Protecting Children from Abuse and Neglect: Developing and Maintaining Effective Support Systems for Families.* San Francisco, Jossey-Bass, 1980.

Gray K, Threlkeld C, Lorentson H, et al: *Reimbursing Family/Friends for Home Care: A Demonstration Project.* Presented at the 33rd Annual Meeting of the Gerontological Society, San Diego, CA, November 1980.

Gross-Andrew S, Zimmer A: Incentives to families caring for disabled elderly: Research and demonstration project to strengthen the natural support system. *J Gerontol Social Work* 1978;1(2):119–138.

Hickey T: *Neglect and Abuse of the Elderly: Implications of a Developmental Model for Research and Intervention.* Presented at the 32nd Annual Meeting of the Gerontological Society, Washington, DC, November 1979.

Horowitz A, Shindelman LW: *The Impact of Caring for an Elderly Relative.* Presented at the 33rd Annual Meeting of the Gerontological Society, San Diego, CA, November 1980.

Information and Assistance Program, Elderly Services. Spokane, WA, Spokane Community Mental Health Center, December 1980.

Innovative Developments in Aging: Area Agencies in Aging. Select Committee on Aging, US House of Representatives, December 1979.

Kahana E, Felton B: Social context and personal need: A study of Polish and Jewish Aged. *J Social Issues* 1977;33(4):56–64.

Kosberg J: *Family Maltreatment: Causality and Practice Issues.* Presented at the 33rd Annual Meeting of the Gerontological Society, San Diego, CA, November 1980.

Lebowitz B: Old age and family functioning. *J Gerontol Social Work* 1978;1(2): 111–119.

Mellor J, Getzel G: *Stress and Service Needs of Those Who Care for the Aged.* Presented at the 33rd Annual Meeting of the Gerontological Society, San Diego, CA, November 1980.

Myllyluoma J, Soldo B: *Family Caregivers to the Elderly: Who Are They?* Paper presented at the 33rd Annual Meeting of the Gerontological Society, San Diego, CA, November 1980.

O'Brien J, Whitelaw N: *Planning Options for the Elderly.* Portland, OR, Institute on Aging, Portland State University, 1978.

Robinson B, Regnier V: *Informal Services Provided by Business and Community Organizations: An Investigation of Existing Non-Service Supports.* Presented at the 33rd Annual Meeting of the Gerontological Society, San Diego, CA, November 1980.

Robinson B, Thurnher M: Taking care of aged parents: A family cycle transition. *Gerontologist* 1979;19(6):586–594.

Ross H: The neighborhood family. *Aging* 1978, 27–32.

Ross H, Ross MS: The neighborhood family—Five years later, a program in preventive community health care of the elderly. Unpublished paper, 1979.

Ruffini J, Todd HF Jr: A network model for leadership development among the elderly. *Gerontologist* 1979;2(19):158–162.

Silverman A: *As Parents Grow Older: A Community-based Intervention Strategy.* Presented at the 32nd Annual Meeting of the Gerontological Society, Washington, DC, November 1979.

Silverman A, Kahn B, Anderson G: A model for working with multi-generational families. *Social Casework* 1977;58(3):131–135.

Toseland R, Decker J, Bliesner J: A community outreach program for socially isolated older persons. *J Gerontol Social Work* 1979;1(3):211–225.

Treas J: Family support systems for the aged: Some social and demographic characteristics. *Gerontologist* 1977;17(6):486–491.

Wagner D, Gleason D: *Later Life Frailty and Social Networks.* Presented at the 33rd Annual Meeting of the Gerontological Society, San Diego, CA, November 1980.

Zarit S, Reaver K, Bach-Peterson J: Relatives of the impaired elderly: Correlates of feelings of burden. *Gerontologist* 1980;20(6):649–655.

Zimmer A, Gross-Andrew S, Frankfather D: *Incentives to Families Caring for Disabled Elderly: Research and Demonstration Project to Strengthen Natural Support Systems.* Paper presented at the 30th Annual Meeting of the Gerontological Society, San Francisco, CA, 1977.

Zimmer A, Sainer J: *Strengthening the Family as an Informal Support for their Aged: Implication for Social Policy and Planning.* Presented at the 31st Annual Meeting of the Gerontological Society, Dallas, November 1978.

SUGGESTED READINGS

Bard M, Zacher J: The prevention of family violence: Dilemmas of community intervention. *J Marriage and the Family* 1971;33:677–682.

Campbell R, Chenoweth B: *Peer Support System.* Presented at the 33rd Annual Meeting of the Gerontological Society, San Diego, CA, November 1980.

Cantor M: *Neighbors and Friends: An Overlooked Resource in the Informal Support System.* Presented at the Annual Meeting of the Gerontological Society, San Francisco, CA, November 1977.

Danis B: *Stress in Individuals Caring for Ill Elderly Relatives.* Presented at the 31st Annual Meeting of the Gerontological Society, Dallas, November 1978.

Froland C, Pancoast D, Chapman N, et al: *Helping Networks and Human Services.* Beverly Hills, CA, Sage, 1981.

Garbarino J: The human ecology of child maltreatment. *J Marriage and the Family* 1977;39:721–735.

Garrison J, Howe J: Community intervention with the elderly: A social network approach. *J Am Geriatr Soc* 1976;24(1).

Gottlieb B: *Social Networks and Social Support.* Beverly Hills, CA, Sage, 1981.

Howells D: *Reallocating Institutional Resources: Respite Care as a Supplement to Family Care of the Elderly.* Presented at the 33rd Annual Meeting of the Gerontological Society, San Diego, CA, November 1980.

Johnson E, Bursk B: Relationships between the elderly and their adult children. *Gerontologist* 1977;17(1):28.

Levy LH: Self help groups: Types and psychological processes. *J Applied Behav Sci* 1976;12:310–322.

Networks for Helping: Illustrations from Research and Practice. Proceedings of the Conference on Networks, Portland State University, Portland, OR, November, 1978.

Pilisuk M, Minkler M: Supportive networks: Life ties for the elderly. *J Social Issues* 1980;36(2):1450–1452.

Rose MA: Problems families face in home care. *Am J Nursing* 1976;76(3):416–418.

Schmidt MG: *Personal Networks: Assessment, Care, and Repair.* Presented at the 26th Annual Meeting, Western Gerontological Society, Anaheim, CA, 1980.

Steinitz L: *The Church as Family Surrogate for the Elderly.* Presented at the 33rd Annual Meeting of the Gerontological Society, San Diego, CA, November 1980.

24 Elderly Abuse in a Hospital: A Nursing Perspective

Elizabeth Reynolds
Sheila Stanton

The nurse, as a primary health care provider, plays a key role in the recognition and reporting of abuse. We shall attempt to see whether nurses are accepting this responsibility through a discussion of the role of the nurse in elderly abuse.

The 1970s saw the beginning of an expanded role for the nurse. Nurses now have prominent roles not only in a hospital, but are key contributors in the health care of the community. The 1980s will see the nurse not as a skilled technician but as a diversified, educated professional. The registered nurse practicing her profession in today's complex technological society is an autonomous practitioner with her own values, and she must make educated decisions. Autonomy also means increased responsibilities, many of which are cyclical. The more assertive nurses will carry these responsibilities of health care not only to the client, but to their profession as well.

BACKGROUND

"Elderly Abuse" was included in a schedule of topics to be prepared for a series of monthly public education programs by our professional organization, The Emergency Department Nurses Association. In studying the topic we found the emergency nurse is in a prominent position to recognize abuse. Inflation is one factor causing difficulties for many of our elderly. Frequently users of the emergency department are the people who cannot afford the care of a private practitioner. Additionally, with a 20% to 25% hospital admission rate from the emergency department, general duty nurses would also be involved.

There is little in the nursing literature relative to elderly abuse. According to one study we could expect to see a 4% incidence of elderly abuse (Block 1979). Another source placed the figure at 10% (*Congressional Record,* 1980). We used Block's definition of the types of abuse: physical, psychological, material, and violation of rights. Still, available data did not reflect accurately the actual incidence of abuse. Reports varied from 600,000 to 2.5 million cases annually.

Surely thousands of cases were being treated in emergency departments in hospitals all over the country. We offered to contribute to the collection of data by the House Select Committee, and our offer was enthusiastically accepted. A continued effort is being made to define the role of the nurse in elderly abuse in the hospital.

A SURVEY

To provide data for this chapter, an exploratory study of nurses from our area of the country was undertaken, to answer the following questions:

1. Are nurses aware of elderly abuse as a social and medical problem?
2. Are they recognizing cases of elderly abuse in their practice?
3. Are they reporting cases of elderly abuse for investigation and follow-up?

We mailed 500 questionnaires to members of the Emergency Department Nurses Association living in South and Central Florida. A self-addressed stamped envelope was enclosed and a signature was not required. Space for additional comments was provided. Responses from 206 individuals were received (40.2%). Many of the respondents wrote comments reflecting their concern about treatment of the elderly.

Awareness

Awareness of elderly abuse as a social and medical problem is indicated by the responses shown in Table 24-1:

Table 24-1
Awareness of Elderly Abuse

	Total	Percent
Aware	183	88.8
Not Aware	21	10.2
No Response	2	1.0
	206	100.0

Thus, being conscious of the problem, nurses should be readily able to identify situations of abuse if they encountered cases in their practice.

The significant news media coverage of problems of the elderly contributes to awareness in our area. Frequent feature stories and weekly newspaper columns keep the topic in the mind of the public.

Recognition

The study found that nurses are encountering situations of abuse, and were able to categorize the four types of abuse we described: physical, including malnutrition and injuries; psychological, including verbal assaults and threats; material, including theft or misuse of money or property; and violation of rights, including personal freedom. A total of 171 (83%) respondents recognized situations of abuse (Table 24-2). Some respondents reported more than one type of abuse, accounting for the higher total. "Other" usually denotes a combination of types. Neglect, abandonment, withholding of or overdosing of medication, allowing loss of self-respect or dignity, and "dumping" are all mentioned. The dumping syndrome describes a familiar phenomenon. For example:

Table 24-2
Description of Abuse Encountered

	Total	Percent
Physical	140	34.1
Psychological	117	28.5
Material	75	18.2
Violation of Rights	69	16.8
Other	10	2.4
	411	100.0

394

The ambulance brought him to the hospital Emergency Department, an elderly gentleman in his eighties. The nurse examined him and what struck her immediately was not his physical appearance, but the sad look on his face, a look that said "I am not loved." She carefully assessed the man and found him to be well oriented, but poorly nourished, so poorly nourished that she could feel his ribs through the hospital gown. He had bruises in different stages on his legs and back. His skin was dehydrated, and he was dirty. There was a conspicuous absence of family. His son finally called two days later and said they wanted him placed in a nursing home. They no longer wanted to care for him. "Another dump," said the nurse." (Turlis L, Director of Staff Development, Imperial Point Hospital, Fort Lauderdale, Florida, personal communication, 1980).

Many elderly patients are brought to hospitals when families are no longer willing or able to care for them. In some cases, they can no longer cope with the responsibility. At other times, such as at holidays, emergency departments are filled with elderly whose families do not want the burden of caring for them because it restricts their own freedom.

In their descriptions of abuse encountered, many nurses specifically identified patients admitted from nursing homes as victims. Gross neglect is described: lack of oral hygiene, malnutrition, dehydration, soiled linen, and decubitus ulcers. Concerned with preserving the dignity of the aged, one nurse commented: "In this day and age when it is becoming increasingly acceptable to place the elderly in nursing homes and retirement homes, I feel it is very important that we remember that they need to above all retain their dignity and preserve the essence of their necessity to us, in our 'youth-geared' world." Another nurse stated, "I supported my way through nursing school by working in an old age home, and I've always had a concern in my heart for the elderly since then."

We asked for an estimation of what percentage of the patients cared for by our respondents were over age 60 (Table 24-3). It is significant that 114 nurses or 55.5% of the respondents report that between 31% and 60% of their patient population are over 60 years of age. This is probably a higher average than in many other parts of the country, and may afford the Florida nurse a greater opportunity to observe and report problems of the elderly.

Reporting

When a nurse assumes care for a patient, establishing a nurse/patient relationship, she is responsible for a care plan that must encompass his immediate needs as well as a discharge plan for follow-up of care. Established standards require this. Reporting to the proper authority or

Table 24-3
Percent of Patients Over Age 60

	Total	Percent
Less than 5%	6	2
5%–10%	11	5
11%–20%	12	6
21%–30%	24	12
31%–40%	37	18
41%–50%	37	18
51%–60%	40	19.5
61%–70%	19	9.6
71%–80%	11	5.3
81%–higher	9	4.3
	206	100.0

Table 24-4
Observation and Reporting of Abuse

	Total	Percent
Observed	171	83.0
Reported	74	35.9

Table 24-5
Reporting of Elderly Abuse

	Total	Percent
Social service	44	40.0
Nursing supervisor	31	27.4
Police	23	20.4
Administration	10	8.8
Other	5	4.4
	113	100.0

social agent when a problem is identified is an essential component of care, and our study indicates a deficiency on reporting (Table 24-4). A breakdown of persons to whom the cases were initially reported shows that the majority of cases were referred to social service for follow-up. Many cases were reported to more than one person or agency (Table 24-5).

Florida is one of 22 states with an adult protective service law requiring the reporting of adult abuse. A statewide, toll-free telephone number has been established to facilitate prompt reporting and intervention. The following case study illustrates how easily this may be accomplished:

Mary T, a 79-year-old woman was admitted to the Emergency Department during a busy afternoon shift. Recorded on the admission sheet as patient complaint was: "arm bitten by daughter." Physical assessment revealed four bite wounds on her right arm. Mary was alert, cooperative, and well mannered. Establishing rapport was not difficult. She became slightly defensive, however, and almost apologetic when questioned about the circumstances surrounding her injury. Her main concern was being attended by the doctor so she could be on her way. Her daughter Peggy, a well-dressed, well-groomed, 45-year-old woman who had accompanied her to the hospital stated, "I did that, but it was not my fault — the Republicans and Democrats told me to." Further questioning revealed a ten-year history of psychiatric problems with frequent hospitalization and current outpatient treatment. The interviewer accepted this information without judgment, and Peggy went on to describe a remarkable account of family conflict. A second daughter, Margo, had recently moved into the home and was "causing all the problems." The sisters, both unemployed, fought because Peggy was "good" and tried to do the right thing and Margo was "bad" — she wore too much makeup and slept with men. After all wasn't she, Peggy, the person who brought Mother to the hospital and tried to resist the voices when they told her to do terrible things to Mother? Margo, on the other hand, often hit Mother and pushed her down and left her on the floor, unable to get up, and emptied out her pills.

Now that this much information had been shared, Mary seemed relieved and was ready to accept help. She admitted to living in "constant fear" that someone would be hurt.

The hospital social service coordinator was notified and arranged for immediate investigation. This was accomplished efficiently and effectively through use of the Adult Abuse Hot Line. She also arranged for a visiting nurse to provide follow-up wound care since the daughters appeared unreliable.

Follow-up of this case revealed that the second daughter was removed from the family setting, reducing the conflict to a manageable level. Mary was no longer the victim of abuse. The outcome of this case might have been very different if the nurse caring for this patient had been concerned only with Mary's physical needs.

Conclusion of Study

1. Nurses are aware of elderly abuse as a medical and social problem.
2. They recognize elderly abuse in their practice.

3, They need to be encouraged to report suspected cases of elderly abuse for investigation and follow-up.

We have so far concentrated on emergency nursing. In the following discussion we will include all professional nurses involved in direct patient care.

THE ROLE OF THE NURSE AS ADVOCATE

"By the year 2000, there will be almost 32 million elderly. Those over 75 are the most vulnerable to the physical, mental and social assaults that lead to the need for care and services" (Brody, 1980). The elderly present a special nursing challenge, one that is sometimes not met. We must monitor our own profession and recognize its strengths and weaknesses in the care of the elderly. The nurse is in a prime position to be advocate for the elderly. This is not as easy as it sounds. Attitudes of some health care professionals will have to change, attitudes that represent society's attitudes toward the aged as a whole. One may hear a health care professional state "I am so tired of taking care of these old people." Poor attitudes show up in poor care.

Why is this attitude common? There are differences in caring for Jim, age 25, who is having his gallbladder removed and Martha, age 80, who is having the same surgical procedure. "The medical profession is geared toward diagnosing and treating the acute illness and quick return on effort is desired" (Johnson, Williamson, 1980). This is possible with the 25-year-old, but usually not with the 80-year-old. The majority of the elderly have chronic underlying conditions, eg, heart disease or diabetes which may complicate and prolong their recovery. Their care does not offer the immediate satisfaction obtained from care of a younger patient.

The rewards are different, but they are there, and the nurses are best equipped to take up the cause. They can develop sensitivity to the needs of the elderly and become role models for the staff and colleagues to emulate. The elderly must be treated with dignity and respect. "Respect for the older patient's views and wishes is the cornerstone of patient's advocacy" (King et al, 1978).

THE ROLE OF THE NURSE IN THE HOSPITAL

When the patient is admitted to a hospital, the nurse's role is to formulate a nursing care plan, including the psychosocial as well as the physical aspect of nursing care. This problem-solving approach will allow the nurse to assess the patient's problem, plan his care, implement this plan, and evaluate the results.

The purpose of nursing care planning is to provide patient-centered, rather than task-oriented care. This means that the patient and his family's input is included in his plan of care, to give the patient a more autonomous role and to provide for continuity of care so important to the elderly. "It is often said if you keep an old patient in bed for a week, you will have no difficulty in keeping him there for the remainder of his life" (Kemp, 1978).

Identifying the patient's problem is accomplished by interviewing, observing, and examining the patient. This interview is important in the overall assessment and is the data base for the care plan. With an abused patient, if the nurse is astute and attuned to the patient as an individual, not just his diagnosis, she may assess the problem on the initial interview. An interview is not an interrogation, and much valuable information may be missed by appearing hurried and inattentive. The older person's sense of time is slower, and the behavior of the nurse should not communicate impatience. An atmosphere of trust needs to be established in a short time. This can be accomplished if the nurse displays warmth and a willingness to listen. She also needs to use her various other senses; smell, touch and sight. She must observe the patient's behavior and recognize the effects of his illness as well as underlying problems. Nurses have many demands on their time. They are hurried and harried, due, in part, to an acute shortage of nurses. It is not, however, the quantity of time spent with the patient, but the quality.

Recognition of abuse may not be easy. If the patient is admitted with contusions on his body or is poorly nourished and dirty, then physical abuse should be suspected. Psychological abuse is different because it will probably not be the immediate problem, but one that is covert. Taking a social history may uncover some problems within the home. Usually much attention is paid to the physical assessment of the patient, but very little to the psychological and social assessment.

What could a social history uncover? History of alcohol abuse or mental illness is important, either by the patient or a member of his family. How many people are living in the household? How old are they? Sincere interest and questioning about living conditions sometimes uncovers problems or potential problems. Recent weight loss or weight gain may denote depression, or absence of a nurturing caretaker. The patient's environment must be considered. This is not 79-year-old Mr. Jones with a fractured right hip, it is Mr. Jones who is living with his schizophrenic daughter who, when she stops taking her medication, loses control and pushes her father around.

Mr. Jones's emotional status should be observed: Is he anxious, withdrawn, or passive? How is he reacting to the stress of being in the hospital? What are his expectations? Mr. Jones should present some behavioral clues that he has been abused. He may appear helpless and hopeless. Hopelessness may be characterized by indifference, apathy, and a flat emotional state. He may appear passive and almost uninterested in what is happening to him. Hopelessness is characterized by a person's no longer taking responsibility for his actions. Mr. Jones may be reluctant to participate with plans for his own care. He may even attempt to undermine it by refusing to eat or to get out of bed. He may not even want to get well. Wellness to him would mean returning to his present environment and a repetition of the same situation.

Verbal threats and derogatory remarks are also used as mechanisms to control the elderly. Mrs. Webster was ready to be discharged on Friday, but she asked to remain over the weekend. When asked why, she replied, "I do not want to go home, my daughter is always yelling at me." This is an example of psychological abuse that needs to be further investigated. However, it is more likely that something will be done about it if the problem is uncovered early in the hospital admission rather than on the day of discharge.

Discharge Planning

Discharge planning is an important aspect of nursing care, and it should begin the day of admission. Many nurses balk at the idea. How am I going to know what discharge planning this patient will need the day he is admitted? If the initial interview and assessment has been worthwhile, there is much that can be foreseen. Meaningful questions the nurse could ask are: What are the dependency needs of this patient? Is he autonomous, needing few services, or has the disease changed the needs? A patient who has had a cerebrovascular accident may need to go to an extended care facility for further rehabilitation.

Many older patients, even in the face of debilitating afflictions, may very much want to maintain their independence. This is their right. Nursing home placement against a patient's will, unless they are declared legally incompetent, is a violation of their civil rights. However, this is often done by well-meaning physicians and families. The more active a patient has been in planning his care, the more confidence he will have in his capabilities for controlling his life. This can be implemented through effective discharge planning and patient education.

Patient Education

When a patient is discharged, the nurse should ask herself:

1. What does the patient need to know about his medication ie, side effects, dosage, and times he should be taking

them? Included in this are diabetic education and insulin administration. Dietary restrictions should be discussed along with proper skin care and urine testing. A list of written instructions is helpful, because demonstration is more effective and meaningful.

2. What should be known about dietary restriction?
3. What procedures is he expected to perform at home?
4. If his activities are restricted, what services may he need to supplement these restrictions?

There should be a multidisciplinary approach to patient care, including the family physician, nurse, social worker, and patient educator. (The patient educator is a resource nurse whose expertise includes patient instruction in various aspects of health care, eg, diabetic teaching. The role of the patient educator has become more prominent in recent years and has been valuable in discharge planning.) The elderly can often remain autonomous with a few adjunctive services, eg, visiting nurses, and meal on wheels, but these needs must be assessed before the patient is discharged.

When Abuse is Not Abuse

Many families take the responsibility of caring for their elderly relatives who may be severely physically impaired. They may be readmitted to the hospital in what appears to be a sad state of neglect. They may have decubitus ulcers, and their nutritional state may be poor. Abuse may be suspected; but, in reality, these families were not given sufficient education to care for their elderly relatives, and needed services were not made available to them. It is difficult for a senile 86-year-old man to care properly for his physically impaired 84-year-old wife. But, many patients leave emergency departments and hospital units with inadequate patient education and haphazard assessment of their needs.

Resources Available

The nurse in a hospital should report any suspicion of elderly abuse to the physician, social worker, and nursing administration. The social worker, according to our survey, has been the most relied on as facilitator. The next most important resource, especially in the emergency department, has been the police.

The nurse, according to our survey, has observed instances of elderly abuse, but has not reported them, usually because of fear of legal action. To protect herself legally, the nurse needs to document her observations and physical findings when abuse is suspected. The observations do not have to be labeled abuse. Nursing records will be her defense, just as in cases of suspected child abuse.

The nurse should also be aware of the protective services available in the community. Not all abuse cases are seen in the hospital. Abuse might be taking place next door. These resources are: (1) Health and Rehabilitation Services (aging and adult services); (2) guardianship programs; (3) ombudsman committee; and (4) toll-free numbers to be called in cases of suspected abuse.

COMMUNITY HEALTH CARE

Elder abuse also has implications for the community-based nurse, as well as for the hospital-based nurse.

Visiting Nurses Association (VNA)

The VNA is one of the oldest community organizations providing multiple health care services, including nursing in the home. These services include family health counseling, direct and supervisory patient care, assessment and monitoring of family situations, and patient education.

These nurses not only have the responsibility of identifying possible elderly abuse, but also are in the position of assessing stressful situations in which potential abuse may occur. The VNA nurse's interaction, ie, providing a health care aide to relieve stress on a burdened family, may not resolve the complicated family dynamics in which abuse occurs. However, these interactions may reduce family tensions enough to prevent a crisis situation which would result in abuse. These nurses also have access to financial information in their financial screening procedure that may uncover possible theft or misuse of property of the elderly.

Public Health

Public health services vary from state to state, depending on budgetary systems. Some departments will provide home care components and geriatric clinics. They will also do pre-admission screening for Medicare and Medicaid for nursing home placement. Again, the nurse is in a position to assess abuse or potential abuse and evaluate and make recommendations for other services.

Outpatient Clinics

These clinics may encompass mental health and/or family health. Many clinics are being staffed by the nurse practitioner. The nurse practitioner program is relatively new, and requires one year of advanced education in a nursing specialty in a university. The programs offered vary with each institution, but specialties range from pediatric nurse practitioner to a practitioner in gerontological nursing.

NURSING EDUCATION

Nursing and in-service educators should be aware of the problem of elderly abuse, and programs should be developed to present the information. The authors are now, through the Association of South Florida Nurse Educators, going to 13 hospitals in Broward County, presenting a program on elderly abuse. This program is offered for 2 continuing education units of which 24 units are mandatory in the state of Florida for relicensure. The reception of the program has been gratifying. We have found that the majority of nurses are concerned about the needs of the elderly. They have offered much information about their own problems in caring for an elderly relative and examples of abuse they have observed. This education and sharing of information are valuable. Community education in care of the elderly might play a part in the prevention of abuse.

Public education should include nursing care of the elderly; lifting and moving techniques; skin care; nutritional needs; bowel and bladder care; lists of services available for elderly, eg, elderly day care centers; and development of elderly advocacy programs.

Psychological aspects of care should include methods of dealing constructively with problems of elderly persons and counseling services available for troubled families.

This list is far from complete. The authors have planned a community education program for presentation to the public on "Abuse of the Elderly." We will present this program with other professionals, including a geriatric psychiatrist, social worker, and law enforcement officer.

Health care is no longer only curing the disease, but now encompasses rehabilitation and the prevention of illness. The recognition of elderly abuse is important, but even more essential is that health care professionals expand their roles and become more involved in the community. The nurse has much to offer, and the rewards are worth the effort made.

BIBLIOGRAPHY

Block, MR, Sinnott, JD: *The Battered Elder Syndrome: An Exploratory Study.* University of Maryland, Center on Aging, College Park, MD, November 1979.

Brody SJ: *Hospitals Health Care for the Aged.* May 1980, p 63.

Congressional Record. Adult abuse. June 11, 1980.

Johnson ES, Williamson, JB: *Drugs, Dollars, and Hospitals: Growing Old, the Social Problems of Aging.* New York, Holt, Rinehart and Winston, 1980, p 115.

Kemp J: Planning hospital care, Part 15, *Nursing Times* 1978;74:198–199.

King G, Vaughn S: The challenge of geriatric care: New ways to cope. You may be the ageds' only advocate, Part I. *RN* 1978;41:47–52.

25 Intervention for the Victimized Elderly and Sensitization of Health Professionals: Therapeutic and Educational Efforts

Kenneth Solomon

In a previous chapter, the frequency of psychopathologic syndromes in the elderly and the relationship of victimization and psychopathology were discussed. In addition, the role of the health provider was examined. In this chapter, the author will discuss intervention with the victimized elderly, examining pharmacologic and nonpharmacologic aspects. Mechanisms to sensitize the health worker to both the problem of elder victimization and the input of the health worker will also be discussed, with an emphasis on education.

INTERVENTION WITH PATIENT AND FAMILY

The principles of intervention with the abused elderly and their families are no different from those of intervention with the elderly with any functional disorder. In all disturbances, the interventions should be specific for the problem. Intervention generally follows a predictable sequence of events (Goldfarb, 1968, 1974; Solomon, 1981b, in press b). There is some overlap in the sequence to allow for maximal therapeutic flexibility when working with the elderly person with a functional disturbance. These principles of intervention hold whether or not the abuse is primary or secondary to the psychologic problem and whether or not the patient's disturbance is primarily organic or functional.

Intervention is divided into two phases (Solomon, 1981b). First, the phase, crisis intervention, is the reversal of the psychodynamic sequence noted in Chapter 9. The second phase, long-term psychotherapy, is relevant only for those individuals who have a lifelong history of inadequate coping skills or those who wish to pursue further personal growth. For chronically dysfunctional families, long-term family therapy or individual psychotherapy for other family members may also be indicated.

Before psychotherapeutic intervention, the health professional must determine whether there is physical danger to or from the patient. Protection of patient and others is the first priority. Hospitalization or temporary placement in a nursing home, foster home, halfway house, or with friends, neighbors, or relatives, may be necessary. This, however, should be done cautiously, so as not to substitute one form of victimization for another.

Crisis Intervention: Pharmacologic

The first step in the first phase is a direct attack on symptomatology. In the presence of severe psychotic or depressive symptoms appropriate drugs are indicated. Before prescription of psychotropic medications to an elderly patient, certain guidelines (Hall, 1973) should be observed, which will help prevent further iatrogenic physical abuse. They are:

1. Know the pharmacologic action of the drug, particularly how it is metabolized and excreted.
2. Use the lowest effective dose for the individual patient.
3. Use the fewest number of drugs needed.
4. Elucidate the cause of symptoms before treating.
5. Do not withhold drugs because of advanced age, especially when pharmacotherapy may enhance the quality of life.
6. Do not use a drug if its side effects are worse than the symptoms it relieves.
7. Do not continue a drug once it is no longer needed.

One must be careful with psychopharmacologic agents in the elderly. Because of changes in absorption, metabolism, storage, binding, and excretion of these drugs, there is generally more active drug available to the brain for a therapeutic or toxic effect (Friedel, 1977; Solomon, 1980a). Increased sensitivity of brain cells and a breakdown of the brain's barrier to drugs also increases therapeutic action or the risk of toxic side effects.

The quality of research in clinical geriatric psychopharmacology is poor (Solomon, 1980a, Strauss and Solomon, 1980). The few published studies have many methodologic problems. The drug recommendations below are based on a cautious interpretation of this literature, supplemented by the author's clinical experience.

If the individual has delusions, hallucinations, or manic symptoms, or has severe brain failure and is extremely agitated and disruptive and other attempts at structuring the environment have not helped, an antipsychotic medication is indicated. One should use a drug that was previously effective in the patient or first-degree relative when faced with similar symptoms (Ayd, 1975, Solomon, 1980b). In the absence of a patient's previous exposure to a drug, one chooses the drug which will avoid side effects that would be most detrimental to the older individual. Should an antipsychotic drug be necessary as a chemical restraint, the guidelines developed by Covert et al (1977) should be followed.

If the person has vegetative symptoms of depression (eg, loss of appetite, sleep disturbance) and is not experiencing a normal grief reaction, antidepressants are indicated. If the patient has manic symptoms, either because of an affective or organic disorder, treatment with lithium is indicated. The principles of lithium use are similar to those in younger patients.

Once it is determined that a particular medication is absolutely necessary, one starts with a low dose of drug and increases the dose less frequently and by smaller increments than with a younger patient. Once per day dosage of the drug may be helpful in minimizing the development of side effects of the drug (DiMascio, 1975).

Crisis Intervention: Psychotherapeutic

If the symptoms are other than these, other treatments are helpful. Acting up, defined as inappropriate social or interpersonal behavior not under conscious control and unrelated to transference issues (Solomon, 1976b), whether it be aggressive, dependent, or helpless, is managed with behavioral paradigms that emphasize environmental manipulation and limit setting of inappropriate behavior. Certain specific neurotic symptoms, such as compulsions and phobias, may respond to classic behavior modification techniques (Schaefer and Martin, 1969; Wolpe, 1969).

If anxiety is the predominant symptom, nonpharmacologic measures may help. There is some question about the efficacy of benzodiazepines in treating anxiety (Solomon, 1976; Solomon and Hart, 1978).

Nonpharmacologic modalities give the patient control over his/her symptoms. These measures include breathing exercises and relaxation exercises as used by Jacobson (Jacobson, 1938; Wolpe, 1969) or by the Lamaze method of childbirth (Bing, 1969), massage, transcendental meditation, Tantric or other forms of yoga, and jogging or other regular exercise. Acupressure to the junction of the mastoid process and base of the skull may be helpful in the treatment of tension headache.

Following the direct attack on symptoms, appropriate ventilation of the underlying affects of fear, anger, or loss is necessary. For men, who in particular have difficulty expressing or labeling affect, it may be necessary to give permission to verbalize and ventilate what is being actively avoided (Solomon, 1980b, in press a). The abused individual may be extremely fearful of verbalizing these feelings. He/she may fear repercussions from the family or institutional staff and may be suspicious of confidentiality, as his/her trust may have been repeatedly broken. This may cause the victimized elderly person to deny problems or minimize the intensity of his rage, sadness, loss, and resignation (Solomon and Zinke, 1981). For individuals whose affect is expressed behaviorally, the behaviors must be translated into verbalization of the affect. For those who overly express affect, an attempt must be made to put some limits on the expression of the affect so that it is expressed in a way conducive to therapy.

The next step in intervention is minimization of helplessness and dependency. The major modalities used in this part of therapy are environmental manipulation and behavioral techniques. The patient is given graduated behavioral tasks that the therapist knows he can definitely manage. At first these tasks should be graded according to the individual's current level of functioning. For example, severely depressed individuals may be required just to get out of bed by a certain time. A better functioning individual may be required to attend a senior center or take care of certain tasks in his environment. It is frequently necessary to enlist the aid of family members or other community resources to aid in the accomplishment of these tasks, especially if the individual suffers from brain failure. Remotivation and rehabilitative therapies are also useful at this juncture.

Next is increasing the patient's sense of mastery. This not only involves the minimization of helplessness and dependency but also requires that the elderly patient be told that he is responsible for his behavior. This responsibility is more than just an existential statement, for without responsibility there can be no need to master and alloplastically manipulate one's environment. Mastery requires that the older person have choice. This choice may have to be limited for the individual with brain failure if he is to make decisions. For the individual without brain failure, however, these choices require that the therapists give and even create options appropriate for the individual person's problems, so that he may be able to choose from many options to resolve the problems that led to the development of symptoms.

The last step in this initial phase is to attempt to reverse the nature of the stress. If the stressor involves losses that may be regained with the help of social agencies, referral to these agencies and aid in advocacy for the older individual is necessary. Losses in the social support system are frequently managed by helping the individual create a new support system. For example, the older person may either attend a senior center, reestablish contact with other family members and friends, or find a new job. Loss of role requires that the individual seek out new meaningful roles, find positive valence to old roles, realign himself with old interests, or attempt to create new roles. The memory deficits of brain failure may be partially reversed with reality orientation.

For those who are societally abused, political and attitudinal consciousness raising becomes an important part of this phase of therapy. The older person is taught to recognize the feelings about age in society and within himself and peers. The effects of ageist attitudes and stereotypes upon the individual and society at large are explored. An active stance, using social and political action rather than resignation, is favored for both therapist and client. The author recommends that his elderly clients join activist organizations such as the Gray Panthers, as a way of increasing their knowledge of the ageism in society and themselves and, through political action, reverse the helplessness and loss of mastery that triggers psychopathology. This action also gives the victimized older person an appropriate target for ventilation of his/her rage, rather than turning it against him/herself.

If the family is the source of the abuse, a similar process of crisis intervention is recommended. Family members are encouraged to ventilate affect appropriately, reverse their sense of helplessness and loss of mastery, and reverse the stress. If the identified patient suffers from an irreversible dementia, as many physically abused elderly do, the education and support from the local chapter of the Association of Alzheimer's Disease and Related Disorders may be of great importance to the future well-being of the patient (Miller, 1981). A similar process may be used for institutional staff (Warschawski and Spiegel, 1979; Warschawski, 1981).

For older persons who are in the first two groups of individuals with inadequate coping skills noted above, this may be all that is necessary. For those who are overwhelmed by stress, relief of the symptomatology and rectification of the stressful situation may allow the person to use previously acquired coping mechanisms and problem-solving skills. This allows for growth and better coping with other stresses in the future. For the individual with brain disease, although there is some capability for growth, these individuals are not capable of working in or benefiting from long-term psychotherapy once stresses are relieved and symptoms have been improved. For the family rendered acutely dysfunctional by the accumulated stresses on its older members, a return to premorbid family functioning, or better, is the usual result.

Long-Term Intervention

Those individuals with a lifelong history of inadequate coping skills or those who seek further growth and self-knowledge, then enter the second stage of intervention, the stage of psychotherapy. Older individuals are often motivated for help and resistances are fewer (LeShan and LeShan, 1961). They are amenable to various psychotherapeutic modalities, including psychoanalytic psychotherapy and psychoanalysis. If the problems are primarily intrapsychic, either of these psychotherapies or Gestalt or primal therapy may be of benefit. If the problems are primarily interpersonal, then group psychotherapy, psychoanalytic psychotherapy, family or marital therapy, or transactional analysis is indicated. For those individuals who are not good candidates for insight-oriented psychotherapy, such as those with an overlay of somatization or those who are not psychologically minded or who cannot tolerate a transference relationship, long-term supportive psychotherapy may also be of aid to help the individual cope with future stress.

At all stages in the therapeutic process it is necessary for the therapist to avoid infantilization or parentification of the patient. The therapist should not relate to the older person with the societal stereotypes of the elderly, for this will also minimize therapeutic response (Solomon, in press a), as noted in Chapter 9.

Older people are probably more motivated for growth and behavioral change in psychotherapy than are the members of any other age group, perhaps because they are aware of their limited life span (LeShan and LeShan, 1961). In addition, they have frequently undergone many years of self-examination, making the beginning of the therapeutic process easier, as they enter therapy with a fair degree of insight. Resistances are diminished, which makes therapy with the elderly simpler and more rapidly progressing. Even in the presence of brain disease, there is remaining brain that is capable of learning, feeling, responding, and modifying behavior. This, coupled with accurate diagnosis and appropriate interventions, will lead the therapist to be successful in most of his work with older patients.

INTERVENTION WITH HEALTH WORKERS:
CONSULTATION AND EDUCATION

Health professionals are a major source of victimization and abuse of the elderly, much of which is secondary societal stereotypes and attitudes held by health workers. Another major source is ignorance. Rarely have students in the health professions had any training in gerontology and geriatrics; most students escape any exposure to this segment of their professional work. Thus, any attempt to minimize victimization by health professionals and to sensitize them to the results and processes of victimization of the elderly must recognize a need to make an impact on both the attitudes and knowledge of the health worker.

A clear relationship has been demonstrated between the improvement in attitudes and the acquisition of factual knowledge of the elderly. In studies that used professionals or professional students as subjects, all showed that training was important in positive changes noted (Kayser and Minningerode, 1975; Johnson and Wilhite, 1976; Hickey et al, 1976; Romaniuk et al, 1977; Brennan and Moravec, 1978; Holtzman and Beck, 1978, 1979; Solomon and Vickers, 1980). Only in the study by Beck and colleagues (1979) was there a negative change; this was the only study in which a formal didactic component was lacking.

As the didactic component of these studies is of such great importance, knowledge of the curriculum would be helpful. Unfortunately these were not described by Kayser and Minningerode (1975), Johnson and Wilhite (1976), Romaniuk et al (1977), Holtzman and Beck (1978, 1979), or Robb (1979). Many gerontology and geriatrics curricula have been developed and not published; they frequently include small mental health components. There are at least 12 fellowships in geropsychiatry in the country, but their curricula have not been published. Furthermore, these training programs in geriatric mental health are usually limited to one discipline (eg, Jacobson and Juthani, 1978; Blumenthal et al, 1979 for geropsychiatry). If the programs are interdisciplinary, such as the geropsychiatry fellowship program at Boston University School of Medicine, available to trainees in psychiatry, neurology, or internal medicine (Weinstock and Leiff, 1980), their curricula have not been published. Thus, statements of objectives and descriptions of content and teaching methodologies in geriatric mental health as interdisciplinary training are sparse.

The program of Hickey and associates (1976) was limited and attempted only to teach about sensory deprivation in the elderly in a three-hour training session. It included a film, lecture, discussion, and experiential exercises designed to simulate sensory impairment through the use of goggles and earplugs.

Brennan and Moravec (1978) described their program in more depth in a three-day seminar attended by psychiatrists, internists, social workers, psychologists, and nurses. It included discussions of sexuality, crime, loneliness, and independence in the elderly; videotapes and films; and on-site interaction of the professionals with elderly clients in remotivation therapy.

With Michael Romaniuk, PhD and Jean G. Romaniuk, PhD, the author developed a program to train Virginia's Medicaid Pre-Screening Committees in assessment of the elderly. The members of these committees ranged from physicians, social workers, and public health nurses to high school graduates with no professional training. They worked in areas with many community resources and in poor, rural areas. Their experience with and knowledge of the elderly ranged from sophisticated and extensive to virtually nonexistent. A program consisted of lectures on assessment techniques and dementia and small and large group discussion of real clients, the discussions emphasizing assessment and clinical problem solving. Slides were used as adjuncts to lectures. Evaluation of this training revealed a positive change in the knowledge of the participants.

A second project, described by Solomon and Vickers (1980), consisted of an intensive four-day workshop for adult protective service workers in Virginia. The first day included three exercises described below.

The second day was didactic, with lectures and discussions on normative biologic, psychologic, and social aging, the psychogeriatric evaluation, mental status examination and social examination, dementia and pseudodementia, and affective disorders. On the third day, lectures and discussions studied death, dying, grieving, other psychopathology and social disorders in the elderly, and treatment and intervention modalities. Slides were used here too.

Also on the third day case material was provided for discussion. Discussions and problem solving emphasized the assessment and intervention with each particular case. The fourth day included discussion of two other cases. Following this, there was discussion of issues pertaining to the treatment and assessment of these older people in the community. The program was videotaped so that it could be used for training of other adult protective service workers in the state.

All participants received the Tuckman-Lorge Questionnaire (Tuckman and Lorge, 1953) before beginning of the first exercise and after the third case discussion, as a measure of their acceptance of stereotypes of older persons. Solomon and Vickers (1980) avoided the problem noted by McTavish (1971) and Kogan (1979) of not using the Tuckman-Lorge Questionnaire to assess the attitudes of these workers. The post-training scores showed a moderate degree of acceptance of stereotypes of older persons had diminished significantly on 6 out of 13 factors. On one other factor, the difference in scores approached significance. The mean scores also diminished significantly.

A third project developed by the author was the development of two graduate courses in the Departments of Gerontology and Psychology at Virginia Commonwealth University. These courses were entitled "Clinical Assessment and Treatment of the Elderly."

The first course consisted of lectures, a term paper, and a final examination. Slides were used as an adjunct to the lectures. The students were interdisciplinary, consisting of graduate students in nursing, clinical psychology, social work, and gerontology; the faculty was also interdisciplinary, consisting of a geropsychiatrist, a clinical geropsychologist, and two clinical psychologists. Evaluations of the students showed an increase in knowledge of the mental health of the elderly.

The second course was taken by the same students as the first and was a clinical practicum augmented by lectures, with this author providing clinical supervision. The psychologists developed a series of complementary lectures and discussion groups. The students were assigned responsibility for three to five geropsychiatry outpatients whom they evaluated and with whom they did therapy with for eight to ten weeks. A major objective of increasing the students' comfort with geriatric patients and a concomitant increase in practical and technical knowledge were accomplished..

The author has also offered another course, on normative aging, to medical and graduate students. It follows the same basic format as the other training, using a combination of values clarification, lecture, and discussion of appropriate topics.

Two final projects have been recently completed. One involves the training of staff in geropsychiatry at several senior centers in Baltimore (Solomon, 1981c). A training consultation model was used, aimed at the agency rather than clinical cases (Cooper, 1975). Consultation included training to provide conceptualization of and information on normal aging as well as psychopathologic and behavioral difficulties of the elderly, assessment of psychiatric problems of the elderly, and training in basic techniques of intervention with behavioral and cognitive disorders in the elderly. The secondary goal was to develop the abilities of selected residents in psychiatry and family medicine at the University of Maryland School of Medicine to understand some of the mental health needs of the elderly in the community, to design and conduct appropriate training, consultation, and education services, and to offer this training to agencies in the community.

Following the work of Cohen (1973), and Harris and Solomon (Harris and Solomon, 1977; Solomon, 1979b, in press b), the author emphasized the multidisciplinary clinical roles of the direct service staff of the senior center worker, primarily to assure access of the elderly to needed services (Kammerman and Kahn, 1976; Gottesman et al, 1979; Ishizaki et al, 1979). Second, it was hoped that recognition and assessment of and timely intervention with the normative psychosocial stresses of aging (eg, grief, retirement) by senior center staff would serve as primary prevention of major psychiatric disorders (Caplan, 1964), notably depression. Third, following the work of Solomon and Vickers (Solomon, 1978, 1979a; Solomon and Vickers, 1979, 1980), it was hoped that the training would modify stereotypes of the elderly held by senior center staff, and increase recognition of psychopathologic processes and appropriate intervention, thus reducing victimization.

Training topics varied slightly by center but a critical core was developed. Slides, movies, and poetry became an integral part of each session. The educational process included a combination of experiential exercises, group discussion, and informal or semiformal lectures. A selected bibliography in geropsychiatry was developed, and a curriculum manual will be developed.

To see if training of this sort can modify stereotypes toward the elderly, the Tuckman-Lorge Questionnaire (Tuckman and Lorge, 1953) was given to all participants at the beginning of the first session and the end of the last session. As with the Virginia adult protective service workers (Solomon and Vickers, 1980), analysis of the data suggests that the agency workers have demonstrated a lessening of the stereotyped views they held of the elderly.

The other project involved training the direct service staff at the Waxter Center for Senior Citizens in Baltimore. This project brings the staff of various disciplines together weekly for instruction in geropsychiatry. This instruction is accomplished by lecture, discussions, slides, values clarification, and experiential exercises. These exercises are similar to those used in the adult protective service worker project.

In all these projects, there are certain similarities. They demonstrate that a particular approach to stereotyping may lead to changes in the degree of stereotyping of older people held by clinical workers. The author's enthusiasm carried into the training sessions and may have presented older people in a positive way. In addition, the didactic material usually began with data about normative aging. Throughout the courses, emphasis was placed on the coping abilities, plasticity, and motivation of older people who encounter psychologic or social difficulties; this was in distinction to the usual emphasis on psychopathology. Thus, for the duration of the course, participants were immersed in a positive social context for aging. This has been consistent with the ideas of Cook (1962).

By reexamining their own aging, the participants began to see themselves as aging persons in a more positive light. This then had the effect of changing the perceived status of older people; from a negative status, older people were perceived more as traditional elders with wisdom and experience that they could share with younger people. Older people were seen as good clients. They became attractive, intelligent, verbal, and motivated clients, rather than stereotyped as hypochondriacs. This perceived higher status of the elderly and of one's own aging may have diminished the fear and stress associated with aging, thereby diminishing adherence to stereotyping. It also diminished cognitive dissonance, insofar as the perception of one's future in aging became more consistent with objective data about aging. This, too, diminished stress.

Experiential exercises to examine one's own aging were also used in the study by Hickey et al (1976) with success. As older people began to be viewed without labels and with positive attributes of growth, experience, and wisdom, the participants began to change their response to the stereotypes. The workers' actual behavioral responses to older people also underwent modification. No longer were older people expected to behave in a way consistent with the stereotype of older people, but rather, workers tended to realize the individuality of each older individual. This feedback would then tend to continue to minimize stereotyping of older people with these workers, which would suggest that long-term change in their views was possible.

The focus of these projects were on the individual worker working with the individual older person. By emphasizing the individuality of the client, the adult protective service worker would then be able to individualize intervention, use the strengths of his client, and render more appropriate and relevant care to the older client in the community. The worker would then minimize his/her own input into the process of victimization and help prevent further victimization of and by the client. Although the emphasis was on general geropsychiatry, the presentation of this material in the context of societal abuse of the elderly further sensitizes the health worker toward issues of victimization and abuse of the elderly.

To sensitize health professional students to the problems of victimization and abuse of the elderly specifically, another course has been developed, the goals of which are to:

1. create an awareness of the problem of victimization of the elderly among medical students and other health care providers;
2. teach students the place of victimization in a societal context that examines the interaction between specific instances of elderly abuse and social structure;
3. teach the techniques to be used by medical students and other health care providers to identify abuse in the elderly;

4. teach the students to be able to identify and use referral resources for abuse in the elderly;

5. modify negative stereotypes of the elderly held by medical students and health care providers, thus reducing attitudinal victimization of the elderly by the health care community, and;

6. modify attitudes regarding awareness of the problem held by medical students and other health care providers and assist them in developing a plan for dealing with this problem.

The course is divided into five modules. Self-study assignments include selected readings, interviews, and identification of real life situations of victimization.

The first unit consists of the following values clarification exercises and a review of the basic concepts of gerontology.

Values Clarification Exercise No. 1: This exercise serves as the pretest for the evaluation component of this course. The students complete the following questionnaires:

A. Tuckman-Lorge Questionnaire (Tuckman and Lorge, 1953) (to assess adherence to stereotyping the elderly);

B. Rosenkranz-McNevin Semantic Differential (Rosenkrantz & McNevin, 1969) (to assess attitudes toward the elderly);

C. Palmore Facts on Aging Quiz (Palmore, 1977) (to assess basic knowledge about the elderly).

This exercise gives the students an opportunity to question their ideas about the elderly in a conflict-free way that allows values and beliefs to be expressed anonymously.

Values Clarification Exercise No. 2: The students form small groups, without a facilitator. Each of the following topics is discussed by each group while responses are compiled:

1. What I like about old people;
2. What I dislike about old people;
3. Sexual attributes of old people;
4. Me at 75.

Following this discussion, all the groups share their responses while a facilitator examines and clarifies themes.

The purpose of this exercise is to allow students to examine some of their personal likes, dislikes, and beliefs about the elderly in the safety of a small group of peers. The absence of a facilitator in this small group allows for greater sharing of feelings in a nonjudgmental environment. Anonymity is also preserved in the large group, since the students identify with their group.

Values Clarification Exercise No. 3: Students are paired with another student whom they do not know well. One student is selected as the follower and is blindfolded, has earplugs in his/her ears, and is barefoot. He/she may not talk. The other student is the leader and is responsible for giving the follower a sensory experience. Followers are led into different parts of the building, for example, or have other non-threatening experiences. The leaders may talk to anyone except the follower. After 20 minutes, all students return to the large group and the experience is processed.

The purpose of this exercise is to expose students to the experience of sensory deprivation and its concomitant affects. Issues of trust, dependency, and responsibility are also explored.

Values Clarification Exercise No. 4: The students are given 20 minutes to write their own obituaries which are then shared and processed. This forces students to confront their own mortality and the meaning of their lives.

Values Clarification Exercise No. 5: Following relaxation exercises, the students are told to close their eyes and imagine themselves at 100 years of age. They are told that they have only 30 minutes left in life and are guided through a personal life review, back to birth. They are then asked to experience their own dying. These experiences are then processed in the group. This exercise allows the students to experience their own lives from the perspective of the elderly, as well as to examine mortality and meaning in their lives.

The introductory large group lecture reviews the basic concepts of gerontology. The scope of the subject plus a demographic overview of gerontology is included in this didactic session. In addition, the effects and types of victimization to be covered in the course are briefly reviewed. The lecture concludes with an overview of societal structure and its relationship to victimization.

The second module deals with didactic information on role and attitudinal victimization and stereotyping and includes such topics as role theory as it relates to victimization of the elderly, social factors in the development of stereotypes, individual factors in the acceptance of stereotypes, and bridges between society and the individual. It consists of three large group didactic sessions dealing with role and attitudinal victimization. The first lecture deals with role victimization. In addition to a definition of role victimization, an overview of role theory is provided, followed by a discussion of role shift and strain in the elderly. The macrosocietal factors which cause role shift and strain concludes this session.

The next two lectures are devoted to attitudinal victimization and stereotyping of the elderly. The first defines attitudinal victimization and stereotyping and reviews current research on stereotyping. The second presents the social factors in the development of stereotypes and individual factors in the acceptance of stereotypes. A bridge between the society and the individual is presented by a discussion of status inconsistency, attribution theory, and labelling theory.

The third module deals with economic victimization and includes such items as the monies with which social, political, and economic processes operate to encourage or discourage systematic financial and medical abuse of the aged, an overview of income and medical assistance programs, and a review of the relationship between economic victimization and both health status and health care.

The economic abuse module is presented in three large group classes and a small group discussion. The first session begins with a nongraded test designed to generate discussion concerning the importance of social policies to older patients and the degree to which victimization of the elderly is an institutionally based phenomenon. This session also includes a discussion about the degree to which the low income and vulnerable elderly's needs are met in the political process.

The second large class lecture presents an overview of the economics of aging, an examination of the economic status of the elderly, income maintenance programs, and the income abuse of certain disadvantaged groups of elders. The types of abuse to which older Americans are subjected in the work force is also discussed.

Economic abuse within the health care system is included. Students present case studies that illustrate possible medical abuse, eg, overmedication or the turning away of a Medicare patient. The goal is to analyze the degree to which these problems represent the failure of individuals or institutions to meet the needs of elderly patients. Then there is a lecture about links between poverty and health problems, a review of health care programs, and an analysis of the economic factors that encourage and discourage abuse in the health care system.

Physical abuse of the elderly includes such topics as crimes of violence, family abuse, and medical abuse. The first lecture presents crimes of violence, including a discussion of personal crimes of purse snatching, muggings, rape, terrorism by others in the neighborhood, and vandalism which engenders fear. Also discussed are property crimes and how the value of heirlooms increases the emotional impact as well as the attractiveness of robbery. This session concludes with the relation of violent crimes to the impairments of age.

The second session presents issues related to family abuse, such as types of covert and overt neglect plus physical, verbal, and psychological abuse. This is followed by small group discussions about predisposing factors leading to abuse by families. Students are asked to react in the group to factors such as dementia, long-standing family maladjustment, financial and living space strain, and the unwillingness of the family to allow institutionalization secondary to a financial dependence on the patient's pension or social security checks despite the family's physical inability or lack of desire to provide care for the elderly impaired victim.

Medical abuse by the health professional and the hospital is discussed. Sources of both overt and covert abuse (physicians' lack of availability to avoid the paperwork of Medicare or the problems of multiple diseases, their lack of accessibility regarding ambulance services, house calls, or evening hours), the use of dementia as an excuse for poor diagnostic effort, or abandonment of patients with terminal illness to nursing homes are discussed.

A session deals with the contribution of the medical establishment and the nursing home to abuse. Included are such topics as Medicare's failure to pay for preventive care or education, discharge of mentally incompetent patients into a community ill-prepared to care for them, nursing homes that, because of a high turnover rate, provide inadequate caretakers, and the abrogation of rights and sexual expression of the elderly in nursing homes.

The fifth section summarizes the emotional effects of victimization and identifies the health care provider's responsibility. It emphasizes the information previously presented.

A lecture presents the emotional effects of victimization through a discussion of coping, the psychology of the oppressed, and psychopathology of aging. A second lecture presents the health care provider's responsibility. There is a discussion of real life situations from newspapers, the media, or one's experiences. The members react as to each one's responsibility as a health care provider. Short segments are recorded on videotape and used as a springboard.

A third session includes the movie "Peege" which depicts the abandonment of an elderly grandmother in a nursing home and the gradual connection made to this older woman by one caring grandson. Then a small group session repeats the first exercise, allowing for expression of personal feelings about the film. The students again complete the Tuckman-Lorge Questionnaire, Rosenkranz-McNevin Semantic Differential, and Palmore Facts on Aging Quiz. This activity closes the course.

SUMMARY

Abuse of the elderly may take many forms and occur in a variety of settings. Physical abuse stems from a violence increasingly indigenous to our society and perpetrated on the weak and helpless, whether child or adult. Neglect extends throughout the entire caregiving spectrum from family member to physician to hospital, nursing home, and community.

The policymakers in government play a significant role in perpetuating this victimization through reimbursement procedures and bureaucratic intervention and dicta. Even the health care providers who profess tremendous concern can be easily perceived as playing a significant role through a patronizing attitude (Blank, 1978) and act as accomplices to family and institutional abuse and mismanagement.

This chapter has examined techniques of intervention with the client, family, and health professional. Its goal has been to sensitize health professionals to the therapeutic needs of the elderly victim and the professional's roles as accomplice, healer, teacher, and student. In addition to the latter role, the author urges all health professionals working with the elderly to raise their consciousness to the ageism within and around them and to add social and political action to their activities with the elderly. This constitutes primary prevention of psychologic disability and can do more good for the elderly than all positive results of intervention and education.

BIBLIOGRAPHY

Ayd FJ Jr: Treatment-resistant patients: A moral, legal and therapeutic challenge, in Ayd FJ Jr (ed): *Rational Psychopharmacotherapy and the Right to Treatment.* Baltimore, Ayd Medical Communications, 1975, pp 37–61.

Beck JD, Ettinger RL, Glenn RE, et al: Oral health status: Impact on dental student attitudes toward the aged. *Gerontologist* 1979;19:580–584.

Bing E: *Six Practical Lessons for an Easier Childbirth.* New York, Bantam, 1969, pp 36–52.

Blank ML: Ageism in gerontologyland. Presented at the 31st Annual Meeting of the Gerontological Society, Dallas, TX, Nov. 17, 1978.

Blumenthal MD, Davie JW, Morycz RK: Developing a curriculum in psychogeriatrics. *Am J Psychiatry* 1979;136:1157–1161.

Brennan SJ, Moravec JD: Assessing multidisciplinary continuing education as it impacts on knowledge, attitudes and behavior in caring for the elderly. Presented at the 31st Annual Meeting of the Gerontological Society, Dallas, TX, Nov. 19, 1978.

Caplan G: *Principles of Preventive Psychiatry.* New York, Basic Books, 1964.

Cohen RE: The collaborative co-professional: Developing a new mental health role. *Hospital Comm Psychiatry* 1973;24:242–246.

Cook SW: The systematic analysis of socially significant events: A strategy for social research. *J Soc Issues* 1962;18:66–84.

Cooper S: A C.M.H. intervention model. Mimeo. 1975.

Covert AB, Rodrigues T, Solomon K: The use of mechanical and chemical restraints in nursing homes. *J Am Geriatr Soc* 1977;25:85–89.

DiMascio A: Innovative drug administration regimens and the economics of health care, in Ayd FJ Jr (ed): *Rational Psychopharmacotherapy and the Right to Treatment.* Baltimore, Ayd Medical Communications, 1975, pp 118–130.

Friedel RO: 1977. Pharmacokinetics of psychotherapeutic agents in aged patients, in Eisdorfer C, Friedel RO (eds): *Cognitive and Emotional Distur-*

bance in the Elderly. Chicago, Year Book Medical Publishers, 1977, pp 139–149.

Goldfarb AL: Clinical perspectives, in Simon AL, Epstein LJ (eds): *Aging in Modern Society.* Washington, American Psychiatric Association, 1968, pp 170–178.

Goldfarb AL: Minor maladjustments of the aged, in Arieti S, Brody EB (eds): *American Handbook of Psychiatry,* vol 3, ed 2. New York, Basic Books, 1974, pp 820–860.

Gottesman LE, Ishizaki B, MacBride SM: Service management—Plan and concept in Pennsylvania. *Gerontologist* 1979;19:379–385.

Hall MRP: Drug therapy in the elderly. *Br Med J* 1973;4:582–584.

Harris M, Solomon K: Roles of the community mental health nurse. *J Psychiatric Nursing Mental Health Serv* 1977;15:35–39.

Hickey T, Rakowski W, Hultsch DF, Fatula BJ: Attitudes toward aging as a function of in-service training and practitioner age. *J Gerontol* 1976;31:681–686.

Holtzman JM, Beck JD: The impact of medical and dental education on student's attitudes toward the aged. Presented at the 31st Annual Meeting of the Gerontological Society, Dallas, TX, Nov. 19, 1978.

Holtzman JM, Beck JD: Palmore's Facts on Aging Quiz: A reappraisal. *Gerontologist* 1979;19:116–120.

Ishizaki B, Gottesman LE, MacBride SM: Determinants of model choice for service management systems. *Gerontologist* 1979;19:385–388.

Jacobson E: *Progressive Relaxation.* Chicago, University of Chicago Press, 1938.

Jacobson SB, Juthani N: The nursing home and training in geropsychiatry. *J Am Geriatr Soc* 1978;26:408–410.

Johnson DM, Wilhite MJ: Changes in nursing students' stereotypic attitudes toward old people. *Nursing Res* 1976;25:430–432.

Kammerman SB, Kahn AJ: *Social Services in the United States.* Philadelphia, Temple University Press, 1976.

Kayser JS, Minningerode FA: Increasing nursing students' interest in working with aged patients. *Nursing Res* 1975;24:23–26.

Kogan N: Beliefs, attitudes, and stereotypes about old people. A new look at some old issues. *Research on Aging* 1979;1:11–36.

LeShan L, LeShan E: Psychiatry and the patient with a limited life span. *Psychiatry* 1961;24:318–323.

McTavish DG: Perceptions of old people. A review of research methodologies and findings. *Gerontologist* 1971;(Part II):90–101.

Miller N: Alzheimer's Disease self-help groups for patients and families: A national perspective. Presented at the 53rd Annual Meeting of the American Orthopsychiatric Association, New York, NY, Mar. 31, 1981.

Palmore E: Facts on Aging. A short quiz. *Gerontologist* 1977;17:315–320.

Robb SS: Attitudes and intentions of baccalaureate nursing students toward the elderly. *Nursing Res* 1979;28:43–50.

Romaniuk M, Hoyer FW, Romaniuk J: Helpless self-attitudes of the elderly: The effect of patronizing statements. Presented at the 30th Annual Meeting of the Gerontological Society, San Francisco, CA, November 1977.

Rosenkranz HA, McNevin TE: A factor analysis of attitudes toward the aged. *Gerontologist* 1969;9:55–59.

Shaefer HH, Martin PL: *Behavioral Therapy.* New York, McGraw-Hill, 1969.

Solomon K: Benzodiazepines and neurotic anxiety. Critique. *NY State J Med* 1976;76:2156–2164.

Solomon K: An objection to the use of the term "acting out." *Hosp Comm*

Psychiatry 1976b;27:773.

Solomon K: The development of stereotypes of the elderly: Toward a unified hypothesis. Presented at the 31st Annual Meeting of the Gerontological Society, Dallas, TX, Nov. 19, 1978.

Solomon K: The development of stereotypes of the elderly: Toward a unified hypothesis, in Lewis EP, Nelson LD, Scully DH, et al (eds): *Sociological Research Symposium Proceedings (IX)*. Richmond, Virginia Commonwealth University, 1979a, pp 172–177.

Solomon K: The geropsychiatrist and the delivery of mental health services in the community. Presented at the 32nd Annual Meeting of the Gerontological Society, Washington, DC, November 1979b.

Solomon K: Haloperidol and the geriatric patient: Practical considerations, in Ayd FJ Jr (ed): *Haloperidol Update: 1958–1980*. Baltimore: Ayd Medical Communications, 1980a, pp 155–173.

Solomon K: Psychosocial crises of older men. Presented at the 133rd Annual Meeting of the American Psychiatric Association, San Francisco, CA, May 7, 1980b.

Solomon, K: Personality disorders and the elderly, in Lion JR (ed): *Personality Disorders: Diagnosis and Management*, ed 2. Baltimore, Williams and Wilkins, 1981a pp 310–338.

Solomon K: The elderly patient, in Spittell JR (ed): *Clinical Medicine, vol 12 Psychiatry*. Hagerstown, MD, Harper and Row, 1981b, pp 1–14.

Solomon K: Geropsychiatry training for senior center staff—Curriculum and process. *Gerontol Geriatr Ed* 1981c;2:9–13.

Solomon K: The older man, in Solomon K, Levy NB (eds): *Men in Transition: Theory and Therapy*. New York, Plenum, in press a.

Solomon K: The roles of the psychiatric resident on a community psychiatry team. *Psychiatric Quarterly,* in press b.

Solomon K, Hart R: Pitfalls and prospects in clinical research on antianxiety drugs. Benzodiazepines and placebo—A research review. *J Clin Psychiatry* 1978;39:823–831.

Solomon K, Vickers R: Attitudes of health workers toward old people. *J Am Geriatr Soc* 1979;27:186–191.

Solomon K, Vickers R: Stereotyping the elderly: Changing the attitudes of clinicians. Presented at the 33rd Annual Meeting of the Gerontological Society of America, San Diego, CA, November 1980.

Solomon K, Zinke MR: Group psychotherapy with the depressed elderly. Presented at the 53rd Annual Meeting of the American Orthopsychiatric Association, New York, NY, March 1981.

Strauss DW, Solomon K: Psychopharmacologic treatment of depression in the elderly. Presented at the 33rd Annual Meeting of the Gerontological Society of America, San Diego, CA, November 1980.

Tuckman J, Lorge I: Attitudes toward old people. *J Soc Psychol* 1953;37:249–260.

Warschawski P: Therapeutic patient and nursing staff groups in a chronic geriatric hospital. Presented at the 53rd Annual Meeting of the American Orthopsychiatric Association, New York, NY, Mar. 1981.

Warschawski P, Spiegel R: Therapeutische patienten- und pflegepersonalgruppen im geriatriespital. *Aktuelle Gerontologie,* 1979;9:329–335.

Weinstock G, Leiff J: The geriatric fellowship: Issues we face and have faced in planning. Presented at the 33rd Annual Meeting of the Gerontological Society of America, San Diego, CA, November 1980.

Wolpe J: *The Practice of Behavior Therapy*. New York, Pergamon Press, 1969.

26 Federal Legislation to Protect the Elderly

Mary Rose Oakar
Carol Ann Miller

Abuse of older persons by family and caregivers has recently been brought to the attention of federal legislators as a national problem demanding legislative action. To provide a perspective on the role of federal legislators in protecting older Americans from abuse, this chapter will review the history of federal legislation related to various aspects of family violence. Additionally, information will be given about the current status of federal legislation to prevent and resolve our national problem of elder abuse.

CHILD ABUSE LEGISLATION

The first aspect of family violence to come to the attention of the American public was child abuse. In 1874 child abuse surfaced as a problem when a concerned neighbor of an abused ten-year-old child, Mary Ellen Wilson, pleaded with Mr. Henry Bergh, founder and president of the American Society for the Prevention of Cruelty to Animals (ASPCA), to come to her aid. This concerned neighbor sought the help of the ASPCA because there were laws to protect animals from mistreatment, but there were no laws to protect children from abuse. Mr. Eldridge T. Gerry, the lawyer who represented the ASPCA on behalf of the child, took the case to the Supreme Court and argued that a child was a member of the animal kingdom, and therefore entitled to the same protections afforded to animals under the law. Mr. Bergh and Mr. Gerry were successful in winning the case of Mary Ellen Wilson, and the child's legal custodian was found guilty of assault and battery. Soon after this case was ended, Mr. Gerry founded the New York Society for the Prevention of Cruelty to Children in December, 1874.

As a result of the publicity generated by the Wilson case, primarily by the *New York Times,* New York enacted this country's first child abuse law. The law authorized "cruelty societies" to file complaints for the violation of any laws related to children and required law enforcement and court officials to aid the societies. Other cities followed the lead of New York, and by 1922 there were 56 Societies for the Prevention of Cruelty to Children. Because of the gradually increasing involvement of government in child welfare, the number of these private organizations has now declined.

In the early 20th century, advances in medical technology contributed to the recognition of child abuse as a widespread social problem. Before 1900 one of the main factors that prevented the prosecution of suspected child abusers was the lack of scientific evidence to determine whether the physical injuries were deliberately caused or accidental. The development of sophisticated techniques in pediatric radiology allowed the detection of abnormal fractures and other injuries caused by deliberate assault.

In 1962, Dr. C. Henry Kemp, a pediatrician in Denver, Colorado, first reported on "The Battered Child Syndrome" in an article published in the *Journal of the American Medical Association.* Dr. Kempe strongly and actively urged the federal government to convene a national conference on child abuse. Following his suggestion, the United States Department of Health and Human Services Children's Bureau convened a national meeting to develop model legislation and propose guidelines for federal legislation dealing with child abuse. Before the national conference, no state had mandatory reporting laws on child abuse and neglect. By 1964, largely as a result of the efforts of the Children's Bureau, 20 states had enacted child abuse legislation.

Child abuse was first brought to public attention as a national social problem in December 1963 by an important broadcasting company in Washington, D.C. A public affairs documentary and editorial by

WMAL radio and television stations emphasized the need to protect children against willful physical abuse. The editorial stated "Until medical reports on suspected abuse cases are mandatory, an accurate count of actual child abuse cases is impossible. However, reliable estimates indicate that 50% of the children who suffer physical harm eventually die from repeated abuse." Further, the editorial urged the introduction of legislation which would mandate reporting of suspected cases of child abuse and grant immunity for doctors who reported cases in the city of Washington, D.C. On January 16, 1964, Representative Abraham J. Multer of New York, a member of the House District Committee, responded to this public plea by introducing H.R. 9652 "to provide for the mandatory reporting by physicians and institutions in the District of Columbia of certain physical abuses of children."

Although this bill was not passed during the 88th session of Congress, it was reintroduced in both the House (Multer, H.R. 3394) and Senate (S 1318) in 1965. On September 30, 1965, a bill (H.R. 10304) similar to the original Multer bill was finally approved by both houses and signed into law.

By 1966, 49 states had endorsed legislation requiring mandatory reporting of physical abuse of children, and by the end of 1977, all 50 states had a mandatory child abuse reporting law. Although laws existed in all states and the District of Columbia aimed at protecting children, very few services were available to prevent or treat those children in need of protective services. As incidences of child abuse became more widely recognized as a serious and widespread national problem, the need for federal legislation and funding became more apparent.

Recognizing the need for federal financial support of programs to provide protective and rehabilitation services for abused children and their parents, Congressman Mario Biaggi of New York introduced the first National Child Abuse Act (H.R. 11584) in 1969. This bill provided for the protection of children under the age of 16 years who were physically injured or threatened with physical injury by those responsible for their care. Additionally, the bill: (1) required mandatory reporting by doctors, teachers, social workers, and welfare workers; (2) made failure to report a misdemeanor; (3) granted immunity to any persons filing a report in good faith; and (4) provided for a child identification system through the issuance of Social Security numbers to infants at birth.

The media continued to be influential in focusing attention on the problem of child abuse and the need for additional services and legislation to deal with this serious national problem. The *Detroit News* published a series of articles "Michigan's Battered Babies," in May 1969; and a *New York Times* article in that same month reported a 30% increase in the number of cases of child abuse reported to the New York

State Department of Social Welfare. In November 1969, columnist Jack Anderson described child abuse as a "national scandal that has been kept in the shadows." He cited statistics of the American Humane Society estimating that "10,000 children are beaten, burned, boiled, and deliberately starved in the U.S. each year by parents, relatives and guardians."

Despite continuing public attention to the problem of child abuse, Congress did not act on the National Child Abuse Act for several years. On March 16, 1972, Congressman Biaggi and 26 cosponsors again reintroduced the bill and stated

> the insidious crime of child abuse and neglect by persons responsible for a child's care is the number one cause of death among children under the age of five. . . . In New York City alone the incidence of child abuse rose 549% from 1969 to 1970. This is only a fraction of the total, however, since the majority of these abuses go unreported.

In March and April 1973, Senate hearings were held before the Subcommittee on Children and Youth of the Committee on Labor and Public Welfare. These hearings emphasized the need for federal funds for comprehensive programs to provide protective services for thousands of abused and neglected children. Several members of Congress and expert witnesses at the hearings testified that the legislation was too narrow. One member of Congress pointed out that "there are lots of horrible crimes committed against persons above the age of eighteen. There are lots of old folks being abused" (Rep. David C. Treen, 1973).

On January 31, 1974, the Child Abuse Prevention and Treatment Act (P.L. 93-247) was enacted to provide federal financial assistance for the identification, prevention, and treatment of child abuse and neglect. This act provided for the establishment of a National Center on Child Abuse and Neglect to collect and disseminate information about and incidence of child abuse and neglect. Additionally, it mandated the creation of an Advisory Board on Child Abuse and Neglect to assist the Secretary in developing federal standards for child abuse programs. This federal legislation was effective in prompting changes in state legislation; the number of states eligible for funding under the state grant program increased from 3 in 1974 to 41 in 1980.

In the 1977 Congressional hearings on the "Extension of the Child Abuse Prevention and Treatment Act," the question of the narrow scope of the legislation was raised. Testimony from expert witnesses recommended that the program consider the entire scope of violence in the family. On April 24, 1978, the Child Abuse Prevention Act was amended to extend the authorizations until fiscal year 1982; however, the scope of the legislation was not expanded in any way. The Omnibus Reconciliation Act of July 1981 authorized $7 million for each of the fiscal years 1982 and 1983.

DOMESTIC VIOLENCE BILLS

As American society and legislators began to recognize and deal with the problem of child abuse, it became increasingly evident that abuse of children was only one aspect of family violence. Research and attention to the problem of societal violence in America uncovered statistics such as the following:

Over one million children were abused each year, physically, sexually, or through neglect. About 240,000 children are victims of physical abuse and at least 2000 of them die of their injuries (DHEW, 1978).

In any one year, approximately 1.8 million wives are beaten by their husbands. Over 25% of all American couples engage in at least one violent episode during their relationship (Straus, 1977).

In 1977, nearly 20% of all murder victims in the United States were related to the assailants. About half of these intrafamily murders were husband-wife killings (USDJ, 1977).

In addition to research on family violence, issues related to wife beating have been brought to the attention of the public by the media. This growing awareness of the prevalence and seriousness of family violence prompted action by the federal government. In 1977, during the 95th Congress, bills were introduced in both the House of Representatives and the Senate to establish a federal office on domestic violence and to make grants for shelters and other projects to assist domestic violence victims. The Senate passed their version of the bill, but the House failed to act during the session, and the measure died.

During the 96th Congress, bills were again introduced in both the House and the Senate to provide federal funds for programs to prevent domestic violence, assist victims of domestic violence, and to provide for the coordination of federal programs pertaining to domestic violence. Domestic violence bills were passed in the House and Senate in December 1979 and September 1980, respectively. However, the final conference report was never acted on by the Senate, and the measure again died at the end of the session.

In January 1981, Representative Mario Biaggi of New York introduced the "Domestic Violence Prevention and Services Act" (H.R. 1007) which essentially contained the provisions of the final conference report from the bills acted on but not passed in the 96th Congress. The purposes of this Act are: (1) to increase participation by states, local public agencies, local communities, nonprofit private organizations, and individual citizens in efforts to prevent domestic violence and to provide immediate shelter and other assistance for victims and dependents of victims of domestic violence; (2) to provide technical assistance and training relating to domestic violence programs; (3) to establish a federal interagency council to coordinate federal programs and activities relating to domestic violence; and (4) to provide for information gathering and reporting programs relating to domestic violence. Additionally, this bill would mandate that the Secretary of Health and Human Services conduct a study of the nature and incidence of abuse of elderly individuals. To carry out the purposes of this bill, $65 million would be authorized over a three-year period. This bill was referred to the Committee on Education and Labor, and no hearings had been scheduled as of September 1981.

Congressional Hearings on Elder Abuse

Elder abuse was first brought to the attention of Congress during a House Subcommittee hearing on "Research into Violent Behavior: Domestic Violence," in February 1978. At the hearing in Washington, D.C., Dr. Suzanne Steinmetz cited incidences of the battering of elderly parents by their kin and noted that this is a growing phenomenon. She stated:

> Our knowledge about the battered elderly parent mirrors our knowledge of the extent of child abuse in the early 60s or the extent of our knowledge about wife abuse in the early 70s. If we were to label the 60s as the decade of interest in child abuse, and the 70s as the decade of wife abuse studies, then I predict, given the generally increasing concern for the elderly and more specifically concern of abuse of the elderly in public institutions, that the 80s will be the decade of the Battered Parent.

The first Congressional hearing dealing exclusively with the physical and psychological abuse of older persons was held on June 23, 1979, by the House Select Committee on Aging in Boston, Massachusetts. Representative Robert Drinan, who chaired the hearing, emphasized that little hard information about elder abuse was available and expressed the hope that the hearing would sensitize the public to the extent and seriousness of elder abuse in the United States. Witnesses at the hearing repeatedly pointed to the lack of knowledge about elder abuse as a hindrance in finding solutions. Mr. James Bergman, regional director of the Legal Research and Services for the Elderly in Boston, stated that many cases of abuse remain unreported for various reasons. He speculated that victims of abuse would be more willing to come forward after media attention had been focused on the problem and further legislative hearings were held.

Other witnesses at the hearing on "Elder Abuse: The Hidden Problem" cited examples of elder abuse from the case files of their agencies.

One incident reported by Meg Harari, caseworker at the Family Services Association of Greater Boston, is as follows:

> A typical case is Mrs. X who is 76 years old, physically handicapped, using a walker. Mrs. X lives with a 34-year-old grandson who has a history of drug addiction and alcoholism. He is separated from his wife and children whom he abused. . . . He stole all her money and food and walked out on her. She was referred to us by home care after a report from her homemaker was filed. Mrs. X was given additional homemaker service and financial help. Contact was made with her family and the names on her bank accounts were changed. A week later, the grandson called and Mrs. X welcomed him back, denying that he was anything but an exemplary grandson. It may take months to work out a better life for Mrs. X until she can accept a plan where she is assured the kind of care she needs without being so dependent on the grandson. The worker will also attempt to involve the grandson in counseling and set up liens against his maltreatment of his grandmother.

A second field hearing on "Domestic Violence Against the Elderly" was held by the Subcommittee on Human Services of the House Select Committee on Aging on April 21, 1980, in New York City. In his opening statement, Representative Mario Biaggi, chairman of the Subcommittee, referred to elder abuse as "a burgeoning national scandal." He referred to his previous efforts aimed at the prevention of domestic violence, citing his National Child Abuse and Neglect Prevention and Treatment Act which became law in 1974. He also gave statistics estimating that at least 500,000 persons aged 65 and over who live with younger members of their families are physically abused by them. Additionally, he pointed out that these numbers are conservative, because thousands of cases go unreported each year. Other subcommittee members at the hearing emphasized the need for legislative solutions such as supportive services for the elderly and their families and mandatory reporting of suspected cases of elder abuse.

At the New York hearing on domestic violence against the elderly, victims of elder abuse were witnesses for the first time at a Congressional hearing and gave first-hand accounts. One victim, Mrs. C, stated her case as follows:

> My sister and my nephew were stealing from me and they threw me out of the house. . . . How they happened to come there was because my mother wasn't feeling well and I let my mother into the house, and my brothers to help her. My brother let my sister in to help my mother. My sister started stealing from me and she started abusing me but on account of my mother being sick I couldn't do anything about it. She helped out a little bit, but not much; but then later on when my mother died she stayed there and started robbing me and was going to kill me if I didn't give her money. They threw me out of the house and I had to get the police in there. They broke walls in the house and stole rugs that I had and different things.

My sister hit me and her son hit me and they were trying to get my property and they really came there not to help my mother, they came there to rob me because they had spent all their money, and my sister has a lot of money. I mean, she gets three times more than I have in a month.

My sister stole money and they threatened me they were going to kill me. They threw me out of the house and they were going to kill me if I stayed there. Her son twisted my arm and she hit me. I have a fractured finger because of it. It will never be all right.

When questioned by the members of the subcommittee, Mrs. C stated she was physically assaulted "many times," and that she frequently reported the incidents to the police who "were there almost every day." When asked how she resolved the problem, she said she had to hire a lawyer, because she could not qualify for Legal Aid services due to the fact that she owned a home—although "the house is a very inexpensive place, it was only $2,500." After legal intervention, Mrs. C was able to return to her home, without her relatives; however, she continued to suffer from the physical injuries sustained from her nephew and sister.

One week after the New York hearing, a similar hearing was held in Union, New Jersey. As in previous hearings, emphasis was placed on the need for more information about the problem of elder abuse, as well as legislative solutions to the problem. One of the witnesses at this hearing, Veronica Kane of the New Jersey Federation of Senior Citizens, who was 75 years old, stated: "Abuses of the elderly are many, and they include physical, verbal, and psychological assaults, financial abuse, misuse of money, belongings and property, and violation of their rights as a person." She further pointed out, "We must now realize that children and battered women are not the only family members who take beatings from their loved ones. The battering of aged parents has joined the ranks for many reasons, first to control their behavior, to force their signature on wills, force them to turn over stock and bonds or money in the bank." Veronica Kane, as well as other witnesses, cited numerous examples of abuse of elderly by their caregivers.

In June 1980, the House and Senate Committees on Aging held a joint hearing in Washington, D.C. to explore the problem of elder abuse. Members of the House and Senate cited research and statistics indicating the seriousness of the problem of elder abuse, and suggested various legislative remedies which should be considered. Senator Lawton Chiles opened the hearing by commenting, "I have attended many hearings that have focused on unfortunate problems, but perhaps never have I attended one on a problem as regrettable as elder abuse." Representative Claude Pepper, Chairman of the House Select Committee on Aging, stated that "although the majority of families are doing a good job of caring for their older parents, about 10% of all dependent elderly are abused by their families."

Witnesses at this joint hearing included three victims of elder abuse as well as their counselors or caregivers who helped them deal with the incidence of abuse. One of the victims, Mr. Jones, gave the following account:

> Five years after my wife's death I had to get help to take care of my financial affairs because I could not make the checks out. My son interfered and entered his name on my checking account. After that, he began to not give me any money and I didn't have a chance to get anything to eat . . . I had only one meal a day and I had to live off greens and turkey wings all week and the next week was chicken wings and noodles, which had maggots in them, they finally got sour. I had to fend for myself. My son shoved me over a chair and told me he wasn't going to do anything for me. I told him I was human and don't be doing that to me. He said he didn't care.

Additional examples of elder abuse were cited by caseworkers at agencies which dealt with the problem of elder abuse. Several witnesses described programs that have been implemented to assist abused older persons and their families.

In March and April 1981, the Select Committee on Aging held hearings in Cambridge, Massachusetts and San Francisco, California, in conjunction with the two-site National Conference on Abuse of Older Persons sponsored by the Legal Research Service for the Elderly, under a grant from the Administration on Aging. The March hearing in Cambridge on "Abuse of Older Persons" was held by the Subcommittee on Human Services, and the April hearing in San Francisco was held by the Subcommittee on Retirement Income and Employment. Witnesses at these hearings discussed actual cases of elder abuse as well as recent research on the subject. Additionally, recommendations for federal action were presented as a summary of the conference. The recommendations presented by Mr. James Bergman, Director of the Boston Legal Research and Services for the Elderly, and convener of the National Conference on Abuse of Older Persons were:

1. Federal legislation, such as H.R. 769, is needed to provide financial incentives to the states to pass mandatory elder abuse reporting laws.
2. Research funds are vital to enable medical, mental health, legal, and social science researchers to conduct much more analysis of the nature and scope of the elder abuse problem.
3. Model project funds are vitally needed to develop more elder abuse programs.
4. Current health, social, mental health, and legal services

must not be cut back or eliminated for the very vulnerable victims of elder abuse, neglect and exploitation.

Government Report on Elder Abuse

In addition to the six Congressional hearings on elder abuse, a national study of the problem of elder abuse was carried out by the House Select Committee on Aging. The report of this study, "Elder Abuse: An Examination of a Hidden Problem," was released on April 3, 1981. The report includes hundreds of documented examples of abuse which the Committee received in response to questionnaires sent to police departments, protective service workers, visiting nurses, state agencies, and other organizations. Also included in the report are summaries of studies done in Iowa, Florida, Maine, Maryland, Massachusetts, Michigan, Missouri, New Hampshire, and Ohio on elder abuse. Additionally, theories for why elder abuse exists were presented in the report and results of a survey of state human service departments and state statutes were presented. Finally, recommendations were made for policy alternatives for federal, state, and local governments.

Some of the report's major conclusions are:

- Elder abuse is a full-scale national problem which exists with a frequency and rate only slightly less than that of child abuse.
- An estimated 4% of the nation's elderly, one million older Americans, are victims of some sort of abuse, from moderate to severe, each year.
- While one out of three cases of child abuse is reported, only one out of six cases of elder abuse comes to the attention of the authorities.
- The victims are likely to be very old — 75 or older. Women are more often abused than men. The victims are usually in a position of dependency, ie, they rely on others, often the persons who abuse them, for their care and protection.
- The probable abuser will undoubtedly be experiencing great stress. Alcoholism, drug addiction, marital problems, and long-term financial difficulties are often factors in abuse of older persons.
- The most likely abuser is the son of the victim (21% of cases) followed by the daughter (17% of cases). The third most frequent abuser is the spouse who acts in a caregiver role, with the male spouse more likely to be the abuser than the female spouse.

- Older persons are less likely to report abuse because they are ashamed, do not wish to bring trouble to the family, are afraid of reprisals, or do not have the physical ability to register complaints.

Significant conclusions of the committee survey of the 50 state human service departments and state statutes are:

- 26 states have what they consider to be adult protective service laws, which vary in scope.
- Only 16 of these 26 states also require the mandatory reporting of elder abuse cases.
- An additional 20 states have bills pending in their state legislatures.
- The majority of states agreed that their statutes relating to adult protective services are ineffective and do not meet the needs of abused elders.
- 63% of the states reported that the greatest hindrance to their ability to help the abused elderly was lack of appropriate statutory authority.
- The second most frequent hindrance was lack of skilled staff, community resources, and funding.
- Averaged nationally, only 6.6% of state funds for protective services are spent on services for abused older persons.

Federal Legislation on Elder Abuse

The first federal legislation relating to elder abuse, "The Prevention, Identification, and Treatment of Adult Abuse Bill (H.R. 7551)" was introduced by Representatives Mary Rose Oakar and Claude Pepper on June 10, 1980. In announcing the introduction of this bill, Representative Oakar stated:

This bill will relate not only to the elderly who are often the victims of abuse, neglect, and exploitation, but also to other vulnerable adults such as women and mentally and physically handicapped persons. It is long overdue that the millions of elderly persons who are the victims of abuse and neglect be provided the services and protection to which they are entitled. The deliberate abuse of individuals who are least able to protect themselves is a national disgrace.

The purposes of the Adult Abuse Bill of 1980 (H.R. 7551) were to provide financial assistance for programs of prevention, identification, and treatment of adult abuse, neglect, and exploitation; and to establish a National Center for Adult Abuse. This bill would provide federal funds to states which had mandatory reporting laws and provided for immunity from prosecution for persons reporting incidents of abuse, neglect, and exploitation. Additionally, states must have trained personnel and services available to abused, neglected and exploited adults.

After the Adult Abuse Bill was introduced at a Joint Hearing of the Senate and House Committees on Aging, the bill was referred to the Committees on Interstate and Foreign Commerce, and Education and Labor. No committee action was taken during the 96th Congress, although 39 Members of Congress had cosponsored the bill.

In January 1981, in the beginning of the 97th Congress, Representative Oakar introduced an Elder Abuse Bill (H.R. 769) which was essentially the same as H.R. 7551 except that the provisions were limited to adults over the age of sixty. Although Representative Oakar felt that a comprehensive adult abuse bill was necessary, the original bill was revised and limited to older Americans because much of the opposition to H.R. 7551 was due to the the broad scope of the bill. Additionally, since the Select Committee on Aging was the primary supporter of the legislation, the focus of Congressional hearings had been limited to elder abuse.

The Elder Abuse bill was referred jointly to the Committees on Education and Labor and Energy and Commerce in January 1981. The Congressional Budget Office estimated that federal funding to support this legislation would be $4.5 million in 1982 and would increase to $12.5 million by 1986. Although neither committee held hearings on H.R. 769, there were approximately 50 cosponsors by September, 1981.

Legislation Needed to Prevent Elder Abuse

Although little research has been done to identify the causes of elder abuse, it has been found that the caregivers who abuse dependent persons are often experiencing a high degree of stress as a result of the dependency relationship. Because there are so few community supports to assist the older persons who choose to remain in their own homes, the burden of caring for elderly persons is left to the family and friends. The Select Committee on Aging has found that 80% of the care given to older persons in the community is provided by family and friends.

This lack of support systems and the long-lasting responsibility on a caregiver often results in heavy financial and emotional strains. Legislation is necessary to provide a system of supports which will relieve some of the strain presently felt by caregivers who provide services to older persons.

Additional home health care services, such as homemaker/chore services, adult day care centers, respite care, temporary full-time nursing services, and home delivered meals must be provided to those older persons who wish to remain in the community. Preventive and rehabilitative counseling should be available to assist families and friends who care for older persons. Tax credits should be given to persons who care for a dependent adult in their own homes. Foster care homes, emergency housing shelters, and safe housing alternatives must be made available to older persons who do not have adequate housing and need supportive services. Low interest loans should be made available to persons who need to adapt or expand their homes to accommodate a dependent person. Persons who receive SSI payments should not be penalized by a reduction in benefits if they reside with someone who provides in-kind services.

The Budget Reconciliation Act for the 1982 Federal Budget allows states to provide home-based care as an alternative to institutional care for chronically ill individuals. Services such as respite care, adult day care, homemaker/home health aide, nursing care and other support services could be covered by Medicaid, as long as the cost of these services did not exceed the cost of institutional care. These community-based services would be one step toward providing support to the families and other caregivers who now provide 80% of home-based care to elderly persons who live in the community.

BIBLIOGRAPHY

Anderson J: Grand jury investigates abuse of helpless children in institutions. *New York Daily News,* November 24, 1969. Reprinted in the *Congressional Record—House.* 91st Congress, 1st Session. November 25, 1969, p 35866.

Biaggi M: Legislation to curb child abuse. *Congressional Record—House.* 92nd Congress, 2nd Session. March 16, 1972, p 8801.

Carlton R, O'Brien K: Michigan's battered babies: Are they the victims of their parents' rage? Of social workers snarled in red tape? Or of a society that doesn't care? *Detroit News* May 1979.

Carlton R, O'Brien K: Abused children take a beating: Children get hurt while social workers fight legal forms, red tape. *Detroit News* May 1969.

Carlton R: Battered baby rescued by social worker: A 53-hour drama. *Detroit News* May 1969.

Carlton R: Abused children: Their parents were abused kids. *Detroit News* May 1969.

Carlton R: Battered babies: Lots of organizations but tragically little service. *Detroit News* May 1969.

Carlton R: Battered babies: Victims of their parents or of society? *Detroit News* May 1969.

Chiles L: Joint Hearing before the Special Committee on Aging, United States

Senate and the Select Committee on Aging, United States House of Representatives: Elder abuse. June 11, 1980, p 2.

Kemp CH: The battered child syndrome. *JAMA* 1962;181:17-24.

Pepper C: Joint Hearing before the Special Committee on Aging, United States Senate and the Select Committee on Aging, United States House of Representatives: Elder abuse. June 11, 1980, p 6.

Rusk HA: Rise in Child abuse: Problem requires more trained help, more funds and the cooperation of all. *New York Times* May 1969. Reprinted in the *Congressional Record—House,* 91st Congress, 1st Session. May 27, 1969, p 14136.

Steinmetz SK: Overlooked aspects of family violence: Battered husbands, battered siblings and battered elderly. Testimony presented to the United States House Committee on Science and Technology, February 15, 1978.

Straus MA: Wife beating: How common and why? *Victimology: An International Journal* 1977;2:445.

Treen DC: National center on child abuse and neglect. *Congressional Record—House.* 93rd Congress, 1st Session. December 3, 1973, p 39231.

United States Department of Health, Education and Welfare: New light on an old problem. DHEW 1978, p 5.

United States House of Representatives, Select Committee on Aging: Elder abuse: The hidden problem. Boston, MA, June 23, 1979, pp 24-25.

United States House of Representatives, Select Committee on Aging, Subcommittee on Human Services: Domestic abuse of the elderly. Union, NJ, April 28, 1980, p 26.

United States House of Representatives, Select Committee on Aging, Subcommittee on Human Services: Abuse of older persons. Cambridge, MA, March 23, 1981, p 14.

United States House of Representatives, Select Committee on Aging. Elder abuse: An examination of a hidden problem. April 3, 1981.

United States Department of Justice: FBI uniform crime reports: Crime in the United States, 1977. October 18, 1978, p 9.

Abandonment, 139, 298
Abuse
  conceptual definitions of, 122–124
  Connecticut protective services program
    on, 297
  definition of, 152
  domestic, 115–132
  elderly women and, 221, 224
Accidents, automobile, 240
ACTION, 331
Administration on Aging (AOA), 308,
    430
  advocacy and, 342–343
  anticrime programs and, 324, 331
Adult Abuse Bill of 1980, 432–433
Adult day care workers, 125, 126, 128
Adult protective services, see Protective
    services
Advocacy, 326
  case study of, 340–353
  community involvement and, 349–350
  definition of, 339
  lobbying by, 337, 340
  maltreatment and, 348–349
  neglect and, 346–347
  nurses and, 397
  nursing homes and, 339–353
  physical abuse and, 347–348
  problem resolution of, 345–349
  psychological abuse and, 347
  public policy and, 350–351
  quality of care monitoring by, 344–345
Age
  black elderly abuse and, 196–197
  fear of crime and, 28, 29, 31, 34
  nursing home residents and, 89
  stress in family and, 141
  risk of crime and, 44, 46, 48, 64
Age Discrimination Act of 1975, 305
Alcoholism, 265
  black family abuse and, 197
  domestic abuse and, 119, 126, 139, 398
  nursing homes and, 99
Alienation, 165
Alzheimer's disease, 150, 175
American Association of Retired Persons,
    328
American Bar Association, 310, 322
Anger, 165
Anomie, 165
Anticrime programs, 316–332
  components of, 319–322
  crime prevention concept in, 318–319
  elderly women and, 229–231

fear of crime and, 32
neighborhood, 255
opportunity reduction in, 319
public housing and, 255, 256–257, 259
resources in, 331–332
trends in, 329–331
victim assistance programs and, 322–329
Anxiety, 406
Arbitration, 312
Arteriosclerosis, 175
Arthritis, 238–239
Arthritis Foundation, 73, 239
Assault
  fear of, 27
  National Crime Survey (NCS) on, 42,
    44, 45
Attorneys, 157
Automobile accidents, 240
Automobile theft, 42, 56
Avoidance behavior, 30–31

Bank examiner scheme, 225–226
Behavior
  criminal incidents and changes in, 63
  fear of crime and, 21, 24–25
  institutionalization and, 94
  learned helplessness in nursing homes
    and, 97–99
  physician in identification of problems
    in, 151–152
  victims and limitations on, 10–11, 63
Benzodiazepines, 406
Bias, antiage, 172, 173
Black American elderly, 187–202
  age, sex, health, and income of, 196–
    197
  alcoholism, drug addiction, and mental
    health problems and, 197
  characteristics of, 196–197
  crime risk and, 47, 48, 49
  family-kin-community factors in, 192–
    196, 199–200
  family violence and, 188–189
  fear of crime and, 25, 27
  high crime neighborhoods and, 191–192
  incidence of abuse of, 188–190
  multigenerational households and, 192–
    193
  non-nuclear family members and, 193
  nursing home residency by, 90
  poverty and, 191
  precipitating factors in abuse of, 197,
    198–199
  risk factors for abuse of, 190–197

societal variables affecting, 191–192
stress and, 198–199
systems model for, 190–191
treatment and prevention and, 197–201
value systems and rates of abuse of, 195–196
women as household heads and, 191
Block clubs, 321, 328
Blood-feud, 5, 6
Blue Cross–Blue Shield, 180
Boiler room operation, 73
Bone fractures, 239
Bureaucracy, governmental, 7
Burglary, 42
elderly women and, 221, 222, 225
fear of, 27

Cerebrovascular arteriosclerosis, 175
Cerebrovascular accident (CVA), 236–238
Child abuse 2, 120, 188–189
community intervention in family and, 382–383
later parent abuse and, 268
legislation on, 422–425
Child Abuse Prevention and Treatment Act, 425
Child Abuse Protection Act, 425
Children Anonymous, 383
Christianity, 5, 6
Chronic illness, 235
Health Maintenance Organization (HMO) and, 174
nursing homes and, 88
Cities, see Inner cities; Urban areas
Class, and criminal justice system, 11
Cleveland Protective Services for Old Persons program, 210–211
Collective responsibility, 5–6
Commission on Legal Problems of the Elderly, 310
Commodities fraud, 72–73
Commodities Futures Trading Commission (CFTC), 82
Community
advocacy in nursing homes and, 349–350
black elderly abuse and, 192–196, 199–200
crime prevention services in, 317
elderly women and, 221, 230–231
fear of crime and, 27, 33
nurses in, 401–402
risk of crime and, 64
Community Anticrime Program (LEAA), 254
Community intervention, see Interventions
Community mental health centers, 150–151
Community Mental Health Centers Act, 305

Community Services Administration, 324, 331
Community Service Society, 381
Compensation programs, 3–4, 324, 330–331
early work in, 3, 7
elderly women and, 230
insurance and, 4
Confidence games, 225–227, 265
Conflicts
resolution techniques for, 146–147
role reversals in families and, 137, 212–213, 243
Connecticut, 292–302
case resolution in, 301–302
ombudsman program in, 292–294, 298–301
protective services in, 294–296
types of abuse in, 296–298
Connecticut Elderly Protective Services Law, 139
Consent, in intervention, 285
Conservator, 283, 295; see also Guardianship
Consumer advocacy, see Advocacy
Consumer fraud, 227
Consumer laws, 111
Contextual family therapy model, 357–358
Control, in nursing homes, 95–100
Coping, 165–166, 240, 418
Costs
guardianship, 285
medical care, 176, 179
Counseling, 312
families of physically disabled and, 245–246
peer, 329–330
victim assistance programs with, 324, 326, 329–330, 331
Counselors, and domestic abuse, 125, 127–128
Criminal justice system
bureaucratic government and, 7
case monitoring in, 321–322
collective responsibility concept in, 5–6
historical perspective on, 4–7
neighborhood dispute resolution and, 313
nursing home fraud and, 114
victim and, 2, 4, 11, 66
Crime
black elderly abuse and, 191–192
consequences of, 54–58
data on, 41, 42–43
elderly women and impact of, 229
fear of, see Fear of crime
injuries from, 54, 55
juvenile offenders in, 51–52, 53

limit on victim's behavior and, 10–11, 63
medical attention needed after, 54–55
multiple offenders in, 52–53
multivariate analysis of seriousness of, 57–58
offender profile in, 50–54
personal crimes in, 40–66
physical and financial consequences of, 21, 23–24
profile of incident in, 49–54
programs to combat, see Anticrime programs
public housing and, 251–252
reactions to incident of, 58–60
reporting of, see Reporting
research on 8–11
risk of, 44–49
time and place of occurrence of, 50
victim as integral part of, 1–2, 3
victim-offender relationship in, 50–54
vulnerability of elderly and, 264
work loss due to, 55
Crime Control Act of 1976, 230
Crime insurance, 230
Crime rates, 1, 41
selected variables in, 44, 46–48
Crisis intervention, 326
drugs in, 403–406
psychotherapy in, 406–409
Cross-cultural studies of crime, 26–27

Day care workers, 125, 126, 128
Day treatment centers, 156
Death and dying
acceptance of, 177–178
geriatrician and, 177–178
Death rates
nursing homes and, 93–94, 96, 205
relocation and, 94
Deinstitutionalization, 151, 306
Dementia, 150, 175, 214, 238, 242, 301
Denial of disability, 242
Dental students, 156, 157
Department of Health and Human Services, 80, 105, 114, 309
Department of Health, Education and Welfare (HEW), 336
Department of Housing and Urban Development, 254, 259, 331
Department of Justice, 114, 230
Department of Labor, 78
Dependency, 208–210
categories of, 142, 144–145, 208
intervention and, 407
multigenerational family and, 137–138
physical disability and, 240
solutions to, 209

stages of, 142, 143
stereotyping by health professionals and, 159
stress and, 142–145
Depression, 150, 207, 241, 398
drugs for, 406
health worker abuse and, 159, 165, 166
hospitalization and, 181
nursing homes and, 91, 96, 98
physical illness and, 207, 237, 238, 239
stereotyping by health professionals and, 159
Diagnosis, 174–175
Dietitians, 181
Dispute resolution, 312–314
Dispute Resolution Act, 312
Distributorship fraud, 72
Domestic neglect and abuse, 115–132
causes of, 124–128
characteristics of individual and family in, 269–270
conceptual definitions of abuse in, 122–124
conflict-resolution techniques and, 146–147
cycle of violence and, 268
generational inversion and, 136–139
incidence of, 116, 118, 139
legislation on, 426–434
mental health counselors and, 127–128
middle-aged caregivers and, 134–138
parent-child conflicts in, 137
physically disabled and, 235–236
recent research and studies on, 116–122
response system for, 128–132
risk for, 122
service providers and, 148
stress and dependence and, 137–138
Drug addiction
black family abuse and, 197
domestic abuse and, 119, 126, 139
Drugs for elderly, 350
crisis intervention and, 404–405
inappropriate prescription of, 158
nursing homes and, 89, 111–112
Due process, 306

Ebenezer Society, 381
Economic abuse
health workers and, 152–153
intervention and, 417
Economic consequences of crime, 21, 23–24.
Economic dependency, 208
Economic stress, and domestic abuse, 119, 126, 138, 139
Education
for families, 381–382

fear of crime and, 28–30
of nurses, 402
of patient in hospital, 399–400
risk of crime and, 44, 47, 48
Elderly
economic productivity and, 135
increasing number of, 134–135
victimology and, 12–14
Emergencies, and guardianship, 288, 289
Emergency Department Nurses Association, 392
Emergency rooms
abuse of elderly in, 159
domestic abuse seen in, 127, 128
Emotional dependence, 138
Emotional stress
caregiving in family and, 379
domestic abuse and, 119, 126, 138
Employment Retirement Income Security Act (ERISA), 78
Environmental factors
advocacy and, 347
anticrime programs with, 322
fear of crime and, 33–34
public housing and, 257–261
Escort services, 321
Estate planning, 305
Ethnic factors, 267
Exchange theory, 162–163
Exploitation of elderly, 139, 298
Extended care facilities, 205

Family
abuse of elderly within, see Domestic abuse and neglect
assessment of, 271
black elderly abuse and organization of, 192–196
burden of caregiving in, 378–379
caregiving function of, 361, 378–381
child abuse and later parent abuse in, 268
as closed system, 266
cost of abuse to, 269
counseling for, 245–246
crisis intervention and, 408
educational programs for, 381–382
failure to report abuse and, 267–268
hospitalization of elderly and, 181–182
increased longevity of family and, 136
intervention training and, 417–418
Medicaid billing in nursing home and, 106
mentally disabled elderly and, 211–214
multigenerational, see Multigenerational family
pairing of volunteers with, 382–383
physically disabled and, 211–214, 235,

241–243, 245–246
protective services for, 272–273
race and violence in, 188–189
role reversals and, 243–244, 270–271
skills for caregiving in, 379–380
support systems for, 272–273, 380, 381–382
training programs for, 215–216
vulnerability of elderly and, 263–274
Family/Friends Support Project, 381
Family Service Association of Greater Lawrence (Massachusetts), 139
Family therapy, 409
clinical gerontology and, 356–359
contextual family therapy model in, 357–358
elderly person's right to define own needs in, 365
problem-centered system and, 358–359
task-centered approach in, 355–374
Family violence, see Domestic neglect and abuse
Fast food franchises, 71–72
Fear, 165
Fear of crime, 15, 21–36, 41
age and, 28
anticrime programs and, 32
avoidance behavior and, 30–31
city size and, 27
community integration and, 27
correlates and causes of, 25–32
cultural factors in, 26–27
elderly women and, 221, 229, 231–232
fear of inability to recover from crime and, 31–32
future research on, 35
importance of, for elderly, 251
income, education, and race and, 28–30
neighborhood and, 27
perceived vulnerability and, 31, 32
physical and financial consequences of crime and, 23–24
psychological and behavioral consequences of crime and, 24–25
public housing and, 27
reducing, 32–34
risk for victimization and, 21, 22–23
sex and, 28
social isolation and, 65
vulnerability and, 251–252
Federal Bureau of Investigation (FBI), 80, 113, 114
Federal Crime Insurance Program, 229–230
Federal Emergency Management Agency (FEMA), 230
Federal Trade Commission, 71, 76, 82, 111

Feuds, 5, 6
Filial maturity, 213
Financial abuse
  elderly women and, 229
  nursing homes and, 345
Financial consequences of crime, 21,
  23–24
Food service, hospital, 181
Fractures, 239
Franchise fraud, 71–72
Fraud, 68–83, 265
  commodities in, 72–73
  distributorships in, 72
  elderly women and, 221, 222, 225–227
  franchises and, 71–72
  funeral abuses in, 75–77
  hearing aids and, 77–78
  home improvement schemes in, 74–75
  insurance frauds in, 81
  jurisdiction over, 82
  land fraud in, 74
  medical quackery and, 73–74
  Medicare and Medicaid in, 79–80
  nursing homes and, 104–114
  pension funds and, 78–79
  risk for, 23
  securities and, 71
  solutions to, 82–83
  types of, 70–81
  work at home schemes in, 70–71
Funeral abuses, 75–77

General Accounting Office (GAO), 105,
  108, 109
Geriatricians, 172–182
  acceptance of, 173
  Diagnostic Profile used by, 174–175
  dying and death and, 177–178
  hospital and, 180–182
  Medicare and, 178–180
  obligation of, 173
  physical examination and, 174–175
Gerontology, and family therapy, 356–359
Gestalt therapy, 409
Government, and criminal justice system,
  7
Gray Panthers, 408
Groups
  mutual help, 386
  psychotherapy, 409
Guardianship, 283–291, 306
  choice of guardians in, 288
  Connecticut protective services program
    with, 295, 296
  consequences of, 284–285
  cost of, 285
  emergencies and, 288, 289
  incompetence definitions in, 283, 287–288

issues in, 283–285
  legislative reform in, 285–291

Health, Education and Welfare (HEW)
  Department, 336
Health insurance, 55
  elderly women and, 227
  fraud in, 79–81
Health Maintenance Organization (HMO),
  173–174
Health professionals, 150–167
  attitudes toward elderly of, 154–157
  coping abilities and, 165–166
  economic victimization by, 152–153
  exchange theory and, 162–163
  family in elderly abuse and, 266
  identifying and assessing problems in
    elderly by, 151–152
  impact of victimization on, 158–160
  intervention and, 410–418
  learned helplessness in elderly and,
    160–161
  patronizing attitude of, 159
  physical victimization by, 157–158
  psychologic effects of abuse on elderly
    and, 160–166
  role victimization by, 153–154
  sick role and, 163
  stereotyping of elderly by, 154–155,
    158, 159, 160, 163–164
  victimization of elderly by, 152–158
Health status
  after age 70, 135
  black elderly abuse and, 196–197
  fear of crime and, 30
  nursing home residents and, 88–89
Hearing aid fraud, 77–78
Hearings, guardianship, 283–285, 288,
  289
Helplessness, 407
  health care workers and, 160–161
  learned, 97–99, 160–161
  nursing homes and, 97–99
  stereotyping by health professionals
    and, 159
Hip fractures, 239
Historical perspectives
  involuntary intervention in, 280–282
  nursing homes in, 85–86
  victim in, 4–8
Home improvement fraud, 74–75
Homes for the aged, see Nursing homes
Homicide, 221, 222
Hospitals and hospitalization, 391–402
  abuse of elderly in, 159
  crime reporting and, 62
  criminal attacks and, 54–55
  discharge planning in, 399

geriatric medicine and, 180–182
domestic abuse seen in, 127, 128
nurse's role in, 397–401
patient education in, 399–400
House calls, 174, 176
House of Representatives, 271
House Select Committee on Aging, 433
frauds and, 68, 69, 70, 78
Health Maintenance Organization
(HMO) before, 173–174
hearings on elder abuse before, 427–430
Medicare and, 172, 178
nursing homes and, 104, 105, 113–114
report on elder abuse from, 431–432
Housing and Community Development
Amendments of 1980, 230
Housing and Urban Development Depart-
ment (HUD), 254, 259
Housing, public, *see* Public housing
Human services workers, 273; *see also*
Health professionals

Income
black family abuse and, 191, 196–197
fear of crime and, 28–30
risk of crime and, 44, 47, 48
Incompetency definitions, 283, 287–288,
289
Infantilization of elderly, 160
Injuries
from crime, 54, 55
disability in elderly from, 239–240
Inner cities
anticrime programs in, 317
blacks in, 194
fear of crime and, 25, 27
victimization risk and, 21, 22
see also Urban areas
Institutionalization, 150, 376
black elderly abuse and, 195
deaths and, 205
physically disabled and, 246
see also Nursing homes
Insurance, 305
compensation programs with, 4
see also Health insurance
Intergenerational family, *see* Multigenerational family
Internal Revenue Service, 109
Intervention, 214–216, 277–434
advocacy and, 352
black elderly and, 198
client consent for, 285
at community level, 376–388
domestic abuse and, 129
emergencies in, 288, 289
family support systems in, 381–383
guardianship and, 283–285

health professionals and, 410–418
historical development of, 280–282
least needed restriction used in, 286
legislative reform in, 285–291
limits of governmental power in, 290
long-term, 409
mutual help groups and, 386
natural helpers in, 377–378
neighbors in, 385
networks in, 376–377
ombudsman programs in, 292–294
pairing volunteers with families at
risk in, 382–383
physically disabled and, 246
reporting in, 384
strategies for, 383–387
task-centered approach in, 355–374
training in, 411–418
see also Protective services
Isolation
black family violence and, 193, 200
caregivers' feelings of, 242
elderly women and, 221
family therapy and, 360
family violence and, 270
vulnerability of elderly and, 264
Italian Americans, 267

Justice Department, 114, 230
Justice system, *see* Criminal justice system
Justice System Improvement Act of 1979,
230
Juvenile offenders, 51–52, 53

Land fraud, 74
Larceny, 42, 44, 45
Law Enforcement Assistance Administration (LEAA), 230
neighborhood dispute resolution programs of, 312
public housing and, 254
victim assistance programs and, 322,
324
Laws and legislation, 422–434
adult protective services and, 272–273
advocacy and, 351, 352
child abuse and, 422–424
domestic violence under, 426–434
due process and, 306
historical evolution of, 4
intervention and, 285–291
need for, 271–272, 272–273, 433–434
neighborhood dispute resolution and,
312–314
nursing homes and, 306–307
overview of, 303–307
reform in, 8
Law schools, 310

Learned helplessness, 97–99, 160–161
Legal Aid Society, 343
Legal Research Service for the Elderly, 430
Legal services, 307–312
    definition of, 307–308
    fees in, 310–311
    private bar and, 310–312
    pro bono basis in, 310
    public bar and, 308–310
    services available in, 308–312
    types of services and tasks under, 308
Legal Services Corporation, 308–309
Legislation, see Laws and legislation
Life-support systems, 175, 178
Living will, 290
Long-term care facility, 86–87; see also
    Nursing homes
Loss, 165, 238
Low-income families, 228

Mail fraud, 70, 73–74, 227
Maltreatment
    advocacy in nursing homes and, 348–349
    conceptual definitions of, 122–124
Marital status
    fear of crime and, 30
    nursing home residents and, 89, 90
    risk of crime and, 45–49, 64
Marital therapy, 409
Media, 231, 245
    child abuse and, 424–425
    fear of crime and, 22, 24
Mediation, 312
Medicaid, 175, 303, 304, 305, 401
    advocacy in nursing homes and, 345, 351
    buying and selling nursing homes and, 109–110
    costs unrelated to patient care billed under, 106–107
    dummy invoices in, 109
    fraud in, 79–80
    kickbacks in nursing homes and, 112
    Medicare duplicate payments and, 108
    nursing homes and, 104–105, 106–109, 306, 336, 337
    nursing home therapy charges under, 111
    payments for discharged or dead patients under, 108–109
    payroll padding with, 107–108
    pharmaceutical charges in nursing homes and, 112
    supplements from family to nursing home and, 106
    unreported income and costs in, 108

Medical abuse of elderly, 152
Medical fraud, 23
Medical insurance, see Health insurance
Medical quackery, 73–74, 227, 265
Medical schools, 412
    attitude toward elderly of students in, 155–156, 157
    geriatric patient and, 173, 179
Medicare, 153, 159, 173, 178–180, 303, 304, 401, 418
    buying and selling nursing homes and, 110
    costs of medical care and, 173, 175, 176
    costs of senior citizens of, 179
    coverage with, 178–179
    factors influencing, 179–180
    fraud and, 79–80
    geriatricians and, 179–180
    kickbacks in nursing homes and, 113
    nursing home abuse of, 153, 337
Medication, see Drugs for elderly
Men
    fear of crime by, 28, 29, 31
    see also Sex
Mental dependency, 208
Mental health counselors, 125, 127–128
Mental health problems, and abuse of elderly, 197
Mentally impaired elderly, 206–208, 211–214
Mexican-Americans, 196
Minority groups, 267; see also Black American elderly
Missouri Division on Aging, 364–367
Mobility, and family stress, 138
Multigenerational family, 136–139, 268–269
    black elderly abuse and, 192–193
    contextual family therapy model and, 357
    stress and dependency in, 137–138
    support systems for, 382
Murder, 26

National Center for Adult Abusers, 271–272
National Child Abuse Act, 424
National Coalition for Nursing Home Reform, 343, 351
National Council of Senior Citizens, 316, 328
National Crime Survey (NCS), 23, 24, 42–43
    National Sample and Cities Sample in, 42
    offender characteristics from, 51–52
    risk of personal victimization taken from, 44–49

National Elderly Victimization Prevention and Assistance Program, 328, 330
National Support Program, New York City, 380, 381
Neglect
  advocacy and, 346–347
  conceptual definitions of, 122–124
  Connecticut protective services on, 297–298
  domestic, 115–132, 139
Neighborhoods
  black elderly abuse and, 191–192, 194–195, 200
  community interventions with, 377, 378, 385
  dispute resolution in, 312–314
  fear of crime and, 27
  public housing and, 253–255
  risk of crime and, 54
  watch programs in, 321
Networks, 200, 376–377
  natural helpers in, 377–378, 381, 383–384
Nurses, 391–402, 411
  as advocate, 397
  attitudes toward elderly of, 155, 157
  awareness of abuse by, 393
  community health care and, 401–402
  discharge planning and, 399
  education of, 402
  geriatric medicine and, 180, 182
  hospital and role of, 397–401
  identification of patient's problem by, 398
  outpatient clinics and, 402
  patient education and, 399–400
  physically disabled and, 246
  recognition of abuse by, 393–394
  reporting by, 394–396
  resources available to, 400–401
  survey of, 392–397
Nursing homes, 84–101, 335, 339
  abuse of elderly in, 159–160
  advocacy in, 339–353
  attitudes toward elderly in, 156
  blacks in, 195
  buying and selling abuses in, 109–110
  causes of substandard conditions in, 88
  characteristics of residents of, 88–90
  civil rights of elderly in, 345–346
  consumerism in, 339–340
  control and choice by elderly in, 95–100
  cutting expenses for profits in, 110–111
  deaths in, 205
  detrimental effects of, 91
  fraud in, 104–114
  free market and, 338

"giving-up, given-up" complex in, 92–93
  growth of, 335–336
  hidden charges in, 111
  historical background to, 85–86
  impact of institutionalization in, 90–94
  issues in, 337–338
  kickbacks in, 112–113
  learned helplessness in, 97–99
  legal problems with, 306–307
  long-term care facility definition in, 86–87
  Medicaid and, 307
  medical abuses in, 104–105, 106–109
  Medicare coverage of, 179
  Medicare fraud by, 153
  ombudsmen in, 309
  organized crime in, 87, 113–114
  passivity in, 96–97
  pharmaceutical charge frauds in, 111–112
  predictors of death in, 93–94
  privacy and territoriality in, 92
  quality of care in, 307, 344–345
  reform strategies for, 338–340
  self-destructive behavior and, 99–100
  symptoms, development, and prognosis of institutionalization in, 92, 93
  theft of patients' funds in, 105–106
  therapy charge frauds in, 111
  training in intervention and, 418
  transfer trauma and, 307
  unionization in, 338

Obesity, 99
Occupational therapists, 111, 113
Older Americans Act, 309–310
Ombudsmen
  Connecticut program with, 292–294, 298–301
  nursing homes and, 309
Omnibus Crime Control and Safe Streets Act of 1968, 230
Operation Identification, 320
Organic brain disease, 206–207
Organized crime
  nursing homes and, 87, 113–114
  pension fraud and, 78–79
Osteoarthritis, 239

Panic, 166
Parentification of elderly, 160
Parents Anonymous, 383
Passivity, and nursing homes, 95, 96–97
Patient education, 399–400
Peer counseling, 329–330
Personal crime, see Crime
Pharmaceuticals, see Drugs for elderly
Pharmacies, 114
Phobia, 166

Physical abuse
  advocacy in nursing homes and, 347–348
  domestic, 116, 139
  health professionals and, 157–158
  intervention training and, 417
Physical consequences of crime, 21, 23–24
Physical dependency, 138, 208
Physical examination, and geriatrician, 174–175, 177
Physically disabled, 204–205, 234–238
  abuse of, 234–238
  arthritis and, 238–239
  characteristics of, 240–241
  depression and, 207
  diabetes and, 238
  elderly women and, 221, 228
  family interactions with, 211–214, 241–243
  government programs and, 305–307
  incidence of abuse against, 236
  injuries and, 239–240
  recommendations for dealing with, 245–246
  social issues and, 243–245
  stroke and, 236–238
Physical stress, and abuse, 119, 126, 138
Physical therapists, 111, 113
Physicians, 151, 382
  abuse of elderly by, 159
  identifying and assessing problems of elderly and, 151–152
  physically disabled and, 246
Pigeon drop scheme, 225, 226–227
Police
  anticrime programs and, 320
  crime reporting and, 60–63
  domestic abuse and, 125, 127
  training for, 328
  victim and, 2
  victim assistance programs and, 324, 325–326
Policy, see Public policy
Political activity, 229
Postal Service, 73–74, 81, 82
Poverty, 307
  black elderly abuse and, 191
  crime and, 191–192
Prepaid health plans, 114
Prevention
  black family abuse and, 197–201
  crime and, see Anticrime programs
  domestic abuse and, 129
Primal therapy, 409
Privacy, in nursing homes, 92
Problem-centered systems family therapy, 358–359, 362, 363
Problem solving, within family, 146–147

Progressive Farmers Association (PFA), 71
Project-Be-My-Guest, 385
Property-marking programs, 320, 328
Protective services, 210–211, 272–273, 279–291
  attitude toward elderly in, 157
  characteristics of, 279–280
  Connecticut programs in, 292–302
  consequences of using, 60
  definition of, 279
  domestic abuse and, 130–132
  family and, 266
  need for, 294
  as reaction to criminal incident, 59–60
Protestantism, 6
Psychiatrists, 411
  attitude toward elderly by, 156, 157, 159
Psychiatry, 159
Psychoanalysis, 409
Psychoanalytic psychology, 357, 409
Psychological abuse
  advocacy in nursing homes and, 347
  coping abilities and, 165–166
  domestic, 116
  health workers and, 160–166
  learned helplessness and, 97–99, 160–161
  self-destructive behavior in nursing homes and, 99–100
  sick role and, 163
  stereotyping of elderly and, 163–164
Psychological consequences of crime, and fear of crime, 21, 24–25, 33
Psychological costs of abuse, 269
Psychological dependence, 138
Psychological problems
  institutionalization and, 94
  physician in identification of, 151–152
Psychologists, 246
Psychotherapy
  crisis intervention with, 406–409
  for elderly, 155
  nursing home charges for, 111
Public health, and nurses, 401
Public Health Service Act, 305
Public housing, 251–261
  age segregation in, 254–255, 256–257
  anticrime programs in, 320, 321
  crime in, 251–252
  elderly women and, 228
  environmental design and, 257–261
  fear of crime and, 27
  neighborhood self-help programs and, 253–255
  surveillance programs in, 258, 260
  territorial reinforcement in, 260

446

vulnerability of elderly in, 251-252
Public Housing Security Program, 230
Public policy
    advocacy and, 350-351
    public housing and, 253
Purse snatching, 221, 222, 223-224

Quality of care in nursing homes, 307,
    344-345
Quality of life
    crime and, 33, 41
    elderly and, 136

Race
    family violence and, 188-189
    fear of crime and, 28-30
    incidence of elder abuse and, 189-190
    nursing home residents and, 89-90
    offender characteristics and, 52, 53
    risk of crime and, 47, 49, 64
    types of victimization by, 221-222
Rage, 165
Rape and attempted rape
    elderly women and, 221, 222-223
    National Crime Survey (NCS) on, 42,
        44, 45
Reagan administration, 309
Religion, 3
Reporting, 60-63, 65, 352, 376
    failure in, 267-268
    medical treatment and, 61-62
    nurses and, 394-396
    reasons for failure in, 62-63
    training programs for, 384
Research
    domestic neglect and abuse in, 116-122
    limitations and risks of, 11-12
    victimology and, 8-12
Revenge, 5
Rheumatoid arthritis, 239
Risk
    black elderly abuse and, 190-197
    elderly women and, 228
    fear of crime and, 21, 22-23
    variations in, 64
Robbery
    elderly women and, 221, 222
    fear of, 27
    National Crime Survey (NCS) on, 42,
        44, 45
Roles
    adult caregiver and reversals in, 212-
        213, 243-244
    sick, 163, 241
    vulnerability of elderly and, 270-271
Rural areas, 299
    blacks in, 194
    risk of crime for, 44, 46

Sacrifice, 3
Schizophrenia, 207-208
Securities and Exchange Commission, 82
Securities fraud, 71
Security programs, in housing, 320
Self-destructive behavior, 99-100
Self-esteem, 165
Self-help programs, 253-255
Senate, 337
Senate Committee on Aging, 433
    hearings before, 429-430
    nursing home fraud in, 80, 88, 105,
        106, 108, 112
Senate Committee on Labor and Public
    Welfare, 425
Senate Permanent Subcommittee on In-
    vestigations, 78
Senate Subcommittee on Long-Term
    Care, 104, 110
Senility, 89, 159
Senior Block Information Service, 385
Senior Citizen Action Network (SCAN),
    253
Senior citizen centers, 151, 385
Sex
    black elderly abuse and, 196-197
    fear of crime and, 28, 29, 31, 34
    nursing home residency and, 89
    risk of crime and, 47, 48, 49, 64
    types of victimization by, 221-222
Sick role, 163, 241
Social consequences of crime, 24, 63, 64-
    65
Social costs of abuse, 269
Social dependency, 208
Social engineering, 8
Social gerontology, 356
Social isolation, see Isolation
Social issues
    black elderly abuse and, 191-192, 201
    crime and, 50-52
    historical perspective on victim and, 4-8
    physically disabled and, 243-245
    stereotyping of elderly in, 154-155
Social sciences, 8-9
Social Security Act of 1935, 86, 305, 335
Social Security system, 13, 304, 305,
    306, 310
Social stress, 138
Social workers
    attitude toward elderly of, 157
    black elderly abuse and, 200
    family in elderly abuse and, 266
    physically disabled and, 246
Socioeconomic class, 11
Specialists, 174
Stage theory, 240
States

compensation programs of, 330–331
criminal justice system and, 7
frauds and, 82
nursing homes and consumer laws of, 111
Stereotyping of elderly, 154–155, 158, 159, 160, 161, 163–164
Street crime, 320
Street patrols, 321
Stress
    black elderly abuse and, 198–199
    characteristics of family and, 141–142
    conflict-resolution techniques and, 146–147
    dependency and, 142–145
    family caregivers and, 212, 380
    family therapy and, 360
    middle-aged caregivers and, 134–138, 141–142
    multigenerational family and, 137–138, 140–147
    physically disabled and, 241–243
    provisions of care and, 142–146
    types of, 138
Stroke, 236–238
Suburban areas, 299
Suicide, 14, 150
    nursing homes and, 99–100
Supplemental Security Income (SSI) programs, 304, 306, 310
Supportive services, for families, 272–273, 380, 381–383
Systems model, for elderly abuse, 190–191

Task-centered approach to intervention, 355–374
    application of, 365–367
    basic features of, 359–360
    client needing help in, 364–365
    factors assisting caretaker in, 363
    illustration from field in, 367–373
    issues relevant to, 359–361
    in service context, 364–367
Tax credits, 201, 434
Telephone assurance programs, 321
Theft
    consequences of, 55–57
    fear of, 26
    nursing homes and, 105–106
    value of property in, 56
Therapy charges, nursing home, 111
Third-party payers, 175
Training programs
    anticrime programs and, 328, 329
    consumer advocacy and, 343
    family and, 215–216
    intervention and, 411–418
    police and, 328

reporting and, 384
values clarification exercises in, 415–416
Transactional analysis, 409
Transportation, 265, 326
Trials, see Criminal justice system

Uniform Probate Code, 287
Unionization, nursing home, 338
Urban areas, 299
    elderly women in, 228
    fear of crime and, 32–33
    protective measures in, 60
    risk of crime for, 44, 46
    see also Inner cities

Value clarification exercises, 415–416
Value systems, and black elderly abuse, 195–196
Veterans Administration, 156, 305
Veterans' benefits, 304–305
Victim Assistance Program for Older Adults (VAOA) (Florida), 330
Victim assistance programs, 322–327
    components of, 325–327
    crime prevention programs and, 327–329
    crime victim's experience and, 322–323
    follow-up component of, 327
    objectives of, 325
    older volunteers in, 332
    referral process in, 326–327
    trends in, 329–331
Victim compensation programs, see Compensation programs
Victims, 1–15
    concept and terminology in, 2–4
    criminal justice system and, 2, 4, 11, 66
    elderly and, 12–14
    historical perspective on, 4–8
    as integral part of crime situation, 1–2, 3
    limits on behavior of, 10–11
    offender relationship with, 50–54
    police and, 2
    research on, 8–12
Violence
    black aged and, 189–190, 196
    elderly women and, 222–224
    income and, 191, 196
    physically disabled and, 235–236
    race and, 188–189
    social isolation and, 193
Visiting Nurses Association (VNA), 401
Vulnerability, 263–274
    domestic abuse and, 122
    elderly women and, 227–229
    fear of crime and perception of, 31, 32
    intergenerational problems and, 268–269

public housing and, 251–252
reasons for, 264–265
role definitions and, 270–271

White House Conference on the Aging, 41
Widow-to-Widow Program, 386
Wills, 305
Withdrawal, in nursing homes, 96, 99
Witnesses, 2, 323
Women, 220–232, 299
  abuse of, 224
  as abusers, 243
  bank examiner scheme and, 225–226
  black elderly abuse and, 196–197
  black households headed by, 191
  burglary and, 225
  as caregiver for elderly, 213, 378
  community organization efforts and, 230–231
  confidence games and, 225–227
  consumer fraud and, 227
  diabetes and, 238
  fear of crime and, 28, 29, 31, 231–232
  fraud and, 225–227
  living alone by, 228–229
  pigeon drop scheme and, 226–227
  purse snatching and, 223–224
  rape and, 222–223
  strategies for change and, 229–231
  stress in family and, 141
  types of victimization of, 220, 221–222
  vulnerability of, 228–229
  see also Sex
Work at home schemes, 70–71
Work loss, and crime, 55

DATE DUE

FEB 0 1 1985		
MAR 25 1986		
FE 27 '87		
AG 03 '87		
AG 03 '87		
FE 19 '88		
NO 19 '88		
AP 04 '93		
NO 09 '93		
JUN 10 '97		
DEC 1 2 2000		
JUN 1 4 1997		

DEMCO 38-297